Applying Quality of Life Research

Best Practices

Series editor

Helena Alves, Department of Management and Economics, University of Beira Interior, Covilhã, Portugal

This book series focuses on best practices in specialty areas of Quality of Life research, including among others potentially: community development, quality of work life, marketing, healthcare and public sector management.

In today's world, governments, organizations and individuals alike are paying increasingly more attention to how their activities impact on quality of life at the regional, national and global levels. Whether as a way to tackle global resource shortages, changing environmental circumstances, political conditions, competition, technology or otherwise, the far-reaching impact of decisions made in these and other areas can have a significant impact on populations regardless of their level of development. Many lessons have been learned; yet many are still to be realized. Across a number of volumes on diverse themes, this book series will address key issues that are of significant importance to decision makers and participants across all sectors. The series will be invaluable to anyone with an interest in applying quality of life knowledge in contemporary society.

More information about this series at http://www.springer.com/series/8364

Ana María Campón-Cerro
José Manuel Hernández-Mogollón
José Antonio Folgado-Fernández
Editors

Best Practices in Hospitality and Tourism Marketing and Management

A Quality of Life Perspective

Springer

Editors
Ana María Campón-Cerro
School of Business, Finance and Tourism
University of Extremadura
Cáceres, Spain

José Manuel Hernández-Mogollón
School of Business, Finance and Tourism
University of Extremadura
Cáceres, Spain

José Antonio Folgado-Fernández
School of Business, Finance and Tourism
University of Extremadura
Cáceres, Spain

ISSN 2213-994X ISSN 2213-9958 (electronic)
Applying Quality of Life Research
ISBN 978-3-319-91691-0 ISBN 978-3-319-91692-7 (eBook)
https://doi.org/10.1007/978-3-319-91692-7

Library of Congress Control Number: 2018950089

Printed on acid-free paper

This Springer imprint is published by the registered company Springer International Publishing AG part of Springer Nature.
The registered company address is: Gewerbestrasse 11, 6330 Cham, Switzerland

Contents

List of Contributors and Reviewers

Contributors

Juan Miguel Alcántara-Pilar University of Granada, Granada, Spain

Tanja Armenski University of Novi Sad, Novi Sad, Serbia

Andrés Artal-Tur Technical University of Cartagena, Murcia, Spain

Salvatore Bimonte University of Siena, Siena, Italy

Viviana Calzati University of Bologna, Bologna, Italy

Ana María Campón-Cerro University of Extremadura, Badajoz, Spain

Maria João Carneiro University of Aveiro, Aveiro, Portugal

Lisa Chase University of Vermont, Burlington, VT, USA

Mª de los Ángeles Plaza-Mejía Huelva University, Huelva, Spain

Verónica Nobre de Oliveira Polytechnic of Leiria, Leiria, Portugal

Paola de Salvo University of Perugia, Perugia, Italy

Elide Di-Clemente University of Extremadura, Badajoz, Spain

Carmelita D'Mello Goa University, Taleigão, India

Celeste Eusébio University of Aveiro, Aveiro, Portugal

José Antonio Folgado-Fernández University of Extremadura, Badajoz, Spain

José Manuel García-Gallego University of Extremadura, Badajoz, Spain

Irene Gil-Saura University of Valencia, Valencia, Spain

José Manuel Hernández-Mogollón University of Extremadura, Badajoz, Spain

Pilar Jiménez-Medina Technical University of Cartagena, Murcia, Spain

M. Joseph Sirgy Virginia Polytechnic Institute and State University, Blacksburg, VA, USA

Kaustubh Kamat Goa University, Taleigão, India

Hyelin (Lina) Kim University of Nevada, Reno, NV, USA

Elena Konovalov James Cook University, Townsville, Australia

Ines Küster-Boluda University of Valencia, Valencia, Spain

Joana Lima University of Évora, Évora, Portugal

Rubén Camilo Lois González University of Santiago de Compostela, Santiago, Spain

Tomás López-Guzmán University of Córdoba, Córdoba, Spain

Jose Trinidad Marin-Aguilar University of Valencia, Valencia, Spain

Antonio Chamorro-Mera University of Extremadura, Badajoz, Spain

Gianna Moscardo James Cook University, Townsville, Australia

Guzmán A. Muñoz-Fernández University of Córdoba, Córdoba, Spain

Laurie Murphy James Cook University, Townsville, Australia

Vanja Pavluković University of Novi Sad, Novi Sad, Serbia

Jesús C. Pérez-Gálvez University of Córdoba, Córdoba, Spain

Yamilé Pérez Guilarte University of Santiago de Compostela, Santiago, Spain

Nuria Porras-Bueno Huelva University, Huelva, Spain

María-Eugenia Ruiz-Molina University of Valencia, Valencia, Spain

Noelia Sánchez-Casado Technical University of Cartagena, Murcia, Spain

Miriam Scaglione University of Applied Sciences Western Switzerland, Delémont, Switzerland

Stefano Soglia University of Siena, Siena, Italy

Subhash Kizhakanveatil Bhaskaran Pillai Goa University, Taleigão, India

Muzaffer Uysal Virginia Polytechnic Institute and State University, Blacksburg, VA, USA

Alfonso Vargas-Sánchez Huelva University, Huelva, Spain

Celeste Amorim Varum University of Aveiro, Aveiro, Portugal

Natalia Vila-Lopez University of Valencia, Valencia, Spain

Klaus Weiermair York University Toronto, Toronto, Canada

Eunju Woo Kangwon National University, Chuncheon, Republic of Korea

Reviewers

Juan Miguel Alcántara-Pilar University of Granada, Granada, Spain

Andrés Artal-Tur Technical University of Cartagena, Murcia, Spain

Subhash Kizhakanveatil Bhaskaran Pillai Goa University, Taleigão, India

Rebecca Biggins York St John University, York, UK

Viviana Calzati University of Bologna, Bologna, Italy

Maria João Carneiro University of Aveiro, Aveiro, Portugal

Lisa Chase University of Vermont, Burlington, VT, USA

Paola de Salvo University of Perugia, Perugia, Italy

Mª de los Ángeles Plaza-Mejía Huelva University, Huelva, Spain

Celeste Eusébio University of Aveiro, Aveiro, Portugal

José Manuel García-Gallego University of Extremadura, Badajoz, Spain

Pilar Jiménez-Medina Technical University of Cartagena, Murcia, Spain

Hyelin (Lina) Kim University of Nevada, Reno, NV, USA

Joana Lima University of Évora, Évora, Portugal

Tomas López-Guzman University of Córdoba, Córdoba, Spain

Antonio Chamorro Mera University of Extremadura, Badajoz, Spain

Gianna Moscardo James Cook University, Townsville, Australia

Brendan Paddison York St John University, York, UK

Jesús C. Pérez-Gálvez University of Córdoba, Córdoba, Spain

Yamilé Pérez Guilarte University of Santiago de Compostela, Santiago, Spain

Nuria Porras-Bueno Huelva University, Huelva, Spain

María-Eugenia Ruiz-Molina University of Valencia, Valencia, Spain

Noelia Sánchez-Casado Technical University of Cartagena, Murcia, Spain

Alfonso Vargas-Sánchez Huelva University, Huelva, Spain

Celeste Amorim Varum University of Aveiro, Aveiro, Portugal

Natalia Vila-Lopez University of Valencia, Valencia, Spain

Margarita Zobnina NRU HSE, Moscow, Russia

Part I
Introduction

Chapter 1
Quality of Life (QOL) in Hospitality and Tourism Marketing and Management: An Approach to the Research Published in High Impact Journals

Ana María Campón-Cerro, José Manuel Hernández-Mogollón, José Antonio Folgado-Fernández, and Elide Di-Clemente

Abstract According to the importance that quality of life (QOL) in tourism research is acquiring, we propose a literature review on QOL in hospitality and tourism marketing and management by considering the published works in top journals listed in the Journal Citation Reports (JCR) in the category of "Hospitality, Leisure, Sport & Tourism" in 2016. We developed a literature review based on a content analysis, in which 20 articles were identified as an illustrative sample of the state-of-the-art and the level of development of this topic. The results show a synthesis of what is being published, who are the authors dedicated to this topic and their affiliations, in which journals these works received major acceptance, among other issues. The current body of knowledge existing is the result of diverse contributions dealing with the topic from multiples points of view, going from tourists perceived impacts of tourism on their personal QOL, to the evaluations by host communities about QOL enhancements caused by tourism development. Moreover, important contributions made by theoretical works were identified.

Keywords Quality of life (QOL) · Tourism marketing · Tourism management · Literature review · High impact journals

1.1 Introduction

Research on happiness and related concepts has traditionally been a "playground for speculative philosophy" (Veenhoven 2009: 45), however it has recently caught the attention of social scientists (Nawijn et al. 2010) as travel industry is selling

A. M. Campón-Cerro (✉) · J. M. Hernández-Mogollón · J. A. Folgado-Fernández
E. Di-Clemente
University of Extremadura, Cáceres, Spain
e-mail: amcampon@unex.es; jmherdez@unex.es; jafolgado@unex.es; ediclemente@unex.es

A. M. Campón-Cerro et al. (eds.), *Best Practices in Hospitality and Tourism Marketing and Management*, Applying Quality of Life Research,
https://doi.org/10.1007/978-3-319-91692-7_1

products that go far beyond the achievement of satisfaction and loyal intentions, it is rather selling moments capable of determining how people feel and how fulfilling they perceive their lives (Nawijn et al. 2013). Richards (1999) maintains that the contribution of tourism experiences to people's quality of life (QOL) is threefold as holidays provide physical and mental recovery, personal development and the achievement of personal interests.

Tourism literature has showed a growing consensus about the benefits that individuals can get from tourism experiences and meaningful travels (Chen and Petrick 2016; Chen et al. 2016; Neal et al. 1999). These benefits have been defined and labelled with different terms such as life satisfaction, happiness, QOL, subjective well-being, etc., which are often used interchangeably (Kim et al. 2015).

A growing body of research in tourism and leisure literature has deepened into the relationships underpinning holiday-taking and improvements in QOL (Dolnicar et al. 2012, 2013). Several works focused on specific aspects related with holidays and QOL or equivalent concepts. Outcomes are diverse with respect of whether tourism experiences increase tourists' or residents' QOL, whether the perception of increased QOL is real or illusory, is higher in the pre-trip, post-trip or during the experience itself (Nawijn et al. 2013; Nawijn 2011a), is momentary or long-lasting (Kroesen and Handy 2014; Nawijn et al. 2010; Nawijn, 2011b). Apart from these specific issues, the generally accepted conclusion is that holiday-taking positively impact tourists' QOL, and that the tourism industry enhances the host communities' perceived well-being (Campón-Cerro et al. 2017; Gilbert and Abdullah 2004; Jeon et al. 2016; Kim et al. 2013; Kim et al. 2015; Sirgy et al. 2011; Woo et al. 2015).

Results achieved in this research line, are being spread through different channels such as international conferences, publications in forms of books, book chapters and journal articles, and also the edition of specialised journals.

Examples of the importance that QOL is gaining in research can be seen in the development of annual conferences, such as the annual meeting organised by the *ISQOLS- International Society for Quality-of-Life Studies* and the edition of specific journals such as *Applied Research in Quality of Life*, edited since 2006 by Springer and listed in the Journal Citation Report (JCR). Some book series specifically dedicated to this topic have already been launched by Springer, the first publisher in the Economics field according to the ranking elaborated by the Scholarly Publishers Indicators in Humanities and Social Sciences (SPI) in 2014.

Additionally, a significant group of books and monographs on tourism and QOL is making useful inroads in the scholarly tourism literature. Hitherto, the most comprehensive book dealing the topics of tourism and QOL is the *Handbook of Tourism and Quality-of-Life Research: Enhancing the Lives of Tourists and Residents of Host Communities* (Uysal et al. 2012), edited by Springer. Some other books are worth to be mentioned as, even though considering QOL in wider terms, they contribute significantly to this body of knowledge. To mention few of them: Smith and Puczkó (2009, 2014) authored in 2009 the first books on wellness and QOL, titled *Health and Wellness Tourism,* and expanded in a second edition published in 2014, with the new title of *Health, Tourism and Hospitality: Spas, Wellness and Medical*

Travel; Pearce et al. (2010) published *Tourists, Tourism and the Good Life*; Bushell and Sheldon (2009) edited the book *Wellness and Tourism: Mind, Body, Spirit, Place*. More recently Prebensen et al. (2014) released a work entitled *Creating Experience Value in Tourism,* focused on deepening into the value of vacation experiences for tourists' life satisfaction (Uysal et al. 2016). All these works prove that QOL is a pushing and dynamic topic in the current tourism literature which deserves more research efforts, as it still offers many research paths to be further explored.

It is also important to highlight that tourism is a multidisciplinary work field, then it is possible to identify significant contributions in multiple types of journals depending on their focus: management, marketing, economics, geography, sociology, psychology….

Uysal et al. (2016) developed an exhaustive literature review about QOL and well-being in tourism in an article published in *Tourism Management*. This work makes a clear description of the findings achieved so far by existing researches, highlights the methods applied for data collection and puts forward a constructive discussion on the issue of construct measurement. The results achieved show that more research is needed in order to identify both tangible and intangible benefits of the tourism activities on QOL and well-being, with regard to different groups of interest, such as consumers, providers, host communities and employees of the hospitality industry. The authors conclude that the tourism ability to improve the QOL of all the involved stakeholders is the key point to ensure the long term success, the sustainability and the competitiveness of tourism in the future. This aspect presents new challenges to academics and practitioners which will need to be addressed with more comprehensive researches on the topic.

As the first step of this collective book about QOL in hospitality and tourism marketing and management we propose a literature review by considering the published works in top journals included in the JCR of 2016 in the category of "Hospitality, Leisure, Sport & Tourism". The works identified represent an illustrative sample of the state-of-the-art and the level of development of this topic. As Hernández et al. (2011) assert, literature review is a fundamental step in any scientific work, since it allows identifying authors and research groups, topics, methodologies, future research lines, etc.

We aim to make a compendium of the most significant results to know what is being published, who are the authors dedicated to this topic and their affiliations, in which journals these works received major acceptance, among other issues. Its purpose is to offer to the scientific community an overview of the research published on this topic from another point of view. The present work is different from previous ones by focusing its attention on journals specialized in hospitality and tourism and listed in JCR.

This chapter was divided into five sections. The first one presents the focus of this work and its main purpose. Next, the theoretical context is introduced, followed by the methodology used. Finally, the conclusions are specified, along with limitations and future lines of research.

1.2 QOL in Hospitality and Tourism

The search for improvements in QOL is a central policy goal for the modern economic systems. According to Sato et al. (2014) governments and policy makers are increasingly interested in developing programs capable of promoting people's QOL. New social indicators are gaining momentum as suitable tools to measure the wellness and health of a society, with a decreasing attention to gross domestic product (GDP) and other statistical economy-based indicators. Concepts such as life satisfaction, happiness, subjective well-being and QOL, among others, are becoming of focal interest (Diener and Suh 1997; Diener 2006; Kittiprapas et al. 2007; Powdthavee 2007; Sirgy et al. 2006; Uysal et al. 2016). Tourism is an industry characterised by a strong commitment with the positive development of communities and destinations and travelling has been identified as a suitable opportunity to experience positive emotions which, in turn, affect the individuals' personal well-being and happiness (Dolnicar et al. 2013; Gilbert and Abdullah 2004; Sirgy et al. 2011). Therefore, QOL and similar concepts are receiving increasing attention by tourism researchers and practitioners as innovative outputs of the modern tourism systems.

In tourism research, several attempts to link holiday-taking and individuals' QOL can be found. According to Chen and Petrick (2013) the majority of the contributions in this field confirmed the positive relation between holiday-taking and individuals' well-being. Broadly speaking, in tourism literature there is a general consensus on considering tourism activities as QOL's enhancers (Bimonte and Faralla 2014, 2015; Bosnjak et al. 2014; Chen and Petrick 2016; Dolnicar et al. 2012, 2013; Eusébio and Carneiro 2011; Gilbert and Abdullah 2004; Kim et al. 2015; Kruger et al. 2013; Mactavish et al. 2007; McCabe and Johnson 2013; McCabe et al. 2010; Michalkó et al. 2009; Morgan et al. 2015; Nawijn 2011a; Neal et al. 1999, 2004, 2007; Pagan 2015; Richards 1999; Sirgy et al. 2011; Su et al. 2015; Tse 2014; Uysal et al. 2016; Wei and Milman 2002), however some authors (Chen et al. 2013; Kroesen and Handy 2014; Kühnel and Sonnentag 2011; Nawijn 2010, 2011a) have questioned this approach and offered theoretical and empirical evidences that tourism-based perceptions of increased QOL tend to fade out over the long-term.

Apart from specific issues, the researches that confirm the positive impact of holiday-taking on tourists' personal evaluation of life are more numerous than the ones that put it into question (Gilbert and Abdullah 2004; Kim et al. 2015; Sirgy et al. 2011), which confirms that the tourism studies on QOL gave birth to a dynamic and fruitful research field.

The contribution of travels to QOL is formally explained by the Bottom-up Spillover Theory which considers a hierarchical model where the overall judgement of one's QOL is the result of the specific satisfaction that spills over from a number of life domains (Kim et al. 2015). Leisure and travel have been extensively confirmed as crucial domains contributing to QOL (Nawijn et al. 2010; Nawijn 2011b; Woo et al. 2016).

From a management and marketing perspective, the connections identified between holiday-taking and QOL offer new opportunities and ideas to market innovative products and to develop new promotion and communication strategies. The enhancement of perceived well-being represents a new output of the tourism proposals which puts forward several potential innovations in the industry.

First, it suggests a novel segmentation base in tourism. According to Dolnicar et al. (2013), not all people need or want to go on vacation. On the other hand, there exists a portion of the population that identifies in travelling a crucial contributor to personal QOL. These consumers attribute a significant importance to vacations which identifies them as a crisis-resistant segment, more likely to keep spending on holiday-taking, regardless of impediments. This suggests that mass marketing strategies are useless and resource-consuming. Specific actions should be addressed to those clients who see in tourism a necessary activity to reach their desired level of QOL. People feeling vacations as essential to their QOL represent the most attractive segment from a managerial and marketing perspective. On the contrary, consumers not feeling this link between holidays and personal well-being may cause a waste of marketing resources, therefore segmenting the market with specific reference to QOL is of germane importance in order to perform effective marketing strategies.

Second, research on QOL offers some useful insights for the achievement of a better explanation and prediction of tourist satisfaction which is a strong determinant of the perception of increased level of QOL (Sirgy 2010).

Third, happy tourists are more likely to have positive future behaviours. When the main goal of travelling goes beyond the search for rest and relaxation, but it is rather to foster personal well-being, then satisfactory tourism experiences can lead to new intentions to patronise the behaviour that led to a desired output: the enhancement of the perceived QOL, in this case. The feeling that a specific tourism practice has contributed to personal well-being can activate future loyal behaviours, namely, the desire to visit again a destination, the intention to recommend the experience, or re-buy a certain product/service linked to a travel. Some contributions have already empirically confirmed the positive relation between tourism experiences, perceived enhancements in QOL, and subsequent loyal behaviours (Kim et al. 2012, 2015; Lam and So 2013; Lee et al. 2014; Lin 2014). QOL is figuring out as an innovative and experiential marketing output, which can outline new and more effective marketing and communication strategies that can foster loyal and durable relationships with the tourist clients. Deep research in QOL can bring to a better understanding of the concept on both its theoretical content and empirical application and can, therefore, layout a new tool for the management of innovative tourism systems, strongly committed with the consumers' well-being and forward-looking.

While most research has treated the relation between tourism experiences and tourists, there exists an emerging research stream which is focusing the attention on the perception of QOL enhancements due to tourism activities for residents and host communities.

The interest on this aspect is twofold. By the one side, the connection between tourism and residents well-being represents a supportive strategy for sustainable tourism development, amending the social negative impacts of certain tourism systems. By the other side, the improvements that tourism makes on host communities' QOL make residents more collaborative for the further development of tourism in a specific destination (Nunkoo and So 2015). Kim et al. (2015) contribute to the existing literature on tourism and host communities' QOL by examining the residents' perceived value of tourism development. The authors used economic and non-economic indicators to test the perceived value and concluded that tourism development impacts material and non-material domains of life satisfaction and that greater perceived value of tourism development is associated with higher levels of non-material/material life domain satisfaction which, in turn, enhances the supportive attitude of residents towards tourism development.

Ridderstaat et al. (2016a) explore the connection between tourism development, residents' QOL and economic growth of a tourism destination. The authors confirm a bilateral and positive relationship between tourism development and QOL over the long term.

Andereck and Nyaupane (2011) made a major contribution to the research on the tourism impacts on residents' QOL by developing a specific calculation tool based on a subjective approach with the aim of providing a more accurate assessment of the perception that the host community has of the benefits that tourism activities brings to its life. According to their results, those who gain the most from tourism are the most supportive of existing and additional tourism development. The economic impacts of tourism activity are the true responsible for determining enhancements in QOL perception. Therefore, the tourism industry, in order to be a QOL enhancer for residents, needs to be an economic contributor.

1.3 Methodology

Literature review is an essential step when a research begins. It allows to know what other authors have done, which method they used, the conclusions achieved, etc., that means to be familiar with the state-of-the-art and to understand which would be the own contribution to the field of study (Losada and López-Feal 2003). It consists on "detecting, obtaining and consulting the bibliography and other materials that are useful for the purposes of the study" (Hernández et al. 2007, p. 23–24).

This literature review is based on a content analysis, which is defined as "a technique for collecting, classifying and analysing the information contained in communications expressed orally or in writing through an objective, systematic and quantitative procedure" (Bigné 1999, p. 259), by reducing a large amount of textual data to a few categories, and obtaining the frequencies that each one has (Callejo 2007).

This literature review was conducted using the key database considered by academics, the Web of Science (WOS), which collects the main scientific publications of any discipline. The journals selected for this literature review were identified from the Journal Citation Reports (JCR), considered a tool for assessing the quality of publications by using a numerical indicator known as impact factor, IF (Grande-Esteban 2013).

According to Albacete and Fuentes (2010), the selection of the journals under review could be complicated due to the difficulty of covering all the existing ones. However, the authors conclude that this could not provide more information that the extracted from a good sample. In the opinion of Hernández et al. (2011), the multidisciplinary character of tourism has led authors to publish in journals of a wide variety of areas. Thus it is even more difficult to identify the publications to conduct an exhaustive literature review.

Due to these reasons, we understand that it is possible to obtain an interesting approach to the literature published on hospitality and tourism marketing and management using, as a sampling procedure, the selection of the journals listed in JCR in the category of "Hospitality, Leisure, Sport & Tourism" in 2016, as in that year was the last update. That category is composed by 45 listed journals. From them, the journals that are related to hospitality and tourism were taken into account. Thus 20 journals were identified (see Table 1.1).

The selection of the articles published on the topic under study has been carried out by searching for the keywords "quality of life" and "QOL" appearing in the title of the work. In that way, the articles identified could be clearly considered as significant contributions to our topic. Even though, all the articles detected were assessed regarding its belonging to our aim. Other keywords such as "happiness" or "satisfaction with life" were discarded. As explained before, these concepts are very close to each other. However, there are some nuances in their meanings which suggest differentiating them. As a result, 20 articles were identified in 7 journals. The last update of this literature review was conducted in November 2017 (see Table 1.2).

1.4 Results

In Fig. 1.1 it is possible to observe that the contributions on QOL in hospitality and tourism marketing and management appear in 2010. Since that year, 20 articles were published in the selected journals, being possible to identify at least one article per year. The most prolific year was 2016, followed by 2013. Even though the last update of the literature review has been done in November 2017, it could be possible to include one article from 2018, as it is already available as a forthcoming content in the WOS database.

Taking into account the results of these literature review, M. Joseph Sirgy and Muzaffer Uysal, professors and researchers from the Virginia Polytechnic Institute and State University of USA, are the authors of reference with 3 articles published on the subject (see Fig. 1.2).

The majority of the literature published in this field has been coauthored by 3 or more authors, having identified just 2 articles with a single author. In the opinion of Sánchez and Marín (2003), a lower proportion of work in groups compared to those of single authorship could be indicative of the lack of consolidation of the research on the topic. Therefore, research in tourism and QOL appears as a growing body of research, acquiring consistency.

Table 1.1 Journals selected

Journal	ISSN	Publisher	Country[a]	IF (2016)
Tourism Management	0261-5177	Elsevier SCI LTD	UK	4.707
Journal of Travel Research	0047-2875	Sage Publications INC	USA	4.564
Annals of Tourism Research	0160-7383	Pergamon-Elsevier Science LTD	USA	3.194
Journal of Sustainable Tourism	0966-9582	Channel View Publications	UK	2.978
International Journal of Hospitality Management	0278-4319	Elsevier SCI LTD	UK	2.787
Cornell Hospitality Quarterly	1938-9655	Sage Publications INC	USA	2.657
Journal of Hospitality & Tourism Research	1096-3480	Sage Publications INC	USA	2.646
Current Issues in Tourism	1368-3500	Routledge Journals, Taylor & Francis LTD	UK	2.451
International Journal of Tourism Research	1099-2340	Wiley-Blackwell	UK	1.857
Tourism Geographies	1461-6688	Routledge Journals, Taylor & Francis LTD	UK	1.663
International Journal of Contemporary Hospitality Management	0959-6119	Emerald Group Publishing LTD	UK	1.623
Journal of Destination Marketing & Management	2212-571X	Elsevier Science BV	Netherlands	1.556
Journal of Travel & Tourism Marketing	1054-8408	Routledge Journals, Taylor & Francis LTD	USA	1.453
Journal of Vacation Marketing	1356-7667	Sage Publications LTD	UK	1.148
Tourist Studies	1468-7976	Sage Publications INC	USA	1.147
Scandinavian Journal of Hospitality and Tourism	1502-2250	Routledge Journals, Taylor & Francis LTD	Norway	1.091
Asia Pacific Journal of Tourism Research	1094-1665	Routledge Journals, Taylor & Francis LTD	UK	1.051
Tourism Economics	1354-8166	Sage Publications LTD	UK	0.826
Journal of Tourism and Cultural Change	1476-6825	Routledge Journals, Taylor & Francis LTD	UK	0.732
Journal of Hospitality Leisure Sport & Tourism Education	1473-8376	Elsevier SCI LTD	UK	0.206

Source: JCR 2016

[a]UK: United Kingdom; USA: The United States of America

Table 1.2 Articles identified

Journal	Authors	Year	Title
Annals of Tourism Research	Dolnicar et al.	2012	The contribution of vacations to quality of life. *39*(1), 59–83.
Asia Pacific Journal of Tourism Research	Liao et al.	2016	Residents' perceptions of the role of leisure satisfaction and quality of life in overall tourism development: case of a fast-growing tourism destination–Macao. *21*(10), 1100–1113.
	Min	2014	The relationships between emotional intelligence, job stress, and quality of life among tour guides. *19*(10), 1170–1190.
International Journal of Tourism Research	Chancellor et al.	2011	Exploring quality of life perceptions in rural midwestern (USA) communities: an application of the core–periphery concept in a tourism development context. *13*(5), 496–507.
	Lee et al.	2015	Does consumers' feeling affect their quality of life? Roles of consumption emotion and its consequences. *17*(4), 409–416.
	McCabe et al.	2010	Understanding the benefits of social tourism: linking participation to subjective well-being and quality of life. *12*(6), 761–773.
Journal of Sustainable Tourism	Polonsky et al.	2013	Using strategic philanthropy to improve heritage tourist sites on the Gallipoli Peninsula, Turkey: community perceptions of changing quality of life and of the sponsoring organization. *21*(3), 376–395.
	Ridderstaat et al.	2016a	A two-way causal chain between tourism development and quality of life in a small island destination: an empirical analysis. *24*(10), 1461–1479.
Journal of Travel Research	Andereck and Nyaupane	2011	Exploring the nature of tourism and quality of life perceptions among residents. *50*(3), 248–260.
	Bronner and De Hoog	2016	Crisis resistance of tourist demand: the importance of quality of life. *55*(2), 190–204.
	Kaplanidou et al.	2013	Quality of life, event impacts, and mega-event support among South African residents before and after the 2010 FIFA World Cup. *52*(5), 631–645.
	Ridderstaat et al.	2016b	The tourism development–quality of life nexus in a small island destination. *55*(1), 79–94.
	Sirgy	2010	Toward a quality-of-life theory of leisure travel satisfaction. *49*(2), 246–260.

(continued)

Table 1.2 (continued)

Journal	Authors	Year	Title
Tourism Management	Kim et al.	2013	How does tourism in a community impact the quality of life of community residents? *36*, 527–540.
	Kim et al.	2015	Tourism experience and quality of life among elderly tourists. *46*, 465–476.
	Lee et al.	2018	Impact of a gaming company's CSR on residents' perceived benefits, quality of life, and support. *64*, 281–290.
	Liang and Hui	2016	Residents' quality of life and attitudes toward tourism development in China. *57*, 56–67.
	Lin et al.	2013	Promoting frontline employees' quality of life: Leisure benefit systems and work-to-leisure conflicts. *36*, 178–187.
	Uysal et al.	2016	Quality of life (QOL) and well-being research in tourism. *53*, 244–261.
International Journal of Hospitality Management	Meng and Choi	2017	Theme restaurants' servicescape in developing quality of life: The moderating effect of perceived authenticity. *65*, 89–99.

Source: Authors

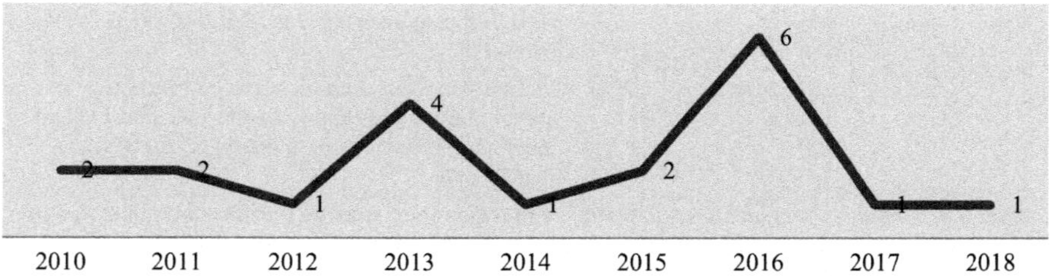

Fig. 1.1 Evolution. (Source: Authors)

The most prolific journal on the research topic is *Tourism Management* (6). Then, it is possible to state that this type of research is particularly attractive for the elaboration of new management strategies in tourism. *Tourism Management* is followed by the *Journal of Travel Research* (5) and the *International Journal of Tourism Research* (3) (see Fig. 1.3).

Regarding the quality of the journals in which the articles have been published, it is necessary to highlight that they have a high JCR IF. 5 out of the 7 journals are located in Q1 of JCR 2016 in the category of "Hospitality, Leisure, Sport & Tourism", and 3 of them are Q1 also in other categories. The other two journals are located in Q2 and Q3 (see Table 1.3). This points out the high quality of the researches published in these top journals and signals the consolidation of this research line in the academy.

Fig. 1.2 More prolific authors. (Source: Authors)

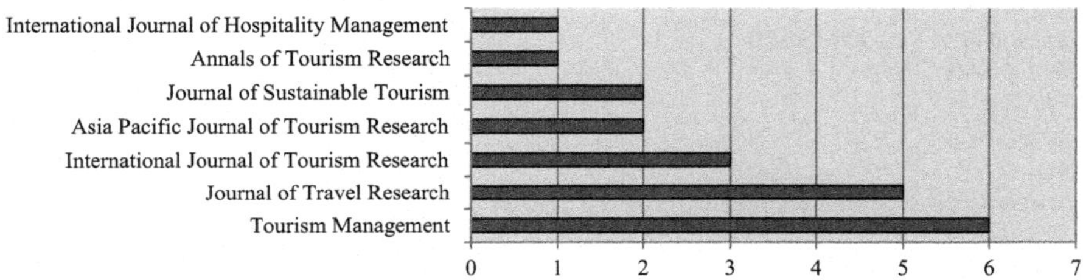

Fig. 1.3 Journals. (Source: Authors)

Keywords have been analysed in each one of the articles selected. Some of them were grouped when considered similar or working with the same content. The most recurrent keyword was "quality of life" (Quality of life/ overall quality of life/ perceived quality of life) (20), followed by "tourism development" ("Tourism development/ attitudes toward further tourism development/ rural tourism development") (7), and "well-being" (Subjective well-being/ wellbeing/ leisure wellbeing/ goal theory of subjective well-being) (6). Another concept that could be studied with QOL is "satisfaction" (Leisure satisfaction/ satisfaction with trip experience/ leisure life satisfaction) (6) (see Table 1.4).

The two main focus through which QOL is approached in scientific literature, the residents' perspective and the tourists' perspective, are also reflected in specific keywords. In the case of residents ("Community resident/ residents/ residents' support/ quality of life of community residents"), related keywords appear with a frequency of 6 and in the case of tourists ("Tourist demand/ tourist well-being/ tourists' quality-of-life") with a frequency of 3 (see Table 1.4)

When a researcher cites a previous work, what he/she is doing is recognizing the utility that work has had in his/her own study. It is the reason why citations are considered an indicator of the influence and the interest it arouses in other colleagues and the utility the work has for the scientific community. Then citations have become an essential indicator to analyse the significance of the scientific production of countries, institutions and researchers to a certain field (Delgado and Torres-Salinas 2013).

Table 1.3 Journal ranking

Journal	IF(2016)	Hospitality, leisure, sport & tourism	Management	Environmental studies	Sociology	Green & sustainable science & technology
Tourism Management	4.707	Q1	Q1	Q1	–	–
Journal of Travel Research	4.564	Q1	–	–	–	–
Annals of Tourism Research	3.194	Q1	–	Undefined	Q1	–
Journal of Sustainable Tourism	2.978	Q1	–	–	–	Q1
International Journal of Hospitality Management	2.787	Q1	–	–	–	–
International Journal of Tourism Research	1.857	Q2	–	–	–	–
Asia Pacific Journal of Tourism Research	1.051	Q3	–	–	–	–

Source: JCR 2016

Table 1.4 Keywords

Keywords or group of keywords	Count
Quality of life/overall quality of life/perceived quality of life	20
Tourism development/attitudes toward further tourism development/rural tourism development	7
Subjective well-being/wellbeing/leisure wellbeing/goal theory of subjective well-being	7
Leisure satisfaction/satisfaction with trip experience/leisure life satisfaction/	6
Community resident/residents/residents' support/quality of life of community residents	6
Life satisfaction	3
Tourist demand/tourist well-being/tourists' quality-of-life	3
Economic development/growth	2
Small island destination/small island destination	2
Tourism/heritage tourism	2
Tourism benefits/tourism impact	2

Source: Authors

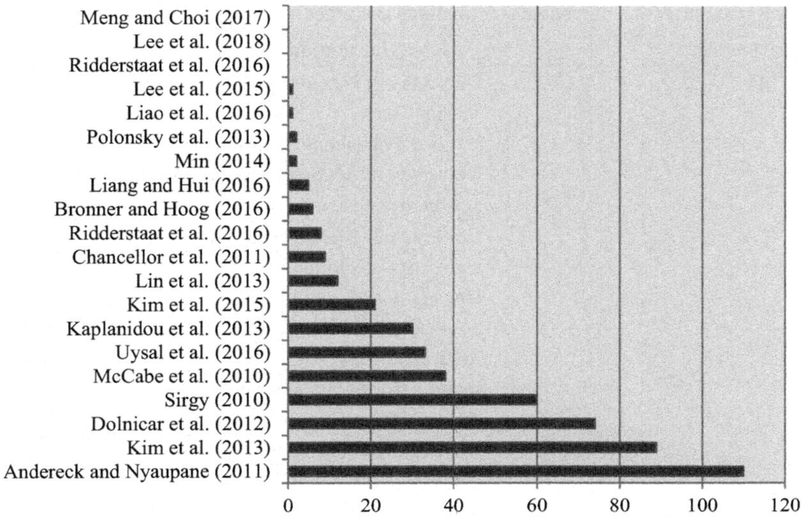

Fig. 1.4 Citations received per article in WOS database. (Source: Authors)

As we can see in Fig. 1.4, in our literature review there are works that have influenced notably the work of other researches such as the contributions of Andereck and Nyaupane (2011), Kim et al. (2013), Dolnicar et al. (2012), and Sirgy (2010). It is important to highlight that several of the most recent works have few cites or they do not have at all, possibly due to their very recent availability for the scientific community.

It is also important to show the relevance of offering a geographical vision of the research capacity (López and López 2008). By analysing the universities and other institutions more frequently linked to the research topic analysed, it is possible to identify the heading country. The leader country appears to be USA with 14 universities working on this subject. Other outstanding countries with universities or different institutions investigating the relationship between QOL and tourism are Taiwan (4), Australia (3), China (3), The Netherlands (3) and Turkey (3) (see Table 1.5).

Regarding the main focus of the research, 10 out of the sample are focused on residents' perceptions of QOL, while 4 are focused on tourists' perspective. With regard to the remaining 6 articles, four have diverse focuses (clients in restaurants, tourism industry frontline employees, tourist guides and attendants of a festival); and two out of the sample were identified as theoretical. Then it is possible to conclude that, hitherto, the research on QOL in hospitality and tourism marketing and management is mainly focused on exploring the assessment that residents and tourists make of tourism activities and experiences.

Regarding the type of data used to conduct the researches it is worth noting that the majority of the works considered (16) collected primary data, while 2 of them performed analysis of secondary data. Finally, 2 of them are theoretical.

Table 1.5 Countries and universities' affiliations and other institutions

Country (count)	University/institution
USA (14)	University of Nevada-Las Vegas
	Virginia Tech
	Virginia Polytechnic Institute and State University
	University of Southern Mississippi
	University of Nevada
	University of Massachusetts Amherst
	University of Florida
	University of Central Florida
	Southern New Hampshire University
	Iowa State University
	Indiana University Bloomington
	Auburn University
	Arizona State University
	University of Central Florida
Taiwan (4)	Yuan Ze University
	National Kaohsiung University of Hospitality and Tourism
	National Chiayi University
	Ming Chuan University
Australia (3)	University of Wollongong
	Swinburne University of Technology
	Deakin University
China (3)	University of Macau
	Sun Yat-sen University
	Shanxi University
The Netherlands (3)	University of Twente
	University of Amsterdam
	Free University of Amsterdam
Turkey (3)	Trakya University
	Mugla University
	Canakkale Onsekiz Mart University
South Korea (2)	Kyung Hee University
	Dong-A University
UK (2)	Nottingham University Business School
	Family Holiday Association
Aruba (1)	Central Bank of Aruba
France (1)	NEOMA Business School-Rouen Campus
Republic of Korea (1)	Kangwon National University
Singapore (1)	National University of Singapore
South Africa (1)	Tshwane University of Technology

Source: Authors

SEM and path analysis are the most preferred techniques employed for data analysis (9). Other studies use regressions (4) or a combination of different statistical tools.

1.5 Conclusions

This work proposes a literature review including all those works dealing with the topic of QOL within the context of hospitality and tourism marketing and management. It is expected that the information extracted from these analysis could be useful for the scientific community, since it offers information about networks of researchers and universities and institutions to which they belong, treated topics, focuses used to approach the subject and current trends or methodologies applied.

Unlike other works, it focuses its attention on the most consolidated journals in the field of hospitality and tourism. A selected sample of contributions has been identified and analysed with the aim of exploring the actual degree of development of the subject under study from a theoretical and empirical perspective.

The current body of knowledge existing on QOL in hospitality and tourism marketing and management is the result of a diverse contributions dealing with the topic from multiples points of view, going from tourists perceived impacts of tourism on their personal QOL, to the evaluations by host communities about QOL enhancements caused by tourism development. Moreover, it is not to disregard the important contributions made by theoretical works in such a new research area. Definition and conceptual contents of QOL and similar concepts still deserve major research efforts to translate theoretical ideas into practical proposals and strategies capable of providing the tourism industry with new value for both consumers and practitioners.

The main goal of this chapter was to present a clear snapshot of the current state of development of the research on QOL in hospitality and tourism marketing and management with the main aim of, by the one side, highlighting the importance that this topic is gaining in tourism research and practice and, by the other side, inspiring new research paths, starting from the significant knowledge that already exists on the subject.

Regarding the limitations of this work, it is possible to point out the difficulty of conducting an exhaustive literature review in a multidisciplinary work field as tourism is. That led to limit the searches applying several criteria following the assertion of Albacete and Fuentes (2010) about the importance of obtaining a good sample of data. The final results of this literature review can be interpreted as a new approach to this research line, from the different angle that the analysis of top journals offers, and as a standpoint to continue working on this subject.

This collective book is the result of the effort that many researchers from over the world have done to contribute to this outstanding research line. The reader can find a compilation of significant theoretical and empirical contributions, as well as case studies related to QOL in hospitality and tourism marketing and management. This book seeks to continue contributing with research results to the advancement of the relationship between QOL and tourism due to the repercussions that this has for the quality of life of residents, and of tourists, offering therefore the quality of life as a fundamental factor to take into account in the development of new tourism practices. Finally, this book is a mean to disseminate the last research conducted on QOL in hospitality and tourism marketing and management with the expectation it could influence and inspire new research paths.

References

Albacete, C. A., & Fuentes, M. M. (2010). Difusión de la investigación española sobre turismo en revistas internacionales. *Análisis Turístico, 9*, 14–29.

Andereck, K. L., & Nyaupane, G. P. (2011). Exploring the nature of tourism and quality of life perceptions among residents. *Journal of Travel Research, 50*(3), 248–260. https://doi.org/10.1177/0047287510362918.

Bigné, J. E. (1999). El análisis de contenido. In F. J. Sarabia (Ed.), *Metodología para la investigación en marketing y dirección de empresas* (pp. 255–271). Madrid: Pirámide.

Bimonte, S., & Faralla, V. (2014). Happiness and nature-based vacations. *Annals of Tourism Research, 46*, 176–178. https://doi.org/10.1016/j.annals.2014.02.002.

Bimonte, S., & Faralla, V. (2015). Happiness and outdoor vacations appreciative versus consumptive tourists. *Journal of Travel Research, 54*(2), 179–192. https://doi.org/10.1177/0047287513513171.

Bosnjak, M., Brown, C. A., Lee, D.-J., Yu, G. B., & Sirgy, M. J. (2014). Self-expressiveness in sport tourism: Determinants and consequences. *Journal of Travel Research, 55*(1), 125–134. https://doi.org/10.1177/0047287514535845.

Bronner, F., & de Hoog, R. (2016). Crisis resistance of tourist demand: The importance of quality of life. *Journal of Travel Research, 55*(2), 190–204. https://doi.org/10.1177/0047287514541006.

Bushell, R., & Sheldon, P. (2009). *Wellness and tourism: Mind, body, spirit, place*. Elmsford: Cognizant Communication Books.

Callejo, J. (2007). Análisis de documentos. In J. Gutiérrez (Ed.), *La investigación social del turismo, perspectivas y aplicaciones* (pp. 179–194). Madrid: Thomson.

Campón-Cerro, A. M., Folgado-Fernández, J. A., & Hernández-Mogollón, J. M. (2017). Rural destination development based on olive oil tourism: The impact of residents' community attachment and quality of life on their support for tourism development. *Sustainability, 9*(9), 1624. https://doi.org/10.3390/su9091624.

Chancellor, C., Yu, C. P. S., & Cole, S. T. (2011). Exploring quality of life perceptions in rural midwestern (USA) communities: An application of the core–periphery concept in a tourism development context. *International Journal of Tourism Research, 13*(5), 496–507. https://doi.org/10.1002/jtr.823.

Chen, C.-C., & Petrick, J. F. (2013). Health and wellness benefits of travel experiences: A literature review. *Journal of Travel Research, 52*(6), 709–719. https://doi.org/10.1177/0047287513496477.

Chen, C.-C., & Petrick, J. F. (2016). The roles of perceived travel benefits, importance, and constraints in predicting travel behavior. *Journal of Travel Research, 55*(4), 509–522. https://doi.org/10.1177/0047287514563986.

Chen, Y., Lehto, X. Y., & Cai, L. (2013). Vacation and well-being: A study of chinese tourists. *Annals of Tourism Research, 42*, 284–310. https://doi.org/10.1016/j.annals.2013.02.003.

Chen, C. C., Petrick, J. F., & Shahvali, M. (2016). Tourism experiences as a stress reliever: Examining the effects of tourism recovery experiences on life satisfaction. *Journal of Travel Research, 55*(2), 150–160. https://doi.org/10.1177/0047287514546223.

Delgado, E., & Torres-Salinas, D. (2013). La evaluación de las publicaciones científicas. In F. J. Sarabia (Ed.), *Métodos de investigación social y de la empresa* (pp. 219–246). Madrid: Pirámide.

Diener, E. (2006). Guidelines for national indicators of subjective well-being and ill-being. *Journal of Happiness Studies, 7*(4), 397–404. https://doi.org/10.1007/s11482-006-9007-x.

Diener, E., & Suh, E. (1997). Measuring quality of life: Economic, social and subjective indicators. *Social Indicators Research, 40*(1), 189–216.

Dolnicar, S., Yanamandram, V., & Cliff, K. (2012). The contribution of vacations to quality of life. *Annals of Tourism Research, 39*(1), 59–83. https://doi.org/10.1016/j.annals.2011.04.015.

Dolnicar, S., Lazarevski, K., & Yanamandram, V. (2013). Quality of life and tourism: A conceptual framework and novel segmentation base. *Journal of Business Research, 66*(6), 724–729. https://doi.org/10.1016/j.jbusres.2011.09.010.

Eusébio, C., & Carneiro, J. C. (2011). Determinants of tourism impact on tourists' quality of life. *International Journal of Leisure and Tourism Marketing, 2*(4), 313–336. https://doi.org/10.1504/IJLTM.2011.043788.

Gilbert, D., & Abdullah, J. (2004). Holidaytaking and the sense of well-being. *Annals of Tourism Research, 31*(1), 103–121. https://doi.org/10.1016/j.annals.2003.06.001.

Grande-Esteban, I. (2013). Bases de datos para la investigación. In F. J. Sarabia (Ed.), *Métodos de investigación social y de la empresa* (pp. 139–165). Madrid: Pirámide.

Hernández, R., Fernández, C., & Baptista, P. (2007). *Fundamentos de metodología de la investigación*. Madrid: Mc Graw Hill.

Hernández, J. M., Campón, A. M., & Folgado, J. A. (2011). La investigación en turismo en España a través de las revistas de dirección de empresas. *Revista de Análisis Turístico, 12*, 1–9.

Jeon, M. M., Kang, M. M., & Desmarais, E. (2016). Residents' perceived quality of life in a cultural-heritage tourism destination. *Applied Research in Quality of Life, 11*, 105–123. https://doi.org/10.1007/s11482-014-9357-8.

Kaplanidou, K., Karadakis, K., Gibson, H., Thapa, B., Walker, M., Geldenhuys, S., & Coetzee, W. (2013). Quality of life, event impacts, and mega-event support among South African residents before and after the 2010 FIFA World Cup. *Journal of Travel Research, 52*(5), 631–645. https://doi.org/10.1177/0047287513478501.

Kim, I., Jeon, S. M., & Hyun, S. S. (2012). Chain restaurant patrons' well-being perception and dining intentions the moderating role of involvement. *International Journal of Contemporary Hospitality Management, 24*(2–3), 402–429. https://doi.org/10.1108/09596111211217888.

Kim, K., Uysal, M., & Sirgy, M. J. (2013). How does tourism in a community impact the quality of life of community residents? *Tourism Management, 36*, 527–540. https://doi.org/10.1016/j.tourman.2012.09.005.

Kim, H., Woo, E., & Uysal, M. (2015). Tourism experience and quality of life among elderly tourists. *Tourism Management, 46*, 465–476. https://doi.org/10.1016/j.tourman.2014.08.002.

Kittiprapas, S., Sawangfa, O., Fisher, C., Powdthavee, N., & Nitnitiphrut, K. (2007). Happiness as a new paradigm for development and public policies. *Chulalongkorn Journal of Economics, 19*(3), 242–281.

Kroesen, M., & Handy, S. (2014). The influence of holiday-taking on affect and contentment. *Annals of Tourism Research, 45*, 89–101. https://doi.org/10.1016/j.annals.2013.12.006.

Kruger, S., Rootenberg, C., & Ellis, S. (2013). Examining the influence of the wine festival experience on tourists' quality of life. *Social Indicators Research, 111*(2), 435–452. https://doi.org/10.1007/s11205-012-0013-0.

Kühnel, J., & Sonnentag, S. (2011). How long do you benefit from vacation? A closer look at the fade-out of vacation effects. *Journal of Organizational Behavior, 32*(1), 125–143. https://doi.org/10.1002/job.699.

Lam, D., & So, A. (2013). Do happy tourists spread more word-of-mouth? The mediating role of life satisfaction. *Annals of Tourism Research, 43*, 646–650. https://doi.org/10.1016/j.annals.2013.06.001.

Lee, D.-J., Kruger, S., Whang, M.-J., Uysal, M., & Sirgy, M. J. (2014). Validating a customer well-being index related to natural wildlife tourism. *Tourism Management, 45*, 171–180. https://doi.org/10.1016/j.tourman.2014.04.002.

Lee, S. A., Manthiou, A., Jeong, M., Tang, L. R., & Chiang, L. L. (2015). Does consumers' feeling affect their quality of life? Roles of consumption emotion and its consequences. *International Journal of Tourism Research, 17*(4), 409–416. https://doi.org/10.1002/jtr.1988.

Lee, C. K., Kim, J. S., & Kim, J. S. (2018). Impact of a gaming company's CSR on residents' perceived benefits, quality of life, and support. *Tourism Management, 64*, 281–290. https://doi.org/10.1016/j.tourman.2017.09.002.

Liang, Z. X., & Hui, T. K. (2016). Residents' quality of life and attitudes toward tourism development in China. *Tourism Management, 57*, 56–67. https://doi.org/10.1016/j.tourman.2016.05.001.

Liao, X. Y., So, S. I., & Lam, D. (2016). Residents' perceptions of the role of leisure satisfaction and quality of life in overall tourism development: Case of a fast-growing tourism destination–Macao. *Asia Pacific Journal of Tourism Research, 21*(10), 1100–1113. https://doi.org/10.1080/10941665.2015.1107111.

Lin, C.-H. (2014). Effects of cuisine experience, psychological well-being, and self-health perception on the revisit intention of hot spring tourists. *Journal of Hospitality & Tourism Research, 38*(2), 243–265. https://doi.org/10.1177/1096348012451460.

Lin, J. H., Wong, J. Y., & Ho, C. H. (2013). Promoting frontline employees' quality of life: Leisure benefit systems and work-to-leisure conflicts. *Tourism Management, 36*, 178–187. https://doi.org/10.1016/j.tourman.2012.12.009.

López, J. M., & López, L. M. (2008). Producción científica española en marketing turístico. *Estudios Turísticos, 177*, 35–50.

Losada, J. L., & Lopez-Feal, R. (2003). *Métodos de investigación en Ciencias Humanas y Sociales*. Madrid: Thomson, Paraninfo.

Mactavish, J. B., MacKay, K. J., Iwasaki, Y., & Betteridge, D. (2007). Family caregivers of individuals with intellectual disability: Perspectives on life quality and the role of vacations. *Journal of Leisure Research, 39*(1), 127–155.

McCabe, S., & Johnson, S. (2013). The happiness factor in tourism: Subjective well-being and social tourism. *Annals of Tourism Research, 41*, 42–65. https://doi.org/10.1016/j.annals.2012.12.001.

McCabe, S., Joldersma, T., & Li, C. (2010). Understanding the benefits of social tourism: Linking participation to subjective well-being and quality of life. *International Journal of Tourism Research, 12*(6), 761–773. https://doi.org/10.1002/jtr.791.

Meng, B., & Choi, K. (2017). Theme restaurants' servicescape in developing quality of life: The moderating effect of perceived authenticity. *International Journal of Hospitality Management, 65*, 89–99. https://doi.org/10.1016/j.ijhm.2017.06.011.

Michalkó, G., Kiss, K., Kovács, B., & Sulyok, J. (2009). The impact of tourism on subjective quality of life among Hungarian population. *Hungarian Geographical Bulletin, 58*(2), 121–136.

Min, J. (2014). The relationships between emotional intelligence, job stress, and quality of life among tour guides. *Asia Pacific Journal of Tourism Research, 19*(10), 1170–1190. https://doi.org/10.1080/10941665.2013.839459.

Morgan, N., Pritchard, A., & Sedgley, D. (2015). Social tourism and well-being in later life. *Annals of Tourism Research, 52*, 1–15. https://doi.org/10.1016/j.annals.2015.02.015.

Nawijn, J. (2010). The holiday happiness curve: A preliminary investigation into mood during a holiday abroad. *International Journal of Tourism Research, 12*(3), 281–290. https://doi.org/10.1002/jtr.756.

Nawijn, J. (2011a). Determinants of daily happiness on vacation. *Journal of Travel Research, 50*(55), 559–566. https://doi.org/10.1177/0047287510379164.

Nawijn, J. (2011b). Happiness through vacationing: Just a temporary boost or long-term benefits? *Journal of Happiness Studies, 12*(4), 651–665. https://doi.org/10.1007/s10902-010-9221-y.

Nawijn, J., Marchand, M. A., Veenhoven, R., & Vingerhoets, A. J. (2010). Vacationers happier, but most not happier after a holiday. *Applied Research in Quality of Life, 5*(1), 35–47. https://doi.org/10.1007/s11482-009-9091-9.

Nawijn, J., Mitas, O., Lin, Y., & Kerstetter, D. (2013). How do we feel on vacation? A closer look at how emotions change over the course of a trip. *Journal of Travel Research, 52*(2), 265–274. https://doi.org/10.1177/0047287512465961.

Neal, J. D., Sirgy, M. J., & Uysal, M. (1999). The role of satisfaction with leisure travel/tourism services and experience in satisfaction with leisure life and overall life. *Journal of Business Research, 44*(3), 153–163. https://doi.org/10.1016/S0148-2963(97)00197-5.

Neal, J. D., Sirgy, M. J., & Uysal, M. (2004). Measuring the effect of tourism services on travelers' quality of life: Further validation. *Social Indicators Research, 69*(3), 243–277. https://doi.org/10.1007/s11205-004-5012-3.

Neal, J. D., Uysal, M., & Sirgy, M. J. (2007). The effect of tourism services on travelers' quality of life. *Journal of Travel Research, 46*(2), 154–163. https://doi.org/10.1177/0047287507303977.

Nunkoo, R., & So, K. K. F. (2015). Residents' support for tourism: Testing alternative structural models. *Journal of Travel Research, 55*, 847–861. https://doi.org/10.1177/0047287515592972.

Pagan, R. (2015). The contribution of holiday trips to life satisfaction: The case of people with disabilities. *Current Issues in Tourism, 18*(6), 524–538. https://doi.org/10.1080/13683500.2013.860086.

Pearce, P., Filep, S., & Ross, G. (2010). *Tourists, tourism and the good life*. London: Routledge/Taylor & Francis Group.

Polonsky, M., Hall, J., Vieceli, J., Atay, L., Akdemir, A., & Marangoz, M. (2013). Using strategic philanthropy to improve heritage tourist sites on the Gallipoli Peninsula, Turkey: Community perceptions of changing quality of life and of the sponsoring organization. *Journal of Sustainable Tourism, 21*(3), 376–395. https://doi.org/10.1080/09669582.2012.699061.

Powdthavee, N. (2007). Economics of happiness: A review of literature and applications. *Chulalongkorn Journal of Economics, 19*(1), 51–73.

Prebensen, N., Chen, J., & Uysal, M. (Eds.). (2014). *Creating experience value in tourism*. London: CABI.

Richards, G. (1999). Vacations and the quality of life: Patterns and structures. *Journal of Business Research, 44*(3), 189–198.

Ridderstaat, J., Croes, R., & Nijkamp, P. (2016a). A two-way causal chain between tourism development and quality of life in a small island destination: An empirical analysis. *Journal of Sustainable Tourism, 24*(10), 1461–1479. https://doi.org/10.1080/09669582.2015.1122016.

Ridderstaat, J., Croes, R., & Nijkamp, P. (2016b). The tourism development–quality of life nexus in a small island destination. *Journal of Travel Research, 55*(1), 79–94. https://doi.org/10.1177/0047287514532372.

Sánchez, M., & Marín, M. B. (2003). La investigación en turismo y economía de la empresa publicada en revistas especializadas españolas: 1996–2001. *Papers de Turisme, 33*, 6–39.

Sato, M., Jordan, J., & Daniel, F. (2014). The role of physically active leisure for enhancing quality of life. *Leisure Sciences: An Interdisciplinary Journal, 36*(3), 293–313. https://doi.org/10.1080/01490400.2014.886912.

Sirgy, M. J. (2010). Toward a quality-of-life theory of leisure travel satisfaction. *Journal of Travel Research, 49*(2), 246–260. https://doi.org/10.1177/0047287509337416.

Sirgy, M. J., Michalos, A. C., Ferriss, A. L., Easterlin, R. A., Patrick, D., & Pavot, W. (2006). The quality-of-life (QOL) research movement: Past, present, and future. *Social Indicators Research, 76*(3), 343–466. https://doi.org/10.1007/s11205-005-2877-8.

Sirgy, M. J., Kruger, P. S., Lee, D.-J., & Yu, G. B. (2011). How does a travel trip affect tourists' life satisfaction? *Journal of Travel Research, 50*(3), 261–275. https://doi.org/10.1177/0047287510362784.

Smith, M., & Puczkó, L. (2009). *Health and wellness tourism*. Oxford: Butterworth.

Smith, M., & Puczkó, L. (2014). *Health, tourism and hospitality: Spas, wellness and medical travel*. Abingdon: Routledge.

Su, L., Huang, S., & Chen, X. (2015). Effects of service fairness and service quality on tourists' behavioral intentions and subjective well-being. *Journal of Travel & Tourism Marketing, 32*(3–4), 290–307. https://doi.org/10.1080/10548408.2014.896766.

Tse, T. (2014). Does tourism change our lives? *Asia Pacific Journal of Tourism Research, 19*(9), 989–1008. https://doi.org/10.1080/10941665.2013.833125.

Uysal, M., Perdue, R., & Sirgy, M. J. (2012). *Handbook of tourism and quality-of-life research: Enhancing the lives of tourists and residents of host communities*. Dordrecht: Springer Science & Business Media.

Uysal, M., Sirgy, M. J., Woo, E., & Kim, H. L. (2016). Quality of life (QOL) and well-being research in tourism. *Tourism Management, 53*, 244–261. https://doi.org/10.1016/j.tourman.2015.07.013.

Veenhoven, R. (2009). The international scale interval study: Improving the comparability of responses to survey questions about happiness. In *Quality of life and the millennium challenge* (pp. 45–58). Dordrecht: Springer.

Wei, S., & Milman, A. (2002). The impact of participation in activities while on vacation on seniors' psychological well-being: A path model application. *Journal of Hospitality & Tourism Research, 26*(2), 175–185. https://doi.org/10.1177/1096348002026002006.

Woo, E., Kim, H., & Uysal, M. (2015). Life satisfaction and support for tourism development. *Annals of Tourism Research, 50*, 84–97. https://doi.org/10.1016/j.annals.2014.11.001.

Woo, E., Kim, H., & Uysal, M. (2016). A measure of quality of life in elderly tourists. *Applied Research in Quality of Life, 11*(1), 65–82. https://doi.org/10.1007/s11482-014-9355-x.

Part II
Quality of Life in Tourism and Its Impact on Local Community

Chapter 2
Tourism Marketing As a Tool to Improve Quality of Life Among Residents

Natalia Vila-Lopez, Ines Küster-Boluda, and Jose Trinidad Marin-Aguilar

Abstract Quality of life can be achieved improving certain subjective factors, such as attitudes, rather than emphasize objective factors. The born of this concept and the concern to use systematic and scientific methods for its evaluation are relatively recent.

Based on this premise, this chapter aims to analyze from a theoretical point of view, how certain tourism measures could improve both city-brand attitudes and sustainability attitudes among city residents', with the final purpose to increase their quality of life.

The philosophy of quality of life can be used to determine the effectiveness of the marketing mix, as far as each part of the mix should have a positive impact on quality of life. Thus, the quality of life from a marketing point of view starts with the devolvement of market products able to generate long-term benefits and to minimize negative effects; promoting favorable city-brand attitudes and sustainability attitudes among city residents'. All of this with a final purpose: improving their quality of life.

That is, the quality of life can be achieved by applying tourism marketing strategies capable of affect attitudes among citizens. On one hand, the attitudes towards sustainability (if tourism strategies are built based on economic, social and/or environmental sustainability) and, on the other, the attitudes towards the city-brand (as long as the public institutions use these strategies to strengthen a destination brand). The ultimate goal is to improve the quality of life as far as better attitudes lead to higher levels of quality of life among residents.

Keywords Quality of life · Tourism · Experiential marketing

N. Vila-Lopez · I. Küster-Boluda (✉)
Marketing Department, Faculty of Economics, University of Valencia, Valencia, Spain
e-mail: Natalia.Vila@uv.es; Ines.Kuster@uv.es

J. T. Marin-Aguilar
Marketing Department, Centro de Ciencias Económicas y Administrativas, Zapopan, Mexico

A. M. Campón-Cerro et al. (eds.), *Best Practices in Hospitality and Tourism Marketing and Management*, Applying Quality of Life Research,
https://doi.org/10.1007/978-3-319-91692-7_2

2.1 Introduction

Interest in the quality of life has existed long time ago (Baker and Palmer 2006). However, the emergence of the concept, and concerns about the systematic and scientific methods to evaluate this concept, are relatively recent (Baker and Palmer 2006; Sirgy et al. 2006; Sirgy 2001). The idea became popular in the late 1960s and today this concept has expanded too many different areas, such as: health, mental health, education, economics, politics and the world of services in general (Gomez and Sabeh 2001). Nowadays, and according to Fredrickson (2000), there has been renewed interest in the study of this concept, considering it as a positive effect of human emotions which includes many multi-dimensional attributes. At the same time and from the earliest literature (i.e. Aristotle) and even among the most renowned contemporary writers, the study of quality of life is understood as a field that reaches multiple disciplines (Baker and Palmer 2006).

In this framework, this chapter seeks to identify the relationship between residents' quality of life and marketing strategies, as far as public and private companies can develop tourism marketing strategies in a city to improve citizens' attitudes towards a place (community attachment) which will lastly augment their satisfaction with living in a particular place. To this end, we have done a theoretical revision about the origin and evolution of the quality of life concept within the marketing philosophy in order to demonstrate how some tourism marketing strategies could improve quality of life among city residents'.

In that way, is possible to understand that the quality of life is a complex multi-dimensional construct, difficult to define. The World Health Organization (WHO) *-is a specialized agency of the United Nations that is concerned with international public health* (WHO 1948)- considers that the quality of life corresponds to the perception of people regarding their position in life in the context of value systems and culture in which they live and in relation to its objectives, expectations, standards and concerns (WHOQOL 1995). From a marketing perspective, quality of life (or well-being) has been measured adopting a subjective approach using subjective indicators representing satisfaction. In this vein, and following Uysal et al. (2016), 246, we can conclude that marketing tourism strategies help to improve residents' attitudes, and this will lastly augment residents' quality of life (understood quality of life as the satisfaction with living in a particular place).

As regards to residents of a particular place, its quality can be improved through tourism products that are held in that city; such as festivals, restaurants, natural and cultural attractions, and opportunities for outdoor recreation among other. All of them lead to improve city brand attitudes among residents and, by extension, to increase their quality of life (Andereck et al. 2007). This is because the quality of life can be seen through a better standard of living, rising incomes, increasing employment opportunities and economic diversity (Andereck et al. 2007). All these items will improve when various events in the city are celebrated. Thus, then the concept of quality of life, as well as their evolution, is the final step of the link between tourism marketing strategies and those attitudes which are improved with them (sustainability attitudes and city brand attitudes with).

2.2 Quality of Life: Concept and Evolution

The quality of life of citizens in different cultures is a psychological and entirely subjective question (Sirgy 2001), and has been studied from different marketing perspectives such as tourism, communication, sociology and psychology (Neal et al. 2007).

The quality of life concept has been defined from different approaches. (i) The quality of the living conditions of a person. (ii) The satisfaction experienced by the person with certain conditions. (iii) A combination of objective and subjective components, for example, the mixture the life conditions of a person and the satisfaction that they produced. And, finally, (iv) a combination of living conditions and personal satisfaction weighted by the scale of values, aspirations and personal expectations (Borthwick- Duffy 1992; Felce and Perry 1995; Gomez and Sabeh 2001).

Research on quality of life has become a growing concern for individuals, communities and governments. That's because all try to find and maintain satisfaction, happiness and belief in a better future in a rapidly changing world (Eckersley 1999; Compton 1997; Lloyd and Auld 2002; Mercer 1994).

The quality of life origins date back to the first public debates about the environment and the deteriorating conditions of urban life (Felce and Perry 1995; Rogerson et al. 1988). During the late 1950s and early 1960s, the growing interest in learning about human welfare and concern about the consequences of society, raise the need to measure this reality using objective data (Gomez and Sabeh 2001). From the social sciences approach, some statistical indicators to measure social data and facts relating to the welfare of a population were developed (Gomez and Sabeh 2001). These indicators had their own evolution, evolving from objective, economic and social conditions to subjective elements able to approximate the quality of life concept (Perry and Felce 1995; Rogerson et al. 1988).

In the mid 1970s and early 1980s, some specific indicators based on social conditions were proposed to measure quality of life. They remain nowadays (Fernández-Ballesteros 1998). From this point, quality of life began be conceived as an inclusive concept that encompasses all areas of life (multidimensionality). Its improvement is related to a good economy, but also, to a favorable environment, social integration and social order, while accepting differences among members of the same community or a city (Fernández-Ballesteros 1998).

In this sense, the quality of life involves all areas in a comprehensive manner so that citizens perceive a better quality of life when all the above elements work together harmoniously to improve its welfare state (Fernández-Ballesteros 1998); encompassing, thereafter, objective conditions and subjective components (Gomez and Sabeh 2001; Schalock 1996). With regard to individual dimensions, quality of life includes: the quality of working life, the quality of family life, satisfaction with personnel health, the quality of leisure, economic well-being and satisfaction with the city among others (Carley 1986). Table 2.1 shows some examples of well-accepted quality of life dimensions in the context of citizens.

Table 2.1 Common dimensions of quality of life in the context of citizens

Context	Subjective indicators	Objectives indicators
Global	Satisfaction with life.	As the standard of living.
Health	Satisfaction with personnel health.	Global measure of fitness.
Work	Job satisfaction.	Absenteeism.
		Stay at work.
Family	Satisfaction with family and marriage.	The permanence in marriage.
		Amount of time spent with family.
Community	Satisfaction with neighborhood and community.	Number of crimes, educational facilities, leisure and cultural activities, transportation, environmental pollution, etc.
Home	Satisfaction with own home conditions.	Number of rooms by number of households, the level of equipment, the quality of furniture, quality of public services, etc.
Transport	Satisfaction with the conditions of the transportation itself.	The time spent in transport.
		Transport costs.
Education	Satisfaction with educational attainment themselves.	Educational attainment.
	Satisfaction with existing educational opportunities.	Number of quality educational programs available to a consumer segment.

Source: Sirgy and Lee (1996)

Based on the above and following Dennis et al. (1993), quality of life can be analyzed following alternative approaches that can be summed up into two types. On one hand, quantitative approaches, aimed at operationalizing the quality of life concept. To do this, different indicators have been proposed: (i) social indicators (which are based on external conditions related to the environment such as health; social welfare, friendship, standard of living, education, public safety, leisure, neighborhood, housing, etc.); (ii) psychological indicators (which are based on the subjective reactions of the individual to the presence or absence of certain life experiences); and (iii) ecological indicators (which based on the measurement of the fit between subjective resources and demands of the environment). On another hand, qualitative approaches, aimed at the interpretation of the quality of life concept by listening individuals' personal experiences, challenges and problems, and how social services have been used to support them effectively.

Moreover, the quality of life must be translated directly into the welfare of the whole society, using subjective and objective indicators to determine whether people are satisfied with their way of life, with the products and services offered by companies and governments (Andrews and Withey 2012). In this sense, the concept can be used for different purposes; including the assessment of the needs of people and their levels of satisfaction, the evaluation of the results of programs and human services, the direction and guidance in the provision of future services and the development of national and international policies aimed at the general population and/or at more specific audiences (Schalock 1996).

Researchers have become increasingly concerned with the identification and measurement of some key strategies that could be used to improve quality of life. Thus, numerous studies have included marketing strategies focused to leisure activities (such as, vacations alternatives, free time options and leisure facilities), as a mechanism for generating quality of life (Moller 1992; Unger and Kernan 1983). In this context, a marketing event has been considered as a key source to generate quality of life, because it would improve attitudes among citizens after experiencing a mega-event in a particular place. If the event is designed from a sustainable perspective (i.e. protects the environment, includes recycling policies etc.), it will improve city-brand attitudes but also and sustainability attitude.

Osborne (1992) suggests that the quality of life assessed from the perspective of leisure activities should be studied under two criteria: the living conditions and the life experience. He proposed the use of the some terms centered on where the tourist event (condition) is performed and focused on the person (experiences) (Compton 1997). A first approach is to use objective criteria (for example, the frequency of use of urban parks, sports facilities or services) to measure the quality of life in external terms to the experiences of the person (Allen 1991). The other approach tries to use subjective criteria that seek to measure quality of life in terms related to the experiences of the person (for example, the attitude with entertainment and leisure satisfaction) (Ragheb and Tate 1993). Strictly speaking, the quality of life is a natural reflex of the enjoyment and satisfaction of the experiences that a person lives in a particular place (Ragheb and Tate 1993).

Then, in successive lines, the relationship between quality of life and marketing will be developed.

2.3 Quality of Life and Marketing

Literature review (Armario 1993; Bell and Emery 1971; Dawson 1969; Farmer 1967; Feldman 1971; Fisk 1973; Kotler 1977, 1986, 2003; Lee and Kotler 2001; Rothe and Benson 1974; Sirgy and Lee 1996) shows that quality of life philosophy can be used to determine the efficacy of marketing mix strategies (product, price, place, and promotion). In this sense, marketing strategy objectives should consider the positive and measurable impact of quality of life (Sirgy and Lee 1996).

Once the specific marketing objectives have been stated, it is important to measure their efficacy. As Fig. 2.1 shows, the link between quality of life philosophy and marketing is present when marketing mix objectives and strategies turn around the development of products, services and programmers that can improve the consumers' welfare (Sirgy and Lee 1996). This means that companies have to market their products in an effective and efficient way in order to decrease the secondary and negative effects for consumers, and for another targets, while trying to find long-term benefits (Sirgy and Lee 1996).

From a marketing perspective, quality of life is similar to customer satisfaction, that is, to find the welfare of the consumer in all its meanings (Sirgy et al. 2006;

Fig. 2.1 Conceptual framework: quality of life & marketing. (Source: Sirgy and Lee 1996)

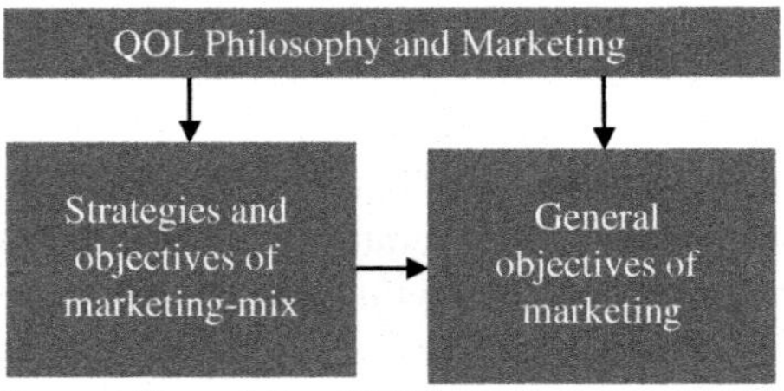

Sirgy 2001). Traditionally, marketing managers have defined marketing performance in terms of sales, economic profits, and market share in relation of a product, for a specific period of time (Aaker 1984; Day 1984; Shetty 1979). However, from an economic perspective, marketing objectives are oriented to reach financial growth and it is possible that companies act in a wrong and irresponsible way, socially speaking (Cespedes 1993; Preston and Richard 1986).

If marketing philosophy is defined in order to create quality of life, companies must focus their marketing activities in products, services and programs to improve consumers' welfare (Cespedes 1993; Preston and Richard 1986). For this reason, quality of life has received increased attention among marketing researchers (Sirgy 2001). For example, some authors have related quality of life with several marketing strategies, where the main objective is to create a better way to live among citizens (Armario 1993; Cuenca 2000; Lamb et al. 2002; Sandhusen 2002; Stanton et al. 2004).

More specifically, from a social marketing perspective, quality of life can be enhanced through the services offered to citizens, including entertainment and leisure (Cuenca 2000). Lloyd and Auld (2002) explain some studies that interrelate leisure and quality of life, indicating that they have mainly study how leisure activities are held on (e.g., frequency of use of entertainment venues), tending to forget the central criterion of quality of life, which is the person himself (i.e. satisfaction with leisure experience).

Leisure marketing has been studied in the social marketing context. In this framework; mega-events emerge as powerful tools to generate a form of tourism through entertainment or leisure, capable of generating a recreation for those who attend those (Dolles and Söderman 2010). Leisure is an area of human experience and a key aspect of quality of life that includes five different dimensions: playful, creative, festive, environmental-ecological and solidarity. These dimensions are shown in Table 2.2 (Cuenca 2000).

In summary, from a marketing perspective, it is possible to establish diverse actions/strategies able to generate an increased perception of quality of life of a given place. Among them, tourism marketing strategies are an alternative that can help in this way because these strategies can be formulated trying to develop some of the above five dimensions. For example, a company can generate quality of life from a playful, festive, environmental-ecological and solidarity dimension. An

Table 2.2 Leisure dimensions as drivers of quality of life

Dimension	Definition
Playful	How people enjoy at the various stages of life. It corresponds to hobbies, sports and other entertainment fields.
Creative	Formative, expressive and cultural experience. It refers to cultural access and creation, educational processes, lifestyles
Festive	Hallmark of cultures and societies. Traditional festivals, major events and theme parks.
Environmental – ecological	Related to physical and urban environment of the community and the experience of leisure in nature. Tourism, natural parks, outdoor sport among others.
Solidarity	Leisure is understood as a social, engaged and altruistic experience. Exemplified by volunteer groups and associations.

Source: Adapted from Cuenca (2000)

example would be to choose an event-marketing strategy, capable of enhancing the quality both from a playful-festive dimension (thanks to the experiences at the event) and from a solidarity-ecological-environmental dimension (thanks to the design of the event from a prism of sustainability, for example having environmentally conscious sponsors, promoting solidarity and respect for the environment actions etc.).

In summary, and following Cuenca (2000), the link between quality of life and marketing is articulated on four key aspects. These are:

1. To improve consumers welfare (residents and tourists) through the commercialization and/or consumptions of products (touristic products).
2. To reduce the negative and secondary effects associated to the commercialization and/or the consumption.
3. To reduce these negative and secondary effects with other targets.
4. To find long term effectiveness.

The next section shows, more specifically, how tourism marketing connects with quality of life. In this way, two marketing strategies (experiential marketing strategy and green marketing strategy) have been chosen in the tourism marketing context, because they seem useful tools to improve city brand attitudes and sustainability attitudes, which ultimately ends up increasing the quality of life.

We start addressing the relationship between city-brand and quality of life.

2.4 Quality of Life and Tourism Marketing

As Constanza et al. (2007) states, and as show before, quality of life is a way to satisfy people needs. So, quality of life also can be understood as the perceived satisfaction in diverse live contexts, taking into account their needs and expectative.

In this context, the quality of life concept is susceptible to study in the tourism field. Thus, several specialists have explored the contribution that tourism makes generally to various aspects of quality of life, both hosts (residents destination site) and visitors (tourists) (Neal et al. 1999, 2007; Moscardo 2009; Perdue et al. 1999).

Related to hosts, local population has been increasing recognized as part of tourism resources, and as such, the importance of community participation has been recognized (Andereck and Vogt 2000; AP 1992; Hardy et al. 2002; Simmons 1994). Thus, once a community becomes a tourist destination, the lives of residents in that community are affected by tourist activities (Jurowski et al. 1997). In this situation, the community support is essential for the proper development, planning and implementation of the strategic plan (Jurowski 1994). The successful development of tourism in a destination incorporates the cultural concerns of all stakeholders from the start of a project (Singal and Uysal 2009).

A number of studies have investigated how tourism marketing strategies can improve residents' attitudes. These studies have analyzed the community as a homogenous group of people, rather than a diversified mix of individuals with differences in status, class and power. This is problematic because it often disadvantaged social groups are those who suffer the most negative consequences of tourism development of a specific destination (Lui 2003).

Indeed, a growing number of complaints and concerns from some residents of any city with regard to how certain measures related to the development of tourism can impair their quality of life. These concerns can be classified as: (1) economic, such as taxation, inflation and labor supply; (2) sociocultural, as the image of the community; and (3) environmental, such as crowding, pollution of air, water and hearing, destruction of flora and fauna and waste generation (Andereck 1995a, b; Toro 1991; Christensen 1994; Marcouiller 1997; Pearce 1989; Ryan 1991).

McKercher (2003) points out that tourism promoters' should work actively in collaboration with local leaders and minority groups to ensure that the community retains control over the development of tourism, to soften the concerns outlined in previous lines. In fact, the participation of residents, in the planning process through a resident advisory council, emerged as an important indicator of sustainability to measure the development of community tourism (Choi and Sirakaya 2006).

On the other hand, Bass et al. (1993) focus on the role of ethnicity to look for patterns of use, environmental perception and behavior in recreational activities outdoors, finding differences in preferences between different ethnic groups. Mackay et al. (2002) found that the development of parks, recreational opportunities, historical and cultural sites, and special events, received the highest level of support from residents of the community; not, development of services used by tourists as lodging and tours.

2.4.1 Improving Residents' Attitudes to Increase Their Quality of Life

Following the City Marketing Theory, tourism marketing strategies can be used to increase the added value of a place and to improve the quality of life among its residents (Stanton et al. 2004). More specifically, tourism marketing strategies such as those promotion experiential events can be used to this end. As Getz and Page (2016, p. 599) have supported, this kind of events mainly focused to residents are "viewed as valued traditions, and perform essential roles within the community… they cannot exist independently of their host community. In this vein, evidence suggests that positive attitudes towards tourism may be related to how residents feel about living in community groups. According to Long et al. (1990), a positive attitude towards tourism strategies among city residents' was positively correlated with heaving a greater concern about the economic future of their community.

Some years early, Johnson et al. (1994) suggested also that attitudes towards tourism could be the result of self-image and feelings of group identity, and no so much, on the belief that tourism will result in personal benefits.

However, and Based on Ross (1992) suggestions, differences in the degree of quality of life can be also attributed to use of different indicators to measure satisfaction feelings. More specifically, there are three basic concepts used to measure the degree of satisfaction: (a) place of birth or duration of residence, (b) feelings about the community and (c) participation in the community. A more recent study showed that the concept of attachment is composed of two elements: feeling and involvement (Jurowski 1998). The results of this study indicate that those willing to commit time and energy to improve their community were less optimistic about the impacts of tourism than those who give higher evaluations to their quality of life and their emotional attachment to the community.

In the next two sections we will analyze how tourism marketing can help to improve the quality of life as long as tourism strategies are capable of stimulate two types of favorable attitudes among citizens: (i) attitudes towards sustainability (sustainability attitudes) and (ii) attitudes towards the city that promotes such strategies (city-brand attitudes).

2.4.2 Impact of Sustainable Attitudes on Residents' Quality of Life

Moscardo (2009) proposed a framework to examine the impact of tourism on the quality of life among residents. This framework argues that different types or approaches to tourism development can have different impacts on different forms of capital (human, construction, natural resources, political, social). The five main stakeholder groups described in this framework are:

- Tourists.
- Residents of the regions where tourists leave (source regions).
- Residents of the regions where tourists pass on their way to other destinations (transit regions).
- Residents of destination regions.
- People working in tourism.

Similarly, Moscardo (2009) also provides an example of the implementation of the framework of the quality of life by analyzing the different ways in which the travel experience can detract from, or add to, the experiences of individual tourists. These issues, then, draw attention to the different types of capital (human, cultural, political, and social) with particular emphasis on understanding the processes and mechanisms that link the characteristics of tourism with the elements and dimensions of the experience lived by tourist (Moscardo 2009). The underlying idea is the desire to promote attitudes toward tourism that are able to influence the quality of life. One important part tourism attitudes are those that have to do with sustainability, understood from the triple perspective: economic sustainability, social sustainability and environmental sustainability.

In sum, the various measures taken to promote tourism development in a specific area can boost or not sustainable attitudes to the environment. Those tourism strategies that are sustainable (economically, socially and environmentally), encourage positive attitudes towards sustainability, thus the quality of life will be enhanced.

Below we will show what is meant by sustainable tourism strategies (economic, social and environmental), capable of promoting sustainable attitudes and therefore capable to impact positively on the quality of life among residents.

2.4.2.1 Economic Impact

Tourism has been identified as a powerful tool for economic development. It can help depressed regions to restructure and reduce poverty (Edwards and Llurdes 1996; Gordon and Raber 2000; Hall and Lew 2009; Xie 2006). Among the benefits of tourism development that a region can obtained, the most relevant is probably the one related to economic issues. These include higher tax revenues, increased employment opportunities, additional income, increased public spending, and in some cases, foreign exchange earnings and an increase in the tax base of local governments based on the increase income. These indicators are usually labeled as "indicators of quality of life", because they represent how tourism impacts move to residents' benefits. These benefits contribute, individually or collectively, economic and material welfare of the community of destination (Moscardo 2009; Sirgy et al. 1995).

2.4.2.2 Sociocultural Impact

Tourism development affects different sociocultural characteristics of residents such as habits, daily routines, beliefs and values (Dogan 1989). Brunt and Courtney (1999) mention that tourism can help to improve community services, additional parks, recreation and cultural services; and the promotion of cultural activities. Such improvements, will also improve the welfare of the residents of the tourist destination. Liu and Var (1986) also predict that tourism can increase entertainment, historical and cultural exhibitions impact (i.e. tourism development plays a role increasing cultural exchange events, and identity). These improvements contribute to emotional well-being of residents and participants.

2.4.2.3 Environment Impact

Sometimes, tourism development causes significant environmental damages. That happens when the destination is developed to meet the needs of tourists regardless of environmental damage (Andereck et al. 2005). Andereck (1995a, b) identified several potential environmental consequences of tourist development: air pollution (such as emissions from vehicles and aircraft); water pollution (such as wastewater discharge); destruction of wildlife because of hunting; the destruction of flora; and deforestation.

However, the environmental impacts can also be positive. For example, Liu and Var (1986) study reported that half of the residents perceived that tourism provides more parks and recreation areas or also public facilities. Contrary, these residents did not perceive ecological deterioration because of tourism in their city. Perdue et al. (1990) also found a positive environmental impact of tourism. They mentioned that the development of tourism improves the appearance of the city and results in greater opportunities for recreation and parks than before.

Nevertheless, a major concern exists about how tourism can negatively influence to the quality of life among residents. These negative impacts can be in the form of overcrowding, traffic and parking problems, higher crime, higher cost of living, friction between tourists and residents and so on (Ap and Crompton 1993; McCool and Martin 1994; Bastias-Perez and Var 1995; Ross 1992; Tooman 1997).

2.4.3 Impact of City-Brand Attitudes on Residents' Quality of Life

Tourism strategies are not only capable to influence residents' sustainability attitudes. They can also improve (or worsen) their attitudes toward the destination, and more specifically, to the brand of the city in which such strategies are applied.

Indeed, those destinations managers that choose to manage the image of a city as a brand need to develop a communication policy of the city considering different targets: residents' tourists, investors and potential residents (Kotler et al. 1999). To promote a city-brand several communication tools can be used. One of the most promising instrument is to hold events that lead to feel experiences and arouse emotions among tourist and residents.

Similarly, in a context of local competition, some cities have used advertising campaigns in a film to present positive aspects of a city that want to attract new residents; for example presenting the advantages of local housing, with good communications channels, and other aspects that assure the quality of life of the place announced. Contrary, on a framework of national or international competition, this medium has been only used to attract tourists and visitors, but not new residents (Elizagarate 2003).

Also, in a context of local competition, some cities have used advertising campaigns in film to present aspects that are interesting to attracting new residents; in particular presenting the advantages of local housing, with good communications, and other aspects of quality of life. In a context of national or international competition, this medium is only used in order to attract tourists and visitors (Elizagarate 2003).

Actually, the relevance of the resident is not questionable. Following Elizagarate (2003), the internal communication policy of a city should have, as a main objective, to strengthen the self-image of the city, which means to reinforce the image of the city among residents. To this end, and according to Noisette and Vallerugo (1998), urban marketing managers could work on the following aspects:

Strengthen the relationship of citizens with their city, which implies to maintain a positive view towards the city. That is, to get positive opinions towards a city, residents' satisfaction must be reached first. Therefore, public policy managers should be capable to provide citizens with what they expect of the city where they live (Elizagarate 2003).

Convert each resident in an active communicator of the positive image of his/her city among other people. In this line, many cities have used the so-called civic spirit, bonding with success the promotional efforts of all operators in the city (businessmen, chambers of commerce and business associations, traders, etc.) (Elizagarate 2003). All can be ambassadors of their city, being the synergistic effect between them highly productive.

In short, city-brand attitudes among residents are the consequence of several marketing strategies, which lastly explain the quality of life that they feel. Therefore, a touristic destination cannot turn our backs on the potential of marketing tools. In this line, Lee and Sirgy (2004) highlight three key benefits associated with the marketing of a touristic destination that justify the relevance of this discipline to improve the quality of life: (1) marketing is a key success factor in the economy of enterprises, organizations and nations (2) that's because the marketing acts directly on improving the quality of life of people living in these nations, (3) the marketing generates more competitive firms and destination.

The relationship between marketing and quality of life benefits the entire society as it provides support to facilitate the lives of people and helps to improve the performance of any organization (Lamb et al. 2002; Sandhusen 2002; Stanton et al. 2004).

Thus, the managers of a particular tourist destination should go for the marketing, promoting the development of tourism strategies able to consolidate a strong brand-destination which, ultimately, will improve the quality among resident.

2.5 Conclusions

Residents' quality of life is an important objective to reach. The tourism marketing has a lot to do with the levels of quality of life that can be finally achieved. Specifically, various tourism marketing strategies can be used to improve the quality of life among residents of a particular place as long as such strategies are able to develop first positive attitudes towards both, the city that promotes such strategies (city brand attitudes) and the sustainability of the place where such strategies are applied.

The quality of life is the most desired end to live in a certain place. Previous research has supported the positive relation between city-brand attitudes and perceived quality of life. This implies that a timely strategy for the governors who are interested in enhancing the quality of life among residents of a place needs to improve their city-brand attitudes first, generating a pride in the place where they live.

To get this, it becomes a priority for public managers to innovate applying some marketing strategies that can be build recognizable cities which will bring benefits to local residents in terms of perceived quality of life. Among these marketing strategies two options are raising weight in recent years. On one side, experiential/leisure marketing strategies, that can be based on the development of emotional mega-events in the city to encourage residents' emotions. On another side, green marketing strategies that can be based on stimulating sustainable behaviors among firms and residents to encourage their compromise with the city. The final result of these measures will be higher levels of quality of life among residents in a place.

In sum, the quality of life of citizens in different cultures is a psychological and totally subjective question, so that the efforts made by local governments to change the behavior of citizens can lead to increase this characteristic of social perception. The citizens' way of life is a reflection of the services and strategies developed by governments. So it is the responsibility of each government to give citizens some quality events, enough infrastructure, efficient public services,, ecological rules etc.

Future studies should paid attention to cultural differences in order to test to what extent marketing strategies must be adapted to the context. That is, to demonstrate if residents' attitudes could be improve using different strategic ways with the final end of augmenting residents' quality of life. For example, in high context cultures, experiential mega-events could be used to stimulate residents' emotions because this kind of cultures encourage greater participation and immersion. Also, green marketing strategies could be applied, as far as greater concern for environmental issues will exist among collectivist citizens (high-context cultures). As Font et al. (2016, p. 69) have demonstrated, "Latin America had the highest mean score for institutional collectivism value", and it also had "high in-group collectivism values".

References

Aaker, D. (1984). *Strategic market management*. New York: Wiley.
Allen, L. (1991). Benefits of leisure services to community satisfaction. In B. Driver, P. Brown, & G. Peterson (Eds.), *Benefits of leisure* (pp. 332–350). State College: Venture Publishing Inc.
Andereck, K. L. (1995a). Environmental consequences of tourism: A review of recent research. In: S. F. McCool & A. E. Watson (Eds.), *Linking tourism, the environment, and sustainability* (General Technical Report No. INT-GTR 323, pp. 77–81).
Andereck, K. L. (1995b). Environmental consequences of tourism: A review of recent research. In *Linking tourism, the environment, and sustainability* (General Technical Report No. INT-GTR-323). Annual meeting of the National Recreation and Park Association, 1994.
Andereck, K. L., & Vogt, C. A. (2000). The relationship between residents' attitudes toward tourism and tourism development options. *Journal of Travel Research, 39*(1), 27–36.
Andereck, K. L., Valentine, K. M., Knopf, R. C., & Vogt, C. A. (2005). Residents' perceptions of community tourism impacts. *Annals of Tourism Research, 32*(4), 1056–1076.
Andereck, K. L., Valentine, K. M., Vogt, C. A., & Knopf, R. C. (2007). A cross-cultural analysis of tourism and quality of life perceptions. *Journal of Sustainable Tourism, 15*(5), 483–502.
Andrews, F. M., & Withey, S. B. (2012). Social indicators of well-being: Americans' perceptions of life quality. Springer Science & Business Media.
AP, J. (1992). Residents' perceptions of tourism impacts. *Annals of Tourism Research, 19*, 665–690.
AP, J., & Crompton, J. L. (1993). Residents strategies for responding to tourism impacts. *Journal of Travel Research, 32*(1), 47–50.
Armario, M. (1993). *Marketing*. Barcelona: Ariel Economía.
Baker, D. A., & Palmer, R. J. (2006). Examining the effects of perceptions of community and recreation participation on quality of life. *Social Indicators Research, 75*(3), 395–418.
Bass, J. M., Ewert, A., & Chavez, D. J. (1993). Influence of ethnicity on recreational and natural environment use patterns: Managing recreation sites for ethnic and racial diversity. *Environmental Management, 17*, 523–529.
Bastias-Perez, P., & Var, T. (1995). Perceived impacts of tourism by residents. *Annals of Tourism Research, 22*(1), 208–210.
Bell, M. L., & Emory, C. W. (1971). The faltering marketing concept. *Journal of Marketing, 75*, 37–42.
Borthwick-Duffy, S. A. (1992). Quality of life and quality of care in mental retardation. In L. Rowitz (Ed.), *Mental retardation in the year 2000* (pp. 52–66). Berlin: Springer.
Brunt, P., & Courtney, P. (1999). Host perceptions of sociocultural impacts. *Annals of Tourism Research, 26*, 493–515.
Carley, K. (1986). An approach for relating social structure to cognitive structure. *Journal of Mathematical Sociology, 12*(2), 137–189.
Cespedes, F. V. (1993). Ethical issues in distribution. In N. C. Smith & J. A. Quelch (Eds.), *Ethics in marketing* (pp. 473–490). Homewood: Irwin.
Choi, H. C., & Sirakaya, E. (2006). Sustainability indicators for managing community tourism. *Tourism Management, 27*(6), 1274–1289.
Christensen, N. A. (1994). *A study of the relationships of tourism and potential impacts on Montana counties*. Missoula: The University of Montana.
Compton, D. (1997). *Rehabilitation, medicine, and quality of life* (Unpublished Visiting Scholar Lecture). University of Sydney.
Constanza, R., Fisher, B., Ali, S., Beer, C., Bond, L., Boumans, R., Danigelis, N. L., Dickinson Hudspeth, T., & Mahoney, D. (2007). Quality of life: An approach integrating opportunities, human needs, and subjective well-being. *Ecological Economics, 61*(2–3), 267–276.
Cuenca, C. M. (2000). *Ocio humanista. Dimensiones y manifestaciones actuales del ocio* (Documento de Estudios de Ocio 16). Instituto de Estudios de Ocio, Universidad de Deusto, España.

Dawson, L. M. (1969, December). The human concept: New philosophy for business. *Business Horizons, 12*, 29–38.

Day, G. S. (1984). *Strategic market planning*. St Paul: West Publishing.

Dennis, R. E., Williams, W., Giangreco, M. F., & Cloninger, C. J. (1993). Quality of life as context for planning and evaluation of services for people with disabilities. *Exceptional Children, 59*(6), 499–512.

Dogan, H. Z. (1989). Forms of adjustment: Sociocultural impacts of tourism. *Annals of Tourism Research, 16*, 216–236.

Dolles, H., & Söderman, S. (2010). Addressing ecology and sustainability in mega-sporting events: The 2006 football world cup in Germany. *Journal of Management & Organization, 16*, 587–600.

Eckersley, R. (1999). *Quality of life in Australia: An analysis of public perceptions* (Discussion Paper 23). The Australia Institute Ltd, Lyneham, ACT.

Edwards, J., & Llurdes, J. (1996). Mines and quarries: Industrial heritage tourism. *Annals of Tourism Research, 23*, 341–363.

Elizagarate, V. (2003). *Marketing de ciudades*. Madrid: Ediciones Pirámide.

Farmer, R. N. (1967). Would you want your daughter to marry a marketing man? *Journal of Marketing, 31*, 1–10.

Felce, D., & Perry, J. (1995). Quality of life: It's definition and measurement. *Research in Developmental Disabilities, 16*(1), 51–74.

Feldman, L. P. (1971, July). Societal adaptation: A new challenge for marketing. *Journal of Marketing, 35*, 54–60.

Fernández-Ballesteros, R. (1998). Calidad de vida: Concepto y Contribución. In J. Adair, D. Belanger, & K. Dion (Eds.), *Avances en la Ciencia Psicológica* (Vol. 1). Sussex: Psicología.

Fisk, G. (1973). Criteria for a theory of responsible consumption. *Journal of Marketing, 37*(2), 24–31.

Font, X., Garay, L., & Jones, S. (2016). A social cognitive theory of sustainability empathy. *Annals of Tourism Research, 58*(6), 5–80.

Fredrickson, B. L. (2000, March 7). Cultivating positive emotions to optimize health and well-being. In *Prevention and Treatment 3*, Article 0001a., Retrieved January 16, 2002, from http://journals.apa.org/prevention/volume3/pre0030001a.htm

Getz, D., & Page, S. J. (2016). Progress and prospects for event tourism research. *Tourism Management, 52*, 593–631.

Gomez, M., & Sabeh, E. (2001). *Calidad de vida. Evolución del concepto y su influencia en la investigación y la práctica*. Salamanca, Instituto Universitario de Integración en la Comunidad, Facultad de Psicología, Universidad de Salamanca.

Gordon, R., & Raber, M. (2000). *Industrial heritage in Northwest Connecticut: A guide to history and archaeology*. New Haven: Connecticut Academy of Arts and Sciences.

Hall, C. M., & Lew, A. (2009). *Understanding and managing tourism impacts: An integrated approach*. New York: Routledge.

Hardy, A., Beeton, R. J. S., & Pearson, L. (2002). Sustainable tourism: An overview of the concept and its position in relation to conceptualization of tourism. *Journal of Sustainable Tourism, 10*, 475–496.

Johnson, J., Snepenger, D. J., & Akis, S. (1994). Residents' perceptions of tourism development. *Annals of Tourism Research, 21*, 629–642.

Jurowski, C. (1994). *The interplay of elements affecting host community resident attitudes toward tourism: A path analytic approach*. Unpublished doctoral dissertation, Virginia Polytechnic Institute and State University, Blacksburg.

Jurowski, C. (1998). A study of community sentiments in relation to attitudes toward tourism development. *Tourism Analysis, 3*(1), 17–24.

Jurowski, C., Uysal, M., & Williams, D. R. (1997). A theoretical analysis of host community resident reactions to tourism. *Journal of Tourism Research, 36*, 3–11.

Kotler, P. (1977). From sales obsession to marketing effectiveness. *Harvard Business Review, 55*(6), 67–75.

Kotler, P. (1986). *Principles of marketing* (3rd ed.). Englewood Cliffs: Prentice-Hall.

Kotler, P. (2003). *Fundamentos de marketing*. México: Prentice Hall.

Kotler, P., Asplund, C., Rein, I., & Heider, D. H. (1999). *Marketing places Europe: Attracting investments, industries, residents and visitors to European cities, communities, regions and nations*. London: Pearson Education.

Lamb, C., Hair, H., & McDaniel, C. (2002). *Marketing*. (6th ed.). International Thomson Editores.

Lee, N., & Kotler, P. (2001). *Social marketing: Influencing behaviors for good* (4th ed.). Los Angeles: SAGE.

Lee, D. J., & Sirgy, M. J. (2004). Quality-of-life (quality of life) marketing: Proposed antecedents and consequences. *Journal of Macromarketing, 24*, 44–58.

Liu, J. C., & Var, T. (1986). Resident attitudes toward tourism impacts in Hawaii. *Annals of Tourism Research, 13*(2), 193–214.

Lloyd, K., & Auld, C. (2002). The role of leisure in determining quality of life: Issues of content and measurement. *Social Indicators Research, 57*, 43–71.

Long, T. P., Perdue, R. R., y Allen, L. (1990). Rural resident tourism perceptions and attitudes by community level of tourism. *Journal of Travel Research, 28*(3), 3–9.

Lui, Z. (2003). Sustainable tourism development: A critique. *Journal of Sustainable Tourism, 11*, 459–475.

MacKay, K. J., Andereck, K. L., & Vogt, C. A. (2002). Understanding vacationing motorist niche markets. *Journal of Travel Research*, 40(4), 356–363.

Marcouiller, D. W. (1997). Towards integrative tourism planning in rural America. *Journal of Planning Literature, 11*, 337–357.

McCool, S. F., & Martin, S. R. (1994). Community attachment and attitudes toward tourism development. *Journal of Travel Research, 32*(3), 29–34.

McKercher, B. (2003). *Sustainable tourism development – Guiding principles for planning and management*. Presented at the National seminar on Sustainable Tourism Development, November 5–9, Bishkek, Kyrgyzstan.

Mercer, C. (1994). Assessing liveability: From statistical indicators to policy benchmarks. In C. Mercer (Ed.), *Urban and regional quality of life indicators* (pp. 3–12). Brisbane: Institute for Cultural Policy Studies/Griffith University.

Moller, V. (1992). Spare time use and perceived Well-being among black south African youth. *Social Indicators Research, 26*, 309–351.

Moscardo, G. (2009). Tourism and quality of life: Toward a more critical approach. *Tourism and Hospitality Research, 9*(2), 159–170.

Neal, J. D., Sirgy, J. M., & Uysal, M. (1999). The role of satisfaction with leisure travel/tourism services and experiences in satisfaction with leisure life and overall life. *Journal of Business Research, 44*(3), 153–164.

Neal, J. D., Uysal, M., & Sirgy, M. J. (2007). The effect of tourism services on travelers' quality of life. *Journal of Travel Research, 46*(2), 154–163.

Noisette, P., & Vallerugo, F. (1998). *Le marketing des villes* (pp. 216–266). París: Les Édition d'Organisation.

Osborne, S. (1992). The quality dimension.Evaluating quality of service and quality of life in human services. *British Journal of Social Work, 22*, 437–453.

Pearce, D. (1989). *Tourist Development*. London: Longman.

Perdue, R. R., Long, P. T., & Allen, L. R. (1990). Resident support for tourism development. *Annals of Tourism Research, 17*(4), 586–599.

Perdue, R. R., Long, P. T., & Kang, Y. S. (1999). Boomtown tourism and resident quality of life: The marketing of gaming to host community residents. *Journal of Business Research, 44*(3), 165–177.

Perry, J., & Felce, D. (1995). Objective Assesment of quality of life: How much do they agree with each other? *Journal of Community and Applied Social Psychology, 5*, 1–19.

Preston, I. L., & Richard, J. (1986). The relationship of miscomprehension to deceptiveness in FTC cases. In R. Lutz (Ed.), *Advances in consumer research* (Vol. 13, pp. 138–142). Provo: Association for Consumer Research.

Ragheb, M., & Tate, R. (1993). A behavioural model of leisure participation, based on leisure attitude, motivation and satisfaction. *Leisure Studies, 12*, 61–70.

Rogerson, R. J., Findlay, A. M., & Morris, A. S. (1988). *Quality of life in British cities: A summary report*. Dpto. de Geografía Universidad de Glasgow, Escocia.

Ross, G. F. (1992). Resident perceptions of the impact of tourism on an Australian city. *Journal of Travel Research, 30*(3), 13–17.

Rothe, J. T., & Benson, L. (1974). Intelligent consumption an attractive alternative to the marketing concept. *MSU Business Topics*, (Winter), 29–34.

Ryan, C. (1991). *Recreational tourism: A social science perspective*. London: Routledge.

Sandhusen, L. (2002). *Mercadotecnia* (1a ed.). México: Compañía Editorial Continental S.A.

Schalock, R. L. (1996). Reconsidering the conceptualization and measurement of quality of life. In R. L. Schalock (Ed.), *Quality of life: Conceptualization and measurement* (Vol. 1, pp. 123–139). Washington, DC: American Association on Mental Retardation.

Shetty, Y. K. (1979). New look at corporate goals. *California Management Review, 22*(Winter), 73.

Simmons, D. G. (1994). Community participation in tourism planning. *Tourism Management, 15*, 98–108.

Singal, M., & Uysal, M. (2009). Resource commitment in destination management: The case of Abingdon,Virginia. *Tourism Review, 57*(3), 329–344.

Sirgy, M. J. (2001). *Handbook of quality-of-life research: An ethical marketing perspective* (Vol. 8). Dordrecht: Kluwer Academic Publisher.

Sirgy, M. J., & Lee, D. J. (1996). Setting socially responsible marketing objectives a quality-of-life approach. *European Journal of Marketing, 30*(5), 20–34.

Sirgy, M. J., Meadow, H. L., & Samli, A. C. (1995). Past, present, and future: An overview of quality-of-life research in marketing. In M. Joseph Sirgy & A. C. Samli (Eds.), *New dimensions of marketing and quality-of-life research* (pp. 335–364). Westport: Greenwood Press.

Sirgy, M. J., Michalos, A. C., Ferriss, A. L., Esaterlin, R. A., Patrick, D., & Pavot, W. (2006). The quality-of-life (QOL) research movement: Past, present, and future. *Social Indicators Research, 76*, 343–466.

Stanton, W., Etzel, M., & Walker, B. (2004). *Fundamentos de Marketing* (13rd ed..) Mc Graw Hill.

The WHOQOL Group. (1995). The World Health Organization quality of life assessment (WHOQOL): Position paper from the World Health Organization. *Social Science & Medicine, 41*, 1403.

Tooman, L. A. (1997). Tourism and development. *Journal of Travel Research, 35*(3), 33–40.

Toro, F. (1991). *Desempeño y productividad. Contribuciones de la psicología organizacional.* Medellín: Cincel.

Unger, L., & Kernan, J. (1983). On the meaning of leisure: An investigation of some determinants of the subjective experience. *The Journal of Consumer Research, 9*(4), 381–392.

Uysal, M., Sirgy, M. J., Woo, E., & Kim, H. L. (2016). Quality of life (QOL) and Well-being research in tourism. *Tourism Management, 53*, 244–261.

WHO. (1948, August 7). World Health Organization. *The British Medical Journal. BMJ Publishing Group, 2*(4570), 302–303.

Xie, P. (2006). Developing industrial heritage tourism: A case study of the proposed jeep museum in Toledo, Ohio. *Tourism Management, 27*(6), 1321–1330.

Chapter 3
What Is the Nature of the Relationship Between Tourism Development and the Quality of Life of Host Communities?

Eunju Woo, Muzaffer Uysal, and M. Joseph Sirgy

Abstract This chapter addresses an important question: Do tourist communities with higher levels of quality of life (QOL) contribute to tourism development, and vice versa? Based on the research literature, the answer to this question is "yes, but it depends." Yes, tourism communities with higher levels of QOL do contribute to tourism development through a pull (rather than push) process (a concept well-known in the tourism literature). Such communities are attractive to tourists because they have good leisure facilities (rated high on food/beverage establishments, shopping malls, and other sports and recreation facilities), good lodging facilities (nice hotels and other lodging accommodations), good transportation facilities (good subways, trains, buses, taxis, etc.), reasonable cost of living (affordable goods and services), safe from crime (rated high on safety indicators such as low crime and high law enforcement), safe from environmental toxins (rated high on environmental well-being measures such as low water/air/land pollution), access to medical facilities (rated high on healthcare), etc. Based on the research literature, we make an attempt to explain the study findings by arguing that there is a reciprocal link between tourism development and QOL of host communities. We also demonstrate that the QOL effect is not always as strong and positive, which can be explained by

E. Woo (✉)
Department of Tourism Administration, Pukyong National University, Busan, Republic of Korea
e-mail: eunjuwoo@pknu.ac.kr

M. Uysal
Department of Hospitality & Tourism Management, Isenberg School of Management, University of Massachusetts, Amherst, MA, USA
e-mail: muysal@isenberg.umass.edu

M. Joseph Sirgy
Department of Marketing, Pamplin College of Business, Virginia Polytechnic Institute and State University, Blacksburg, VA, USA
e-mail: sirgy@vt.edu

A. M. Campón-Cerro et al. (eds.), *Best Practices in Hospitality and Tourism Marketing and Management*, Applying Quality of Life Research,
https://doi.org/10.1007/978-3-319-91692-7_3

a number of moderator effects. One important moderator is the carrying capacity of the community (the extent to which a community can accommodate large number of tourists with no adverse consequences). Other moderators are identified and discussed. Public policy implications of these relationships are also discussed.

Keywords Quality of life · Tourism development · Life satisfaction

3.1 Introduction

Positive psychology refers to a perspective in psychological research that focuses on the role of positive emotions, character strengths, and institutions that contributes to positive emotions and character strengths (Seligman and Csikszentmihalyi 2000). Positive psychology researchers assert that much of past research on human behavior has focused on behavioral problems (e.g., depression, aggression, fear, anxiety, and stress). Positive psychology seeks to complement past research by focusing on the positive aspects of human psychology (e.g., human happiness, well-being, and the factors that contribute to the good life). This movement in psychology has influenced other social and behavioral science disciplines including tourism (e.g., Biswas-Diener 2011; Filep 2014; Marujo et al. 2014; Pearce 2009). As such, research in positive psychology in tourism is now referred to as "positive tourism."

The positive tourism literature is replete with studies that have argued, and to some extent empirically supported, the notion that tourism development improves the economic well-being of communities as destinations through poverty reduction, taxes, income, and employment generated as a result of tourism activities (e.g., Chou 2013; Croes 2012a, b; Lee and Chang 2008; Manyara and Jones 2007; Vanegas 2012). However, the contribution of tourism development to improving well-being of local economies may be a function of the rate of economic multipliers, level of infrastructure and human development, favorable policies, and effective governance systems in the destination community (e.g., Allen et al. 1988; Andereck and Nyaupane 2011; Ap and Crompton 1998; Aref 2011). Some tourism economists (e.g., Croes 2012a; Vanegas 2012) argue that there is a reciprocal relationship between economic growth and tourism. A strong economy makes certain tourism investments possible, and a healthy and growing tourism sector can also help support the growth of the local economy. Recent research on the topic hints at the possibility that tourist communities with higher levels of QOL contribute to tourism development and vice versa. One can also argue that higher levels of QOL in a community may also be a sign of economic stability and growth. Figure 3.1 depicts the general purpose of the chapter, namely a reciprocal link between tourism development and QOL of host communities.

The goal of this chapter is to review the tourism literature to make the case that there is a reciprocal link between tourism development and quality of life of residents of host communities. The chapter proceeds as follows. First, we discuss the concept of tourism development, followed by types of tourism impacts and

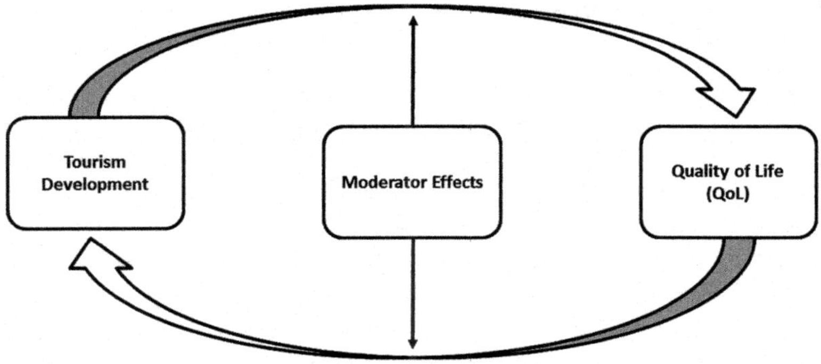

Fig. 3.1 The reciprocal relationships between tourism development and the quality of life of host communities

measures, and residents' perceptions of tourism development impacts. The second section of this chapter focuses on the bi-directional relationship between tourism development and QOL. This third section discusses moderator effects such as stage of tourism development, stakeholder characteristics, involvement in the community, and level of attachment. The conclusion section of the chapter ends with suggestions for future research.

3.2 Tourism Development

Recently, much interest has been shown in marketing and management strategies for tourism destinations (Meng et al. 2010). Some of the research in this area has focused on the social and economic impact of tourism development on host communities (e.g., Allen et al. 1988; Andereck and Nyaupane 2011; Ap and Crompton 1998; Aref 2011). Once a host community becomes a tourism destination, the lives of the residents in that community become affected, both positively and negatively. In other words, tourism development affects the lives of community residents in different ways. Positive impact of tourism development encourages residents' support of the tourism industry, which is essential for tourism destination development. The continued success, competitiveness, and sustainability of the tourism in a given community is dependent on the impact of tourism development on that community (Gursoy et al. 2002; Moscardo et al. 2013). Much research is available documenting the impact of tourism development on the QOL of residents of host communities (e.g., Kim 2002; Perdue et al. 1999). This research can be categorized in three camps: (1) identifying types of tourism impact in a community context; (2) describing tourism impact assessment instruments; and (3) capturing residents' perceptions and evaluations of tourism impact on their community. We will discuss this research organized by these three categories.

3.2.1 Types of Tourism Impact

Early research in tourism impact has focused on the perceived impact of tourism development. (e.g., Allen et al. 1988; Belisle and Hoy 1980; Liu et al. 1987; Liu and Var 1986; Nunkoo et al. 2013; Perdue et al. 1987; Ross 1992; Sharpley 2014; Sheldon and Var 1984). The major dimensions of perceived impact include economic, social, cultural, political, and environment. These tend to be grouped in three major categories: (1) economic, (2) socio-cultural, (3) physical and environmental (Andereck et al. 2005; Uysal et al. 2012b). These three major dimensions of perceived impact have positive and negative aspects. In other words, residents perceive tourism impact as having both positive and negative impact on the economic, socio-cultural, and physical environment of their community (Perdue et al. 1995).

The most prominent community benefits of tourism development are economic, such as more jobs, higher tax revenue, increases in job opportunities, increased public spending, and foreign exchange earnings (e.g., Lankford 1994; McCool and Martin 1994; Uysal et al. 2012b). These benefits individually and collectively contribute to the economic well-being of community residents. As such, economic impact of tourism development has been frequently researched relative to other types of tourism development impact (Mason 2008).

A number of studies not only highlighted the positive economic impact of tourism development on host communities but also identified negative effects. Positive impact of tourism development may include contribution to foreign exchange earnings, increased government revenues, increased employment, greater regional development, and heightened economic quality of life (McCool and Martin 1994). Negative impact of tourism development includes inflation opportunity and over-dependence on tourism (Pearce 1989). A comprehensive examination of the economic impact of tourism development by Liu and Var (1986) also reveal that there is a strong perception among residents of increased employment, investment, and profitability of local retailers. Moreover, their study also noted negative perceptions such as increased cost of living.

Tourism development also influences the community's socio-cultural aspects such as residents' habits, daily routines, beliefs, and values (Doğan 1989). Similar to economic impact, socio-cultural impact also has two dimensions, positive and negative. With respect to the positive dimension of socio-cultural impact, Brunt and Courtney (1999) provided evidence suggesting that tourism helps foster further development of community services such as parks and recreation as well as cultural facilities and activities. The negative dimension of sociocultural impact tend to be captured by concerns with crime, degradation of morality, gambling, drug addiction, vandalism, and crowding of public facilities and amenities. Doğan (1989) also added to this list of negative effects: decline in tradition, materialism, social conflict, and crowding.

Although much of the research has provided evidence for the positive effects of tourism development in relation to economic and socio-cultural benefits, some research shows negative effects on the environment (Andereck 1995; Andereck et al. 2005;

Brunt and Courtney 1999). For example, Andereck (1995) identified emissions from vehicles and airplanes, water pollution such as waste water discharge, wildlife destruction as a result of hunting, plant destruction, and deforestation. However, there are some exceptions (showing positive environmental effects). For instance, Perdue et al. (1995) found that tourism development improves community appearance resulting in increased recreation and park opportunities.

3.2.2 Residents' Perceptions and Evaluations of Tourism Development

Residents' attitudes toward tourism development is a subject of extensive study (e.g., Gursoy et al. 2002). As previously mentioned, residents' perceptions and evaluations of tourism development are taken into account in important planning and policy deliberations (e.g., Haywood 1975). Such information is considered vital in the successful development, marketing, and operation of existing and future tourism programs. As such, a significant number of studies have focused on the link between tourism development and residents' perceptions and evaluations of the impact of tourism development (e.g., Allen et al. 1988; Andereck and Nyaupane 2011; Ap and Crompton 1998; Aref 2011; Nunkoo and Ramkissoon 2011). For example, research on the topic has found that residents' attitudes toward tourism development is generally positive when residents perceive more positive than negative effects; conversely, residents' attitude tend to be negative when they perceive more negative than positive effects (Byrd et al. 2009; Yoon 2002).

Another study conducted in Cairns, Australia (Pearce et al. 1991) examined community residents' attitude to tourism in terms an equity-social representational perspective. This perspective posits that residents' attitude toward tourism are influenced by equity considerations. Residents grouped based on their equity perceptions (perceived costs and benefits from tourism) were found to differ in their perception of tourism's contribution to the community.

Past research has also found that the relationship between tourism development and residents' perceptions and evaluations of tourism development are not consistent across a host of variables such as:

- demographic groups (e.g., Brougham and Butler 1981; Haralambopoulos and Pizam 1996; Liu and Var 1986; Mason and Cheyne 2000; McCool and Martin 1994; Milman and Pizam 1988; Pizam 1978),
- distance from the tourism area of the community (e.g., Liu and Var 1986; Sheldon and Var 1984; Um and Crompton 1987),
- economic dependency on tourism (e.g., Haralambopoulos and Pizam 1996; King et al. 1993; Liu and Var 1986; Pizam 1978; Schluter and Var 1988; Zhou and Ap 2009),
- knowledge about the industry (e.g., Davis et al. 1988), and
- type and form of tourism (e.g., Murphy 1985; Ritchie 1988).

A common finding from past attitudinal studies of tourism development impact is that those residents or stakeholders whose livelihoods depend on tourism activities are more likely to hold positive perceptions of tourism and its impact, thus expressing higher support for tourism development in their communities. The second common thread is that residents' attitude change, negatively or positively, depending on the stage of tourism development cycle—from the introductory stage to growth, from growth to maturity, and decline. Specifically, in the introductory stage of the cycle, residents tend to be euphoric and welcoming; but this attitude dissipates in the later stages of the cycle (i.e., in the maturity and decline stages) (e.g., Butler 2004). Once tourism development begins to take a negative toll on the well-being of residents, their attitude toward tourism development changes from euphoric to annoyance, annoyance to antagonism, and even total rejection.

As previously mentioned, the type of impact and residents' attitude toward tourism development are topics that have been researched extensively since the 1960s. However, tourism development impact does not only affect residents' attitude toward tourism, but also their own QOL (e.g., Hartwell et al. 2016; Uysal et al. 2012a; Yang and Li 2012). Once a community becomes a tourist destination, the QOL of local residents is influenced by tourism development (McKercher and Ho 2012). However, only a few studies have specifically considered the impact of tourism development on residents' QOL (e.g., Andereck and Nyaupane 2011; Uysal et al. 2012a). We will review the research dealing with the relationship between the perceived impact of tourism development and QOL of community residents.

3.3 The Reciprocal Influence of Tourism Development and QOL

In this section we will describe studies that have demonstrated the influence of tourism development on community residents' QOL and conversely the influence of QOL on tourism development.

3.3.1 Influence of Tourism Development on QOL

QOL has become a topic of broad discussion in recent years, and numerous studies have examined the relationship between tourism development and QOL (see Table 3.1 for a list of studies and a brief description). One of the early studies examining tourism impact on QOL explored the impact of the gaming tourism on QOL in host communities (Perdue et al. 1999). These authors used theoretical concepts of tourism development cycle and social disruption to explain the link. The study findings provided support for the concept of social disruption. That is, residents' QOL declines initially and then improves when the community and its resident adapt to the new situation.

Table 3.1 The bi-directional influence of tourism development and residents' QOL

#	Author/date	Purpose	Notes on results
1	Allen et al. (1988)	To investigate whether residents' perceptions of community life satisfaction increased with increased levels of tourism development	Community life satisfaction was perceived to decline as the tourism development increased.
2	Milman and Pizam (1988)	To understand residents' attitude toward tourism development	Most residents perceived that tourism development serves to improve employment opportunities, income, and standard of living, overall tax revenue, and overall quality of life.
3	Perdue and Gustke (1991)	To examine the relationship between tourism development and several objective indicators of QOL	Economic benefits of tourism development, per capita income, per student education expenditures and the quality of available health care facilities all seem to increase with increasing levels of tourism development.
4	Allen et al. (1993)	To investigate residents' attitude toward recreation and tourism development	Residents were significantly more positive toward the effects of recreation on their quality of life compared to the effects of tourism development.
5	Lankford (1994)	To compare attitude toward tourism development and planning at the local and regional level among the key actors (residents, government employees, decision makers, and local business owners)	Resident groups differed significantly from the other three groups regarding the quality of life issues such as noise, crime, litter, and environmental impacts.
6	Carmichael et al. (1996)	To investigate residents' perceptions of the effects of casino and related development on themselves, their towns, and the region	Residents perceived significantly reduced QOL in their towns over time.
7	Perdue et al. (1999)	To analyze the impact of gaming tourism on residents' quality of life in host communities	Residents' QOL initially declined and then improved
8	Roehl (1999)	To test the relationship between resident characteristics, perception of the impact of gaming, and perceived quality of life	Perceived social costs were negatively correlated with QOL; whereas, perceived job growth was positively correlated with QOL. Resident demographic characteristics were unrelated to residents' perceived QOL.
9	Jurowski and Brown (2001)	To examine the relationship between residents' community involvement and their perceptions of tourism-related QOL	Involved residents evaluated their quality of life higher noninvolved residents.
10	Nichols et al. (2002)	To examine the effect of the introduction of casino gambling on residents' quality of life	Depending on different characteristics such as demographic, proximity and relationships with the casino, and moral attitude toward the casino, residents' quality of life was different.

(continued)

Table 3.1 (continued)

#	Author/date	Purpose	Notes on results
11	Ko and Stewart (2002)	To explain the relationship between residents' perception of tourism impacts and residents' community satisfaction	Residents' community satisfaction was positively related to perceived positive impacts
12	Gjerald (2005)	To examine residents' perception of tourism as a detractor of QOL of the local community	Local residents did not view tourism as a detractor of QOL in the local community (at least at this stage of destination development).
13	Urtasun and Gutièrrez (2006)	To explore the impact of tourism on several objective dimensions of the host community's quality of life	Tourism impacts on the residents' QOL varied depending on which dimension of QOL is considered.
14	Andereck et al. (2007)	To investigate the differences between Hispanic and Anglo residents in terms of the effect of tourism development on QOL dimensions	Hispanic residents perceived greater effect of tourism on positive environmental and social cultural QOL variables more so than Anglo residents.
15	Yamada et al. (2009)	To examine how cultural tourism along with four life domains (health, wealth, safety, and community pride) influences life satisfaction	Cultural along with health satisfaction, wealth satisfaction, satisfaction with safety, and community pride were positively related to life satisfaction.
16	Vargas-Sanchez et al. (2009)	To examine the relationship between perceptions of tourism development and satisfaction with community life	Increases in perceived tourism development correlated with increases in overall community satisfaction
17	Meng et al. (2010)	To identify whether significant differences exist among the three groups of provinces with varying levels of tourism development in relation to QOL	The residents of provinces with the highest level of tourism development reported a significantly "better life" than those who are in the regions on medium or low level of tourism development.
18	Matarrita-Cascante (2010)	To examine community's shifting living conditions and its effects on community satisfaction, and quality of life in two communities (Liberia and La Fortuna)	In Liberia shifting living conditions result in decreased perceived community satisfaction and quality of life, while La Fortuna presents contrasting results.
19	Cecil et al. (2010)	To investigate the relationship between value of cultural tourism and resident's overall QOL	Value of cultural tourism is positively related with residents' QOL; however, the impact is inconsistent over time.

(continued)

Table 3.1 (continued)

#	Author/date	Purpose	Notes on results
20	Andereck and Nyaupane (2011)	To examine the relationship between resident perception of the role of tourism in community development and residents' quality of life	Perceived personal benefit derived from tourism mediate the effect of tourism on the economic aspects of QOL.
21	Chancellor et al. (2011)	To examine the relationship between tourism development and residents' quality of life using the CP (Core–periphery) model as a conceptual framework	Tourism development may be contributing to the difference in quality of life scores for the respondents and that the CP (Core-periphery) context might help explain these differences.
22	Renda et al. (2011)	To test the hypothesis that residents' perception of tourism development impacts on their quality of life	In general, residents perceive tourism as causing positive impacts on their quality of life, while recognizing also negative effects, namely those related to emotional and community well-being.
23	Yu et al. (2011)	To explore tourism impacts on resident perceived quality of life	The social cost dimension of tourism development has no significant effect on residents' quality of life; however, both environmental sustainability and perceived economic benefits seem to affect residents' quality of life.
24	Aref (2011)	To investigate the effect of tourism development on residents' quality of life	Tourism development has a positive effect on the quality of life of residents.
25	Manap et al. (2011)	To examine how tourism innovation impact the quality of life of residents	Resident's quality of life can be predicted by levels of tourism innovation through perceived impact in particular life domains, and satisfaction with these life domains seem to influence overall life satisfaction.
26	Nawijn and Mitas (2012)	To examine the relationship between perceived tourism impacts and residents' well-being using cognitive versus affective measure of subjective well-being	Tourism impacts are associated with the cognitive component of subjective well-being (i.e., life satisfaction), not the affective component.
27	Khizindar (2012)	To analyze the direct effects of tourism on the perceptions of residents' quality of life and to investigate relationship between tourism impacts and demographic information	Social, cultural, and environmental impacts seem to influence resident's quality of life and demographic characteristics seem to affect their perception of tourism domains.
28	Kim et al. (2013)	To examine the relationship between tourism impacts and the satisfaction with particular life domains and overall quality of life	Residents perceive tourism impacts in particular life domains, and satisfaction with these domains seem to influence their overall quality of life.

(continued)

Table 3.1 (continued)

#	Author/date	Purpose	Notes on results
29	Woo (2013)	To determine the relationship between perception of tourism impacts and community stakeholders' quality of life	Satisfaction with material and non-material life positively affect residents' overall quality of life.
30	Jeon et al. (2014)	To investigate influences of seasonal attributes on residents' perceptions of tourism impacts and, residents' perceived quality life in a cultural-heritage tourism destination	Seasonal factor attributes adversely affected resident's economic benefits; seasonal attributes positively affected residents' social costs; seasonal attributes inversely influenced residents' environmental sustainability; perception of economic benefits positively impacted residents' perceived quality of life; perceived social costs adversely affected residents' QOL; and perceived sustainability positively affected residents'' QOL.
31	Lipovčan et al. (2014)	To examine the relationship between the quality of tourist destinations and the subjective well-being of people living in these destinations	The quality of tourist destinations was related to residents' life satisfaction and happiness, as well as the satisfaction with personal life domains.
32	Woo et al. (2015)	To examine the reciprocal relationship between local residents 'support for tourism development and residents' quality of life	Residents' perceived value of tourism development positively affects non-material and material life domain satisfaction, which in turn influence overall quality of life. Furthermore, overall quality of life seems to be an effective predictor of support for further tourism development.

Kim (2002) tested a theoretical model that links community residents' perception of tourism impact (economic, social, cultural, and environmental) with residents' satisfaction with particular life domains (material well-being, community well-being, emotional well-being, and health and safety well-being) and overall life satisfaction. Results indicate that residents have well-formed perceptions of tourism impact on the community and this impact influences their sense of well-being in various life domains, which in turn affect their life satisfaction. Recently, Andereck and Nyaupane (2011) also investigated the relationship between resident perception of the role of tourism and QOL. The finding was higher levels of QOL may result from tourism development.

3.3.2 *The Influence of QOL on Tourism Development*

Croes (2012b) discussed the potential bilateral relation between tourism development and QOL; his study provided suggestive evidence of a stable, mutual relationship between tourism development and QOL. However, there is hardly any additional empirical evidence documenting the effect of QOL on tourism development. A number of authors have only suggested such an effect (e.g., Andereck et al. 2005; Ap 1992; King et al. 1993; Uysal et al. 2012a). For example, Uysal et al. (2012a) suggested an integrated model reflective of the current and future research in the effect of tourism development on the QOL of residents. The model postulates that host community residents perceive that their community living conditions, as impacted by tourism development, would affect satisfaction in various life domains, which cumulatively would affect residents' overall community well-being. Moreover, they also argued that if the development of tourism results in a lower QOL, residents may be reluctant to support further tourism development in their community. While, if their QOL is higher enough, residents may agree to further tourism development (see Table 3.1).

Recently, Woo et al. (2015) conducted a study to examine local residents' support for tourism development by exploring residents' perceived value of tourism development, life domain satisfaction, and overall QOL in the community. Using a sample of residents from five different tourism destinations, the results indicated that residents' perceived value of tourism development positively affects domain satisfaction; thereby, it contributes to overall QOL. Furthermore, the study found that QOL is an effective predictor of support for further tourism development. In a nutshell, the relationship between QOL and tourism development is influenced by a host of moderating variables, a subject to which we now turn.

3.4 Moderating and Antecedent Effects

The bi-directional relationship between tourism development and QOL might not always be as strong and positive. Depending on possible moderator and antecedent effects, the relationship could be different and show variation (see Table 3.2).

3.4.1 Stage of Tourism Development in the Community

One important moderator is the stage of tourism development in the community or what some may call 'carrying capacity'. Several studies have examined how residents' QOL can change depending on the level of tourism development (e.g., Allen et al. 1988; Kerstetter and Bricker 2012; Kim et al. 2013; Meng et al. 2010; Perdue et al. 1999). Uysal et al. (2012b) reviewed past research related to tourism development impact using the concept of Tourism Area Life Cycle (TALC); they suggested that depending upon the stage of destination development, residents' attitudes toward economic, sociocultural, and environmental factors might change from positive to negative or negative to positive. Moreover, different stages of tourism development in a community affect residents' QOL differently. For example, the study conducted by Allen et al. (1988) found that tourism development does benefit host

Table 3.2 Moderator and antecedent effects

Author/ date	Purpose	Moderators	Notes on results
Allen et al. (1988)	To determine whether residents' perceptions of community life satisfaction vary with levels of tourism development	Level of tourism development	Residents perceptions of community life satisfaction seem to decline in the later stages of the tourism development life cycle
Meng et al. (2010)	To examine whether significant differences exist among the three groups of provinces with varying levels of tourism development	Level of tourism development	The residents of provinces with the highest level of tourism development were found to lead a significantly "better life" than those who are in the regions of medium or low levels of tourism development.
Uysal et al. (2012b)	To review past research related to tourism development impact using the concept of Tourism Area Life Cycle (TALC)	Level of tourism development	Depending upon the stage of destination's TALC, residents' attitude toward economic, sociocultural, and environmental factors seems to change from positive to negative or negative to positive
Kim et al. (2013)	To investigate how the relationship between tourism development impact and quality of life can change depending on the stage of tourism development in the community	Level of tourism development	Perceptions of tourism impact affecting residents' sense of well-being in various life domains vary depending on the stage of tourism development of the community.
Allen and Gibson (1987)	To compare the perceptions of community leaders and the general public regarding the importance of 22 proposed community work projects and satisfaction with various dimensions of community life	Type of stakeholder group	Health and safety, education, environmental, economic, public administration, community involvement, and leisure were considered important to satisfaction with community life by both groups. However, residents were less satisfied than leaders on every dimension of community life.
Lankford (1994)	To examine the impact of tourism development of business owners, paid government officials, elected, appointed officials, and residents	Type of stakeholder group	Residents were more negative about the impact, or rather more cautious about the benefits of tourism than were government employees, elected/appointed leaders or business owners. Business owners, elected/appointed leaders, and government employees seem to be in agreement regarding tourism impacts.

(continued)

Table 3.2 (continued)

Author/ date	Purpose	Moderators	Notes on results
Byrd et al. (2009)	To investigate differences in perceptions of tourism impact on a rural community among four stakeholder groups: government officials, entrepreneurs, residents, and tourist	Type of stakeholder group	Residents indicated a higher level of agreement than government officials on negative impacts such as increased crime rate and property taxed.
Woo (2013)	To test the relationship between the perception of tourism impact and community stakeholder's quality of life	Type of stakeholder group	Residents affiliated with the tourism industry (compared to those who are not affiliated) perceived greater benefits stemming from tourism and these benefits do play a significant role on their sense of well-being.
McCool and Martin (1994)	To examine the relationship between residents' perceptions of tourism development impact and their level of community attachment	Level of involvement	Highly attached residents were more likely to be concerned about the costs and impact of tourism development, more so than those not attached.
Jurowski and Brown (2001)	To better understand the role of community involvement through community organizations on residents quality of life	Level of involvement	Residents who belonged to no community organizations evaluated the quality of most aspects of their lives lower than those one that were the most involved.
Belisle and Hoy (1980)	To examine whether perceptions of tourist impact varies with the distance a person lives from the tourist zone and with residents' socio-economic status	Distance and residents' socio-economic status	Distance has a significant effect on residents' perceptions of tourism impact. Specifically, as residents move away from the tourist zone, the impact of tourism is perceived less positively.
King et al. (1993)	To investigate residents of Nadi/Fiji perceptions of impact of tourism.	Types of tourism	Residents, depending on types of tourism, can clearly differentiate between its economic benefits and the social costs; and that awareness of certain negative consequences does not lead to opposition towards further tourism development.
Roehl (1999)	To examine the relationship between resident demographic characteristics, perceptions of impact of gaming, and perceived quality of life	Demographics	Residents with less education and urban residents perceived more social costs from legalized gaming.

(continued)

Table 3.2 (continued)

Author/ date	Purpose	Moderators	Notes on results
Perdue et al. (1999)	To investigate the role of distance on residents' perception of impact of gaming tourism and residents quality of life	Distance	The perceived impact of tourism decreased as distance between the individuals' home and the tourism sector of the community increased.
Andereck et al. (2005)	To examine differences between Anglo and Hispanic residents' perceptions regarding the influence of tourism on their QOL	Ethnic group	Hispanic residents perceived significantly greater effects of tourism development on positive environmental and socio-cultural quality-of-life dimensions than Anglo residents.

communities; however, residents perceive community well-being to decline in the later stages of the tourism development life cycle.

More recently Kim et al. (2013) investigated how the relationship between tourism development impact and QOL can change depending on the stage of tourism development in the community. The results indicated that the relationship between the economic and social impact of tourism and the satisfaction with its correspondent life domains (material well-being and community well-being) initially decreased in the growth stage of tourism development and peaked in maturity stage of tourism development. However, when a community enters the decline stage of tourism development, the strength of the relationship between the economic and social impact of tourism and the satisfaction with correspondent life domains decreased.

3.4.2 Type of Stakeholder Group

Other moderator effects may be related to resident's characteristics such as occupation, nationality, and involvement (e.g., Allen and Gibson 1987; Andereck et al. 2005; Byrd et al. 2009; Jurowski and Brown 2001; Lankford 1994; Weiermair and Peters 2012; Woo 2013). For example, two studies compared different types of stakeholder's perceptions of tourism development impact and perceived QOL (Lankford 1994; Woo 2013). Specifically, Lankford (1994) examined the impact of tourism development of business owners, paid government officials, elected/ appointed officials, and residents. The results showed that community residents were more negative about the impact (or rather more cautious about the benefits of tourism) than were government employees, elected/appointed leaders, and business owners. Woo (2013) tested the relationship between the perception of tourism impact and community stakeholder's QOL. The study found that satisfaction with material and non-material life domain (community, emotional, and health and safety) positively affect stakeholders' perceived QOL; and the type of community stakeholder groups (residents affiliated versus those who are not affiliated with the tourism industry) moderates this relationship. Specifically, the residents affiliated with the tourism industry (compared to those who are not affiliated) perceive greater benefits stemming from tourism and these benefits do play a significant role on their sense of well-being. Others studies also indicated that tourism-employed residents were more favorably disposed toward tourists than those who were not tourism-employed (Pizam 1978; Zhou and Ap 2009).

3.4.3 Involvement in Community Affairs and Community Attachment

McCool and Martin (1994) examined the relationship between residents' perceptions of tourism development impact and their level of community attachment. The study found that highly attached residents were more likely to be concerned about the costs and impact of tourism development, more so than those not attached.

Jurowski and Brown (2001) hypothesized community residents' perceptions of tourism-related QOL are likely to differ as a direct function of their level of involvement in community affairs. They conducted a survey using telephone interviews that revealed the following: residents *not* belonging to community organizations evaluated the quality of most aspects of their lives lower than those who reported not to belong to community organizations. That is, the study found a positive relationship between membership in community organizations and resident's satisfaction with the community and their QOL.

3.4.4 Other Demographic and Geographic Characteristics of Community Residents

Roehl (1999) examined the relationship between resident *demographic* characteristics, perception of the impact of gaming, and perceived QOL. The results showed that residents with less education and urban residents perceived more social costs from legalized gaming. Perceived social costs were negatively correlated with QOL, whereas perceived job growth was found to be positively correlated with QOL. Similarly, Andereck et al. (2005) examined differences between Anglo and Hispanic residents' perceptions regarding the influence of tourism on their QOL in southwestern United States. The study found that Hispanic residents perceived significantly greater effects of tourism on positive environmental and socio-cultural QOL dimensions.

Belisle and Hoy (1980) found that *distance* has a significant effect on residents' perceptions of tourism impact. Specifically, as residents move away from the tourist zone, the impact of tourism is perceived less positively. This moderator effect of distance was also hinted by Perdue et al. (1999) who argued that the perceived impact of tourism decreases as distance between the individual's home and the tourism sector of the community increases.

3.5 Conclusion

The preceding discussion points to several key propositions. It is clear that community residents with higher levels of perceived QOL are favorably disposed toward tourism development. This does not, however, imply that residents with lower levels of perceived QOL are less supportive of tourism development. It is also clear that the relationship between tourism development and community QOL is bi-directional. The relationship between these two constructs is also influenced by a host of moderator effects. These moderator effects point to public policy questions. For example, at what point or stage of tourism development do tourism activities begin to adversely influence the QOL of residents? What is the optimal threshold of tourism development? Identifying such thresholds should allow public policy officials and community leaders to regulate tourism development. To do so, community QOL should be measured and monitored over time. There is no question that a good place for home residence is a good place to visit. The challenge is that if tourist communities should strive to enhance and sustain community QOL over time.

Ideas for future research? Scholars interested in tourism and QOL should strive to capture community QOL using *both* objective and subjective indicators. Each set of QOL metrics has its own strengths and weaknesses; hence, there is a need to employ both objective and subjective indicators to better capture residents' QOL. To date, there is no research, if any, using both objective and subjective indicators to measure community QOL. Using objective and subjective indicators conjunctively should allow us to reach more definitive conclusions and provide meaningful results for policy making and long-term community planning.

Also, to better measure community QOL, we need to recognize that the QOL dimensions (i.e., domains) vary in salience. In other words, domains are not all equally important and the importance of each domain may vary across stakeholder groups and contexts. Perhaps future research should incorporate a domain salience construct in the measurement of community QOL.

Resident's perspective of tourism development and its impact on community QOL has been researched since the 1980s. However, there is still relatively limited research that examines direct and indirect impact of tourism development on community QOL. Thus, we conclude with a call to action. Much more research and attention is needed in this area to ensure that tourism development contributes most positively to the QOL of host communities.

References

Allen, L. R., & Gibson, R. (1987). Perceptions of community life and services: A comparison between leaders and community residents. *Community Development, 18*(1), 89–103.
Allen, L. R., Long, P. T., Perdue, R. R., & Kieselbach, S. (1988). The impact of tourism development on residents' perceptions of community life. *Journal of Travel Research, 27*(1), 16–21.
Allen, L. R., Hafer, H. R., Long, P. T., & Perdue, R. R. (1993). Rural residents' attitudes toward recreation and tourism development. *Journal of Travel Research, 31*(4), 27–33.
Andereck, K. L. (1995). *Environmental consequences of tourism: A review of recent research.* General Technical Report-Intermountain Research Station, USDA Forest Service. INT-323, pp. 77–81.
Andereck, K. L., & Nyaupane, G. P. (2011). Exploring the nature of tourism and quality of life perceptions among residents. *Journal of Travel Research, 50*(3), 248–260.
Andereck, K. L., Valentine, K. M., Knopf, R. C., & Vogt, C. A. (2005). Residents' perceptions of community tourism impacts. *Annals of Tourism Research, 32*(4), 1056–1076.
Andereck, K. L., Valentine, K. M., Vogt, C. A., & Knof, R. C. (2007). A cross-cultural analysis of tourism and quality of life perceptions. *Journal of Sustainable Tourism, 15*(5), 483–501.
Ap, J. (1992). Residents' perceptions on tourism impacts. *Annals of Tourism Research, 19*(4), 665–690.
Ap, J., & Crompton, J. L. (1998). Developing and testing a tourism impact scale. *Journal of Travel Research, 37*(2), 120–130.
Aref, F. (2011). The effects of tourism on quality of life: A case study of Shiraz, Iran. *Life Science Journal, 8*(2), 26–30.
Belisle, F. J., & Hoy, D. R. (1980). The perceived impact of tourism by residents a case study in Santa Marta, Colombia. *Annals of Tourism Research, 7*(1), 83–101.
Biswas-Diener, R. (Ed.). (2011). *Positive psychology as social change.* Dordrecht: Springer.
Brougham, J., & Butler, R. W. (1981). A segmentation analysis of resident attitudes to the social impact of tourism. *Annals of Tourism Research, 8*(4), 569–590.
Brunt, P., & Courtney, P. (1999). Host perceptions of sociocultural impacts. *Annals of Tourism Research, 26*(3), 493–515.
Butler, R. W. (2004). The tourism area lifecycle in the twenty first century. In A. A. Lew, C. M. Hall, & A. M. Williams (Eds.), *A companion to tourism* (pp. 159–169). Oxford: Blackwell Publishing Ltd..
Byrd, E. T., Bosley, H. E., & Dronberger, M. G. (2009). Comparisons of stakeholder perceptions of tourism impacts in rural eastern North Carolina. *Tourism Management, 30*(5), 693–703.
Carmichael, B. A., Peppard, D. M., Jr., & Boudreau, F. A. (1996). Megaresort on my doorstep: Local resident attitudes toward Foxwoods Casino and casino gambling on nearby Indian reservation land. *Journal of Travel Research, 34*(3), 9–16.
Cecil, A. K., Fu, Y., Wang, S., & Avgoustis, S. (2010). Cultural tourism and quality of life: Results of a longitudinal study. *European Journal of Tourism Research, 3*(1), 54–66.
Chancellor, C., Yu, C. S., & Cole, S. T. (2011). Exploring quality of life perceptions in rural Midwestern (USA) communities: An application of the core–periphery concept in a tourism development context. *International Journal of Tourism Research, 13*, 496–507.
Choi, H. S. C., & Sirakaya, E. (2005). Measuring residents' attitude toward sustainable tourism: Development of sustainable tourism attitude scale. *Journal of Travel Research, 43*(4), 380–394.
Chou, M. C. (2013). Does tourism development promote economic growth in transition countries? A panel data analysis. *Econometric Modeling, 33*, 226–232.
Croes, R. R. (2012a). Tourism, poverty relief, and quality of life in developing countries. In M. Uysal, R. Perdue, & M. J. Sirgy (Eds.), *Handbook of tourism and quality-of-life research: Enhancing the lives of tourists and residents of host communities* (pp. 85–103). Dordrecht: Springer.
Croes, R. (2012b). Assessing tourism development from Sen's capability approach. *Journal of Travel Research, 51*(5), 542–554.

Davis, D., Allen, J., & Cosenza, R. M. (1988). Segmenting local residents by their attitudes, interests, and opinions toward tourism. *Journal of Travel Research, 27*(2), 2–8.

Doğan, H. Z. (1989). Forms of adjustment: Sociocultural impacts of tourism. *Annals of Tourism Research, 16*(2), 216–236.

Filep, S. (2014). Moving beyond subjective well-being: A tourism critique. *Journal of Hospitality & Tourism Research, 38*(2), 266–274.

Gjerald, O. (2005). Sociocultural impacts of tourism: A case study of Norway. *Journal of Tourism and Cultural Change, 3*(1), 36–58.

Gursoy, D., Jurowski, C., & Uysal, M. (2002). Resident attitudes: A structural modeling approach. *Annals of Tourism Research, 29*(1), 79–105.

Haralambopoulos, N., & Pizam, A. (1996). Perceived impacts of tourism: The case of Samos. *Annals of Tourism Research, 23*(3), 503–526.

Hartwell, H., Fyall, A., Willis, C., Page, S., Ladkin, A., & Hemingway, A. (2016). Progress in tourism and destination wellbeing research. *Current Issues in Tourism*, 1–63.

Haywood, K. (1975). *Criteria for evaluating the social performance of tourism development projects: Tourism as a factor in national and regional development*, Proceedings of the IGU working group on the Geography of tourism and recreation, Trent University, Peterborough, Ontario, pp. 94–97.

Jeon, M., Kang, M., & Desmarais, E. (2014). Residents' perceived quality of life in a cultural-heritage tourism destination. *Applied Research in Quality of life*. https://doi.org/10.1007/s11482-014-9357-8.

Jurowski, C., & Brown, D. O. (2001). A comparison of the views of involved versus noninvolved citizens on quality of life and tourism development issues. *Journal of Hospitality & Tourism Research, 25*(4), 355–370.

Kerstetter, D. L., & Bricker, K. S. (2012). Relationship between carrying capacity of small island tourism destinations and quality-of-life. In M. Uysal, R. Perdue, & J. Sirgy (Eds.), *Handbook of tourism and quality-of-life research: Enhancing the lives of tourists and residents of host communities* (pp. 445–462). Dordrecht: Springer.

Khizindar, T. M. (2012). Effects of tourism on residents' quality of life in Saudi Arabia: An empirical study. *Journal of Hospitality Marketing & Management, 21*(6), 617–637.

Kim, K. (2002). *The effects of tourism impacts upon quality of life of residents in the community*. Blacksburg: Virginia Polytechnic Institute and State University.

Kim, K., Uysal, M., & Sirgy, M. J. (2013). How does tourism in a community impact the quality of life of community residents? *Tourism Management, 36*, 527–540.

King, B., Pizam, A., & Milman, A. (1993). Social impacts of tourism: Host perceptions. *Annals of Tourism Research, 20*(4), 650–665.

Ko, D., & Stewart, W. P. (2002). A structural equation model of residents' attitudes for tourism development. *Tourism Management, 23*, 521–530.

Lankford, S. V. (1994). Attitudes and perceptions toward tourism and rural regional development. *Journal of Travel Research, 32*(3), 35–43.

Lankford, S. V., & Howard, D. R. (1994). Developing a tourism impact attitude scale. *Annals of Tourism Research, 21*(1), 121–139.

Lee, C. C., & Chang, C. P. (2008). Tourism development and economic growth: A closer look at panels. *Tourism Management, 29*(1), 180–192.

Lipovčan, K., Brajša-Žganec, L., & Poljanec-Borić, S. (2014). What is good for tourists should be good for residents too: The relationship between the quality of the touristic offer and subjective well-being of residents. *Tourism Analysis, 19*(6), 719–730.

Liu, J. C., & Var, T. (1986). Resident attitudes toward tourism impacts in Hawaii. *Annals of Tourism Research, 13*(2), 193–214.

Liu, J. C., Sheldon, P. J., & Var, T. (1987). Resident perception of the environmental impacts of tourism. *Annals of Tourism Research, 14*(1), 17–37.

Manap, A. A., Aman, O., & Rahmiati, F. (2011, June 13–14). *The impact of tourism innovation on quality of life residents in the community: A case study of Sungai Melaka*. International conference on management (ICM 2011) proceeding. Penang, Malaysia, pp. 334–342.

Manyara, G., & Jones, E. (2007). Community-based tourism enterprises development in Kenya: An exploration of their potential as avenues of poverty reduction. *Journal of Sustainable Tourism, 15*(6), 628–644.

Marujo, A., Neto, H., & Miguel, L. (Eds.). (2014). *Positive nations and communities: Collective, qualitative and cultural-sensitive processes in positive psychology*. Dordrecht: Springer.

Mason, P. (2008). *Tourism impacts, planning and management*. Burlington: Butterworth-Heinemann.

Mason, P., & Cheyne, J. (2000). Residents' attitudes to proposed tourism development. *Annals of Tourism Research, 27*(2), 391–411.

Matarrita-Cascante, D. (2010). Changing communities, community satisfaction, and quality of life: A view of multiple perceived indicators. *Social Indicators Research, 98*(1), 105–127.

McCool, S. F., & Martin, S. R. (1994). Community attachment and attitudes toward tourism development. *Journal of Travel Research, 32*(3), 29–34.

McKercher, B., & Ho, P. (2012). Cultural tourism and the enhancement of quality-of-life. In M. Uysal, R. Perdue, & R. Sirgy (Eds.), *Handbook of tourism and quality-of-life research* (pp. 341–357). Dordrecht: Springer.

Meng, F., Li, X., & Uysal, M. (2010). Tourism development and regional quality of life: The case of China. *Journal of China Tourism Research, 6*(2), 164–182.

Milman, A., & Pizam, A. (1988). Social impacts of tourism on Central Florida. *Annals of Tourism Research, 15*(2), 191–204.

Moscardo, G., Konovalov, E., Murphy, L., & McGehee, N. (2013). Mobilities, community well-being and sustainable tourism. *Journal of Sustainable Tourism, 21*(4), 532–556.

Murphy, P. E. (1985). *Tourism. A community approach*. London: Methuen & Co. Ltd.

Nawijn, J., & Mitas, O. (2012). Resident attitudes to tourism and their effect on subjective well-being: The case of Palma de Mallorca. *Journal of Travel Research, 51*(1), 531–541.

Nichols, M., Stitt, B. G., & Giacopassi, D. (2002). Community assessment of the effects of casinos on quality of life. *Social Indicators Research, 57*(3), 229–262.

Nunkoo, R., & Ramkissoon, H. (2011). Residents' satisfaction with community attributes and support for tourism. *Journal of Hospitality & Tourism Research, 35*(2), 171–190.

Nunkoo, R., Smith, S. L., & Ramkissoon, H. (2013). Residents' attitudes to tourism: A longitudinal study of 140 articles from 1984 to 2010. *Journal of Sustainable Tourism, 21*(1), 5–25.

Pearce, D. (1989). *Tourist development* (2nd ed.). Harlow/New York: Longman/Wiley.

Pearce, P. L. (2009). The relationship between positive psychology and tourist behavior studies. *Tourism Analysis, 14*(1), 37–48.

Pearce, P. L., Moscardo, G., & Ross, G. F. (1991). Tourism impact and community perception: An equity-social representational perspective. *Australian Psychologist, 26*(3), 147–152.

Perdue, R. R., & Gustke, L. (1991). *The effects of tourism development on objective indicators of local quality of life. Tourism: building credibility for a credible industry*. Travel and Tourism Research Association twenty-second annual conference. California, pp. 191–201.

Perdue, R. R., Long, P. T., & Allen, L. (1987). Rural resident tourism perceptions and attitudes. *Annals of Tourism Research, 14*(3), 420–429.

Perdue, R. R., Long, P. T., & Kang, Y. S. (1995). Resident support for gambling as a tourism development strategy. *Journal of Travel Research, 34*(2), 3–11.

Perdue, R. R., Long, P. T., & Kang, Y. S. (1999). Boomtown tourism and resident quality of life: The marketing of gaming to host community residents. *Journal of Business Research, 44*(3), 165–177.

Pizam, A. (1978). Tourism's impacts: The social costs to the destination community as perceived by its residents. *Journal of Travel Research, 16*(4), 8–12.

Renda, A. I., Mendes, J. C., & Valle, P. O. d. (2011, October 26–29). *A structural model approach of residents' perception of tourism impacts in their own quality of life: The municipality of Loulé, Algarve*. Book of proceedings Vol II, international conference on tourism & management studies – Algarve. Faro, Algarve, Portugal.

Ritchie, J. (1988). Consensus policy formulation in tourism: Measuring resident views via survey research. *Tourism Management, 9*(3), 199–212.

Roehl, W. S. (1999). Quality of life issues in a casino destination. *Journal of Business Research, 44*(3), 223–229.
Ross, G. F. (1992). Resident perceptions of the impact of tourism on an Australian city. *Journal of Travel Research, 30*(3), 13–17.
Schluter, R., & Var, T. (1988). Resident attitudes toward tourism in Argentina. *Annals of Tourism Research, 15*(3), 442–445.
Seligman, M. E. P., & Csikszentmihalyi, M. (2000). Positive psychology: An introduction. *American Psychologist, 55*(1), 5–14.
Sharpley, R. (2014). Host perceptions of tourism: A review of the research. *Tourism Management, 42*, 37–49.
Sheldon, P. J., & Var, T. (1984). Resident attitudes to tourism in North Wales. *Tourism Management, 5*(1), 40–47.
Um, S., & Crompton, J. L. (1987). Measuring resident's attachment levels in a host community. *Journal of Travel Research, 26*(1), 27–29.
Urtasun, A., & Gutièrrez, I. (2006). Tourism agglomeration and its impact on social welfare: An empirical approach to the Spanish case. *Tourism Management, 27*, 901–912.
Uysal, M., Perdue, R., & Sirgy, M. J. (2012a). *Handbook of tourism and quality-of-life research: Enhancing the lives of tourists and residents of host communities*. Dordrecht: Springer Publishers.
Uysal, M., Woo, E., & Singal, M. (2012b). The Tourist Area Life Cycle (TALC) and its effect on the Quality-of-Life (QOL) of destination community. In M. Uysal, R. Perdue, & M. J. Sirgy (Eds.), *Handbook of tourism and quality-of-life research* (pp. 423–443). Dordrecht: Springer Publishers.
Vanegas, M., Sr. (2012). Poverty elimination through tourism dynamics. In M. Uysal, R. Perdue, & M. J. Sirgy (Eds.), *Handbook of tourism and quality-of-life research: Enhancing the lives of tourists and residents of host communities* (pp. 65–82). Dordrecht: Springer.
Vargas-Sanchez, A., Plaza-Mejia, M. d. l. A., & Porras-Bueno, N. (2009). Understanding residents' attitudes toward the development of industrial tourism in a former mining community. *Journal of Travel Research, 47*(3), 373–387.
Weiermair, K., & Peters, M. (2012). Quality-of-life values among stakeholders in tourism destinations: A tale of converging and diverging interests and conflicts. In M. Uysal, R. Perdue, & M. J. Sirgy (Eds.), *Handbook of tourism and quality-of-life research* (pp. 463–473). Dordrecht: Springer.
Woo, E. (2013). *The impacts of tourism development on stakeholders' quality of life (QOL): A comparison between community residents and employed residents in the hospitality and tourism industry*. Blacksburg: Virginia Polytechnic Institute and State University.
Woo, E., Kim, H., & Uysal, M. (2015). Life satisfaction and support for tourism development. *Annals of Tourism Research, 50*(1), 84–97.
Yamada, N., Heo, J., King, C., & Fu, Y. (2009, July 31). *Life satisfaction of urban residents: Do health perception, wealth, safety, community pride and, and cultural tourism matter?* International CHRIE Conference-Refereed Track. Paper 24. http://scholarworks.umass.edu/refereed/Sessions/Friday/24
Yang, L., & Li, X. R. (2012). Ethnic tourism and resident quality-of-life. In M. Uysal, R. Perdue, & J. Sirgy (Eds.), *Handbook of tourism and quality-of-life research* (pp. 373–387). Dordrecht: Springer.
Yoon, Y. (2002). *Development of a structural model for tourism destination competitiveness from stakeholders' perspectives*. Blacksburg: Virginia Polytechnic Institute and State University.
Yu, C., Chancellor, H. C., & Cole, S. T. (2011). Examining the effects of tourism impacts on resident quality of life: Evidence from rural Midwestern communities in USA. *International Journal of Tourism Sciences, 11*(2), 161–186.
Zhou, Y., & Ap, J. (2009). Residents' perceptions towards the impacts of the Beijing 2008 Olympic games. *Journal of Travel Research, 48*(1), 78–91.

Chapter 4
Tourism Development As a Resident-Tourist Exchange Process: an Economic Theoretic Interpretation

Salvatore Bimonte

Abstract Many attemps have been made to theoretically base research in tourism development. However, a discernible bias towards residents' perceptions exists. Since tourism involves the meeting of (at least) two populations, residents' perception ha to be analysed as part of an exchange process where hosts and guests are both considered. This paper presents and partially develops the Exchange Economic Model implemented by Bimonte and Punzo (Tour Manage 55:199–208, 2016) to investigate the possible scenarios and dynamics that tourism development may imply. The theoretical framework takes an economic perspective and assumes that agents' preferences are endogenous. This means that the population's interactions and experiences influence guests' and/or hosts' attitudes and opinions, which may in turn cause structural changes in individuals' preferences. As a consequence, populations may split and inter- and/or intra-community conflict may arise that affects individual quality of life (QOL). The paper addresses this issue theoretically, suggesting some possible solutions.

Keywords Edgeworth Box · Exchange Theory · Residents and Tourist Attitudes · Hosts and guests interaction

4.1 Introduction

Tourism is widely accredited as a major engine of local development (Sharpley 2015) and industry in the world, in terms of job creation and receipts (WTTC 2014). It was recently also acknlowledged as a determinant of quality of life (QOL) and perceived happiness (Neal et al. 2004, 2007; Pearce 2009; Pearce et al. 2011; Uysal et al. 2016). While travelling, people build social relationships, experience positive

S. Bimonte (✉)
Department of Economics and Statistics, University of Siena, Siena, Italy
e-mail: bimonte@unisi.it

A. M. Campón-Cerro et al. (eds.), *Best Practices in Hospitality and Tourism Marketing and Management*, Applying Quality of Life Research,
https://doi.org/10.1007/978-3-319-91692-7_4

emotions, and expand their knowledge. All these aspects have been found to positively affect personal wellbeing (Bimonte and Faralla 2012, 2015; Neal et al. 2007; Sirgy et al. 2011). However, while this may seem to be the case for tourists (guests), it is less certain for those who receive tourists, i.e. local communities (hosts) (Bimonte and Faralla 2016).

In fact, the fast (and often uncontrolled) expansion of tourism, together with benefits, has caused many social and environmental problems. This "epiphenomenon" mainly impinges on local communities (Wall and Mathieson 2006) who have to deal with "development dilemma" (Telfer and Sharpley 2008) or a trade-off between perceived benefits and costs. This is why many authors advise caution with regard to tourist development (Gursoy et al. 2002; Northcote and Macbeth 2006; Saarinen 2006; Saarinen et al. 2011) and hope for a deeper investigation of the relationship between it, residents' perception of tourist impacts and QOL. This is an important issue, because the friendliness of local residents and acceptance of tourists and tourist-related plans by the local community are important requirements for the success and sustainability of any tourist development (Bimonte 2013; Bimonte and Punzo 2011; Jurowski and Gursoy 2004; Lepp 2007; Pérez and Nadal 2005). Should the (perceived) costs of tourism outweigh its (perceived) benefits, then the hosts, or part of them, could withdraw their support for tourism (Lawson et al. 1998; Woosnam 2012). This does not mean that tourism would come to an end, but rather would acquire in an "unfriendly" context, to the detriment of social welfare.[1]

Many studies have investigated the relationships between residents' perception of tourism impacts, QOL and support for tourism development (Gursoy et al. 2010; Nunkoo and Gursoy 2012). Awareness that a balance and equitable distribution of costs and benefits are fundamental to the successful development of tourism (Andriotis and Vaughan 2003), together with recognition of the growing costs associated with tourism development, underlies the now considerable literature on resident perceptions of tourism (Sharpley 2014).

Tourism involves the meeting of two populations: a better known and stable population (residents) and a changing and generally less known one (tourists) (Bimonte 2008a). Populations may also be divided into communities, which implies complex interactions and variegated experiences that may influence guest and/or host attitudes, opinions, and ultimately lifestyles (Sharpley 2008). The quality and nature of the interaction also affects residents' perceptions of tourist development and the tourists' willingness to pay (Bimonte and Punzo 2011). Attention therefore has to be paid to the pay-offs for residents and tourists alike. Only mutually beneficial development can prevent latent conflicts and the sometimes disastrous effects of competition (Bimonte 2008a; Bimonte and Punzo 2007; Getz and Timur 2005; Gursoy and Rutherford 2004).

To analyze, understand and manage this phenomenon, a conceptual framework of host-guest relations is required. Unfortunately, the question has rarely been investigated in such a framework (Sharpley 2014). Since its inception, empirical

---

[1] An example is what is happening in Barcelona. Groups of residents are joining forces to protest over soaring rents fuelled by the big rise in visitor numbers (The Guardian, Juanuary, 29th, 2017).

research has mainly focused on the residents' side, while conceptual frameworks have been developed to theorize the relationship between tourism, residents' perceptions of impacts and residents' responses.

Tourist Area Life Cycle (Butler 1980, 2006) and the Irridex model (Doxey 1975; Fridgen 1991) are the reference frameworks for most studies on resident attitudes to tourism, which involve quantitative analysis based on surveys. Theoretical analysis is less developed and also has a discernible bias toward residents.

In view of these aspects, and building on some well-established and shared theoretical economic concepts, Bimonte and Punzo (2016) developed a guest-host model to explain the relationship between tourism development, residents' perceptions of impacts, and tourists' and residents' responses. To interpret this process they used the Edgeworth Box.[2]

This paper builds on and further develops their theoretical framework. Here, technical aspects are kept simple, as far as possible, in order to make the question understandable to non economists. Our main goal is to understand tourist dynamics and the evolution of attitudes, and to spur reflection on these issues. We aim to contribute to theoretical analysis of the issue and implement a reference framework to support policy makers in implementing suitable instruments for the success and sustainability of tourist development.

4.2 Tourism Development: A Review of the Basic Literature on Interpretative Models

Various theoretical models have been suggested to explain the relationship between tourists and residents (e.g. Ap and Crompton 1993; Bimonte and Punzo 2007; Dogan 1989). However, many studies use the Irridex model (Doxey 1975; Fridgen 1991) and the Tourist Area Life Cycle (TALC) (Butler 1980, 2006) as analytical framework. While telling the same story as for the expected results, they focus on different actors. The former mainly focuses on host community responses to tourism and assumes that locals initially have positive attitudes to tourism, but their perception of impact and their level of acceptance tend to evolve as tourism increases (Teye et al. 2002), though not necessarily in a deterministic and generalizable way (Gursoy et al. 2010; King et al. 1993). It is a deterministic four-stage model in which residents are supposed to pass from a state of euphoria, to apathy, to annoyance, and finally to antagonism. This is because the adverse impacts of tourism produce some degree of irritation in the host community. How much irritation depends on the number of tourists and the degree of incompatibility between residents and tourists.

Borrowing from the theory of product cycle, TALC implicitly focuses on the tourists' response. Like any product, it asserts that a tourist destination follows a pattern that evolves from the discovery to the maturity stage. During this process,

[2] Readers interested in a more technical analysis are referred to Bimonte and Punzo's (2016) paper and any microeconomics textbook, for example Katz and Rosen (1998) and Varian (2010).

the number of tourists initially increases but on approaching the carrying capacity and maturity stage, starts to decline. The model has been criticised (Dyer et al. 2007) especially with regard to its simplistic assumptions and deterministic evolution (Mason and Cheyne 2000; Tosun 2002; Wall and Mathieson 2006).

Though with differences, the models proposed by Dogan (1989) and Ap and Crompton (1993) focus on residents' response to tourism impacts rather than attitudes. The former model draws attention to tourism as a cause of conflict among residents. It considers the possibility that tourism development act as a deflagrating activity, transforming a homogeneous population in a relatively heterogeneous community.[3] This leads to more uncertain and complex results. Regarding the latter aspect, Bimonte and Punzo (2007) analyse the interaction between tourists and residents in terms of conflict and evolutionary game. This permits them to deal with many expected outcomes. None of these models considers the possibility of simultaneous (multiple) outcome.

However, while the development path is important, the fundamental issue isunderstanding of factors that may influence it. With the aim of preventing undesirable results and of obtaining insights for tourism planning, attention has been also paid to aspects that influence or determine residents' perceptions, attitudes and responses to tourism (Harrill 2004; Nunkoo et al. 2013; Sharpley 2014).

Though not always convergent, empirical results have allowed some advances in our understanding of the phenomenon. However, the widespread "atheoretical" approach (Harrill 2004), together with different methods, sampling and segmentations technicques, and the variety of variables investigated, make any generalization difficult (Sharpley 2014; Williams and Lawson 2001).

Although attempts have been made to give a theoretical basis to research on tourism development, the matter remains unclear, especially in explaining or understanding the evolution of residents' perceptions (Sharpley 2014). On this aspect, Social Exchange Theory (SET) is an advance on which a number of studies draw. It postulates that an individual's attitudes towards tourism depends on an evaluation of perceived tourism impacts (Andereck et al. 2005). Therefore, research is aimed at elaborating a cost-benefit appraisal to determine local citizens' inclination to participate in exchange with tourists and to endorse tourist development in their own community (Ap 1992, 1990; Ap and Crompton 1993; Gursoy and Kendall 2006; Jurowski et al. 1997; Kayat 2002). It focuses on the perceived impact of tourism, distinguishing socioeconomic, cultural and environmental impacts (Andereck and Vogt 2000; Harrill 2004).

Social Representation Theory (SRT), on the other hand, emphasizes the social influences and interactions of community. It focuses on "both the content of social knowledge and the way that this knowledge is created and shared by people in various groups, societies or communities" (Pearce et al. 1996: 31). It is therefore supposed to be useful for explaining social conflicts and individual reactions to events. In fact, SRT asserts that the way individuals describe and react to a stimulus "is affected by social knowledge, which is a combination of individual and societal

[3] For a survey and more detailed analysis see Monterrubio-Cordero (2008)

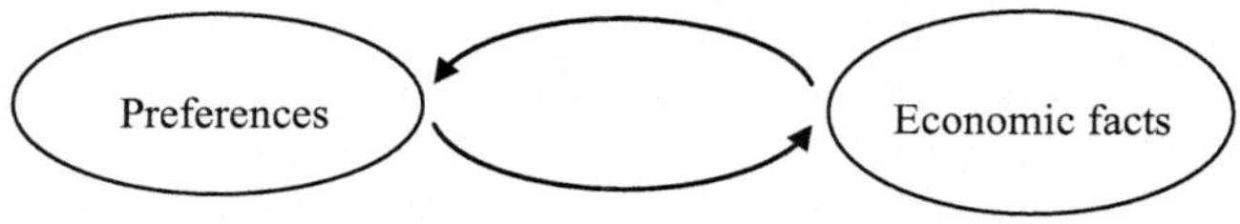

Fig. 4.1 Choices and feed back relations

values, ideas and practices" (Murphy and Murphy 2004). However, although SRT offers a fertile reference framework, its usefulness and value still need to be recognized and confirmed by empirical studies (Monterrubio-Cordero 2008).

Despite these attempts and improvements, it is an indisputable fact that models and empirical research have a discernible bias towards residents, hosts' perceptions and responses. However, as stated before, besides being a complex social phenomenon, tourism is mainly an encounter of two populations and possibly many communities. While this is rarely the case, a conceptual framework of host-guest relations is required to achieve a better understanding of tourism development (Sharpley 2014).

An attempt was recently made by Bimonte and Punzo (2016). Drawing on social exchange theory, they proposed an economic tourist-host exchange model. When deciding whether to engage in tourism, they assumed that the contractors develop an exchange process to optimize their well-being, maximizing benefits while trying to minimize costs. They argue that hosts and guests appraise and compare costs and benefits implied by the exchange: the former determine their Willingness to Accept (WTA) for endorsing tourist development in their community; the latter determine their Willingness to Pay (WTP) for tourist activities.[4] Given participants' preferences and contextual factors, an exchange is presumed to occur when a balance (equilibrium) between costs and benefits emerges for both (all) players. To represent and interpret this process they use the Edgeworth Box, representing the "exchange" in terms of "resource-space", mainly managed by the host community, against income, i.e. the amount of money that guests are willing to invest in travel.

Building on this model and assuming endogenous preferences, the present paper tries to investigate host-guest interactions and envisage outcomes. It assumes that feasible tourist development is an equilibrium path delimited by a spatial-temporal scale. It depends on the players' preferences (or attitudes) and the interaction dynamics between hosts and guests whereby players react to a stimulus and to feedbacks generated by responses.

These aspects are emphasized when a relationship between preferences and economic facts exists (Etzioni 1985). In fact, preferences and economic conditions determine the choice, but the former evolve in turn due to experience associated with the economic choice (Fig. 4.1). In such a context, equilibrium is determined endogenously. For example: because of price increases, an individual may change

[4]WTP (WTA) is the maximum (minimum) payment (compensation) an individual is willing to pay (accept) for a change that leaves her/him just as well off as before (Bellinger 2007; Perman et al. 2011)

her/his decision, choosing a mountain rather than a sea vacation. When the price of the sea vacation returns to its initial level, the individual may still opt for a mountain vacation. The experience induced by the price increase caused a change in the individual's preferences (Candela and Figini 2012).[5] Differences may also exist between expected and experienced utility. We examine this issue later.[6]

4.3 Host-Guest Interactions and Tourist Resources

Tourism is essentially a social phenomenon that entails an interaction between a temporary (tourists) and a stable (residents) population on one hand, and an exchange of resources on the other. The nature and quality of the interaction and exchange determine the tourists' and the residents' experience (Bimonte and Punzo 2007; Reisinger and Turner 2002) and consequently the former's willingness to pay (WTP) and the latter's perceived tourism impacts and response, together with their willingness to accept (WTA) (Andereck and Vogt 2000; Harrill 2004). From an economic perspective, an efficient exchange occurs when these two measures (WTP and WTA) coincide (Bimonte and Punzo 2016).

Since these two populations have different needs and interests to fulfill, they may entertain different expectations with regard to the benefits and costs deriving from the encounter. Considering the type of resources involved (mainly of a public or common pool nature), they have to reach an agreement on how to simultaneously use and/or share local resources and how much to exploit them. Compared with others sectors and exchanges, this may be a difficult task in tourism, because the two populations are probably divided internally into communities, each with its own needs and interests, and different WTP or WTA. The largely indivisible nature of the exchange, caused by the public and common-pool nature of the goods and the dependence between individuals' behavior and utility (externalities) make the equilibrium difficult to achieve or economically and socially unstable.

For the sake of simplicity, we start with the two populations case. One may represent this issue in term of "exchange" between "resource-space" (S) and income/money (I). The former consists of a set of resources (material and immaterial) that tourists "consume" during their stay. Many are produced by the host communities, themselves a locally defined and non-reproducible "tourism product". These resources are goods with economic value and their conservation can be threatened by development of those very activities that valorize them, tourism being one such activity. Their (rate of) usage may often have critical tapping values, beyond which use and often economic value fall sharply, or even completely disappear. They are mostly common-pool resources used simultaneosly by hosts and guests, not necessarily with same aim (for example hunting *vs* watching). Their use may produce

[5] Note that this is not a case of dynamically incoherent preferences but simply of a change in preferences.

[6] This phenomenon is widely analysed in behavioral and neuro economics.

Fig. 4.2 Indifference curves and equilibrium

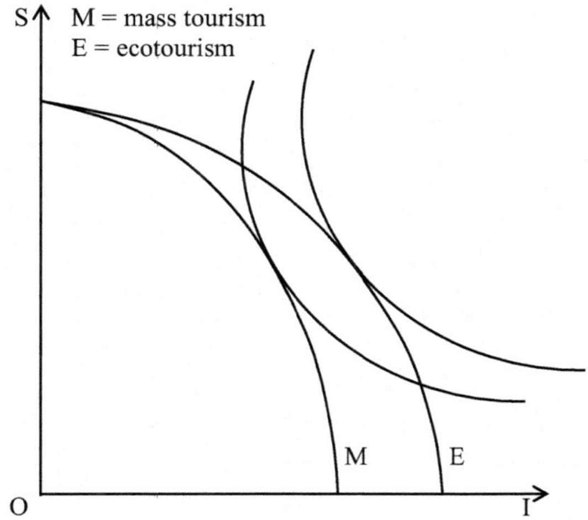

competition (generating congestion effects) or even conflict (generating externality effects). Competition, or even antagonism, is of course all the more acute, the smaller or more fragile the resources available for tourist development.[7] It also depends on how heterogeneous the two populations are, in terms of culture and plans/technologies determining resource usage.

S is mainly managed by the host community, who can decide to prevent tourist development or open their resource-space to tourism in order to obtain benefits, such as additional income. They trade S for I. The latter is the income guests invest in travel. Roughly speaking, it is payment to use S. In a broad sense, it is the reward for local community, and can be thought of as additional income, social development, cultural interchange, better services.

This situation may be represented by a production possibility frontier, which represents the production tradeoff. For given technology, tourist preferences, market conditions and amount and type of resources, the curve shows the maximum quantity of one good one can get for any given level of the other. In the case of a destination, this is the maximum quantity of income (tourist WTP) one can get from a given amount of resource-space made available to tourism.

Increasing tourist demand for a good (say S) entails disbursing the other (I). The latter (I) is the opportunity cost of the former (additional S) (in the case of residents it is the opposite). The ratio of the two variations represents the *marginal rate of transformation* (MRT). It depends on where we are and on the shape of the curve. MRT increases in absolute size as one moves from the top left to the bottom right of the curve. This means that appraisal (productivity) varies with relative scarcity (in quantitative and qualitative terms). It also depends on technology, tourist preferences and type of tourist development. This is evident in Fig. 4.2. For example, it

[7] We assume that the bundle of resources can be quantified by a single indicator and can be put on a single axis of our model. There is no need to complicate the picture to drive our message home.

may be thought of as mass tourism against ecotourism. It is normally acknowledged that mass tourism brings higher costs and lower benefits than ecotourism (Bimonte 2008b). Different development models result in different frontiers (curves).

Besides production conditions, there are also welfare aspects to consider. In our framework, these are represented by indifference curves that denote a consumption trade-off. Given the technology, type and amount of resources, these curves show the maximum amount of resource-space that residents are willing to give-up for a given amount of additional income (*marginal rate of substitution – MRS*). The exchange ratio depends on where we measure it on the curves and the shape of the curve. Since these curves are convex, the opportunity cost is decreasing: it declines in absolute size as one moves from the top left to the bottom right of the curve (this means that WTA goes to infinity). This means that appraisal varies with relative quantitative and qualitative scarcity. As before, the latter are influenced by the model of tourist development and tourist type. Faulkner and Tideswell (1997) argued that the "type of tourist" can condition the attitude of the resident toward tourists and tourism. Among other things, it is claimed that "*the more positive the perception that residents have about the respectful behavior of tourists, the greater is their overall perception that the positive impacts outweigh the negative impacts, and the more favorable is their attitude toward further tourism development*" (Vargas-Sánchez et al. 2014, 583; Vargas-Sánchez et al. 2011).

4.4 A Host-Guest Exchange Scheme

Let us now investigate how the exchange process functions. According to standard neoclassical theory, in a pure exchange economy there are several consumers. Each consumer is described by her/his preferences and goods endowment and is assumed to behave competitively. Agents are therefore price takers and are represented by their utility functions (u_i) and initial endowment (ω_i). The aggregate demand curve for a private good is a continuous and decreasing curve (showing decreasing marginal WTP). It is the sum of individuals' independent demand curves. No interaction between individuals' demand and consumption is allowed. Given preferences and endowments, they trade their goods in order to make themselves better off.

In the case of tourism, things are a slightly different. First of all, tourism is mainly an "experience good" consisting of many (hedonic) attributes. Tourists' WTP and residents' WTA are defined *ex-ante*, according to the importance of each attribute and expected utility (Lancaster 1966). Moreover, given the nature of the resources involved, attributes differentiate in terms of the state of the world, which in turn depends on the behaviour of other individuals. Thus tourist demand is neither unique nor independent of the demand of other individuals, as in the case of pure private goods. Congestion and conflict externalities arise. This implies that the market demand is endogenously determined and steeper[8] than it would be in the case of pure private goods (Bimonte and Punzo 2007).

Under the endogeous assumption, "economic fact" interacts with preferences, which therefore evolve in time, because individuals' utility depends on actual experience, in turn affected by contextual factors, such as crowding, community composition (measured by the different types of tourists simultaneously visiting that destination), views and values shared with host community, and intensity of resource use.[9] Once again, individuals' perceived "utility" and "disutility" depend on technical aspects and players' preferences that in turn depend on the nature of the interactions affecting contextual factors.

With regards the latter aspect, one has to consider that, unlike residents, tourists are a "changing" population. As such, they can use both the voice and exit option. The latter is much more costly for hosts than for guests. Therefore, a tourism-induced change in attitude may have different outcomes: on the host side, it is more likely to generate voice, whereas on the guest side it may generate voice or exit.

Thus market and contextual factors intermingle to determine the final (temporary and/or unstable) outcome. As we said, the relative importance of the two goods generally varies along the relevant curves, as does the marginal rate of substitutions between the two goods: the less of a good left, compared to the other, the higher the assigned value (decreasing marginal utility). Moreover, ceteris paribus, the less resource-space left (or perceived as such), the higher the intercommunity conflict; the higher the conflict, the higher host WTA and the lower guest WTP; the less equitable the tourist development, the greater host intra community conflict, and as a result, host-guest intercommunity conflict. To summarize, WTP and WTA depend on what is left of S, both in qualitative and quantitative sense. This obviously affects the MRS.

From microeconomic theory we know that an efficient equilibrium (outcome) maximizes agents' utility. This condition is met when the indifference curves are tangents to each other and MRT = MRS.[10] However, considering what we said before, what seems to be an *ex-ante* efficient outcome may turn out to be an *ex-post* inefficient and conflictual outcome. Actual experience modifies agents' perception shifting them on a different indifference curve and production frontier with a different expected equilibrium. When populations are divided into communities, multiple equilibria can also emerge.

It is the responsibility of local planners and policy makers to forge balanced, equitable, enduring tourism development. To do so, a private outcome (equilibrium) compatible with social expectations is needed. The latter may be met through policies, such as redistributive (compensative) measures that modify the social marginal rate of substitution in terms of income and services, or else policies that reduce the negative impact of tourism on the local community, or make the intensity of resource-space use (technology) more efficient. Such policies aim to produce a kind

[8] In the case of destinations characterized by the truck effect, the opposite would be true.

[9] For more elaboration of these aspects, see Bimonte and Punzo (2007).

[10] This could be represented by means of a modified Edgeworth Box.

of *pooling equilibrium*. When possible, seasonal or spatial segmentation may be required to reduce conflict and increase welfare. These policies would aim at ensuring multiple equilibria (a kind of *separating equilibrium*). For example, in the case of sea or river tourism, one can have fishers and waterscooters enjoying the same resource but with conflinting needs. In this case, a pooling equilibrium is difficult to obtain. A solution could be to separate users or activities spatially or seasonally.

4.5 Concluding Remarks

This paper is based on the assumption that tourism involves the meeting of at least two, not necessarily homogeneous populations, i.e. hosts and guests. Unlike previous approaches, it focuses simultaneously on both agents and considers the effects of different development paths and interactions. In an attempt to avoid any simplistic syncretism, it combines elements of various models and theories (Irridex model, life cycle model, social exchange theory, carrying capacity) with some basic and well-shared economic concepts, building a theoretical economic framework to analyze tourist development at a destination and residents' attitudes to tourism. It aims to investigate and hopefully answer some of the issues detected in the best known models of the literature.

Drawing mainly on Bimonte and Punzo (2016), and assuming endogenous preferences, it represents tourism as an exchange between guests and hosts. As such, it assumes that both actors try to optimize their well-being while minimizing the costs implied by tourism. Given their preferences, both envisage and compare expected costs and benefits. Based on these expectations, hosts define their WTA tourist development and guests determine their WTP for their visit. Exchange occurs when a balance (equilibrium) between expected costs and benefits emerges for both (all) players. However, depending on contextual factors, the actual outcome may not turn out to be an equilibrium. Non equilibrium outcomes produce friction or conflict that may lead to reappraisal of costs and benefits. This would explain why residents' attitudes to tourism and their perception of tourist impact vary with the tourist season (Bimonte and Faralla 2016; Vargas-Sánchez et al. 2014).

Equilibrium is a necessary condition for any durable tourist development. Market conditions have to be compatible with social conditions and tourists' expectations. When they are, tourism is more likely to contribute to visitors and residents' QOL and well-being. Understandably, this is a major policy issue.

The microeconomic foundation of the present model also allows it to address issues that previous models were unable to deal with. *Ceteris paribus*, the theory of decreasing marginal utility of a good (and the increasing marginal disutility associated with the shrinking of another good) makes it possible to explain not only why a local community may change its attitute to tourism, but also why tourist development may take a certain path (such as that of the Irridex model). This aspect is strongly linked to tourist carrying capacity, a phenomenon with qualitative and quantitave aspects determined in space and time.

Our model also confutes the determinism of the TALC model. Dynamics depend on many factors, such as players' preferences and the nature and history of interactions affecting contextual factors. Moreover, the type of tourism a destination promotes may enhance or dampen intra- and inter-community conflicts, which in turn affect host WTA and guest WTP. There is nothing deterministic about tourist-resident interactions or the fate of a destination.

With respect to the Economic Exchange Model, our model addresses and deals with an additional aspect, i.e. multiple equilibrium. It provides a theoretical foundation to support policies that aim to generate *separating equilibrium*. When possible, separating (as opposed to pooling) equilibrium may maximize host QOL and guest satisfaction, i.e. social welfare.

To conclude, the present interpretative model may be useful for understanding, studying and explaining different situations and for interpreting various outcomes. It may also support policy makers and local planners in their decisions. Hopefully, it may prove to be a suitable reference framework for generalizing results and understanding what residents perceive and why, thereby enhancing the debate on such issues.

The paper is not lacking in limitations. Its analysis is based on a theoretical model. Like any other such model, it is based on assumptions and a simplified representation of the world, the main critical aspect being that it treats populations as homogeneous communities. However, by simplifying, it reduces the dimensions of the problem to an analytically manageable level, without losing the essence of the complex issue(s) at stake. Another aspect to consider is that it addresses the issue of intra-community conflict but does not offer a model to interpret ensuing dynamic evolution, which is a major theoretical and empirical issue.

As shown by Bimonte and Punzo (2016), the model only applies to cases where tourism may be seen as an exchange process. However, in many cases locals do not have a say about tourist development, which is thrust on them by influential groups and powerful elites. In such cases, other analytical frameworks are more appropriate.

In any case, our model offers a tool to enrich our comprehension of the issues at stake, while adding a new (economic) viewpoint to the analysis of tourist development, and endeavouring to establish communication between disciplines.

References

Andereck, K., & Vogt, C. (2000). The relations between resident's attitudes toward tourism and tourism development options. *Journal of Travel Research, 39*(1), 27–37.

Andereck, K., Valentine, K., Knopf, R., & Vogt, C. (2005). Residents' perceptions of community tourism impacts. *Annals of Tourism Research, 32*(4), 1056–1076.

Andriotis, K., & Vaughan, D. (2003). Urban residents' attitudes toward tourism development: The case of Crete. *Journal of Travel Research, 42*(2), 172–185.

Ap, J. (1990). Residents' perceptions research on the social impacts of tourism. *Annals of Tourism Research, 17*(4), 610–616.

Ap, J. (1992). Residents' perceptions on tourism impacts. *Annals of Tourism Research, 19*(4), 665–690.

Ap, J., & Crompton, J. L. (1993). Residents' strategies in responding to tourism impacts. *Journal of Travel Research, 32*(1), 47–50.

Bellinger, W. J. K. (2007). *The economic analysis of public policy*. London/New York: Routledge.

Bimonte, S. (2008a). The "tragedy of tourism resources" as the outcome of a strategic game a new analytical framework. *Ecological Economics, 67*, 457–464.

Bimonte, S. (2008b). Park visitors vs beach tourists: A comparative study in an Italian coastal region. *European Journal of Tourism Research, 1*(2), 112–127.

Bimonte, S. (2013). Sustainable tourism: An interpretative and management paradigm. In P. Diaz (Ed.), *Tourism as a tool for development* (pp. 83–99). Southampton: WIT Press, ISBN 978-1-84564-812-1.

Bimonte, S., & Faralla, V. (2012). Tourist types and happiness. A comparative study in Tuscany. *Annals of Tourism Research, 39*(4), 1929–1950.

Bimonte, S., & Faralla, V. (2015). Happiness and outdoor vacations: Appreciative versus consumptive tourists. *Journal of Travel Research, 54*(2), 179–192.

Bimonte, S., & Faralla, V. (2016). Does residents' perceived life satisfaction vary with tourist season? A two-step survey in a Mediterranean destination. *Tourism Management, 55*, 199–208.

Bimonte, S., & Punzo, L. (2007). The evolutionary game between tourist and resident populations and tourist carrying capacity. *International Journal of Technology and Globalisation, 3*(1), 73–87.

Bimonte, S., & Punzo, L. (2011). Tourism, residents' attitudes and perceived carrying capacity with an experimental study in five Tuscan destinations. *International Journal of Sustainable Development, 14*(3/4), 242–261.

Bimonte, S., & Punzo, F. L. (2016). Tourist development and host–guest interaction: An economic exchange theory. *Annals of Tourism Research, 58*, 128–139.

Butler, R. (1980). The concept of a tourism area cycle of evolution. *Canadian Geographer, 24*(1), 5–12.

Butler, R. (2006). The concept of a tourist area life cycle of evolution: Implication for management of resources. In R. W. Butler, a cura di *The tourism area life cycle: Applications and modifications*. Clevedon: Channel View Publications.

Candela, G., & Figini, P. (2012). *The economics of tourism destinations* (First a cura di). Berlin: Springer.

Dogan, H. (1989). Forms of adjustment: Sociocultural impacts of tourism. *Annals of Tourism Research, 16*(2), 216–136.

Doxey, G. (1975). A causation theory of visitor-resident irritants, methodology, and research inferences. In *Sixth annual conference proceedings of the Travel Research Association*. San Diego, CA, Travel and Tourism Research Association, 195–198.

Dyer, P., Gursoy, D., Sharma, B., & Carter, J. (2007). Structural modeling of resident perceptions of tourism and associated development on the Sunshine Coast, Australia. *Tourism Management, 28*(2), 409–422.

Etzioni, A. (1985). Opening the preferences: A socio-economic research agenda. *Journal of Behavioral Economics, 14*, 183–205.

Faulkner, B., & Tideswell, C. (1997). A framework for monitoring community impacts of tourism. *Journal of Sustainable Tourism, 5*(1), 3–28.

Fridgen, J. D. (1991). *Dimensions of tourism*. Lansing: The Educational Institute of the American Hotel & Lodging Association.

Getz, D., & Timur, S. (2005). Stakeholder involvement in sustainable tourism: Balancing the voice. In W. F. Theobald, a cura di *Global Tourism* (3rd ed., pp. 230–247). New York: Butterworth-Heinemann/Elsevier.

Gursoy, D., & Kendall, K. (2006). Hosting mega events: Modeling locals' support. *Annals of Tourism Research, 33*(3), 603–623.

Gursoy, D., & Rutherford, D. (2004). Host attitudes toward tourism. An improved structural model. *Annals of Tourism Research, 31*, 495–516.

Gursoy, D., Jurowski, C., & Uysal, M. (2002). Resident attitudes: A structural modeling approach. *Annals of Tourism Research, 29*, 79–105.

Gursoy, D., Chi, C. G., & Dyer, P. (2010). Locals' attitudes toward mass and alternative tourism: The case of Sunshine Coast, Australia. *Journal of Travel Research, 49*(3), 381–394.

Harrill, R. (2004). Residents' attitudes toward tourism development: A literature review with implications for tourism planning. *Journal of Planning Literature, 18*(1), 1–16.

Jurowski, C., & Gursoy, D. (2004). Distance effects on residents' attitudes toward tourism. *Annals of Tourism Research, 31*(2), 296–312.

Jurowski, C., Uysal, M., & Williams, D. (1997). A theoretical analysis of host community resident reactions to tourism. *Journal of Travel Research, 36*(2), 3–11.

Katz, M., & Rosen, H. (1998). *Microeconomics* (3rd a cura di). New York: McGraw-Hill Companies Inc.

Kayat, K. (2002). Power, social exchanges and tourism in Langkawi: Rethinking resident perceptions. *International Journal of Tourism Research, 4*(3), 171–191.

King, B., Pizam, A., & Milman, A. (1993). Social impacts of tourism. *Annals of Tourism Research, 20*, 650–655.

Lancaster, K. J. (1966). A new approach to consumer theory. *Journal of Political Economy, 74*(2), 132.

Lawson, R., Williams, J., Young, T., & Cossens, J. (1998). A comparison of residents' attitudes towards tourism in 10 New Zealand destinations. *Tourism Management, 19*(2), 247–256.

Lepp, A. (2007). Residents' attitudes towards tourism in Bigodi Village, Uganda. *Tourism Management, 28*, 876–885.

Mason, P., & Cheyne, J. (2000). Residents' attitudes to proposed tourism development. *Annals of Tourism Research, 27*(2), 391–411.

Monterrubio-Cordero, J. C. (2008). Resident's perception of tourism: A critical theoretical and methodological review. *Ciencia Ergo Sum, 15*(1), 35–44.

Murphy, P., & Murphy, A. (2004). *Strategic management for tourism communities: Bridging the gaps*. Clevedon: Channel View Publications.

Neal, J., Sirgy, M., & Uysal, M. (2004). Measuring the effect of tourism services on travelers' quality of life: Further validation. *Social Indicators Research, 69*(3), 243–277.

Neal, J. D., Uysal, M., & Sirgy, M. J. (2007). The effect of tourism services on travelers' quality of life. *Journal of Travel Research, 46*(2), 154–163.

Northcote, J., & Macbeth, J. (2006). Conceptualising yield in sustainable tourism management. *Annals of Tourism Research, 33*, 199–220.

Nunkoo, R., & Gursoy, D. (2012). Residents' support for tourism: An identity perspective. *Annals of Tourism Research, 39*(1), 243–268.

Nunkoo, R., Smith, S., & Ramkissoon, M. (2013). Resident attitudes to tourism: A longitudinal study of 140 articles from 1984 to 2010. *Journal of Sustainable Tourism, 21*(1), 5–25.

Pearce, P. (2009). The relationship between positive psychology and tourist behavior studies. *Tourism Analysis, 14*(1), 37–48.

Pearce, P., Moscardo, G., & Ross, G. (1996). *Tourism community relationships*. Oxford: Elsevier Science Ltd.

Pearce, P., Filep, S., & Ross, G. (2011). *Tourists, tourism and the good life*. London/New York: Routledge.

Pérez, E., & Nadal, J. (2005). Host community perceptions: A cluster analysis. *Annals of Tourism Research, 32*(4), 925–941.

Perman, R., Ma, Y., Common, M., Maddison, D., & McGilvray, J. (2011). *Natural resources and environmental economics* (4th ed.). Pearson: Harlow.

Reisinger, Y., & Turner, L. (2002). Cultural differences between Asian tourist markets and Australian hosts: Part 1. *Journal of Travel Research, 40*(3), 295–315.

Saarinen, J. (2006). Traditions of sustainability in tourism studies. *Annals of Tourism Research, 38*, 1121–1140.

Saarinen, J., Rogerson, C., & Manwa, H. (2011). Tourism and millennium development goals: Tourism for development? *Current Issues in Tourism, 14*(3), 201–203.

Sharpley, R. (2008). *Tourism, tourists and society* (4th ed. a cura di). Huntingdon: Elm Publications.

Sharpley, R. (2014). Host perceptions of tourism: A review of the research. *Tourism Management, 42*, 37–49.

Sharpley, R. (2015). Tourism: A vehicle for development. In: R. Sharpley & D. Telfer, a cura di *Tourism and development: Concepts and issues* (pp. 3–30). Bristol: Channel View Publications.

Sirgy, M. J., Kruger, P., Lee, D., & Yu, G. (2011). How does a travel trip affect tourists' life satisfaction? *Journal of Travel Research, 50*(3), 261–275.

Telfer, D., & Sharpley, R. (2008). *Tourism and development in the developing world*. Abingdon: Routledge.

Teye, V., Sonmez, S. F., & Sirakaya, E. (2002). Residents' attitudes towards tourism development. *Annals of Tourism Research, 29*, 668–688.

Tosun, C. (2002). Host perceptions of impacts: A comparative tourism study. *Annals of Tourism Research, 29*(1), 231–253.

Uysal, M., Sirgy, M., Woo, E., & Kim, H. (2016). Quality of life (QOL) and well-being research in tourism. *Tourism Management, 53*, 244–261.

Vargas-Sánchez, A., Porras-Bueno, N., & Plaza-Mejia, A. (2011). Explaining residents attitudes to tourism. Is a universal model possible? *Annals of Tourism Research, 38*(2), 460–480.

Vargas-Sánchez, A., Porras-Bueno, N., de los, A., & Plaza-Mejia, M. (2014). Residents' attitude to tourism and seasonality. *Journal of Travel Research, 53*, 581–596.

Varian, H. (2010). *Intermediate microeconomics* (8th a cura di). New York: W.W. Norton and Company.

Wall, G., & Mathieson, A. (2006). *Tourism: Change, impacts and opportunities*. Harlow: Pearson Prentice Hall.

Williams, J., & Lawson, R. (2001). Community issues and resident opinions of tourism. *Annals of Tourism Research, 28*(2), 269–290.

Woosnam, K. M. (2012). Using emotional solidarity to explain residents' attitudes about tourism and tourism development. *Journal of Travel Research, 51*(3), 315–327.

WTTC. (2014). *Travel and tourism economic impact 2014*. London: s.n.

Chapter 5
An Exploration of Links between Levels of Tourism Development and Impacts on the Social Facet of Residents' Quality of Life

Elena Konovalov, Laurie Murphy, and Gianna Moscardo

Abstract Tourism is often recognized as having significant impacts on the quality of life (QOL) of the people who live and work in tourism destinations. Despite an extensive body of literature on tourism impacts, very little research has focused detailed attention on tourism and the social dimensions of residents' QOL. The available evidence in this area suggests that social impacts of tourism are related to the level and type of tourism development at a destination. This chapter will explore these proposed linkages by comparing three regional Australian destinations with different levels and styles of tourism on a series of measures of residents' QOL. The investigation of social impacts of tourism at the study locations was carried out in 2013–2014 and consisted of two components – an analysis of available relevant secondary data and a survey of residents. Consistent with previous research, a higher scale of tourism development was linked to increased crime, reduced volunteering and perceived influence over community development, and more/better community services. However, the results did not demonstrate a higher emotional connection to place, community pride, and needs fulfilment that are commonly assigned to benefits of tourism development. The chapter describes the complex pattern of results that emerged from the analyses before discussing the implications of these for further research and theoretical development in understanding the social impacts of tourism.

Keywords Tourism impacts · Quality of life (QoL) · Social impacts of tourism · Comparative research · Social facet of QoL · Scale of tourism development · Style of tourism development · The systems theory framework for QoL · The capitals-framework for QoL

E. Konovalov (✉) · L. Murphy · G. Moscardo
James Cook University, Townsville, QLD, Australia
e-mail: e.konovalov@cqu.edu.au

A. M. Campón-Cerro et al. (eds.), *Best Practices in Hospitality and Tourism Marketing and Management*, Applying Quality of Life Research,
https://doi.org/10.1007/978-3-319-91692-7_5

5.1 Introduction

Tourism is often promoted as a development opportunity for rural and regional communities based on the assumption that it will generate income and that higher income equates to improvements in Quality of Life (QOL) in destination communities. Research into community QOL, however, identifies a range of contributing factors often organised into economic, social and environmental dimensions, all of which are important, and progress in one is not always able to substitute for a decline in one of the others (Rogers and Ryan 2001). Despite recognition of this, the majority of tourism impact research has focused on economic indicators with some attention paid to environmental indicators, and only limited research into indicators for social impacts of tourism (Sharma et al. 2008). While discussions of tourism impacts often include a range of social benefits and costs associated with tourism development, there has been little research specifically focusing on identifying and explaining the links between tourism and the social dimensions of residents' QOL.

Planning and managing tourism in a way that positively contributes to local residents' QOL is a major challenge (Epley and Menon 2008). In response to this challenge recent tourism impact research has concentrated on better understanding the links between tourism and the different capitals that have been linked to QOL (cf. Andereck and Nyaupane 2011; McGehee et al. 2010; Moscardo 2009; Moscardo et al. 2013). This chapter is going to explore these links further, focusing on the social aspects of QOL in three Australian regional destinations with different histories and styles of tourism development. The main objective of the study was to investigate relationships between style and scale of tourism development and socials aspects of QOL at the study communities, and then compare the observed relationships to the links proposed by current tourism impact research. The main research question investigated by the study was 'With the current knowledge of tourism impacts, can we predict the social impacts of tourism based on style and scale of tourism development at a destination community?'

The chapter will begin with a short review of the relevant literature identifying the processes that have been proposed or assumed to link tourism to changes in residents' QOL. It will then describe a study that used existing government data and the results from a survey of 597 residents in the three regions to examine whether or not, and how, different levels and types of tourism were linked to social aspects of destination residents' QOL. After describing the complex pattern of results that emerged from the analyses some implications of these for further research, theoretical development and practice in sustainable tourism development will be suggested.

5.2 Research on Social Impacts of Tourism

The term ‘social impacts of tourism’ is used to describe the impacts of tourism on the lifestyle of residents (Butler 1974), their social life, daily routines, habits, beliefs and values (Doğan 1989), and on individual behaviour, family relationships, safety levels, moral conduct, creative expressions, traditional ceremonies and community organizations (Ap 1990). Unlike economic and environmental impacts, social impacts of tourism have proven difficult to quantify and measure (Vanclay 2004).

The majority of research into tourism’s social impacts has examined residents’ perceptions (Sharpley 2014). Researchers commonly rationalise this research position arguing that for planning and managing tourism development residents’ perceptions of tourism are at least equally, or more important, than assessment of the actual tourism impacts (Deery et al. 2012). However, unlike economic and environmental tourism impacts studies, there has been little research into how well these subjective measures (residents’ perceptions) match up to the objective measures (actual impacts) (Northcote and Macbeth 2005).

There is also confusion about theoretical explanations of tourism’s social impacts. Theories proposed by current tourism impact research include Equity theory, Growth Machine theory, Power theory, Stakeholder theory (Easterling 2004), community attachment (McCool and Martin 1994) as well as some others (for more details please see the review by Nunkoo et al. 2013). Three main approaches dominate this area. Social exchange theory is the most common, proposing that resident’s perceptions of tourism result from weighing up the benefits, such as more jobs, against the costs, such as crowding (Ap 1992). The second are cumulative impact approaches like the Life Cycle Model (Butler 1980) and ‘Irridex model’ (Doxey 1975). These models propose that impacts develop as the level of tourism rises until they exceed the coping mechanisms of the residents, resulting in attitudes towards tourism becoming more negative. Finally there is Social Representations Theory which argues that residents’ perceptions are mostly determined by the everyday theories and images that residents have of tourism and tourists (Andriotis and Vaughan 2003; Fredline 2005). The first two approaches assume perceptions closely follow actual impacts, while the third one proposes the existence of only limited links between objective and subjective impact measures. To date, little research has been conducting linking objective and subjective measures of social impacts of tourism (Northcote and Macbeth 2005) and therefore little evidence is available to assess these different approaches. In the present chapter the social impacts of tourism are theorised as interactions between two complex phenomena: (1) the social aspects of community QOL, and (2) the style and scale of tourism development.

5.2.1 Understanding the Social Facet of QOL

QOL is a complex concept used for different research purposes and defined in many different ways (Sirgy et al. 2006). The unit of analysis at which the concept is applied can also vary across individuals or groups of individuals, communities, and nations. The research reported here focused on destination residents' or community QOL. It is important to note here that community well-being is frequently used as a synonym for community QOL as both concepts are very closely related. For this research project community QOL/community well-being was defined as "a function of the actual conditions of … life and what a person or community makes of those conditions" (Michalos 2008, p. 357). Investigation of links between tourism and social aspects of community QOL required a conceptual model of community QOL. A review of existing literature in the interdisciplinary field of QOL research identified two potential concepts: the systems-theory framework and the capitals framework.

The systems theory framework for QOL builds on the work of Veenhoven (2001), who identified three main dimensions: quality of environment (external to an individual conditions of living), quality of performance (inner ability of an individual to respond to external living conditions), and quality of the result (the actual satisfaction/dissatisfaction with life). The systems theory framework, proposed by Hagerty et al. (2001), aligns Veenhoven's three dimensions of QOL with input, throughput and output components of a system and establishes causal relationships between them. The inputs (environment) represent exogenous or independent variables, which affect outputs (subjective well-being of an individual) by affecting throughputs (individual choices). The outputs in this system represent the endogenous or dependent variables, which denote overall contentment with various QOL domains and one's life overall.

The capitals framework sees community QOL as a community's ability to access and utilise various types of capitals/assets/resources (Flora and Flora 2013). Usually seven forms of community capitals are identified including natural, cultural, human, social, political financial and built (Emery and Flora 2006). As this research project was focused on links between tourism and social aspects of QOL, the above list of capitals was reduced to only those that have direct links to the social impacts of tourism.

5.2.2 Proposed Theoretical Framework of the Social Facet of QOL

An analysis of relevant review papers (Andereck et al. 2005; Deery et al. 2012; Easterling 2004) identified four key social dimensions of tourism impacts on local residents' QOL: (1) Human capital, (2) Social capital, (3) Community Identity and Pride (linked to cultural capital) and (4) Community Services (linked to built capital).

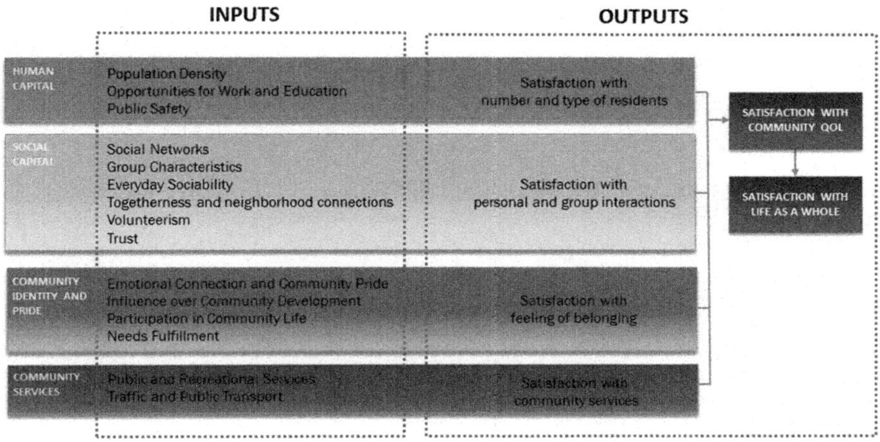

Fig. 5.1 Proposed theoretical framework of social facet of QOL

A simplified systems theory approach was then adopted and input and output measures were identified for each of those capitals. Figure 5.1 details the proposed theoretical framework. Inputs in this framework are the dimensions of the selected capitals representing the social aspects of QOL that have been previously linked to tourism. Outputs are dependent variables that are influenced by changes in inputs and which represent residents' satisfaction with each of the selected aspects of QOL, overall community QOL and the individual's life as a whole. It is proposed that satisfaction with the social aspects of QOL contribute to overall satisfaction with community QOL, which in turn contributes to individual satisfaction with their life overall.

5.2.3 *Style and Scale of Tourism Development*

Tourism development at different destinations varies in its style and scale. Faulkner and Tideswell (1997) proposed that specific tourism impacts at a destination are determined by the following tourism features: (1) stage of tourism development, (2) tourist/resident ratio, (3) types of tourists, and (4) seasonality. Links between those variables and identified social aspects of QOL suggested by previous tourism impact research (see reviews of research in Andereck et al. 2005; Deery et al. 2012; Easterling 2004; Harrill 2004; Nunkoo, et al. 2013; Sharpley 2014) are summarised in Fig. 5.2 (Human Capital), Fig. 5.3 (Social Capital), Fig. 5.4 (Community Identity and Pride) and Fig. 5.5 (Community Services). To date, these links, have not been tested in a consistent way across destinations that differ on the identified tourism features. Furthermore, tourism impact researchers have not yet proposed the nature of relationships between the four tourism features and residents' satisfaction with community QOL and life as a whole (the overall outputs of the theoretical framework).

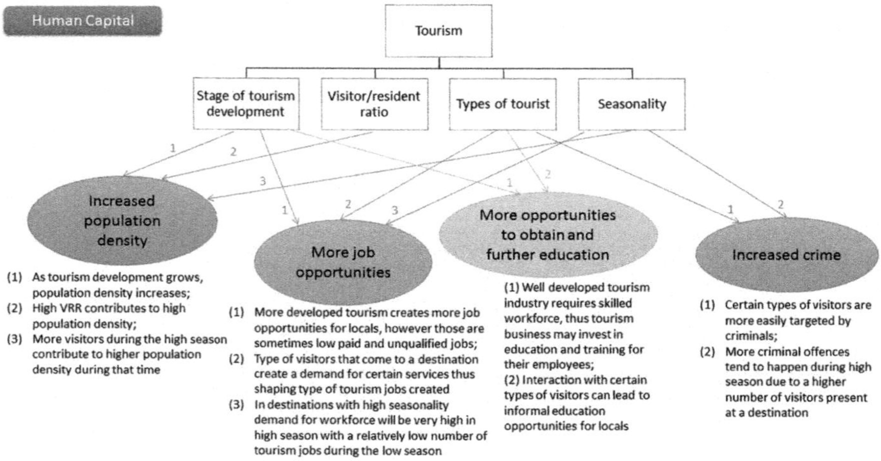

Fig. 5.2 Proposed links between features of tourism and dimensions of human capital

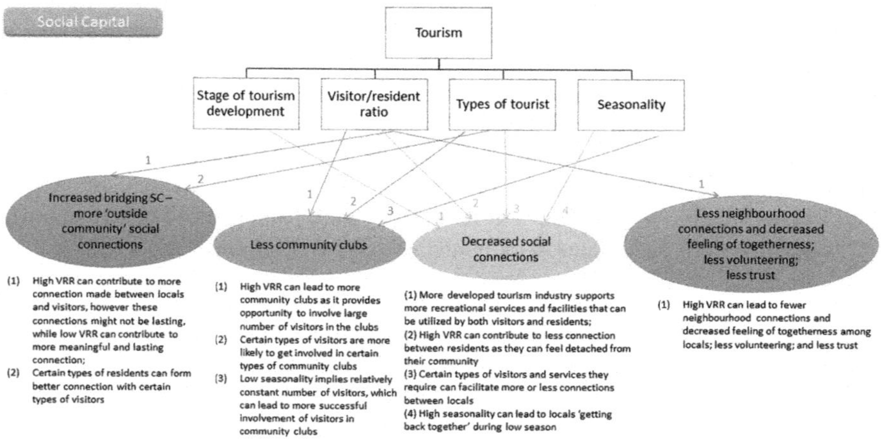

Fig. 5.3 Proposed links between features of tourism and dimensions of social capital

The present study aimed to address the research gaps by developing and implementing a set of measures of the actual features of tourism and of social aspects of QOL at three Australian tropical destinations. The aim of the study was to adopt a comparative approach for identifying specific links between the style and scale of tourism development and social aspects of QOL through combined implementation of objective and subjective measures. Small-N comparative analysis was utilised to achieve this goal with a small number of cases carefully selected by the 'most similar system design' method, with selected cases varying most significantly on the variable of interest – style and scale of tourism development (Druckman 2005).

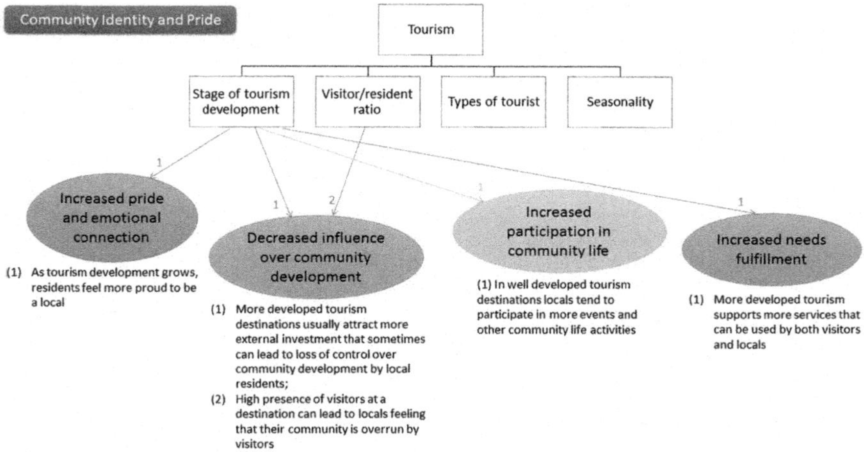

Fig. 5.4 Proposed links between features of tourism and dimensions of community identity and pride

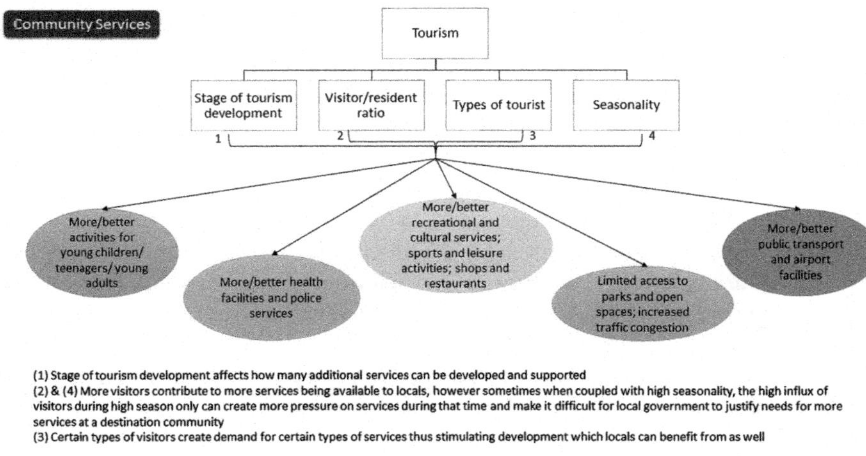

Fig. 5.5 Proposed links between features of tourism and dimensions of community services

5.3 Study Regions

The three selected communities, in North Queensland Australia, vary in their style and scale of tourism development but are relatively similar on main QOL aspects. They share similar climates as they are located within a restricted geographic range in the same state with the same government and business systems, and in a developed country with no major cultural, political, macro-economic or macro-climate

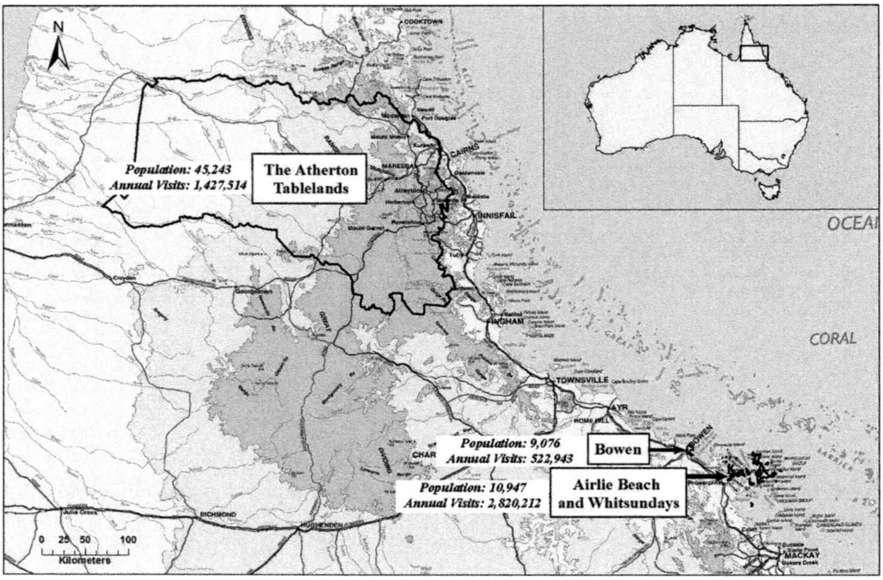

Fig. 5.6 The three study regions: the Atherton Tablelands, Bowen, and Airlie Beach and Whitsunday Islands
Population figures are for 2011; Annual visits is an aggregated number of day visitors and international and domestic visitor nights. Data sources: Australian Bureau of Statistics, Tourism Research Australia, Geoscience Australia and Queensland Government Information Service. Map was generated using ARC Map software

differences. The study communities were: (1) Airlie Beach – a gateway to the Whitsunday Islands which is a high profile tourism destination with a well-developed tourism industry, (2) Bowen – a major industrial port and a local centre for the mining industry with an emerging tourism industry; (3) Atherton Tablelands – an agricultural region with a limited but established tourism industry, where tourism seen as a complementary opportunity for economic development. Figure 5.6 shows their locations.

5.4 Tourism Profiles

The first step in the research process was to construct tourism profiles for each study community. This was done through analysis of available secondary data from various tourism and government bodies (please refer to Konovalov et al. 2013 for methodology and detailed results description). Table 5.1 summarises the findings of that analysis. Airlie Beach is the most developed tourism destination with the highest ratio of visitors to locals, the highest proportion of larger accommodation businesses, and the highest proportion of international and interstate tourists. It does not,

Table 5.1 Tourism measures of the three study regions

	Variables	Available measures	Airlie beach		Bowen		The Atherton tablelands	
Stage of tourism development	Scale and diversity of tourism development (data for larger proxy geographical units used)	Number and type of accommodation establishments (abbreviations: CP – caravan parks, SA – serviced apartments, H – hotels, M – motels, (15+) - with 15 or more rooms, (5–14) – with 5–14 rooms)	Total number – 59		Total number – 23		Total number – 39	
			Hostels	10%	Hostels	13%	Hostels	5%
			Flats/units	8%	Flats/units	4%	Flats/units	2%
			CP	15%	CP	30%	CP	26%
			SA (15+)	24%	SA (15+)	None	SA (15+)	None
			M (15+)	10%	M (15+)	22%	M (15+)	18%
			H (15+)	14%	H (15+)	9%	H (15+)	5%
			H/M/SA (5–14)	19%	H/M/SA (5–14)	22%	H/M/SA (5–14)	44%
		Average bed spaces (excluding H/M/SA(5–14))	220		80		56	
	Economic reliance on tourism	Employment in 'accommodation and food services' industry	Number	1514	Number	363	Number	1097
			% total employment	26.3%	% total employment	9.1%	% total employment	6.2%
Visitor-resident contact	Density of visitors	Average daily visitor density per 1000 population[a]	Between 1071 and 662 per 1000 residents		Between 201 and 62 per 1000 residents		Between 109 and 60 per 1000 residents	
		Average daily visitor density per land area[a]	Between 34 and 21 per km^2		Between 34 and 11per km^2		Between 0.07 and 0.04 per km^2	

(continued)

Table 5.1 (continued)

	Variables	Available measures	Airlie beach		Bowen		The Atherton tablelands	
Type of visitors	Demographic and trip related characteristics	Visitors by length of stay	Day visitors	16%	Day visitors	47%	Day visitors	65%
			1 night	8%	1 night	16%	1 night	8%
			2–4 nights	40%	2–4 nights	23%	2–4 nights	13%
			5–8 nights	27%	5–8 nights	6%	5–8 nights	6%
			9–30 nights	7%	9–30 nights	5%	9–30 nights	7%
			31 or more nights	1%	31 or more nights	3%	31 or more nights	2%
		Travel party + age + length of stay (% of annual domestic and international overnight visitors mean)[b]	Adult couple, 25–64, 2–8 nights – 15%		Friends/relatives, 15–24, 1–4 nights – 12%		Adult couple, 45–64. 1–30 nights – 10%	
			Unaccompanied Traveller, 15–44, 2–8 nights – 12%		Unaccompanied Traveller, 15–64, 2–4 nights – 10%		Friends/relatives, 15–44, 1–4 nights – 7%	
			Family group, 25–44, 2–8 nights – 7%		Adult couple, 45–64, 1–4 nights –8%			
			Friends/relatives, 15–44, 2–4 nights – 6%		Family group, 15–44, 2–4 nights – 6%			
		Percent of international visitors	30%		6%		4%	
		Interstate/intrastate overnight domestic visitors ratio	50 inter- and 50 intrastate visitors per 100 domestic overnight visitors		16 inter- and 84 intrastate visitors per 100 domestic overnight visitors		21 inter- and 79 intrastate visitors per 100 domestic overnight visitors	

Seasonality[a]	Pattern	Seasonal index (tourism seasons correspond to the index above one)	March quarter	0.947	March quarter	0.769	March quarter	0.806
			June quarter	0.860	June quarter	1.019	June quarter	1.019
			September quarter	1.083	September quarter	1.239	September quarter	1.203
			December quarter	1.115	December quarter	0.967	December quarter	0.965
	Amplitude	Low season/high season ratio	77%		62%		67%	

Data Sources: Australian Bureau of Statistics and Tourism Research Australia
[a]95% Confidence Interval
[b]Data on domestic day visitors is not detailed by travel party and age

however, have strong seasonality and has far fewer day-trippers than the other two regions. The tourism industry in Bowen is relatively small and caters mostly to domestic visitors. The Atherton Tablelands is mostly visited by day-trippers from a major adjacent coastal tourism destination, and international and interstate visitors are a minority in the overall visitor mix. The tourism profiles presented in Table 5.1 confirm that the selected destinations have varying degrees and styles of tourism development.

5.5 Proposed Linkages

Connecting these tourism development profiles (Table 5.1) with the links between tourism features and impacts on social aspects of QOL (Figs. 5.2, 5.3, 5.4, and 5.5), allows for the researchers to propose potential relationships between tourism and social aspects of QOL at the three communities. Based on the scale and style of tourism development, tourism impacts at Airlie Beach are expected to be more significant compared to Bowen and Atherton Tablelands. Specifically, we would expect to find here a higher population density, along with more opportunities for work and to obtain or further education. Those benefits for human capital are expected to be offset by higher crime rates. In the area of social capital, in Airlie Beach we would expect to find increased 'outside community' social connections, offset by lower within community connections, including fewer neighbourhood connections, less volunteering, fewer community clubs, decreased feelings of togetherness and less trust of other local residents. It was also expected for Airlie Beach residents to have increased pride and emotional connection to the local area, increased participation in community life and increased needs fulfilment; this however would coincide with decreased ability to influence community development. In the area of community services, overall it would be expected that residents in Airlie Beach would have access to more and/or better community services, compared to residents in Bowen and Atherton Tablelands. Those benefits would be expected to be offset by higher traffic congestion and limited access for local residents to local parks and open/public spaces.

However, the relationships pattern is far from linear and is very complex. The severity of impacts could be lessened in Airlie Beach due to less pronounced seasonality and the diverse mix of visitors. While in Bowen, which relies on particular a type of visitors and has more pronounced seasonality, the actual impacts could be more significant than would be concluded from stage of tourism development and visitor/resident ratio. Thus, further investigation was conducted to identify specific links.

5.6 Methodology

The research adopted an approach in which objective and subjective measures were combined, as well as primary and available secondary data. First, the available secondary data on social aspects of community well-being were compiled for each community. Then, a questionnaire was developed to complement existing secondary data and to measure the components of the proposed theoretical framework relating to residents' experience with, and perceptions of, tourism (the copy of the questionnaire is available from the leading author on request).

The questionnaire included questions utilized in previous research as well as some original questions developed specifically for this research project. Most of the questions were derived from a review of previous research on measures of human capital (Cuthill, 2003; Morton and Edwards 2012), social capital (Burt 2000; Knack 2002; Narayan and Cassidy 2001; Onyx and Bullen 2000; Stone 2001), community identity and pride (Baker and Palmer 2006; McMillan 1996; Peterson et al. 2008), and community services (Grzeskowiak et al. 2003; Sirgy et al. 2000, 2008). The survey questions aimed to collect data for (1) objective measures of the framework's inputs (which could not be obtained from the secondary sources), (2) data for subjective measures of those inputs, and (3) data for outputs of the framework. For example, one of the identified inputs of Community Identity and Pride is 'influence over community development'. This input can be measured objectively (public meeting attendance rate) and subjectively (degree of agreement with an influence statement). As no secondary data was available for public meeting attendance rate, the survey included a question that asked respondents to specify whether or not they attended a public meeting within last 6 months, as well as a question on how much they agreed with a statement "I have a say in what goes on in my community'.

Additionally, the survey was targeting longer-term residents of the study communities. Screening questions on residency type and length were used at the beginning of the survey so that only those participants who reported having lived in the area for more than 6 months were directed to questions about community QOL and perceptions of tourism.

The survey was carried out at the three study regions in late 2013 – early 2014. Qualtrics software was used to administer the survey. The study utilised convenience sampling. A press release was issued in each region with information about the study and a link via which the online survey could be accessed. Key community stakeholders were also asked to distribute the survey information and link among their networks. The online survey was complemented by a one week long site visit at each of the study locations. Passers-by in various public places were invited to take the survey via iPads and survey flyers were distributed throughout the community. This boosted the survey responses and ensured inclusion of people who did not have internet access.

The final sample size for Airlie Beach was 170, for Bowen 180 and for the Atherton Tablelands 247. Table 5.2 provides details on the size of the adult (18+) resident population at each of the regions and specifies the proportion of the population

Table 5.2 Details of the resident survey at the study communities

	Airlie beach	Bowen	The Atherton tablelands
Dates of the survey	February – May 2014	December 2013 – Match 2014	April – July 2014
Sample size	170	180	247
18+ Population[a]	8568	6851	33,061
% of sample in population	1.98%	2.63%	0.75%

[a]Data Source: ABS, Census of Australian of Australian Population and Housing, 2011

sampled, which varied between the regions from 2.63% to 0.75%. The objective of the survey was to explore links and explanatory elements of the research rather than establish absolute ratings and figures; and so while the sample did not necessarily provide a statistically representative analysis of the total population in the three regions, it did represent a diverse cross-section of the study communities. The convenience sampling approach adopted is consistent with other tourism impact research publications (see for example Chen 2016; Mensah 2012; Pranić et al. 2012; Wang and Chen 2015) and was the only feasible option given time and funding constraints.

The main demographic characteristics of the sample are summarised in Table 5.3. Persons' Chi Square test identified that significant differences between the three samples existed only on 'age' and 'length of residence' variables, with respondents in the Atherton Tablelands on average being older and living in the local community longer compared to the other two regions. These sample differences, however, are reflective of differences in the populations of the locations as established from Australian Bureau of Statistics census data and previous research projects at the study locations. Thus the observed differences in measured variables between the study regions are unlikely to be the result of differences in the samples.

5.7 Results

The first step in the analysis examined the underlying processes for the proposed theoretical framework presented in Fig. 5.1 using a series of regression analyses. A series of simple and multiple regression analyses were performed to explore the relationships among the variables. The results are summarized in Table 5.4 and show support for the theoretical model with the inputs contributing significantly to satisfaction with the four social aspects of community QOL, which in turn were significant contributors to satisfaction with overall community QOL, which then contributed to satisfaction with life as a whole.

The second stage of the analysis examined differences between the three regions on the objective and subjective indicators for each of the four social aspects of com-

Table 5.3 Sociodemographic characteristics of the survey respondents

		Airlie beach	Bowen	The Atherton tablelands	
		% in sample	% in sample	% in sample	χ^{2a}
Gender	Male	39.2	33.8	31.8	2.011, df = 2
	Female	60.8	66.2	68.2	$p = .366$
Age	Under 35	17.0	17.3	8.3	25.664*, df = 8
	35–44	19.7	23.2	12.6	
	45–54	21.1	26.1	23.3	
	55–64	21.8	22.5	31.6	
	65 and over	20.4	10.9	24.2	
Education	Some postgraduate work	16.7	14.6	18.3	16.277, df = 6
	Bachelor degree	14.6	13.9	25.8	$p = .012$
	Some post-school qualifications	45.1	38.7	31.9	
	School education or below	23.6	32.8	23.9	
Length of residence	Less than 12 months	8.9	4.5	2.4	17.037*, df = 6
	1 year – Less than 5 years	18.8	19.4	13.5	
	5 years – Less than 10 year	18.8	19.4	15.2	
	10 year or more	53.5	56.7	68.9	
Connection to tourism	I work in tourism	14.4	5.3	11.2	10.996, df = 4,
	I work in industry which benefits from tourism	21.9	23.2	15.6	$p = .027$
	I work in other than tourism industry/I don't work	63.7	71.5	73.5	

[a]Pearson Chi-Square test
*$p < .01$

munity QOL. Results are summarised in Tables 5.5, 5.6, 5.7, and 5.8. Please note that measures typed in bold font represent objective measures, measures typed in normal font are subjective measures, measures typed in italic are output measures and measures marked with (SS) were obtained from secondary data sources. For secondary data, observed differences are reported and for primary data a series of one-way ANOVA with Bonferroni Post Hoc tests were employed where appropriate to determine statistically significant differences in the measures between the study regions. Consistency of the observed links with those established by previous research is reported the following way: ✓✓ – consistent, ✓ – somewhat consistent, × – not consistent. 'Somewhat consistent' implies that the observed highest/lowest measures (as applicable) were consistent with proposed links.

The results for the measures of human capital are summarised in Table 5.5. Only one measure was consistent with the proposed links (see Fig. 5.2) – crime rates in

Table 5.4 Regression analyses: Social facet of community QOL

Independent variable(s)	Dependent variable	β	t
Model 1: Overall life satisfaction		$F(1, 551) = 288.62$, $p = .000$, adjusted $R^2 = .343$	
Satisfaction with community Well-being	Satisfaction with life as a whole	.586*	16.99
Model 2: Community well-being		$F(4, 535) = 131.97$, $p = .000$, adjusted $R^2 = .493$	
Satisfaction with human capital	Satisfaction with community Well-being	.266*	4.82
Satisfaction with social capital		.223*	7.01
Satisfaction with identity and pride		.208*	4.92
Satisfaction with community services		.173*	4.39
Model 3: Human capital		$F(3, 441) = 41.456$, $p = .000$, adjusted $R^2 = .215$	
Population density	Satisfaction with human capital	.310*	10.94
Opportunities for work		.198*	7.06
Opportunities for education		ns	–
Public safety		.163*	3.80
Model 4: Social capital		$F(5, 475) = 30.818$, $p = .000$, adjusted $R^2 = .237$	
Group characteristics	Satisfaction with social capital	.098, $p = .042$	2.04
Everyday sociability		.172*	4.20
Togetherness		.204*	4.42
Neighborhood connections		ns	–
Volunteering		.152*	3.16
Trust		.170*	3.66
Model 5: Community identity and pride		$F(4, 458) = 64.390$, $p = .000$, adjusted $R^2 = .354$	
Emotional connections	Satisfaction with identity and pride	.195*	4.18
Community pride		.301*	6.46
Influence over Community development		.248*	6.18
Participation in community life		ns	–
Needs fulfillment		.080, $p = .046$	2.00
Model 6: Community services[a]		$F(5, 225) = 30.654$, $p = .000$, adjusted $R^2 = .341$	
Activities for young children	Satisfaction with community services	.164*	2.96
Health facilities		.254*	4.21
Shops and restaurants		.185*	3.09
Airport facilities		.283*	4.99

Note: Condition of the roads was excluded due to presence of road works in Tablelands at the time of the survey which affected Tablelands residents' responses

*$p < .01$

[a]Nonsignificant predictors: Activities for teenage children, Activities for young adults, Police services, Recreational services, Cultural activities, Sports and leisure activities, Parks and open spaces, Public transport, Boat ramp facilities

Table 5.5 Measures of human capital

Dimensions	Measures of human capital	AB *M*	B *M*	AT *M*	ANOVA *F*	Observed differences/ Bonferroni Post Hoc	Consistency with previous research
Population density	**Number of persons per km² (SS)**	144	187	>1		B > AB > AT	✓
	Population change preference (7 pt scale from 1 big decrease to7 big increase)	4.69	5.58	4.63	*F* (2, 497) = 37.60*	B > AB & AT	✓
Opportunities for work	**Unemployment rate (%) (SS)**	6.7	10.1	8.2		B > AT > AB	✓
	Residents' evaluation (4 pt scale from 1 severely lacking to 4 more than enough)	2.09	1.45	1.97	*F* (2, 534) = 38.19*	AB & AT > B	✓
Opportunities for education	**% of post-school students (SS)**	4.9	4.0	4.5		AB > AT > B	✓
	Residents' evaluation (as above)	2.07	1.59	2.01	*F* (2, 506) = 19.75*	AB & AT > B	✓
Public safety	**Offences per 1000 residents (SS)**	145	104	89		AB > B > AT	✓✓
	Residents' perceptions (5 pt scale from 1 very unsafe to 5 very safe)	4.08	3.72	4.18	*F* (2, 546) = 13.61*	AT & AB > B	✓
Output	*Satisfaction with number and type of residents* (11 pt scale from 0 not at all to 10 completely satisfied)	*7.09*	*5.60*	*7.70*	*F* (2, 542) = 41.60*	AT > AB > B	✓

*p < .01

Table 5.6 Measures of social capital

Dimensions	Measures of social capital	AB	B	AT	ANOVA	Observed differences/ Bonferroni Post Hoc	Consistency with previous research
		M	*M*	*M*	*F*		
Social networks	**Openness of social networks (%)**	16	21	9		B > AB > AT	✓
	(% who's social networks consist of 'mostly new friends')						
Group characteristics	**Club membership per person**	0.91	0.84	1.57	F (2, 547) = 20.49*	AT > AB & B	✓
	(5 pt scale from 0 none to 5 five or more)						
Everyday sociability	**Frequency of socialising informally**	3.81	3.53	3.73	F (2, 543) = 2.06, p = .129	No difference	×
	(6 pt scale from 1 never to 6 daily)						
	Frequency of socialising in public spaces	3.56	3.28	3.12	F (2, 543) = 5.73*	AB > AT	✓
	(as above)						
Togetherness	Agreement with a statement	3.86	3.49	3.86	F (2, 535) = 11.03*	AB & AT > B	×
	(5 pt scale from 1 strongly disagree to 5 strongly agree)						
Neighbourhood connections	Agreement with a statement	3.46	3.48	3.75	F (2, 534) = 4.10, p = .017	AT > AB & B	✓
	(as above)						
Volunteerism	**% volunteering (SS)**	14.6	17.3	21.8		AT > B > AB	✓✓
	Average hours devoted to volunteering	2.27	1.89	2.83	F (2, 519) = 20.97*	AT > AB > B	✓✓
	(5 pt scale from 1 none to 5 more than 20 h)						
Trust	Trust of people in your community	3.55	3.32	3.88	F (2, 492) = 19.46*	AT > AB > B	✓✓
	(5 pt scale from 1 not at all to 5 to a very great extent)						
Output	*Satisfaction with personal and group interaction*	*6.98*	*5.70*	*7.57*	F (2, 550) = 33.39*	AT > AB > B	✓✓
	(11 pt scale from 0 not at all to 10 completely satisfied)						

*$p < .01$

Table 5.7 Measures of community identity and pride

Dimensions	Measures of community identity and pride	AB *M*	B *M*	AT *M*	ANOVA *F*	Observed differences/ Bonferroni Post Hoc	Consistency with previous research
Emotional connection	Evaluation of living in local community (3 pt scale from 1 live here due to circumstances to 3 love living here)	2.29	2.16	2.55	F (2, 470) = 15.72*	AT > AB & B	×
Community pride	Agreement with a statement (5 pt scale from 1 strongly disagree to 5 strongly agree)	4.18	4.06	4.56	F (2, 537) = 23.74*	AT > AB & B	×
Influence over community development	**Public meeting attendance** (2 pt scale with 1 not attended a meeting and 2 attended a meeting)	1.27	1.46	1.42	F (2, 517) = 7.07*	AT & B > AB[a]	✓
	Agreement with a statement (5 pt scale from 1 strongly disagree to 5 strongly agree)	2.67	2.26	3.02	F (2, 535) = 24.87*	AT > AB > B	✓
Participation in community life	**Event attendance** (2 pt scale with 1 not attended an event and 2 attended an event)	1.73	1.78	1.62	F (2, 507) = 6.19*	B > AT	✓
Needs fulfilment	**Frequency for travelling for purchases** (6 pt scale from 1 never to 6 daily)	2.60	3.01	2.76	F (2, 538) = 6.35*	B > AB & AT	×

(continued)

Table 5.7 (continued)

Dimensions	Measures of community identity and pride	AB *M*	B *M*	AT *M*	ANOVA *F*	Observed differences/ Bonferroni Post Hoc	Consistency with previous research
	Agreement with a statement (5 pt scale from 1 strongly disagree to 5 strongly agree)	2.91	1.96	3.15	F (2, 535) = 55.52*	AT & AB > B	×
Output	*Satisfaction with feeling of belonging* (11 pt scale from 0 not at all to 10 completely satisfied)	*7.28*	*6.00*	*7.85*	F (2, 550) = 30.47*	AT > AB > B	×

*p < .01

[a]Please note that in Bowen and Airlie Beach there were many public consultations held at the time of the survey due to government approval of expansion of a local port

Airlie Beach were higher than in Bowen, and in Bowen higher than at the Atherton Tablelands. For the rest of the input measures some consistency was observed. The observed output measures were also somewhat consistent with the expected pattern of residents' satisfaction with Human Capital being lowest in Bowen. It was however, highest in the Atherton Tablelands rather than Airlie Beach.

Interestingly, despite the crime rates following the expected pattern, residents' perceptions of safety did not follow the same rule, that is despite higher crime rates in Airlie Beach, residents here felt as safe as residents in Atherton Tablelands where the lowest crime rates were observed. Objective and subjective measures also did not align for population density. Despite Bowen already having the highest number of persons per square kilometre, compared to the other two locations residents here indicated a preference for the highest increase in resident numbers in the future. Objective and subjective measures for opportunities for work and education however provided the same information. Of the three regions, unemployment was the highest in Bowen, aligning with lowest resident evaluation of opportunities for decent work. The proportion of post-school students was the highest in Airlie Beach, and residents here also evaluated opportunities to obtain and further education in the community more positively compared to the other two regions.

The results for measures of Social Capital are summarized in Table 5.6. As expected (see Fig. 5.3) it was found that in the region with the lowest tourism presence (Atherton Tablelands) volunteering and trust in people in the local community were the highest. Also compared to the other two regions, there was a higher level of neighbourhood connections and club memberships per person. Frequency of socializing in public places was the highest in Airlie Beach, as expected. However,

Table 5.8 Measures of community services

Dimensions	Measures of community services	AB	B	AT	ANOVA	Observed differences/ Bonferroni Post Hoc	Consistency with previous research
		M	*M*	*M*	*F*		
Activities for young children	**% who are young children (0–12 years old) (SS)**	15	16	17		No difference	–
	Agreement with sufficiency statement (5 pt scale from 1 strongly disagree to 5 strongly agree)	2.72	3.19	3.16	F (2, 404) = 5.42*	AT & B > AB	×
Activities for teenagers	**% who are teenage children (13–19) (SS)**	6	9	9		AT & B > AB	–
	Agreement with sufficiency statement (as above)	2.34	2.68	2.61	F (2, 395) = 2.79, p = .063	No difference	×
Activities for young adults	**% who are young adults (20–25) (SS)**	12	8	5		AB > B > AT	–
	Agreement with sufficiency statement (as above)	2.75	2.42	2.40	F (2, 387) = 3.72, p = .025	AB > AT	✓
Health facilities	**% working in health care/ social assistance (SS)**	5	9	11		AT > B > AB	×
	Agreement with sufficiency statement (as above)	2.99	2.18	2.74	F (2, 515) = 19.96*	AB & AT > B	✓
Police services	**Offences per 1000 residents (SS)**	145	104	89		AB > B > AT	✓✓

(continued)

Table 5.8 (continued)

Dimensions	Measures of community services	AB	B	AT	ANOVA	Observed differences/ Bonferroni Post Hoc	Consistency with previous research
		M	*M*	*M*	*F*		
	Agreement with sufficiency statement (as above)	3.69	3.21	3.24	F (2, 514) = 12.38*	AB > AT & B	✓
Cultural activities	Agreement with sufficiency statement (as above)	2.69	2.97	3.07	F (2, 515) = 6.62*	AT & B > AB	×
Sports and leisure activities	Agreement with sufficiency statement (as above)	3.26	3.30	3.45	F (2, 517) = 2.04, p = .131	No difference	×
Recreational services/shops & restaurants	**Frequency of going out** (6 pt scale from 1 never to 6 daily)	3.47	3.20	2.81	F (2, 521) = 14.13*	AB & B > AT	✓
	Agreement with sufficiency statement (as above)	3.50	2.13	3.07	F (2, 517) = 71.14*	AB > AT > B	✓
Parks and open spaces	**Frequency of visiting** (as above)	4.09	4.26	3.25	F (2, 518) = 33.20*	AB & B > AT	✓
	Agreement with sufficiency statement (as above)	3.74	3.89	3.79	F (2, 517) = 1.29, p = .276	No difference	×
Public transport	**Frequency of using** (as above)	1.53	1.07	1.13	F (2, 520) = 18.42*	AB > B & AT	✓
	Satisfaction with access to public transport (5 pt scale from 1 very dissatisfied to 5 very satisfied)	3.61	2.89	2.46	F (2, 422) = 43.71*	AB > B > AT	✓✓

(continued)

Table 5.8 (continued)

Dimensions	Measures of community services	AB *M*	B *M*	AT *M*	ANOVA *F*	Observed differences/ Bonferroni Post Hoc	Consistency with previous research
Traffic	**Frequency of traffic jams** (as above)	1.37	1.12	2.73	F (2, 520) = 77.85*	AT > AB & B[a]	–
	Satisfaction with road conditions (as above)	2.92	3.20	2.40	F (2, 519) = 25.43*	AB & B > AT[a]	–
Airport facilities	**Frequency of using** (as above)	2.09	1.88	1.80	F (2, 519) = 6.32*	AB > AT & B	✓
	Satisfaction with airport facilities (as above)	4.00	3.09	3.34	F (2, 486) = 31.57*	AB > AT & B	✓
Boat ramp facilities	**Frequency of using** (as above)	1.84	1.79	1.31	F (2, 516) = 16.05*	AB & B > AT	✓
	Satisfaction with boat ramp facilities (as above)	3.61	3.68	3.36	F (2, 335) = 3.82, p = .02	AB & B > AT	✓
Output	*Satisfaction with community services*\ (11 pt scale from 0 not at all to 10 completely satisfied)	*6.40*	*4.74*	*6.42*	F (2, 550) = 31.22*	AB & AT > B	×

*p < .01

[a]Please note that there were extensive road works in the Atherton Tablelands at the time the survey was conducted

togetherness, measured as agreement with 'people in my community get along with each other very well', did not follow the expected pattern and was as high in Airlie Beach as it was in the Atherton Tablelands. Also, somewhat unexpectedly, the openness of social networks measured as a proportion of people who described their social network as consisting of mostly friends they have met in the past 12 months, was the highest in Bowen, and not in the bigger tourism destination, Airlie Beach. Observed output measures for Social Capital followed the expected pattern – satisfaction with personal and group interactions was the highest in Atherton Tablelands and reflected the findings on the inputs. Despite some difficulty in aligning the different measures, both objective and subjective input measures of dimensions of social capital demonstrated that social connections among residents were higher in Atherton Tablelands compared to the other two regions.

The results for measures of Community Identity and Pride are summarized in Table 5.7. Of the three regions, the highest emotional connection, community pride and needs fulfillment were observed in the region with the lowest tourism presence (Atherton Tablelands) which is not consistent with links proposed by previous research (see Fig. 5.4). Measures of participation in community life were somewhat consistent with expectations – respondents reported higher event attendance in Bowen than in Atherton Tablelands, however event attendance by Airlie Beach respondents fell between the other two regions, and was not the highest as would be expected. As expected, perceived influence over community development was higher in the Atherton Tablelands compared to the other two more tourism developed regions. Output measures for Community Identity and Pride were not consistent with previous research (perhaps reflecting inconsistency in inputs), with respondents in more developed tourism regions reporting lower satisfaction with feelings of belonging compared to Atherton Tablelands. In the case of needs fulfillment, both subjective and objective measures demonstrated that respondents' need fulfillment is lower in Bowen compared to the other two regions.

The results for measures of Community Services are summarized in Table 5.8. Very little support for the proposed links (see Fig. 5.5) was found for this social aspect of community QOL. It was confirmed that tourism can contribute to better/more public transport with satisfaction with public transport being highest in Airlie Beach, followed by Bowen and lowest in Atherton Tablelands, with Airlie Beach respondents also reporting using public transport more frequently. The more developed tourism regions, Airlie Beach and Bowen, had more/better services compared to the less tourism developed region, Atherton Tablelands, as measured by frequency of going out and visiting parks and open spaces, and use and satisfaction with airport and boat ramp facilities. Similarly, participants in Airlie Beach evaluated sufficiency of activities for young adults, police services, shops and restaurants more positively compared to Atherton Tablelands and Bowen. However, there was no consistency in observed results for activities for young and teenage children, cultural activities, sport and leisure activities, and sufficiency of parks and open spaces, where either no difference between regions was observed or Atherton Tablelands had higher results compared to more tourism developed Airlie Beach. Bowen respondents evaluated sufficiency of health services in their region lower compared to the other two regions. Of the three regions, satisfaction with community services was the lowest in Bowen, with Airlie Beach and Atherton Tablelands respondents reporting similar, but higher levels. Consistency between objective and subjective measures was evaluated where appropriate and, with the exception of parks and open spaces, information derived about various dimensions of community services through objective and subjective measures was consistent.

Lastly, the results for the overall outputs of the framework, i.e. satisfaction with community QOL and life as a whole, are summarised in Table 5.9. Respondents in all three communities were very satisfied with their life as a whole. That is, on average respondents in all three communities rated their overall life satisfaction above

Table 5.9 Satisfaction scores for main outputs of the theoretical framework for study regions

Satisfaction scores (11 pt scale from 0 not at all to 10 completely satisfied)	Airlie beach	Bowen	The Atherton tablelands	ANOVA *F*	Observed differences/ Bonferroni Post Hoc
Satisfaction with community quality of life	8.57	7.13	9.19	$F\ (2, 553) = 58.519^*$	AT > AB > B
Satisfaction with life as a whole	9.07	8.25	9.08	$F\ (2, 551) = 13.932^*$	AB & AT > B

$^*p < .01$

the national average, which in 2013 was estimated at 7.4 out of 10 (OECD Better Life Index data: http://www.oecdbetterlifeindex.org/). It is worth noting however, that scores in Bowen were lower, compared to Airlie Beach and the Atherton Tablelands, the regions with the most and the least developed tourism industry respectively. Satisfaction with community QOL was also lowest in Bowen, the region with medium tourism development. Thus, no direct link between level of tourism development (i.e. 'stage of tourism development' and 'visitor/resident ratio' features of tourism) and satisfaction with community well-being as well as life overall, was observed at the three study regions. That is, the highest satisfaction scores did not align with the highest or lowest level of tourism development.

5.8 Conclusions and Implications

The chapter described the theoretical underpinning, research process and findings of a study of social impacts of tourism on community QOL in three regional Australian destinations that vary in style and scale of tourism development. A theoretical framework for social aspects of community QOL was proposed and tested, with overall results supporting the framework. A system of measures was used to assess the style and scale of tourism development at each study region. The links between tourism and community QOL proposed by previous research (Figs. 5.2, 5.3, 5.4, and 5.5) were compared to observed links (Tables 5.5, 5.6, 5.7, and 5.8).

Consistent with previous research, it was found that a higher degree of tourism development was associated with (1) higher crime rates (however not necessarily with decreased perceptions of safety by local residents); (2) lower participation in volunteering activities, lower trust of people in the local community, and fewer neighborhood connections and club memberships, but a higher frequency of socialising in public spaces; (3) lower perceived influence over community development; (4) better/more activities for young adults, police services, public transport and airport facilities, recreational services/shops and restaurants, and more frequent visitation of parks and open spaces.

Conversely, some of the observed links contradicted previously assumed patterns of interaction between tourism and community QOL. Specifically: (1) community togetherness was as high in the region with highly developed tourism as it was in the region with low scale tourism development; there was no difference between frequency of socialising informally across the regions, despite substantial differences in the degree of tourism development; (2) the less developed tourism region had higher scores on emotional connection and community pride compared to the more developed tourism regions, and the region with medium tourism development had the lowest scores in the area of needs fulfillment; (3) the regions with lower tourism development had higher scores for activities for young children, cultural activities and there was no difference in scores for activities for teenage children, sports and leisure activities, sufficiency of parks and open spaces.

Some of the observed links did not strictly follow the patterns of the scale of tourism development, i.e. the more/less developed tourism region was not associated with highest/lowest scores as would be expected from previous research. Those links include links between tourism and perceptions of crowdedness, opportunities for work and education, and perceptions of safety (human capital), openness of social networks (social capital), participation in community life (community identity and pride), and health services (community services). This might be explained by the presence of a mitigating effect from either tourism style (including types of visitors and seasonality), or from specific community characteristics.

Consistency between objective and subjective measures was observed in some cases but not others. Both types of measures provided consistent information on opportunities for work and education, needs fulfillment, recreational services/shops and restaurants, public transport, airport and boat ramp facilities, as well somewhat consistent information for measures of social capital. However, there were contradictions between objective and subjective measures of crowdedness, public safety, and parks and open spaces. This overall pattern provides both more support for the Social Representation approach to understanding tourism impacts than the social exchange and cumulative impacts perspectives, and highlights the complexity of these relationships.

And lastly, the research has found no direct link between satisfaction with community QOL and life as a whole and level of tourism development. It appears that these relationships are very complex and mediated by other factors, perhaps including the style of tourism development (i.e. 'types of tourist' and 'seasonality' features of tourism). Additionally, as overall outputs of the proposed theoretical framework, these satisfaction scores are influenced by all the indicators for each of the four social aspects. Bowen scored lower on most of the indicators, and consistently, of the three regions, this destination had the lowest measures for the overall outputs.

The main theoretical contribution of this study was the proposition of a theoretical framework that can be utilized by other researchers and practitioners in the growing field of research on social impacts of tourism on community QOL. Additionally, the process of examining complex relationships between style and scale of tourism and social aspects of community QOL is outlined. This process can be replicated for other study communities with a suitable adjustment of the measures used.

Based on research findings, the following recommendations for future tourism impact research can be made: (1) more research on variations in scale and style of tourism at destinations with the goal to establish some sort of a classification system by which destinations can be assigned to a certain group, for example high visitor/resident ratio, high seasonality, and high reliance on a specific type of visitors; (2) there is a pressing need for more comparative studies to clarify and confirm the links between tourism and community QOL that are commonly assumed/proposed by previous research; and (3) researchers are encouraged to use both objective and subjective measures as this provides greater insight into tourism-community QOL interrelationships.

The authors would like to point out one important limitation of this study – as the study relied on the review of the previous research, the measures included assessed only previously known links between tourism and social aspects of community QOL. Thus some other important links could have being overlooked and not included in the scope of the study. Another point to be made is that research that aims to combine secondary and primary data is bound to face some challenges, such as secondary data availability and level of detail, as well as the presence of inconsistencies in the way secondary data are collected by different government bodies and between years for which data are available. Also, as discussed by McKercher et al. (2015), within the geographical space of a community there tend to be areas that are open to visitors and tourism and those that are relatively closed to outsiders. Tourism impacts are therefore felt/perceived/evaluated differently depending on whether tourism follows the expected geographical pattern in a community or not. For example, although there is a much higher level of tourism development at Airlie Beach, it is mostly located in an area separated from the rest of the town by hills. It is possible to be a resident of this destination and avoid contact with visitors. Similarly, tourist circuits on the Atherton Tablelands are quite separate from residents' pathways. Other variables that could be important in mediating tourism-QOL relationships could include more specific types of tourism, the history of tourism development and the extent to which tourism is connected to other economic activities. These options provide guidance for further research.

The research also has some implications for tourism destination management and tourism development. Firstly, it reinforces calls for greater destination community involvement in, and control over, tourism development and practice (Marzuki and Hay 2013), as increased levels of tourism development were associated with lower levels of perceived influence over community development decision and erosion of various aspects of social capital. In particular, it directs policymakers and destination managers to more carefully and critically assess different types of tourism development in terms of the number and types of job and education opportunities and tourism markets in terms of the extent to which they can contribute to community life. The data supports an approach to tourism planning that focusses on community QoL and assesses potential tourism activities against various contributors to this QoL (cf., Moscardo and Murphy 2014 for an example of this alternative approach). Finally, the data suggested that resident attitudes towards tourism can be influenced as much, and possibly more, by their social representations of tourism than their direct experience of it. This suggests that greater attention could be paid by destination managers to public education about tourism highlighting its positive contributions as well as the processes that are involved in managing its negative impacts (cf., Moscardo 2011 for more information on this type of public education).

In conclusion, it is believed that this study advances tourism impact research by adopting a comparative approach, employing both objective and subjective measures, as well using both secondary and primary data. The study also proposed a theoretical framework for social aspects of community QOL and objectively assessed tourism development differences between the study locations. It is hoped that the methods used will prove useful for other tourism impact researchers and facilitate the advancement of research into understanding the complex relationships between tourism and residents' QOL.

Acknowledgement This research was supported by a research grant from The Cairns Institute, James Cook University.

References

Andereck, K. L., & Nyaupane, G. P. (2011). Exploring the nature of tourism and quality of life perceptions among residents. *Journal of Travel Research, 50*(3), 248–260.

Andereck, K. L., Valentine, K. M., Knopf, R. C., & Vogt, C. A. (2005). Residents' perceptions of community tourism impacts. *Annals of Tourism Research, 32*(4), 1056–1076. https://doi.org/10.1016/j.annals.2005.03.001.

Andriotis, K., & Vaughan, R. D. (2003). Urban residents' attitudes toward tourism development: The case of Crete. *Journal of Travel Research, 42*(2), 172–185. https://doi.org/10.1177/0047287503257488.

Ap, J. (1990). Residents' perceptions research on the social impacts of tourism. *Annals of Tourism Research, 17*(4), 610–616. https://doi.org/10.1016/0160-7383(90)90032-m.

Ap, J. (1992). Residents' perceptions on tourism impacts. *Annals of Tourism Research, 19*(4), 665–690.

Baker, D., & Palmer, R. (2006). Examining the effects of perceptions of community and recreation participation on quality of life. *Social Indicators Research, 75*(3), 395–418. https://doi.org/10.1007/s11205-004-5298-1.

Burt, R. S. (2000). The network structure of social capital. *Research in Organizational Behavior, 22*, 345–423. https://doi.org/10.1016/S0191-3085(00)22009-1.

Butler, R. W. (1974). The social implications of tourist developments. *Annals of Tourism Research, 2*(2), 100–111. https://doi.org/10.1016/0160-7383(74)90025-5.

Butler, R. W. (1980). The concept of a tourist area cycle of evolution: Implications for managers of resources. *Canadian Geographer/ Le Géographe Canadien, 24*(1), 5–12. https://doi.org/10.1111/j.1541-0064.1980.tb00970.x.

Chen, C.-Y. (2016). The impact of the Chinese tourism market on Taiwan residents' attitudes. *Journal of Quality Assurance in Hospitality and Tourism, 17*(1), 1–23. https://doi.org/10.1080/1528008X.2014.988777.

Cuthill, M. (2003). The contribution of human and social capital to building community well-being: A research agenda relating to citizen participation in local governance in Australia. *Urban Policy and Research, 21*(4), 373–391. https://doi.org/10.1080/0811114032000147412.

Deery, M., Jago, L., & Fredline, L. (2012). Rethinking social impacts of tourism research: A new research agenda. *Tourism Management, 33*(1), 64–73. https://doi.org/10.1016/j.tourman.2011.01.026.

Doğan, H. Z. (1989). Forms of adjustment: Sociocultural impacts of tourism. *Annals of Tourism Research, 16*(2), 216–236. https://doi.org/10.1016/0160-7383(89)90069-8.

Doxey, G. V. (1975, September 8–11). A causation theory of visitor resident irritants: Methodology and research inferences. In *Travel and Tourism Research Association sixth annual conference proceedings* (pp.195–198), San Diego, California.

Druckman, D. (2005). Comparative case study approaches. In D. Druckman (Ed.), *Doing research* (pp. 208–226). Thousand Oaks: SAGE.

Easterling, D. S. (2004). The residents' perspective in tourism research – a review and synthesis. *Journal of Travel and Tourism Marketing, 17*(4), 45–62.

Emery, M., & Flora, C. (2006). Spiraling-up: Mapping community transformation with community capitals framework. *Community Development, 37*(1), 19–35.

Epley, D. R., & Menon, M. (2008). A method of assembling cross-sectional indicators into a community quality of life. *Social Indicators Research, 88*(2), 281–296.

Faulkner, B., & Tideswell, C. (1997). A framework for monitoring community impacts of tourism. *Journal of Sustainable Tourism, 5*(1), 3–28. https://doi.org/10.1080/09669589708667273.

Flora, C. B., & Flora, J. L. (2013). *Rural communities: Legacy and change* (4th ed.). Boulder: Westview Press.

Fredline, E. (2005). Host and guest relations and sport tourism. *Sport in Society, 8*(2), 263–279. https://doi.org/10.1080/17430430500087328.

Grzeskowiak, S., Sirgy, M., & Widgery, R. (2003). Resident's satisfaction with community services: Predictors and outcomes. *Journal of Regional Analysis and Policy, 33*(2), 1–36.

Hagerty, M. R., Cummins, R. A., Ferriss, A. L., Land, K., Michalos, A. C., Peterson, M., et al. (2001). Quality of life indexes for national policy: Review and agenda for research. *Social Indicators Research, 55*(1), 1–96.

Harrill, R. (2004). Residents' attitudes toward tourism development: A literature review with implications for tourism planning. *Journal of Planning Literature, 18*(3), 251–266. https://doi.org/10.1177/0885412203260306.

Knack, S. (2002). Social capital and the quality of government: Evidence from the states. *American Journal of Political Science, 46*(4), 772–785. https://doi.org/10.2307/3088433.

Konovalov, E., Murphy, L., & Moscardo, G. (2013, June 23–26). *Measuring tourism: Developing a regional level framework for assessing tourism impacts.* In Conference proceedings of BEST Educational Network Think Tank XIII: Engaging communities in sustainable tourism development (pp. 147–170). Kuala Lumpur, Malaysia.

Marzuki, A., & Hay, I. (2013). Towards a public participation framework in tourism planning. *Tourism Planning & Development, 10*(4), 494–512.

McCool, S. F., & Martin, S. R. (1994). Community attachment and attitudes toward tourism development. *Journal of Travel Research, 32*(3), 29–34.

McGehee, N. G., Lee, S., O'Bannon, T. L., & Perdue, R. R. (2010). Tourism-related social capital and its relationship with other forms of capital: An exploratory study. *Journal of Travel Research, 49*(4), 486–500.

McKercher, B., Wang, D., & Park, E. (2015). Social impacts as a function of place change. *Annals of Tourism Research, 50*, 52–66. https://doi.org/10.1016/j.annals.2014.11.002.

McMillan, D. W. (1996). Sense of community. *Journal of Community Psychology, 24*(4), 315–325. https://doi.org/10.1002/(SICI)1520-6629(199610)24:4<315::AID-JCOP2>3.0.CO;2-T.

Mensah, C. (2012). Residents' perception of socio-economic impacts of tourism in Tafi Atome, Ghana. *Asian Social Science, 8*(15), 274–287. https://doi.org/10.5539/ass.v8n15p274.

Michalos, A. C. (2008). Education, happiness and wellbeing. *Social Indicators Research, 87*(3), 347–366.
Morton, A., & Edwards, L. (2012). *Community wellbeing indicators, survey template for local government*. Sydney: Australian Centre of Excellence for Local Government, University of Technology.
Moscardo, G. (2009). Tourism and quality of life: Towards a more critical approach. *Tourism and Hospitality Research, 9*(2), 159–170. https://doi.org/10.1057/thr.2009.6.
Moscardo, G. (2011). The role of knowledge in good governance for tourism. In E. Laws, H. Richins, J. Agrusa, & N. Scott (Eds.), *Tourist destination governance: Practice, theory and issues* (pp. 67–80). Wallingford: CAB International.
Moscardo, G., & Murphy, L. (2014). There is no such thing as sustainable tourism: Re-conceptualizing tourism as a tool for sustainability. *Sustainability, 6*(5), 2538–2561.
Moscardo, G., Konovalov, E., Murphy, L., & McGehee, N. (2013). Mobilities, community well-being and sustainable tourism. *Journal of Sustainable Tourism, 21*(4), 532–556. https://doi.org/10.1080/09669582.2013.785556.
Narayan, D., & Cassidy, M. F. (2001). A dimensional approach to measuring social capital: Development and validation of a social capital inventory. *Current Sociology, 49*(2), 59–102. https://doi.org/10.1177/0011392101049002006.
Northcote, J., & Macbeth, J. (2005). Limitations of resident perception surveys for understanding tourism social impacts: The need for triangulation. *Tourism Recreation Research, 30*(2), 43–54. https://doi.org/10.1080/02508281.2005.11081472.
Nunkoo, R., Smith, S. L. J., & Ramkissoon, H. (2013). Residents' attitudes to tourism: A longitudinal study of 140 articles from 1984 to 2010. *Journal of Sustainable Tourism, 21*(1), 5–25.
Onyx, J., & Bullen, P. (2000). Measuring social capital in five communities. *The Journal of Applied Behavioral Science, 36*(1), 23–42. https://doi.org/10.1177/0021886300361002.
Peterson, N. A., Speer, P. W., & McMillan, D. W. (2008). Validation of a brief sense of community scale: Confirmation of the principal theory of sense of community. *Journal of Community Psychology, 36*(1), 61–73. https://doi.org/10.1002/jcop.20217.
Pranić, L., Petrić, L., & Cetinić, L. (2012). Host population perceptions of the social impacts of sport tourism events in transition countries: Evidence from Croatia. *International Journal of Event and Festival Management, 3*(3), 236–256. https://doi.org/10.1108/17582951211262684.
Rogers, M., & Ryan, R. (2001). The triple bottom line for sustainable community development. *Local Environment, 6*(3), 279–289. https://doi.org/10.1080/13549830120073275.
Sharma, B., Dyer, P., Carter, J., & Gursoy, D. (2008). Exploring Residents' perceptions of the social impacts of tourism on the sunshine coast, Australia. *International Journal of Hospitality and Tourism Administration, 9*(3), 288–311. https://doi.org/10.1080/15256480802096092.
Sharpley, R. (2014). Host perceptions of tourism: A review of the research. *Tourism Management, 42*, 37–49. https://doi.org/10.1016/j.tourman.2013.10.007.
Sirgy, M., Rahtz, D. R., Cicic, M., & Underwood, R. (2000). A method for assessing residents' satisfaction with community-based services: A quality-of-life perspective. *Social Indicators Research, 49*(3), 279–316.
Sirgy, M., Michalos, A., Ferriss, A., Easterlin, R., Patrick, D., & Pavot, W. (2006). The Qualityy-of-Life (QOL) research movement: Past, present, and future. *Social Indicators Research, 76*(3), 343–466. https://doi.org/10.1007/s11205-005-2877-8.
Sirgy, M., Gao, T., & Young, R. F. (2008). How does residents' satisfaction with community services influence quality of life (QOL) outcomes? *Applied Research in Quality of Life, 3*(2), 81–105.
Stone, W. (2001). *Measuring social capital: Towards a theoretically informed measurment framework for researching social capital in family and community life* (Research Paper No. 24). Canberra: Austalian Institute of Family Studies.

Vanclay, F. (2004). The triple bottom line and impact assessment: How do TBL, EIA, SIA, SEA and EMS relate to each other? *Journal of Environmental Assessment Policy and Management, 6*(3), 265–288. https://doi.org/10.1142/S1464333204001729.

Veenhoven, R. (2001). Quality-of-life and happiness: Not quite the same. In G. DeGirolamo (Ed.), *Salute e qualità dell vida* (pp. 67–95). Torino: Centro Scientifico Editore.

Wang, S., & Chen, J. S. (2015). The influence of place identity on perceived tourism impacts. *Annals of Tourism Research, 52*, 16–28. https://doi.org/10.1016/j.annals.2015.02.016.

Chapter 6
Quality of Life and Perception of the Effects of Tourism: A Contingent Approach

Nuria Porras-Bueno, Mª de los Ángeles Plaza-Mejía, and Alfonso Vargas-Sánchez

Abstract The relationship between the perception of the resident community as far as the effects of tourism and their quality of life is a subject that has recently sparked the interest of researchers. As currently there is no uniformity in either the approach adopted for measuring variables or the significance of their inter-relationships, our study will aim to contribute to the topic by introducing a series of new factors, among which we can highlight the methodology employed, the means of assessing quality of life on the basis of community satisfaction, the disaggregation of the effects of tourism according to typology and the nature of the relationship established between the two variables. Among the results obtained, and in contrast to those obtained from previous studies, the current research reveals that it is not possible to establish a unique relationship between community satisfaction and the effects of tourism as the satisfaction aspect studied as well as the nature and sign (positive or negative) of the effects taken into account condition both the nature and intensity of the relationship established between the two variables.

Keywords Tourism impacts · Residents' perceptions · Community satisfaction · Quality of Life

6.1 Introduction

While studies abound dealing with the resident community's perception of the impact of tourism and the corresponding repercussions on attitudes towards tourism development, far fewer studies have focussed on Quality of Life (QOL). However, it is important to point out that since the publication in 1999 of a special issue of the Journal of Business Research (vol. 44, issue 3) focussing on QOL for both tourists and residents, the number of publications dealing with this subject matter has

N. Porras-Bueno · Mª. d. l. A. Plaza-Mejía · A. Vargas-Sánchez (✉)
University of Huelva, Huelva, Spain
e-mail: vargas@uhu.es

A. M. Campón-Cerro et al. (eds.), *Best Practices in Hospitality and Tourism Marketing and Management*, Applying Quality of Life Research,
https://doi.org/10.1007/978-3-319-91692-7_6

increased significantly. In this regard, particularly noteworthy are the "Handbook of Tourism and Quality of Life Research: Enhancing the Lives of Tourists and Residents of Host Communities" (Uysal et al. 2012) and the review article "Quality of Life and Well-being Research in Tourism" (Uysal et al. 2016).

The fundamental difference between attitude/impact studies and QOL studies lies in the measurement methods employed (Andereck et al. 2007, p. 45): "Attitudes/impact studies largely focus on the way in which tourism is perceived to affect the communities and the environment, whereas quality of life studies are typically concerned with the way these impacts affect individual or family life satisfaction, including satisfaction with community, neighbourhoods and personal satisfaction".

In this study we will focus on one of the dimensions of Quality of Life, namely, community satisfaction, and attempt to observe its influence on the perception of the positive and negative effects of tourism. Our main contributions to this line of research are the following:

1. Few studies have attempted to relate community satisfaction with the perception of the aforementioned effects.
2. Traditionally the relationship has been studied using the effects as the independent variable and community satisfaction as the dependent variable. In our study, and following the trend of more recent contributions, we will attempt to analyse the inverse relationship, where community satisfaction is the independent variable that influences the perception of the impacts.
3. Documented evidence to date groups the effects perceived in tourism into two blocks, positive impacts and negative impacts, while we propose combining this approach with one that disaggregates the effects according to their nature (economic, socio-cultural and environmental).
4. In contrast to other authors, who either measure community satisfaction on the basis of a single item, calculate overall satisfaction on the basis of a series of items, or construct it multi-dimensionally but as a single construct, our study disaggregates the variable into three dimensions.
5. With regard to methodology, in contrast to the majority of studies that use a covariance-based SEM (CBSEM) statistical technique, the exploratory nature of our study and the high number of indicators and latent variables present in our model has led us to opt for the Partial Least Squares method, or PLS (variance-based SEM).

6.2 Theoretical Framework

The article published by Uysal et al. (2016) constitutes the most recent and complete research carried out in an effort to summarise how tourism affects, or may affect, the quality of life of the residents in a tourism destination as well as the tourists themselves. Focussing attention on the residents, the authors review 36 articles and conclude that the most numerous studies are those that use a fundamentally quantitative analysis, use subjective indicators to measure QOL, identify the mediator variables between tourism impacts and QOL and measure satisfaction from an individual perspective.

Below (Table 6.1) is a list of studies that focus the attention on the relationship between perception of impacts derived from tourism and QOL.

QOL is a measurement concept which the authors have used a wide variety of indicators for. One of the components taken into account when analysing the QOL construct is community satisfaction, which will constitute the variable that is the focus of our study.

While QOL and Community Satisfaction are terms that are occasionally used interchangeably they present significant conceptual differences when it comes to research (Matarrita-Cascante 2010). QOL is a more extensive concept that can include community satisfaction. QOL refers to the overall human experience and the evaluation of this experience, while community satisfaction is concerned with an evaluative judgement of how responses are offered to meet the requirements of the community itself.

Along the lines of the above argument, Sirgy et al. (2000) proposed a Community QOL Model which, as seen in Table 6.2, establishes global life satisfaction being determined by satisfaction with the community, in addition to other domains. Simultaneously, satisfaction with the community is susceptible to influence by degree of satisfaction with government, business and non-profit services, which are in turn determined by other factors.

Very few studies exist analysing the relationship between the impacts of tourism as perceived by residents and their degree of satisfaction with their community (Ko and Stewart 2002; Nunkoo and Ramkissoon 2010, 2011; Vargas-Sánchez et al. 2009, 2011).

The studies are very diverse, a fact that is reflected in Table 6.3, in terms of both the nature of the tourism destination being studied (from coastal to interior) and the level of tourism development present at the destination.

All the studies are characterised by building Structural Equation Models in which both the perceived impacts and community satisfaction are measured through the aggregation of numerous items. In general, all of them take into consideration the positive and negative impacts derived from tourism, thought these indicators are constructed from a wide variety of diverse items.

With regard to the community satisfaction variable there would appear to be greater standardisation, the six most employed items being: satisfaction with public services, satisfaction with formal education, satisfaction with the environment, satisfaction with leisure opportunities, satisfaction with the economy and citizen

Table 6.1 Studies dealing with the relationship between the impacts of tourism and quality of life

Milman and Pizan (1988); Allen, Hafer, Long and Perdue (1993); Andereck and Vogt (2000); Nichols, Sttit and Giocopassi (2002); Ko and Steward (2002); Gjerald (2005); Urtasum and Gutierrez (2006); Wheeler and Laing (2008); Yamada, Hen, King and Fu (2009); Vargas-Sanchez, Plaza-Mejía and Porras Bueno (2009); Matarrita-Cascante (2010); Andereck and Nyaupane (2011); Yu, Chancellor and Cole (2011); Aref (2011); Manap, Aman and rahmiau (2011); Nawijn and Mitas (2012); Khzindar (2012); Woo, Kim and Uysal (2015).

Source: Own elaboration

Table 6.2 Community QOL Model

Overall life domain	Community life domain	Community life subdomains	Community life sub-subdomains
Global life satisfaction	Global community satisfaction	Global government services satisfaction	Satisfaction with fire services
			Satisfaction with rescue services
			Satisfaction with police services
		Global business services satisfaction	Satisfaction with banking/ savings
			Satisfaction with insurance
			Satisfaction with department store
		Global non-profit services satisfaction	Satisfaction with alcohol abuses services
			Satisfaction with adoption/ foster care services
			Satisfaction with crisis intervention services
	Other life domains	Global job satisfaction	
		Global family satisfaction	
		Global financial satisfaction	

Source: Own elaboration, based on Sirgy et al. (2000)

Table 6.3 Studies focussing on the relationship between tourism impacts and community satisfaction

Authors	Place studied	Level of tourism development	Sample size
Ko and Stewart (2002)	Cheju Island (Korea) natural scenery of mountains, cultural heritage and playing golf	The most popular destination in Korea. Tourism is the primary business sector of its economy	732 residents
Vargas-Sánchez et al. (2009)	Minas de Riotinto (Huelva, Spain)	For centuries almost totally dependent on open-cast mining. This mining activity stopped in 1986. Since then, its history and urban and natural environment are its main attractions. Low tourism development	359 residents
Nunkoo and Ramkissoon (2010)	Coastal village of Le Morne (Island of Mauritius)	Dependent on fishing, hunting and agriculture. Cultural and heritage attractions.	400 residents
Nunkoo and Ramkissoon (2011)	Coastal Village of grand-Baie (Island of Mauritius)	It has developed from agriculture to a mature and popular tourist resort	363 residents
Vargas-Sánchez et al. (2011)	Province of Huelva (South of Spain)	Tourism industry is a recent phenomenon. Not a mass destination. Medium tourism development	400 residents

Source: Own elaboration

involvement and social opportunities. On occasion the community satisfaction variable is either constructed on the basis of just one of the above items (such as satisfaction with public services in Vargas-Sánchez et al. 2011) or is calculated as an average of the six aforementioned items (Vargas-Sánchez et al. 2009).

The nature of the relationship between local residents' the perception and community satisfaction is the most important difference found in this group of five studies. Ko and Stewart (2002) and Vargas-Sánchez et al. (2009, 2011) suggest that the perception of tourism impacts is the independent variable that influences community satisfaction, which in turn is a mediator variable between the perceived impacts and the attitude towards tourism development (Kaplanidou et al. 2013). This supposes the acceptance of a unidirectional relationship by virtue of which the perception of impacts would affect QOL, which in turn would affect the attitude towards tourism. However, as other authors suggest, the existence of a more complex, reciprocal relationship between the perceived living conditions and the perceived impacts of tourism is a possibility (Vargas-Sánchez et al. 2009; Uysal et al. 2016).

Along the same lines, Nunkoo and Ramkissoon (2010, 2011) propose the opposite relationship. In other words, that it is community satisfaction as the independent variable that influences the perception of impacts and, as such, it is this perception of impacts that directly determines the attitude towards tourism.

In addition to this, the study published by Nunkoo and Ramkissoon in 2011 criticises the fact that previous studies consider community satisfaction as a uni- rather than multi-dimensional variable and, in consequence, disaggregates it into three distinct variables, in line with the approach of Sirgy et al. (2000) and his aforementioned definition of Global Community Satisfaction.

The following Tables (6.4 and 6.5) synthesise the structural relationships proposed in the model by the aforementioned authors, highlighting those studies in bold which the perception of impacts or the attitude towards tourism development and community satisfaction into account.

Finally, Table 6.6 presents the principal conclusions of each of the studies under scrutiny:

The global hypothesis for this research has been formulated based on the conclusions drawn from the studies carried out by Nunkoo and Ramkissoon (2010, 2011) Table 6.6, which can be summarised as follows: "The greater the resident's satisfaction with their community, the greater their perception of the positive effects of tourism and the lesser their perception of the negative effects, independently of the aspect of satisfaction analysed and of the nature of the effects of tourism studied". This global hypothesis will be broken down into a total of 21 hypotheses, due to the disaggregation of the satisfaction construct and the consideration of the different nature and sign of the perceived effects of tourism. This disaggregation will be undertaken and will be explained afterwards in the empirical part of this work.

Table 6.4 Structural relationships

Hypothesis			Ko and Stewart (2002)	Vargas-Sánchez et al. (2009)	Vargas-Sánchez et al. (2011)
PBTD	—(+)→	PPTI	Supported	Supported	Supported
PBTD	—(−)→	NPTI	Not supported	Not supported (*)	Not supported (*)
PBTD	**—(+)→**	**OCS**	**Not supported**	**Not supported (**)**	**Not supported (*)**
PBTD	—(+)→	AATD	Supported	Not supported (**)	Supported
PPTI	—(+)→	AATD	Supported	Supported	Supported
PTI	**—(+)→**	**OCS**	**Supported**	**Supported**	**Supported**
OCS	**—(−)→**	**AATD**	**Not supported**	**Supported**	**Not supported (**)**
NPTI	**—(−)→**	**OCS**	**Supported**	**Not supported (*)**	**Not supported (*)**
NPTI	—(−)→	AATD	Supported	Supported	Not supported (*)

Source: Own elaboration
PBTD Personal Benefit from Tourism Development, *PPTI* Positive Perception of Tourism Impacts, *NPTI* Negative Perception of Tourism Impacts, *OCS* Overall Community Satisfaction, *AATD* Attitude towards Additional Tourism Development
(*) Non-significant relationship (critical ratio below 1.96)
(**) Significant relationship (critical ratio over 1.96), but opposite sign

6.3 Method for Hypotheses Testing

6.3.1 Place Studied

As its territorial framework this study uses 15 municipalities in the province of Huelva, in south-west Spain. These municipalities are notably involved in mining and occupy one third of the area of the province, with a total of 55,244 inhabitants, approximately one tenth of the population of the province as a whole. Despite the enormous potential environmental value in terms of landscape and leisure opportunities that these interior municipalities possess (93% of the surface area is woodland), they are currently experiencing economic and social recession, with reduced population densities, population decrease, high rates of ageing of the population and unemployment as well as low levels of income and education, as compared with coastal areas in the same province.

The current tourism offering in these mining municipalities is characterised by a lack of diversity and can be essentially divided into two segments: rural/environmental tourism and industrial mining tourism, of which the Riotinto Mining Park

Table 6.5 Structural relationships

Hypothesis			Nunkoo and Ramkissoon (2010)	Nunkoo and Ramkissoon (2011)
CS	**—(+)→**	**PDB**	**Supported**	–
CS	**—(−)→**	**PDC**	**Supported**	–
URB	—(+)→	PDB	Not supported	–
URB	—(−)→	PDC	Not supported	–
SLE	—(+)→	PDB	Supported	–
SLE	—(−)→	PDC	Supported	–
EA	—(−)→	PDB	Supported	–
EA	—(+)→	PDC	Supported	–
CSS	**—(+)→**	**PDB**	–	**Supported**
CSS	**—(−)→**	**PDC**	–	**Supported**
CC	**—(+)→**	**PDB**	–	**Not supported**
CC	**—(−)→**	**PDC**	–	**Not supported**
SNC	**—(+)→**	**PDB**	–	**Supported**
SNC	**—(−)→**	**PDC**		**Supported**
PDB	—(+)→	STD	Supported	Supported
PDC	—(−)→	STD	Supported	Supported

Source: Own elaboration
CS Community Satisfaction, *URB* Utilization of Resource Based, *SLE* State of the Local Economy, *EA* Environmental Attitudes, *PDB* Perceived Development Benefits, *PDC* Perceived Development Cost, *STD* Support for Tourism Development, *CSS* Community Services Satisfaction, *CC* Community Commitment, *SNC* Satisfaction with Neighbourhood Conditions

-receiving 89,235 visitors in 2016, with positive growth from 62,492 visitors in 2005- constitutes practically the only experience available.

The case of Riotinto is the best example of industrial tourism existing in the province of Huelva. It is the example par excellence, as far as tourism goes, of the economic diversification process in the Mining Area. This area was ravaged by the collapse of extraction activity at the end of the 1980s and start of the 1990s, which left the municipalities in it in serious economic depression. The search for alternatives for its development became an imperative need, one of these alternatives being to take advantage of its mining heritage for tourism.

In particular, 1987 represents a turning point for the Huelva Pyrite Belt. A region that would witness the closure of the copper line in the Riotinto mining company, resulting in one of the worst socioeconomic crises in the region. In this context of major crisis, all of the social agents (companies, unions, governments at different levels, etc.) reached an agreement to start a foundation which would gather all of the important historic capital of the company and which would at the same time be a driving force behind new alternative initiatives to mining. That is how "Fundación Riotinto para la Historia de la Minería y la Metalurgia" (Riotinto Foundation for the History of Mining and Metallurgy) came into being, with the following purpose:

Table 6.6 Conclusions

Ko and Stewart (2002)	Personal benefits from tourism development do not contribute to attitude towards overall community satisfaction
	Perceived positive tourism impacts are positively correlated with overall community satisfaction
	Perceived negative tourism impacts are negatively correlated with overall community satisfaction
	Overall community satisfaction is not correlated with attitude for additional tourism development
Vargas-Sánchez et al. (2009)	Personal benefits from tourism development do not contribute to attitude towards overall community satisfaction
	Perceived positive tourism impacts are positively correlated to overall community satisfaction. A mutual interaction was found between the perceived positive tourism impacts and the overall community satisfaction, but the influence of PPTI over OCS is stronger than OCS over PPTI
	Perceived negative tourism impacts do not contribute to overall community satisfaction
	Overall community satisfaction is negatively correlated with attitude for additional tourism development
Vargas-Sánchez et al. (2011)	Personal benefits from tourism development do not contribute to attitude towards overall community satisfaction
	Perceived positive tourism impacts are positively related to overall community satisfaction
	Perceived negative tourism impacts do not contribute to overall community satisfaction
	Overall community satisfaction is related to attitude towards additional tourism development, but with a positive sign, not with the negative sign stated in the hypothesis. That is to say, the higher the satisfaction with the community, the more favourable attitude towards tourism
Nunkoo and Ramkissoon (2010)	There is a direct positive relationship between residents' overall community satisfaction and the perceived benefits of the development. Residents who were satisfied with community services were found to perceive that tourisms will result in several benefits.
	There is a direct negative relationship between residents' overall community satisfaction and the perceived cost of the development. Residents who were dissatisfied with community perceived higher costs resulting from development
Nunkoo and Ramkissoon (2011)	There is a direct positive relationship between residents' degree of satisfaction with community services and their perceptions of positive impacts of tourism
	There is a direct negative relationship between residents' degree of satisfaction with community services and their perceptions of negative impacts of tourism
	There is a direct positive relationship between residents' degree of satisfaction with neighbourhood conditions and their perceptions of positive impacts of tourism
	There is a direct negative relationship between residents' degree of satisfaction with neighbourhood conditions and their perceptions of negative impacts of tourism
	There is no relationship between residents' degree of satisfaction with neighbourhood conditions and their perceptions of positive impacts of tourism
	There is no relationship between residents' degree of satisfaction with neighbourhood conditions and their perceptions of negative impacts of tourism

Source: Own elaboration

"the study and research of the History of Mining and Metallurgy, both as far as its technical as well as cultural, social and economic aspects; the preservation and restoration of the whole environment located at the end of Minas de Riotinto, province of Huelva, through establishing a mining park including the pre-existing archaeological areas, the assets of ethnography interest and the natural sites, gardens and parks which of significant historical, artistic, or anthropological interest and the sharing of the historic and artistic values which the area holds."

The Riotinto Mining Park includes:

- Mining and Railway Museum, with a replica of a Roman mine.
- Tourist Mining Railroad.
- English neighbourhood of Bellavista (House 21).
- La Dehesa necropolis (*).
- Open-pit mine of Corta Atalaya (*).
- Open-pit mine (and inner tunnel) of Peña de Hierro.
- Mining facilities.
- Documentation Centre.

(*) Not able to be visited at the time of the finishing of this chapter.

As stated by García-Delgado et al. (2013), "the isolated, scattered nature of the existing tourism initiatives and services clearly condition the destination's low degree of competitiveness", which has proven to be incapable of converting casual day-trippers into a tourists. This tourism activity is offered as an economic alternative to mining activity that for many years constituted the area's main source of revenue but which has experienced a severe crisis over recent decades and has only recently appeared to show some semblance of recovery.

6.3.2 *Sample*

The sample taken consists of 381 residents from towns and villages with the highest rates of tourism activity in the area known as the Cuenca Minera de Huelva (Mining Area of Huelva). The sample is random and multi-stage in terms of gender, age and residence, thereby guaranteeing the statistical representativeness of the reference population with a margin of error of ±5%, a 2σ (95.5%) level of confidence, and a population variance of 50%. The 15 mining municipalities used for the study were Almonaster La Real, Alosno, Cala, Calañas, El Campillo, Campofrío, El Cerro de Andévalo, Cortegana, Minas de Riotinto, Nerva, Puebla de Guzmán, Santa Olalla del Cala, Valverde del Camino, Zalamea La Real and Zufre.

The questionnaires were administered by three interviewers, who were previously trained between September and October 2008. The effective response rate was 100%, and in 87% of the cases (332) the observations obtained were complete (including all of the variables considered).

For better understanding the population being studied, Table 6.7 shows the sociodemographic profile of the sample analysed.

Table 6.7 Sociodemographic profile of the sample under study

Gender	Male: 49,3%	**Age**	From age 18 to 29: 17,1%
	Female: 50,7%		From age 30 to 44: 26,8%
Marital status	Married: 57,5%		From age 45 to 64: 29,4%
	Single: 22,8%		Age 65 and older: 26,8%
	Other: 19,7%		
Level of education	Without education: 21,8%	**Employment situation**	Employee: 30,7%
	Primary: 33,9%		Self-employed: 11,3%
	Secondary: 12,9%		Civil servant: 7,3%
	Professional training: 16,3%		Retired: 18,4%
	University (bachelor's degree or equivalent): 14,7%		Student: 6,0%
			Housework: 19,4%
	University (master or doctorate): 0,5%		Unemployed: 6,8%
Birth place	The same as current place of residence: 36,0%	**Years of residence in locality**	Less than 18 years: 4,2%
			Between 18 and 34: 28,9%
	Other municipalities in the province of Huelva: 52,5%		Between 35 and 51: 29,1%
			Between 52 and 68: 23,9%
	Other Spanish provinces: 10,7%		69 or more: 13,9%
	Abroad: 0,8%		
Is/has your job been associated with mining?	Yes: 11,0%	**¿is/has your job been associated with the tourism sector?**	Yes: 29,1%
	No: 89,0%		No: 70,9%

Source: Own elaboration

6.3.3 Instrument of Measurement

The questionnaire consists of a total of 62 items structured into the following subject areas: social-demographic, economic dependency on tourism, environmental attitude, degree of acceptance by local residents, knowledge of current local and tourism-related reality, contact between tourists and residents and the evaluation of it, evaluation by the residents of the current degree of tourist development in the locality, attitude towards future tourism development, perception by the residents of the impacts of tourism development on their locality and residents' satisfaction with their community. Insofar as only the final two of the aforementioned subject areas have been used for the purposes of this study, we will limit more in-depth explanation to these specific areas (a key is provided in Table 6.8).

Table 6.8 Items in the questionnaire grouped in their corresponding constructs and mean of each one of the observed variables

Constructs and items	Mean	Standard deviation
PECTI: Perception of positive economic impacts		
PECTI1: More development and better standard of living	3,74	1,01
PECTI2: Increased opportunities for employment	3,65	1,01
PECTI3: Increased availability of recreational activities	3,62	1,02
PSCTI: Perception of positive social and cultural impacts		
PSCTI1: Tourism turns this locality into a more attractive and interesting place to live in	3,60	1,02
PSCTI2: Better knowledge of other cultures/communities	3,55	1,05
PSCTI3: The inhabitants of the locality feel prouder about belonging to it	3,56	1,04
PSCTI4: Increase in the quality of public services and the quality of service in restaurants, shops and hotels in the area	3,58	1,02
PSCTI5: Increase in the degree of police and fire protection	3,53	1,04
PSCTI6: An incentive to preserve local culture	3,61	0,98
PSCTI7: Infrastructure improvement (roads, water supply, electricity, telephone, etc.)	3,56	1,01
PENTI: Perception of positive environmental impacts		
PENTI1: Entails an incentive to conserve natural resources	3,62	1,00
PENTI2: Entails an incentive to restore and maintain historic buildings	3,62	0,99
NECTI: Perception of negative economic impacts		
NECTI1: Increase in the cost of living (product and service prices, homes)	3,77	1,02
NECTI2: The profits produced by the tourism activity revert to companies and people outside of the locality	3,53	1,09
NSDTI: Perception of social dysfunctionalities		
NSDTI1: Increase in traffic and parking problems	3,53	0,99
NSDTI2: Increase in theft/vandalism, alcoholism, prostitution, and sexual permissiveness	3,39	1,08
NSDTI3: Local workers are exploited	3,27	1,13
NSCTI: Perception of negative social and cultural impacts		
NSCTI1: Change/loss in way of living and traditional culture	3,13	1,08
NSCTI2: Problems in so far as the social harmony between residents and tourists	2,97	1,11
NSCTI3: Loss of peacefulness in the area	3,29	1,08
NENTI: Perception of negative environmental impacts		
NENTI1: Harm to the natural environment and landscape and increase in pollution (waste, noise, etc.)	3,39	1,02
NENTI2: Uncontrolled growth of the urban areas and urban environment.	3,38	1,02
NENTI3: Decrease in quality and breakdowns in health services, public transport and other local services (long queues and waits in restaurants, shops and tourist attractions)	3,41	1,04
ESS: Economic and sanitary satisfaction		

(continued)

Table 6.8 (continued)

Constructs and items	Mean	Standard deviation
ECS: Economic satisfaction (businesses, cost of living, homes – Price and availability, electricity, water, gas, employment opportunities)	2,25	0,93
SSS: Sanitary system satisfaction (health centres, number of doctors and nurses, speed and quality of service, etc.).	2,76	0,90
SS: Social satisfaction		
PSS: Public services satisfaction (fire protection, social and welfare services, public transport in the locality, public transport between localities, police protection, local government, roads, educational services)	3,03	0,94
ROS: Recreation opportunities satisfaction (cinemas, gyms, parks and open spaces, exhibition halls, museums)	2,66	0,99
CISOS: Citizen involvement and social opportunities (opportunities to be with friends and family members, participation in community decision making, opportunities to be with friends and family, participating in community decision making, organised religion (churches), opportunities to socialise with other neighbours in the locality.)	2,66	0,93
ENS: Environment satisfaction (physical geography, cleaning of natural environment (ground, water, air-, climate, general appearance of municipality)	2,95	0,92

Source: Own elaboration

- The residents' perception of the impacts of tourism development on their locality: a total of 23 items measured using five-point Likert-type scales relating to the overall economic, socio-cultural, environmental (positive and negative) impacts linked to the development of said activity. A variable synthesis is also included using the same Likert scale, designed to aid our understanding of the residents' perception as far as the extent to which the benefits derived from tourism development outweigh the costs, though this is not taken into account in our model.
- Residents' satisfaction with their community: six items measured using a five-point Likert scale in order to gauge the degree of satisfaction with public services, sanitation systems, environment, leisure and entertainment opportunities, economy, citizen involvement and social opportunities.

Most of the items of the questionnaire have been extracted from the review of previous studies published by various authors, mainly those by Johnson et al. (1994), Williams and Lawson (2001), Ko and Stewart (2002), and Kuvan and Akan (2005).

6.3.4 Techniques Applied

For the development of the study we have used Structural Equation Modelling (SEM), which combines an econometric perspective (linear regression models) with a psychometric approach (factor analysis). Given the scarcity of previous studies linking residents' satisfaction with their community to their perception of the effects of tourism, we have opted for a variance-based SEM statistical technique such as Partial Least Squares (PLS) as it would appear better suited than a covariance-based SEM (CBSEM) for an exploratory analysis such as the one we are concerned with here (Roldán and Sánchez-Franco 2012) and insofar as "for application and prediction, when the theoretical model or measures are not well formed, a PLS approach is often more suitable" (Chin and Newsted 1999). Another factor that led us to select this technique as opposed to CBSEM is the high number of indicators and latent variables present in our model (Chin 2010; Hair et al. 2011). The software used for the study was SPSS 13.0 and Smart PLS 3.2.2.

6.4 Results

6.4.1 Descriptive Statistics

The inhabitants living in the mining municipalities perceive both the favourable as well as unfavourable effects linked to tourist activity with limited intensity, which suggests that the mean of the 23 items measured, on a five point scale, moves between 2.97 ("social harmony problems between residents and tourists") and the 3.77 ("rise in the cost of living"), without in going over value 4 or considerably under 3 in none of the items (see Table 6.8). Always within this general trend of muted perception, the most strongly perceived impacts are economic in nature (both favourable and unfavourable), while to the contrary, the residents seem to show confusion or indetermination regarding the sociocultural damage of tourism.

As far as community satisfaction, residents only show a medium amount of satisfaction as far as public services and the environment (mean of 3 on a five point scale), with this being mid-low for the rest of the analysed aspects (economy, health care system, recreational activities and the involvement of citizens and social opportunities) (mean between 2 and 3).

6.4.2 Measurement of Constructs and Hypothetical Approach

In order to determine the suitability of the composition of the various constructs we have been aided by both existing relevant literature and performing two factorial analyses, one for the twenty-three items relating to the "perception of the impacts of tourism", the other for the six items that comprise "resident satisfaction with their community". It was established, in accordance with the combination of these two tools:

- The reflective definition of seven constructs for the "perceived effects of tourism", depending on the varying nature and sign of these effects, and
- Three constructs for "community satisfaction", one of which ("satisfaction with the environment") is to be taken as a unidimensional construct as it consists of just one item.

Table 6.8, which we referred to earlier, shows the various items contained in each of the construct identified.

In the light of them, and in accordance with the global hypothesis formulated in the theoretical section, the 21 hypotheses (H) used for the purposes of contrast are as follows:

H1: Environment Satisfaction is negatively related to Perception of Negative Economic Impacts.
H2: Environment Satisfaction is negatively related to Perception of Negative Environmental Impacts.
H3: Environment Satisfaction is negatively related to Perception of Negative Social and Cultural Impacts.
H4: Environment Satisfaction is negatively related to Perception of Social Dysfunctionalities.
H5: Environment Satisfaction is positively related to Perception of Positive Economic Impacts.
H6: Environment Satisfaction is positively related to Perception of Positive Environmental Impacts.
H7: Environment Satisfaction is positively related to Perception of Positive Social and Cultural Impacts.
H8: Economic and Sanitary Satisfaction is negatively related to Perception of Negative Economic Impacts.
H9: Economic and Sanitary Satisfaction is negatively related to Perception of Negative Environmental Impacts.
H10: Economic and Sanitary Satisfaction is negatively related to Perception of Negative Social and Cultural Impacts.
H11: Economic and Sanitary Satisfaction is negatively related to Perception of Social Dysfunctionalities.
H12: Economic and Sanitary Satisfaction is positively related to Perception of Positive Economic Impacts.
H13: Economic and Sanitary Satisfaction is positively related to Perception of Positive Environmental Impacts.
H14: Economic and Sanitary Satisfaction is positively related to Perception of Positive Social and Cultural Impacts.
H15: Social Satisfaction is negatively related to Perception of Negative Economic Impacts.
H16: Social Satisfaction is negatively related to Perception of Negative Environmental Impacts.
H17: Social Satisfaction is negatively related to Perception of Negative Social and Cultural Impacts.

H18: Social Satisfaction is negatively related to Perception of Social Dysfunctionalities.
H19: Social Satisfaction is positively related to Perception of Positive Economic Impacts.
H20: Social Satisfaction is positively related to Perception of Positive Environmental Impacts.
H21: Social Satisfaction is positively related to Perception of Positive Social and Cultural Impacts.

6.4.3 Measurement Model Assessment

As shown in Table 6.9, all standardized loadings (λ) are greater than 0.707, thereby demonstrating individual item reliability and rendering any "item filtering" unnecessary. With regard to the trustworthiness of the scale or the internal consistency of all the indicators at the time of measuring the construct, Table 6.10 shows that the composite reliabilities (ρ_c) are greater than 0.7 for all ten constructs, thereby complying with the requirement, though Cronbach's alpha coefficient is slightly below said value for the latent variable "Economic and Sanitary Satisfaction" (0.650), possibly due to the recent and pioneering means by which the concept of "community satisfaction" that concerns us here has been approached on a research level.

On the other hand (see Table 6.10), latent variables achieve convergent validity, as their average variance extracted (AVE) widely exceed the 0.5 threshold. Finally, it is worth pointing out that the ten constructs also demonstrate discriminant validity by two distinct methods: the first, the fact that the square root of the AVE for each construct is greater than the correlation of the construct with any other construct, and secondly because the table of cross loadings reveals that each indicator has a higher loading on its own construct than on the remaining latent variables, and that each construct has a higher loading on the indicators it has assigned than on the remaining items.

6.4.4 Structural Model Assessment

To begin with, we should point out that as a measure of goodness of fit for the model we have used the SRMR indicator (Hu and Bentler 1999), the value of which (0.058), being notably inferior to the threshold of 0.08, reveals a good fit (see Fig. 6.1).

Bootstrapping (with 5000 resamples) was used to generate standard errors and t-statistics (Table 6.11). Just nine of the 21 hypotheses proposed have been supported (H5, H7, H8, H9, H10, H11, H19, H20 and H21), a further five were not accepted due to the fact that they revealed non-significant relationships (H1, H2, H3, H4 and H6), and the remaining seven (H12, H13, H14, H15, H16, H17 and H18) reveal significant relationships but of the opposite sign to those hypothesised.

Table 6.9 Outer model loadings and cross loadings

	ENS	ESS	SS	NECTI	NENTI	NSCTI	NSDTI	PECTI	PENTI	PSCTI
ENS	**1.000**	0.366	0.313	−0.067	−0.068	0.018	−0.018	0.088	0.012	0.065
SSS	0.301	**0.720**	0.498	−0.085	−0.164	−0.100	−0.122	−0.119	−0.127	−0.107
ECS	0.333	**0.955**	0.344	−0.303	−0.327	−0.313	−0.123	−0.231	−0.240	−0.294
PSS	0.189	0.259	**0.936**	0.288	0.310	0.403	0.222	0.199	0.275	0.301
ROS	0.475	0.559	**0.759**	0.093	0.077	0.164	0.085	0.002	0.099	0.068
CISOS	0.307	0.528	**0.768**	0.137	0.134	0.220	0.109	0.049	0.109	0.096
NECTI1	−0.030	−0.261	0.180	**0.911**	0.613	0.506	0.339	0.482	0.627	0.530
NECTI2	−0.089	−0.238	0.274	**0.936**	0.586	0.649	0.359	0.458	0.571	0.521
NENTI1	−0.079	−0.297	0.151	0.518	**0.849**	0.511	0.578	0.449	0.473	0.514
NENTI2	−0.074	−0.279	0.238	0.611	**0.943**	0.663	0.575	0.442	0.521	0.513
NENTI3	−0.037	−0.283	0.301	0.621	**0.924**	0.695	0.536	0.471	0.534	0.560
NSCTI1	0.010	−0.335	0.245	0.603	0.628	**0.877**	0.409	0.462	0.469	0.501
NSCTI2	0.011	−0.219	0.341	0.607	0.661	**0.936**	0.513	0.494	0.471	0.530
NSCTI3	0.025	−0.212	0.397	0.504	0.596	**0.898**	0.556	0.449	0.440	0.537
NSDTI1	−0.005	−0.139	0.196	0.328	0.520	0.547	**0.904**	0.364	0.298	0.370
NSDTI2	−0.022	−0.066	0.227	0.339	0.513	0.464	**0.903**	0.345	0.325	0.352
NSDTI3	−0.022	−0.173	0.071	0.338	0.627	0.417	**0.833**	0.344	0.299	0.333
PECTI1	0.085	−0.158	0.135	0.379	0.415	0.431	0.338	**0.889**	0.545	0.702
PECTI2	0.077	−0.179	0.140	0.502	0.460	0.468	0.368	**0.941**	0.614	0.760
PECTI3	0.080	−0.261	0.129	0.501	0.492	0.513	0.384	**0.920**	0.595	0.766
PENTI1	−0.019	−0.245	0.204	0.645	0.542	0.487	0.339	0.606	**0.945**	0.663
PENTI2	0.042	−0.193	0.237	0.570	0.520	0.472	0.317	0.598	**0.941**	0.736
PSCTI1	0.073	−0.251	0.170	0.505	0.441	0.478	0.310	0.786	0.580	**0.832**
PSCTI2	0.091	−0.248	0.137	0.487	0.481	0.463	0.331	0.751	0.597	**0.845**
PSCTI3	0.069	−0.198	0.151	0.478	0.518	0.453	0.341	0.668	0.553	**0.831**
PSCTI4	0.059	−0.240	0.212	0.465	0.485	0.506	0.353	0.660	0.572	**0.854**
PSCTI5	0.013	−0.223	0.264	0.473	0.475	0.518	0.339	0.629	0.611	**0.860**
PSCTI6	0.067	−0.181	0.244	0.487	0.516	0.464	0.334	0.642	0.791	**0.810**
PSCTI7	0.022	−0.242	0.224	0.463	0.535	0.522	0.350	0.670	0.665	**0.867**

Source: Own elaboration

Thus it would appear that we can confirm that the aspect of community satisfaction studied does, in fact, affect the manner in which the effects derived from tourism are perceived, and as such:

(a) Satisfaction with the environment would appear not to influence the manner in which the residents perceive the negative effects of tourism, but would appear to affect, and positively, though not to any great degree, the perception of favourable socio-cultural (0.114) and economic (0.147) effects.
(b) Economic and Sanitary Satisfaction has a significant relationship, negative in sign and of notable magnitude, with the effects perceived in tourism, independently of its nature and sign, meaning that the greater the satisfaction of the residents with the economy and the sanitation system in their locality, the lesser the

Table 6.10 Construct reliability, convergent validity and discriminant validity

Composite Reliability	Cronbach's Alpha	AVE		ENS	ESS	NECTI	NENTI	NSCTI	NSDTI	PECTI	PENTI	PSCTI	SS
1.000	1.000	1.000	ENS	**1.000**									
0.831	0.650	0.715	ESS	0.366	**0.846**								
0.921	0.829	0.853	NECTI	−0.067	−0.269	**0.924**							
0.932	0.891	0.821	NENTI	−0.068	−0.315	0.647	**0.906**						
0.931	0.888	0.817	NSCTI	0.018	−0.282	0.630	0.694	**0.904**					
0.912	0.856	0.775	NSDTI	−0.018	−0.139	0.378	0.618	0.546	**0.880**				
0.940	0.906	0.840	PECTI	0.088	−0.223	0.508	0.501	0.518	0.398	**0.917**			
0.941	0.875	0.889	PENTI	0.012	−0.233	0.645	0.564	0.509	0.348	0.639	**0.943**		
0.945	0.932	0.710	PSCTI	0.065	−0.269	0.568	0.584	0.579	0.400	0.812	0.741	**0.843**	
0.863	0.796	0.680	SS	0.313	0.441	0.250	0.260	0.364	0.196	0.146	0.234	0.241	**0.825**

Source: Own elaboration

Note: Diagonal elements (bold) are the square root of variance shared between the constructs and their measures (AVE). Off-diagonal elements are the correlations among constructs. For discriminant validity, the diagonal elements should be larger than the off-diagonal elements

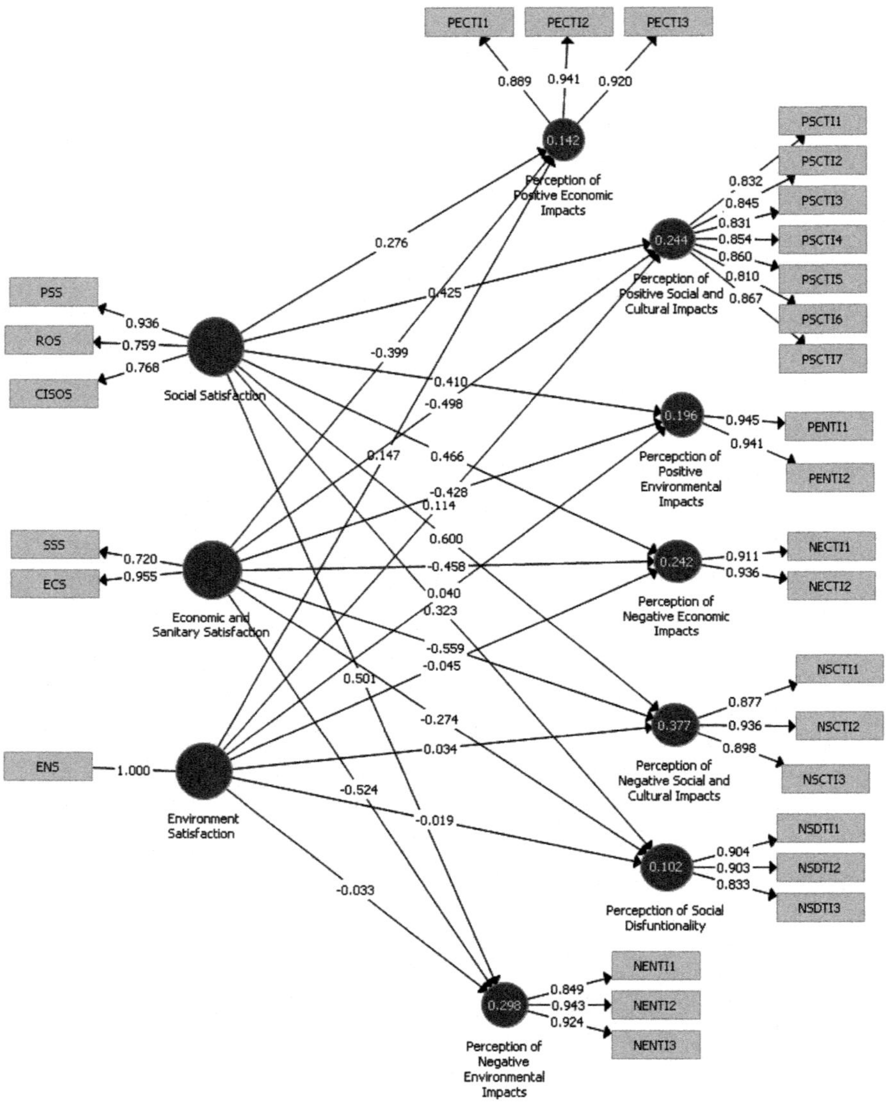

Fig. 6.1 Path coefficients for the model. Indicator of goodness of fit: SRMR Composite Model = 0.058. (Source: own elaboration)

intensity with which they perceive the effects of tourism, be these favourable or unfavourable. The magnitude of this relationship is somewhat lower for favourable effects (from −0.399 to −0.498) than for unfavourable effects (from −0.458 to −0.559), with the exception of the influence on the social dysfunctionalities of tourism, an unfavourable effect with a magnitude notably inferior to that shown by the remaining damaging effects of tourism (−0.274).

Table 6.11 Structural model results. Path significance using percentile bootstrap 95% confidence interval

Hypothesis	Suggested effect	Original Sample (O)	Sample Mean (M)	Standard Deviation	T Statistics	P Values	Support	Percentile bootstrap 95% confidence level		Support
								5.0%	95.0%	
ENS -> NECTI	–	−0.045	−0.046	0.050	0.900	0.184	No	−0.130	0.036	No
ENS -> NENTI	–	−0.033	−0.033	0.048	0.695	0.244	No	−0.110	0.045	No
ENS -> NSCTI	–	0.034	0.034	0.046	0.740	0.230	No	−0.042	0.110	No
ENS -> NSDTI	–	−0.019	−0.020	0.049	0.377	0.353	No	−0.102	0.060	No
ENS -> PECTI	+	0.147**	0.147	0.050	2.959	0.002	Yes	0.066	0.229	Yes
ENS -> PENTI	+	0.040	0.040	0.056	0.718	0.236	No	−0.051	0.132	No
ENS -> PSCTI	+	0.114*	0.114	0.051	2.216	0.013	Yes	0.031	0.198	Yes
ESS -> NECTI	–	−0.458***	−0.456	0.052	8.840	0.000	Yes	−0.541	−0.372	Yes
ESS -> NENTI	–	−0.524***	−0.521	0.055	9.506	0.000	Yes	−0.611	−0.428	Yes
ESS -> NSCTI	–	−0.559***	−0.555	0.050	11.222	0.000	Yes	−0.635	−0.474	Yes
ESS -> NSDTI	–	−0.274***	−0.274	0.074	3.726	0.000	Yes	−0.390	−0.148	Yes
ESS -> PECTI	+	−0.399***	−0.398	0.060	6.631	0.000	No	−0.495	−0.299	No
ESS -> PENTI	+	−0.428***	−0.427	0.056	7.713	0.000	No	−0.517	−0.336	No
ESS -> PSCTI	+	−0.498***	−0.497	0.056	8.926	0.000	No	−0.589	−0.405	No
SS -> NECTI	–	0.466***	0.464	0.054	8.653	0.000	No	0.374	0.551	No
SS -> NENTI	–	0.501***	0.499	0.053	9.467	0.000	No	0.410	0.584	No
SS -> NSCTI	–	0.600***	0.597	0.051	11.670	0.000	No	0.512	0.682	No
SS -> NSDTI	–	0.323***	0.325	0.063	5.104	0.000	No	0.220	0.430	No
SS -> PECTI	+	0.276***	0.275	0.057	4.840	0.000	Yes	0.182	0.368	Yes
SS -> PENTI	+	0.410***	0.408	0.056	7.364	0.000	Yes	0.316	0.499	Yes
SS -> PSCTI	+	0.425***	0.423	0.057	7.428	0.000	Yes	0.329	0.516	Yes

Source: Own elaboration

For n = 5000 subsamples: $^{*}p < .05$; $^{**}p < .01$; $^{***}p < .001$ (based on a one-tailed Student's t (4999) distribution); t(0.05; 4999) = 1645; t(0.01; 4999) = 2327; t(0.001; 4999) = 3092

Depending on its nature, the relationship appears to be the strongest for socio-cultural-type effects, where it reaches and even surpasses 0.5 in value.

(c) Social Satisfaction enjoys a significant relationship of positive sign and generally notable magnitude with the effects perceived in tourism, once again independently of the sign and character of the effect under study. This relationship indicates that, as the residents' satisfaction with the social aspects of their community (public services, social and leisure opportunities and citizen involvement) increases, the intensity with which these residents perceive each and every one of the effects derived from tourism also increases. Once again, as in the previous case, the magnitude of the relationship is shown to be greater for unfavourable effects (from 0.323 to 0.600) then for favourable ones (0.276 to 0.425). Once again it is the socio-cultural effects linked to tourism that show the relationship of greatest magnitude (0.425 for favourable and 6.000 for unfavourable).

As shown in Table 6.12, figures of R^2 are not excessively outstanding. While all the constructs exceed the minimum value of 0.10, only "Perception of Negative Social and Cultural Impacts" ($R^2 = 0.377$) achieves a moderate level, though it is important to bear in mind that "Perception of Negative Environmental Impacts" ($R^2 = 0.298$) also approaches this moderate level. In spite of this, cross-validated redundancy measures show that the theoretical/structural model has a predictive relevant ($Q^2 > 0$). With regard to the f^2 indicator (effect size), which measures the change in R^2 when a specific exogenous construct is omitted from the model, its magnitude is insignificant for the latent variable "Environment Satisfaction", which only reveals a small impact influence on the dependent construct ("Perception of Positive Economic Impacts". However, the remaining two exogenous latent variables ("Economic and Sanitary Satisfaction" and "Social Satisfaction") generally denote a medium (0.15) or even great (0.35) impact influence on the majority of dependent constructs, and are especially important for "Perception of Negative Social and Cultural Impacts" (0.376 and 0.451 respectively). An exception to the final affirmation is the reduced impact influence that these two types of satisfaction exert on the endogenous latent variable "Perception of Social Dysfunctionalities" (0.063 and 0.090 respectively).

Table 6.12 also displays the amount of variance that each antecedent variable explains on each endogenous construct. With regard to this, it is revealed that the exogenous latent variable "Environment Satisfaction" has insignificant participation when it comes to explaining the variance of any of the endogenous constructs (from 0.03% to 1.29%), while it is the remaining two exogenous latent variables ("Economic and Sanitary Satisfaction" and "Social Satisfaction") that explain almost all the variance of the construct "perception of the effects of tourism", sometimes with greater prominence than the former (in the case of "Perception of Positive Economic Impacts", where it explains double the percentage of variance), and sometimes with greater relevance to the latter (as in the case of "Perception of Social Dysfunctionalities"), but in general with very similar participations.

Finally we should point out that the fact that all Inner VIFs are inferior to 5 disproves the existence of indications of multi-collinearity between the antecedent

Table 6.12 Effects on endogenous variables

	R^2	Q^2	f^2	Direct effect	Correlation	Variance explained (%)
NECTI	0.242	0.198				24,3
SS			0.223	0.466	0.250	11,65
ESS			0.207	−0.458	−0.269	12,32
ENS			0.002	−0.045	−0.067	0,30
NENTI	**0.298**	**0.237**				**29,8**
SS			0.279	0.501	0.260	13,03
ESS			0.292	−0.524	−0.315	16,51
ENS			0.001	−0.033	−0.068	0,22
NSCTI	**0.377**	**0.302**				**37,7**
SS			0.451	0.600	0.364	21,84
ESS			0.376	−0.559	−0.282	15,76
ENS			0.002	0.034	0.018	0,06
NSDTI	**0.102**	**0.074**				**10,2**
SS			0.090	0.323	0.196	6,33
ESS			0.063	−0.274	−0.139	3,81
ENS			0.000	−0.019	−0.018	0,03
PECTI	**0.142**	**0.113**				**14,2**
SS			0.069	0.276	0.146	4,03
ESS			0.139	−0.399	−0.223	8,90
ENS			0.021	0.147	0.088	1,29
PENTI	**0.196**	**0.169**				**19,6**
SS			0.163	0.410	0.234	9,59
ESS			0.171	−0.428	−0.233	9,97
ENS			0.002	0.040	0.012	0,05
PSCTI	**0.244**	**0.170**				**24,4**
SS			0.186	0.425	0.241	10,24
ESS			0.245	−0.498	−0.269	13,40
ENS			0.014	0.114	0.065	0,74

Source: Own elaboration

variables of each of the endogenous structures: "Environment Satisfaction" (1.194), "Economic and Sanitary Satisfaction" (1.337) and "Social Satisfaction" (1.284).

6.5 Conclusions, Practical Implications and Recommendations

Few previous studies have analysed the relationship between community satisfaction and the perceived effects of tourism and those that have done so have not coincided in the means of measuring this variable, some considering it as an average of the constituent items (Vargas-Sánchez et al. 2009), some considering it on the basis of a single item (Vargas-Sánchez et al. 2011), and in other cases it is delimited reflectively on the basis of a series of indicators (Nunkoo and Ramkissoon 2010). With regard to how the relationship between the two variables is approached, studies that do so by analysing the incidence of satisfaction on the perception of impacts of tourism usually conclude by recognising a positive sign relationship with respect to the benefits of tourism and a negative sign relationship with respect to the damaging effects of tourism (Nunkoo and Ramkissoon 2010). The implications of these results are clear: residents' satisfaction with their community is discerned as a variable which allows the attitude of the citizen to be predicted as far as major tourism development in their locality: those who are more satisfied with their community will perceive the favourable effects of tourism more and the unfavourable effects less, which means they will be favourable to tourism develop in the area continuing, while those who are unsatisfied with the community will perceive the favourable aspects of tourism development less and perceive the unfavourable ones more, developing an unfavourable attitude towards tourism in the area. Therefore, from this perspective, the message for government agencies should be the following: improve the satisfaction of residents as far as their community and you will get their attitudes to be more favourable towards increasing tourism development.

In order to add new insights, in our case we have approached the study in a contingent manner, disaggregating the effects of tourism not just according to their sign but also to their nature and disaggregating community satisfaction in three constructs (social satisfaction, economic and sanitary satisfaction and environment satisfaction).

The results obtained demonstrate that it is the aspect of community satisfaction analysed, and not the positive or negative character of the effect studied, that conditions the sign of the relationship between satisfaction and effects, so Social Satisfaction shows a significant relationship of positive sign and generally notable magnitude with the perceived effects of tourism, Economic and Sanitary Satisfaction shows a significant relationship of negative sign and notable magnitude with the perceived effects of tourism, and Environment Satisfaction does not appear to influence the manner in which the residents perceive the negative effects of tourism but does appear to influence, with a positive though weak sign, the perception of the favourable socio-cultural and economic effects.

In light of these results, it is impossible to attempt to predict the attitude of residents towards tourism based on the variable "satisfaction with their community", not even disaggregating the variable satisfaction according to its nature, since the residents who are most satisfied with the social aspects, will perceive the favourable effects of tourism with a high degree of intensity, yet also the negative ones, which prevents us from knowing the net or overall result of this perception, with something similar happening, although with the opposite sign, in the most satisfied citizens in economic and sanitary aspects, who will perceive the unfavourable aspects of tourism less, but also the more favourable ones. Not even satisfaction with the natural environment, where the relation with the effects is quite weak and occasionally inexistent, can be a predictor of the attitude towards tourism development.

The practical implications of this study demonstrate that it is not advisable to propose universal models that globally analyse the relationship between community satisfaction and the perceived effects of tourism, and which attempt to predict the residents' attitude towards tourism development based on this overall satisfaction variable. On the other hand, the results of our study lead us to recommend aiming at disaggregating community satisfaction into its various dimensions rather than treating it solely on an overall level and to not claim that the different dimensions of this satisfaction enabled us to anticipate the attitude of citizens in so far as tourism development. In fact, if we refer to this particular research case, we find a medium-low degree of community satisfaction in residents who generally show a low intensity perception in relation to the various effects of tourism (both the positive and negative ones) and yet however they show quite favourable attitudes towards increased tourism develop in their region (mean of 4.2 on a scale of 1 to 5) and towards an increased presence of tourists in the area (mean of 4.1). Other variables, such as the life cycle stage should be explored as moderators of these relationships.

References

Allen, L., Hafer, H., Long, P., & Perdue, R. (1993). Rural residents' attitudes toward recreation and tourism development. *Journal of Travel Research, 31*(4), 2–33.

Andereck, K. L., & Nyaupane, G. P. (2011). Exploring the nature of tourism and quality of life perceptions among residents. *Journal of Travel Research, 50*(3), 248–260.

Andereck, K., & Vogt, C. (2000). The relations between resident's attitudes toward tourism and tourism development options. *Journal of Travel Research, 39*(1), 27–37.

Andereck, K., Valentine, K., Vogt, C., & Knopf, R. (2007). A cross-cultural analysis of tourism and quality of life perceptions. *Journal of Sustainable Tourism, 15*(5), 483–500.

Aref, F. (2011). The effects of tourism on quality of life: A case study of shiraz, Iran. *Life Science Journal, 8*(2), 26–30.

Chin, W. (2010). How to write up and report PLS analyses. In V. Esposito, W. W. Chin, J. Henseler, & H. Wang (Eds.), *Handbook of partial least squares: Concepts, methods and applications* (pp. 655–690). Berlin/Heidelberg: Springer.

Chin, W., & Newsted, P. R. (1999). Structural equation modelling analysis with small samples using partial least squares. In R. H. Hoyle (Ed.), *Statistical strategies for small sample research* (pp. 307–341). Thousand Oaks: Sage Publications.

García-Delgado, F. J., Delgado-Domínguez, A., & Felicidades-García, J. (2013). El turismo en la cuenca minera de Riotinto. *Cuadernos de Turismo, 31*, 129–152.

Gjerald, O. (2005). Sociocultural impacts of tourism: A case study of Norway. *Journal of Tourism and Cultural Change, 3*(1), 36–58.

Hair, J. F., Ringle, C. M., & Sarstedt, M. (2011). PLS-SEM: Indeed a silver bullet. *Journal of Marketing Theory and Practice, 19*(2), 139–152.

Hu, L. T., & Bentler, P. M. (1999). Cutoff criteria for fit indexes in covariance structure analysis: Conventional criteria versus new alternatives. *Structural Equation Modeling: A Multidisciplinary Journal, 6*(1), 1–55.

Johnson, J. D., Snepenger, D. J., & Akis, S. (1994). Residents perceptions of tourism development. *Annals of Tourism Research, 21*(3), 629–642.

Kaplanidou, K., Karadakis, K., Gibson, H., Thapa, B., Walker, M., Geldenhuys, S., & Coetzee, W. (2013). Quality of life, event impacts and mega event support among South African residents before and after the 2010 FIFA World Cup. *Journal of Travel Research, 52*(5), 631–645.

Khizindar, T. M. (2012). Effects of tourism on residents' quality of life in Saudi Arabia: An empirical study. *Journal of Hospitality Marketing & Management, 21*(6), 617–637.

Ko, D. W., & Stewart, W. P. (2002). A structural equation model of residents' attitudes for tourism development. *Tourism Management, 23*(5), 521–530.

Kuvan, Y., & Akan, P. (2005). Residents' attitudes toward general and forest-related impacts of tourism: The case of Belek, Natalia. *Tourism Management, 26*, 691–706.

Manap, A. A., Aman, O., & Rahmiati, F. (2011). The impact of tourism innovation on quality of life residents in the community: A case study of Sungai Melaka. In: *International Conference on Management (ICM 2011) proceedings* (pp. 334–342). Penang, Malaysia.

Matarrita-Cascante, D. (2010). Changing communities, community satisfaction, and quality of life: A view of multiple perceived indicators. *Social Indicators Research, 98*(1), 105–127.

Milman, A., & Pizam, A. (1988). Social impacts of tourism on Central Florida. *Annals of Tourism Research, 15*(2), 191–204.

Nawijn, J., & Mitas, O. (2012). Resident attitudes to tourism and their effect on subjective well-being: The case of Palma de Mallorca. *Journal of Travel Research, 51*(1), 531–541.

Nichols, M., Stitt, B. G., & Giacopassi, D. (2002). Community assessment of the effects of casinos on quality of life. *Social Indicators Research, 57*(3), 229–262.

Nunkoo, R., & Ramkissoon, H. (2010). Residents' satisfaction with community attributes and support for tourism. *Journal of Hospitality & Support for Tourism, 35*(2), 171–190.

Nunkoo, R., & Ramkissoon, H. (2011). Modeling community support for a proposed integrated resort project. *Journal of Sustainable Tourism, 18*(2), 257–277.

Roldán, J. L., & Sánchez-Franco, M. J. (2012). Variance-based structural equation modeling: Guidelines for using partial least squares in information systems research. In M. Mora, O. Gelman, A. Steenkamp, & M. Raisinghani (Eds.), *Research methodologies, innovations and philosophies in software systems engineering and information systems* (pp. 193–221). Hershey: IGI Global.

Sirgy, J., Rathz, D. R., Cicic, R., & Underwood, R. (2000). A method for assessing residents' satisfaction with community-based services: A quality of life perspective. *Social Indicators Research, 49*, 279–316.

Urtasun, A., & Gutiérrez, I. (2006). Tourism agglomeration and its impact on social welfare: An empirical approach to the Spanish case. *Tourism Management, 27*, 901–912.

Uysal, M., Perdue, R., & Sirgy, J. (Eds.). (2012). *Handbook of tourism and quality-of-life research: Enhancing the lives of tourists and residents of host communities*. Dordrecht: Springer.

Uysal, M., Sirgy, J., Woo, E., & Kim, H. (2016). Quality of life (QOL) and well-being research in tourism. *Tourism Management, 53*, 244–261.

Vargas-Sánchez, A., Plaza-Mejía, M. A., & Porras-Bueno, N. (2009). Understanding residents' attitudes toward the development of industrial tourism in a former mining community. *Journal of Travel Research, 47*(3), 373–387.

Vargas-Sánchez, A., Porras-Bueno, N., & Plaza-Mejía, M. A. (2011). Explaining residents attitudes to tourism. Is a universal model possible? *Annals of Tourism Research, 38*(2), 460–480.

Wheeler, F., & Laing, J. (2008). Tourism as a vehicle for liveable communities: Case studies from regional Victoria, Australia. *Annals of Leisure Research, 11*(1–2), 242–263.

Williams, J., & Lawson, R. (2001). Community issues and resident opinions of tourism. *Annals of Tourism Research, 28*(2), 269–290.

Woo, E., Kim, H., & Uysal, M. (2015). Life satisfaction and support for tourism development. *Annals of Tourism Research, 50*, 84–97.

Yamada, N., Heo, J., King, C., & Fu, Y. (2009). Life satisfaction of urban residents: Do health perception, wealth, safety, community pride and, and cultural tourism matter? In: *International CHRIE conference-refereed track* (Paper 24).

Yu, C. P., Chancellor, H. C., & Cole, T. P. (2011). Measuring resident's attitudes toward sustainable tourism attitude scale. *Journal of Travel Research, 50*(1), 57–63.

Chapter 7
Impact of Tourism on Residents' Quality of Life: Segmentation Analysis and Marketing Implications

Celeste Eusébio and Maria João Carneiro

Abstract Tourism has a great potential for enhancing residents' quality of life (QOL). Nevertheless, a limited number of studies have been carried out in this field. In order to overcome this gap this chapter aims to analyse the heterogeneity of residents of tourism destinations regarding perceptions of tourism impacts on several dimensions of their QOL. A survey of residents of two coastal communities located in the Central region of Portugal (Barra and Costa Nova) was undertaken in 2012 (N = 288). Two Principal Component Analyses (PCAs) were carried out to identify the dimensions both of tourism impacts on QOL and of host-tourist interaction. A hierarchical cluster analysis was carried out based on the dimensions of tourism impacts on QOL. Anova, Kruskal-Wallis and Chi-square tests were used to compare the clusters identified. Results reveal that tourism has a considerable impact on residents' QOL and that the residents' communities are heterogeneous regarding the perception of tourism impacts on several dimensions of QOL. Three clusters emerged: Cluster 1 – *The most benefited* (N = 34.4%); Cluster 2 – *The quite benefited* (N = 49.7%); and Cluster 3 – *The least benefited* (N = 16.0%). Statistical significant differences were detected among the clusters regarding several dimensions of host-tourist interaction, place of residence and satisfaction with several issues. Host-tourist interaction emerges as one of the factors with higher positive influence on the perceptions of tourism impacts on residents' QOL. The chapter ends with some contributions to the development and marketing of tourism destinations.

Keywords Residents' quality of life · Cluster analysis · Segmentation · Host-tourist interaction · Satisfaction · Portugal

---

C. Eusébio (✉) · M. J. Carneiro
Department of Economics, Management, Industrial Engineering and Tourism, GOVCOPP – Research Unit in Governance, Competitiveness and Public Policies, University of Aveiro, Aveiro, Portugal
e-mail: celeste.eusebio@ua.pt; mjcarneiro@ua.pt

A. M. Campón-Cerro et al. (eds.), *Best Practices in Hospitality and Tourism Marketing and Management*, Applying Quality of Life Research,
https://doi.org/10.1007/978-3-319-91692-7_7

7.1 Introduction

Nowadays, tourism is one of the most important socioeconomic forces worldwide (Uysal et al. 2015), involving various agents, economic sectors and destinations. Tourism has become an important agent of change (economic, social, cultural and environmental) (Matarrita-Cascante 2010) in all places which are involved in the tourism system (origin region, transit region and destination region). In order to analyse these changes, several studies on residents' perceptions of tourism impacts and on residents' attitudes towards tourism development have been published since the 70s (e.g. Andereck et al. 2005; Brunt and Courtney 1999; Carneiro and Eusébio 2011; Haley et al. 2005). However, tourism impacts on Quality of Life (QOL) studies are gaining prominence, as mentioned by Uysal et al. (2015: 1) "one of the research areas gaining momentum and increased attention is the link between tourism activities, its consequences, and the QOL of those involved in the production or consumption of tourism goods and services". Despite the growing interest in analysing the relationship between tourism and QOL, and the widespread knowledge that tourism has great potential for enhancing residents' QOL, a limited number of studies have examined the impact of tourism on residents' QOL (e.g. Andereck et al. 2007; Aref 2011; Benckendorff et al. 2009; Kim 2002). Moreover, there is also an absence of studies that examine if destination communities are heterogeneous in terms of perceptions of tourism impacts on their QOL and which analyse the factors that may influence this heterogeneity. In order to close this gap, this study aims to analyse the heterogeneity of residents of coastal tourism destinations regarding perceptions of tourism impacts on several dimensions of their QOL. Specifically, this chapter intends to answer the following questions: (i) Does tourism affect the QOL of residents in costal tourism destinations? (ii) What residents' QOL domains are most influenced by tourism? (iii) Is there heterogeneity among residents regarding their perceptions of tourism impacts on the various domains of QOL? (iv) Are the perceptions of tourism impacts on QOL related to the socioeconomic characteristics of residents and their interaction with visitors?

The present study extends the research carried out in this field in two areas. First, the focus of the study is to assess the residents' perceptions of tourism impacts on their QOL in two important coastal tourism destinations located in the Central Region of Portugal (*Barra* and *Costa Nova*), where there are no studies in this topic. Second, this study also extends previous research by presenting and empirically testing a segmentation approach based on residents' perceptions of tourism impacts on several domains of their QOL. These types of studies are of utmost relevance to both public and private agents responsible for designing and implementing tourism development strategies in order to generate positive tourism impacts on residents' QOL. Consequently, this kind of research actions will contribute to increasing the level of residents' satisfaction with the tourism industry. Studies that analyse residents' perception of the impact of tourism on their QOL are also of utmost relevance since, as Andereck et al. (2007) highlight, this kind of studies helps to identify perceptions and residents' attitudes towards tourism and provide important data to evaluate residents' support for additional tourism development and for specific development strategies.

This chapter first presents a literature review on the impact of tourism on residents' QOL and discusses the relevance of carrying out segmentation studies based on the impacts of tourism on residents' QOL. In this context, factors that may influence the perceptions of these impacts, namely socioeconomic features and interaction with visitors – are also examined. This literature review is followed by the description of an empirical study carried out in two Portuguese costal tourism destinations. This part of the chapter begins with a brief description of the costal tourism destinations analysed. Next, a methodology section is provided, where both data collection methods and data analysis methods are explained. The results of this analysis are presented and discussed. Finally, the chapter ends with a description of the most important conclusions of this research, followed by a discussion of the practical implications in order to define tourism development strategies that improve residents' QOL.

7.2 Literature Review

7.2.1 Impact of Tourism on Residents' QOL

It is widely recognized that tourism has great potential to affect the life of local residents. Once a destination engages in tourism development, it will face changes and challenges in several areas (economic, social, cultural, and environmental). As a result, the residents of this destination also face new changes and challenges that influence their QOL and, consequently, their satisfaction with the tourism development process (Matarrita-Cascante 2010). Despite these arguments, a limited number of studies have specifically analysed the impact of tourism on residents' QOL (e.g. Andereck and Nyaupane 2011; Khizindar 2012; Kim et al. 2013). However, it is widely recognized that the improvement of residents' QOL should be a priority of all local authorities. As Yu et al. (2014: 9) highlight, "one of major purposes of tourism development in a destination is to improve the QOL of the host community". Consequently, it is widely recognized that all tourism development strategies should be designed and implemented with the purpose of improving the QOL of all agents involved, the residents being one of the most important agents for the success of a tourism destination.

Defining QOL is a difficult task because it is a subjective experience that may "depend on an individual's perceptions and feelings" (Andereck et al. 2007: 484). More than 100 definitions and models of QOL appear in the literature (Andereck et al. 2007; Eusébio and Carneiro 2014). Despite the wide range of QOL definitions published, there has been agreement in recent years that this is a complex and multidimensional construct comprising many issues of people's life and environments (Andereck et al. 2007; Moscardo 2009). Moreover, terms such as well-being, happiness and life satisfaction have frequently been used practically as synonymous of QOL (Khizindar 2012; Matarrita-Cascante 2010). The QOL construct has been measured using a great range of indicators, such as social indicators, well-being measures and economic indicators (Liu 2015). Globally, this construct has often been measured using two types of indicators: (i) objective indicators that measure specific conditions of people's life (e.g. income level, education level) and (ii) subjective indicators regarding the evaluation of subjective life conditions (e.g. satisfaction with several aspects of life) (Andereck and Nyaupane 2011; Kim 2002). To assess all the domains of resident's QOL influenced by tourism development, as suggested by Jeon et al. (2016: 109) "resident's quality of life should be conceptualized with an aggregation of residents' perception of economic, social, and environmental conditions as well as comprehensive perception of well-being in the host community, embracing residents' subjective well-being and objective well-being".

Recently, the number of studies published that analyse the impact of tourism on residents' QOL has increased considerably. Some of the studies published analyse the impacts of tourism in a global sense (e.g. Andereck et al. 2007; Andereck and Nyaupane 2011; Aref 2011; Khizindar 2012; Kim et al. 2013), while others analyse the effects of specific types of tourism (e.g. gambling/casinos, surf tourism, cultural tourism and rural tourism) on residents' QOL (e.g. Chhabra and Gursoy 2009; Kim 2002; Jurowski and Brown 2001; Usher and Kerstetter 2014). Moreover, some studies published analyse the impacts of events on residents' QOL (e.g. Fredline et al. 2013; Liu 2015). In terms of methodologies, both qualitative (e.g. Matarrita-Cascante 2010; Usher and Kerstetter 2014) and quantitative methods (e.g. Andereck et al. 2007; Andereck and Nyaupane 2011; Chhabra and Gursoy 2009; Fredline et al. 2013; Jeon et al. (2016); Khizindar 2012; Kim 2002; Kim et al. 2013) have been used to analyse the impacts of tourism on residents' QOL. However, there is a prevalence of quantitative studies.

Several authors have studied the relevance of the QOL construct in the tourism literature and its various domains (e.g. Andereck et al. 2007; Kim 2002). Kim (2002) proposes a measure for QOL based on previous literature comprising four domains: material well-being (including two dimensions: income and employment and also cost of living), community well-being, emotional well-being (including two dimensions: leisure well-being and spiritual well-being) and health and safety well-being. Khizindar (2012) uses the four domains of QOL proposed by Kim (2002) to analyse the effects of tourism on residents' QOL in Saudi Arabia and Aref (2011) investigates the effect of tourism on residents' QOL in Shiraz, Iran, also using the domains of QOL proposed by Kim (2002). Moreover, Kim et al. (2013) also use the four domains of QOL proposed in 2002 to analyse the links between community residents' perceptions of tourism impacts (economic, social, cultural, and environmental) and residents' satisfaction with the four domains of life and overall life satisfaction. Kim et al. (2013) test the model developed in several communities of Virginia with different levels of tourism development. Andereck et al. (2007) analyse the existence of significant differences in perceived tourism-related QOL domains between Hispanic and Anglo residents in Arizona, using 38 tourism-related QOL variables categorized into four groups (negative QOL impacts, positive QOL economic impacts, positive QOL sociocultural impacts, positive QOL environmental impacts). Andereck and Nyaupane (2011) examine residents' perception of the impact tourism has on their QOL, and the relationship between QOL perceptions and support for tourism in Arizona, using eight domains of residents' QOL (community well-being, urban issues, way of life, community pride and awareness, natural and cultural preservation, economic strength, recreation amenities and crime and substance abuse).

The studies published which examine the impact of tourism on residents' QOL (e.g. Andereck et al. 2007; Andereck and Nyaupane 2011; Aref 2011; Fredline et al. 2013; Khizindar 2012; Usher and Kerstetter 2014) reveal that tourism has effects on economic, social and cultural dimensions of QOL. These studies show that tourism contributes to increasing job opportunities (Andereck and Nyaupane 2011; Liu 2015; Usher and Kerstetter 2014), to providing additional and improved infrastructures and recreation opportunities (Andereck and Nyaupane 2011; Liu 2015) and to strengthening social and family ties (Usher and Kerstetter 2014). Moreover, other studies (e.g. Aref 2011; Kim 2002; Kim et al. 2013) reveal that tourism has different effects on material well-being, community well-being, emotional well-being and health and safety well-being. For example, the results of Aref's (2011) study reveal that the strongest tourism impacts occurred on emotional well-being, community well-being and income and employment, while health and safety well-being was the QOL domain least influenced by tourism. Despite the majority of the published studies revealing that tourism has a positive effect on residents' QOL (e.g. Andereck et al. 2007; Aref 2011; Kim et al. 2013, Usher and Kerstetter 2014) tourism growth may also negatively influence residents' QOL, when it contributes to loss of cultural identity (Jeon et al. 2016; Liu 2015), environmental degradation (Jeon et al. 2016; Liu 2015), increased cost of living (Andereck and Nyaupane 2011; Jeon et al. 2016; Liu 2015), friction created between residents and tourists (Andereck and Nyaupane 2011; Jeon et al. 2016; Liu 2015), a change in residents' way of life (Jeon et al. 2016; Liu 2015; Andereck and Nyaupane 2011), generating crowding and traffic and parking problems (Andereck and Nyaupane 2011; Jeon et al. 2016), as well as to increasing crime and the use of alcohol and drugs (Andereck and Nyaupane 2011; Usher and Kerstetter 2014). Therefore, tourism growth does not always have a positive impact on residents' QOL. When the tourism costs exceed the benefits perceived, tourism may contribute to a decrease in residents' QOL. Moreover, the effects of tourism on residents' QOL vary from resident to resident. Andereck et al. (2007: 487) report "while tourism development can improve the QOL of some members of a given population, it should not be assumed that a positive effect on QOL of the majority group will necessarily have a similar result for minority groups". This suggests the importance of segmenting residents according to their perception of tourism impacts on their QOL. The relevance of this construct as a segmentation basis will be further analysed in the next section.

7.2.2 Segmentation Based on Impact of Tourism on QOL

Segmentation is a useful tool for identifying distinct groups of consumers that should be approached using different marketing mixes (Kotler et al. 1999). Several reasons point to the relevance of segmenting residents of tourism destinations based on the impact of tourism on QOL. First, as the literature reviewed in the last section shows (e.g. Andereck and Nyaupane 2011; Kim 2002; Kim et al. 2013; Liu 2015; Usher and Kerstetter 2014), tourism may have important impacts on residents' QOL, contributing to enhanced residents' perceptions regarding their lives. Second, residents are important stakeholders of tourism destinations, since they may assume the role of service providers, of cultural brokers or, even, have casual unplanned encounters with visitors that may affect the visitors' experience of the destination (Sharpley 2014). Therefore, it is of utmost importance to ensure that tourism has a positive impact on the hosts' QOL, so that they develop positive attitudes towards tourism. In this context, some research reveals that the residents who perceive more positive impacts of tourism on their QOL are more likely to accept and support future tourism development (Woo et al. 2015) and to develop positive attitudes towards those responsible for the tourism development (Polonsky et al. 2013).

Additionally, some research reveals that the residents' perceptions regarding tourism impacts on QOL may depend on several features, such as the socioeconomic profile of hosts (Andereck and Nyaupane 2011; Chancellor et al. 2011; Jeon et al. 2016; Kim et al. 2013; Meng et al. 2010) and the contact established with visitors (Andereck and Nyaupane 2011; Nawijn and Mitas 2012). This suggests that residents of tourism destinations are heterogeneous regarding the perceptions of tourism impacts on their QOL and that segmentation studies using this segmentation basis may provide important insights to develop tourism development strategies that contribute to improving the QOL of tourism destinations' hosts.

Finally, perceptions regarding tourism impacts on QOL are revealed to be an useful segmentation basis in another context, namely in the segmentation of the visitors' market, giving rise to distinct and considerably large segments of visitors that differ not only in perceptions concerning tourism impacts, but also in several other features. However, regarding this last issue, a literature review undertaken revealed that the use of QOL as a segmentation basis has been confined, in the field of tourism, to the scope of tourists. Moreover, the research segmenting tourists based on this construct (e.g. Dolnicar et al. 2013; Eusébio and Carneiro 2014) is still very limited. As far as residents are concerned, several researchers (e.g. Andriotis 2005; Brida et al. 2010; Sinclair-Maragh et al. 2015) segment residents according to their perceptions about tourism impacts on a specific community. Only one study that identified clusters based on hosts' perceptions regarding tourism impacts on their own QOL was found. This study, undertaken by Fredline et al. (2013), corresponds to a longitudinal research where changes on impacts of tourism on QOL across time are assessed, specifically by analysing modifications in the size of clusters of residents with different perceptions of tourism impacts on QOL.

Looking in further detail to the potential relationships between tourism impacts on QOL and other constructs, namely those defining the socioeconomic profile of the residents, the study of Gu and Wong (2016) shows that, among the homestay operators analysed, the youngest and most highly educated are those who recognize the highest positive impact of tourism on QOL. Similar results regarding age were found in the Andereck and Nyaupane's (2011) study, and concerning education in the Roehl's (1999) study. Gender seems to affect perceptions of some tourism impacts and, consequently, of QOL. For example, in a research with residents of a casino destination (Roehl 1999), men perceived that tourism contributed more to creating jobs and to enhancing their QOL than women. However, the research is very limited in this field. Regarding income, there are contradictory findings that point to a positive influence of that variable on personal benefits in some cases (e.g. Andereck and Nyaupane, 2011) and to no significant influence on QOL in other cases (e.g. Roehl 1999).

A set of researches reveals that the place of residence of hosts may also influence their perceptions. Chancellor et al. (2011) examine the hosts' QOL elements that are affected by tourism development and detect significant differences between the perceptions of core and periphery residents in eight of those elements. Similarly, Roehl's (1999) research reports that urban residents perceive more social costs from casino gambling legalization and, thus, a lower QOL, than rural residents. Literature suggests that some differences in these perceptions may be associated with the level of development of the destination. As Butler (2006) postulates, tourism destinations evolve and hosts' perceptions of tourism impacts are likely to change across the stages of the destination's life cycles. The perceptions tend to become more negative when the number of visitors exceeds some thresholds and the charge capacity is surpassed. In this context, Meng et al. (2010) find that three groups of Chinese regions with different levels of tourism development also have different QOL levels, which suggests that tourism development may affect the residents' perspectives concerning QOL. Kim et al. (2013) go one step further and provide evidences that the relationship between the perceptions of specific tourism impacts (e.g. economic impacts) and the corresponding QOL domain (e.g. material well-being) changes across the stage of tourism development of the destination. Jeon et al. (2016) identify seasonality as another factor that affects perceptions on tourism outcomes, with higher seasonality leading to the perceptions of more social costs, less environmental sustainability and fewer economic benefits from tourism. In the context of socioeconomic features, the major consensus seems to be that those working in tourism are more likely to perceive a higher contribution of tourism to increased QOL (Andereck and Nyaupane 2011; Roehl 1999).

According to social theory, residents and tourists engage in various exchanges of physical and symbolic resources (Sharpley 2014) that may occur in several contexts – when visitors acquire goods or services, when both parties use the same tourism attractions and facilities, and when exchanging information and ideas (De Kadt 1979). There is a little evidence that the contact with tourists often contributes to increase the residents' QOL (Andereck and Nyaupane 2011; Moscardo et al. 2013), probably because of economic benefits derived from commercial exchanges (e.g. sales of goods and services) (Sharpley 2014), but also because tourism offers residents a plethora of opportunities to, among other features, meet new people and, therefore, increase social networks and decrease isolation, have contact with other cultures and expand knowledge (Guo et al. 2014; Kastenholz et al. 2013; Mai et al. 2014). However, as several researchers argue, host-tourist interaction may also have a negative impact on residents (Moscardo et al. 2013; Reisinger and Turner 2002; Tucker 2003), since the impacts of this interaction also depend on several issues such as whether these contacts are planned or voluntary and on the attitudes and expectations of residents and tourists (Sharpley 2014). Therefore, when trying to understand the relationship within host-tourist interactions, it is important to consider not only the frequency of encounters with tourists, but also the satisfaction with those encounters. A limited number of studies (e.g. Nawijn and Mitas 2012) confirm that the hosts with a more positive opinion of contact with tourists are more likely to perceive more benefits of tourism to their QOL.

Research previously analysed suggests the existence of relationships between the residents' perceptions of tourism impacts on QOL, and both the socioeconomic characteristics of residents and their contact with tourists. However, the limited number of studies undertaken in this scope and some contradictory findings do not permit us to draw consensual conclusions regarding the kind of relationships that exist between these constructs.

7.3 Empirical Study

7.3.1 Brief Characterisation of the Study Area

The two coastal communities under analysis in this research – *Barra* and *Costa Nova* – are located on the west coast of Portugal and in the Central Region of this country – in the municipality of *Ílhavo*. The three parishes where these two communities are located have a total of approximately 22,000 residents (INE 2012). These two coastal communities are contiguous and very close to the city of Aveiro, both easily accessible by road and public transports. These two coastal tourism destinations are separated from Aveiro by a Lagoon (known as *Ria*).

Costa Nova, known for its candy-striped beachside houses, was originally a fishing town. However, throughout the nineteenth century this town gradually changed from a fishing community to a summer resort (Turismo Centro de Portugal 2014). Barra is essentially a residential town, known for its stately lighthouse (*Farol da Barra*), considered one of the tallest lighthouses in Portugal. Both beaches are known for their long sandy beaches and also for being windy, attracting many practitioners of water sports, such as surfing and bodyboarding. In these coastal communities there are many facilities supporting tourism and, manly during the peak season, several events are promoted. Moreover, these two beaches have Blue Flag (an eco-label based on several criteria such as environmental education and information, water quality, environmental management and safety and services) and flag of Accessible Beaches. Consequently, these beach tourism destinations are highly demanded, not only by residents from *Aveiro* and *Ílhavo* Municipalities, but also by visitors (domestic and international), namely families and sports' lovers. These two destinations are in the development stage of the life cycle.

Some tourism supply and demand indicators of the municipality of *Ílhavo* reveal that tourism already has some relevance in this municipality. In 2013, seven tourism accommodation establishments, with 380 beds, lodged 15,670 guests, corresponding to 29,948 overnights. The majority of guests are Portuguese (representing 69% of the total), while foreign guests represent only 31%. Spain is the most important foreign market (representing 52% of all foreign guests), followed by the French (16%) and the German (8%) markets (INE 2014).

7.3.2 Data Collection Methods

In order to obtain information about the residents' perception of tourism impacts on their QOL a questionnaire was administered, in 2012, to the residents of the two coastal communities – *Barra* and *Costa Nova* – characterized in the previous section. The questionnaire used was designed based on a literature review and includes questions organized into four groups: (i) perceptions of residents about the impact of tourism on their QOL; (ii) social contact with visitors; (iii) satisfaction; and (iv) socioeconomic profile.

To measure the perceptions of tourism impacts on residents' QOL, 22 features related to several domains of their QOL, selected from an extensive literature review on tourism and residents' QOL studies (e.g. Andereck et al. 2007; Andereck and Nyaupane 2011; Khizindar 2012; Kim et al. 2013, Yu et al. 2014) and on perceived tourism impact studies (e.g. Andereck et al. 2005; Carneiro and Eusebio 2011) were used. Respondents had to answer the question using a 7-point Likert scale from 1 "completely disagree" to 7 "completely agree". To assess the social contact of residents with visitors, residents were invited, using a 7-point Likert type scale from 1 "never" to 7 "very frequently", to report the frequency of 14 types of interactions, identified based on a literature review (e.g. De Kadt 1979; Eusébio and Carneiro 2012; Kastenholz et al. 2015; Reisinger and Turner 1998). Residents were also invited to indicate their level of satisfaction, also using a 7-point Likert-type scale, from 1 "very unsatisfied" to 7 "very satisfied", with three issues: place of residence, contact with visitors and their level of QOL. Finally, the questionnaire ends with some questions related to the sociodemographic profile of residents (e.g. local of residence, duration of residence in the coastal community, job, gender, age, education level and economic activity status).

A quota sampling approach, based on gender and age, using data provided by the National Statistics Institute of Portugal (INE – *Instituto Nacional de Estatística*), was used in this research to identify the sample. Residents of the two coastal regions under analysis (*Costa Nova* and *Barra*) were contacted by qualified interviewers in the street, in their own houses or in commercial establishments. In order to analyse the validity and reliability of the questionnaire used, a pilot test was undertaken with 15 residents of the two coastal communities under analysis. Although 308 responses were obtained, a total of 288 questionnaires were considered valid for this research.

7.3.3 Data Analysis Methods

Two Principal Component Analyses (PCAs) were carried out to identify both the dimensions of the frequency of host-tourist interaction and of residents' perceptions regarding the impact of tourism on QOL. Moreover, in order to identify visitors with distinct perceptions concerning tourism impacts on QOL, a hierarchical cluster analysis was carried out based on the factor scores of the dimensions of tourism impacts on QOL previously identified in the PCA. Ward's method and the squared Euclidean distance were used in the scope of this cluster analysis. ANOVA, Kruskal-Wallis and Chi-square tests were used to compare the clusters identified, not only on the basis of segmentation adopted – perceptions regarding tourism impacts on QOL – but also on socioeconomic features: gender, age, education, economic activity status, job related to tourism, place of residence and duration of residence in the coastal community, and on frequency of interaction with visitors. Finally, the clusters were also compared in terms of their satisfaction with several issues – place of residence, QOL and contact with tourists. ANOVA was used to compare the clusters on quantitative variables while Chi-square tests were undertaken to compare the clusters on nominal or ordinal variables. Kruskal-Wallis tests were undertaken when the assumptions to carry out the ANOVA were not met. All the results presented in the following section correspond to statistical analyses that met all the required assumptions and that may, therefore, be considered valid.

7.4 Results and Discussion

7.4.1 Socioeconomic Profile

The sample is quite balanced regarding gender, including only slightly more men (52.1%) than women (47.9%) and the majority of the respondents are between 25 and 64 years old. There is a prevalence of people with basic education (53.5%), with less than one quarter (23.1%) having higher education. As far as economic activity status and job are concerned, there is a considerable diversity in the sample, since about half of the respondents (49.7%) were employed and half of them (51.7%) had a job related to tourism. Considering the place of residence, about 55.2% of the respondents live in *Barra* whereas 44.8% live in *Costa Nova*. A large part of the respondents reported living in the coastal community where they were interviewed for a considerable period – from 1 to 5 years (30.3%) or even for more than 5 years (62.0%).

7.4.2 Identification of the Clusters Based on Residents' Perceptions of Tourism Impact on their QOL

In order to identify the clusters' profile regarding the residents' perception of tourism impacts on their QOL, a PCA with varimax rotation of the items representing those perceptions was carried out first. Five factors emerged from this PCA (Table 7.1): (i) F1: *economic and sociocultural opportunities*, which encompass both economic and financial opportunities provided by tourism (e.g. having a job, having more financial resources, diversity of economic activities in the community) as well as sociocultural opportunities (e.g. socializing, having contact with people of different cultures, carrying out and participating in leisure and cultural activities); (ii) F2: *opportunities for living in a healthy and quiet environment*; (iii) F3: *heritage preservation and psychological benefits,* which includes the perception that tourism contributes to preserving natural and cultural heritage, but also the perception that tourism brings psychological benefits such as having positive feelings, considering life meaningful and being proud to live in a specific place; (iv) F4: *opportunities of access to supporting facilities*, including transport, health services and some kinds of commercial establishments; (v) F5: *changes in costs of living,* representing changes in the price of goods and services and, specifically, in the price of land, that occur as a result of tourism development. The values of Kaiser-Meyer-Olkin (KMO), Bartlett's test of sphericity, communalities, total variance explained and Cronbach's Alpha attest to the appropriateness of the PCA and the reliability of the factors that emerged from the PCA.

The residents perceive that tourism has a considerable impact on their overall QOL (5.25 in average on a scale from 1 "completely disagree" to 7 "completely agree") (Table 7.2). The impact is higher concerning opportunities of access to supporting facilities (5.50) and economic and sociocultural opportunities (5.42) and somewhat lower in the case of heritage preservation and generation of psychological benefits (5.28), changes in costs of living (5.00) and of opportunities for living in a healthy and quiet environment (4.86). These results attest to the important role that tourism may have in improving the QOL of the residents of tourism destinations either by enhancing the set of facilities and economic and financial opportunities in the community, or by contributing to preserving heritage, to improving the psychological state of the residents or by offering them a wider set of opportunities of socialization or of participation in leisure and cultural activities.

With the aim of identifying homogeneous groups of respondents regarding perceptions of impacts on their QOL, the factor scores of the PCA previously undertaken were used as input for a hierarchical cluster analysis. This analysis was performed using Ward's method and squared Euclidean distance. It was decided, based on the dendrogram and on the agglomeration schedule, to retain a three-cluster solution. ANOVA and Kruskal-Wallis tests were then used to compare the three clusters regarding the residents' perceptions of the impact of tourism on their QOL. Statistical significant differences were detected among the three clusters concerning the perceptions of tourism impacts on QOL. Cluster 1 (*The most benefited*)

Table 7.1 PCA of residents' perceptions of tourism impacts on their QOL

Tourism impacts on residents' QOL domains	Mean	Communality	F1: Economic and sociocultural opportunities	F2: Opportunities for living in healthy and quiet environment	F3: Heritage preservation and psychological benefits	F4: Opportunities of access to supporting facilities	F5: Changes in cost of living
Having more job opportunities	5.27	0.655	0.731				
Having opportunities of contact with people of different cultures	5.80	0.604	0.714				
Having opportunity to carry out recreational activities	5.30	0.658	0.703				
Having opportunities to get more financial resources	5.13	0.635	0.685				
Having opportunity to participate in cultural activities	5.21	0.651	0.679				
Feeling that this place is valued by others	5.66	0.648	0.656				
Having opportunities for socialising	5.53	0.690	0.633				
Having diversity of economic activities	5.49	0.671	0.628				
Living in an unpolluted environment	4.98	0.799		0.870			
Living in a quiet environment	4.64	0.792		0.806			
Having a healthy life	5.26	0.747		0.800			

Feeling safe	5.11	0.731		0.782			
Living without traffic jams and people	4.24	0.711		0.757			
Having positive feelings	5.19	0.790			0.765		
Feeling proud to live in this place	5.54	0.718			0.708		
Preserving natural environment	5.35	0.727			0.678		
Preserving cultural heritage	5.31	0.739			0.656		
Having a meaningful life	5.01	0.724			0.620		
Having access to good transport	5.52	0.799				0.800	
Having facilities to promote mobility/ accessibility	5.40	0.737				0.696	
Having access to health services	5.20	0.766				0.695	
Having restaurants and other commercial establishments	5.89	0.682				0.605	
Changes in prices of goods and services	4.83	0.753					0.801
Occurence of valuation of real estate and land	5.16	0.588					0.462
Eigenvalue			10.940	2.609	1.288	1.175	1.003
Comulative variance explained (%)			20.717	37.939	52.416	65.065	70.894
Cronbach's alpha			0.910	0.902	0.891	0.854	0.607
KMO = 0.927 Bartlett's test of sphericity = 4700.761 (p = 0.000)							

Table 7.2 Cluster profile regarding residents' perceptions of tourism impacts on their QOL (ANOVA and Kruskal-Wallis tests)

Profile of clusters – tourism impacts on residents' QOL domains	Total sample	Cluster 1 The most benefited	Cluster 2 The quite benefited	Cluster 3 The least benefited	ANOVA	Kruskal-Wallis test
	(N = 288) (100%)	(N = 99) (34.4%)	(N = 143) (49.7%)	(N = 46) (16.0%)	F (p-value)	Chi-square (p-value)
F1: Economic and sociocultural opportunities	**5.42**	**6.33**[c]	**5.34**[b]	**3.71**[a]	187.867 (0.000)	
Having more job opportunities	5.26	6.33	5.21	3.11		97.038 (0.000)
Having opportunities of contact with people of different cultures	5.79	6.52	5.67	4.63		74.705 (0.000)
Having opportunity to carry out recreational activities	5.28	6.25[c]	5.16[b]	3.52[a]	91.233 (0.000)	
Having opportunities to get more financial resources	5.13	6.18	5.02	3.28		106.658 (0.000)
Having opportunity to participate in cultural activities	5.20	6.11[c]	5.16[b]	3.33[a]	86.338 (0.000)	
Feeling that this place is valued by others	5.66	6.50	5.40	4.62		89.647 (0.000)
Having opportunities for socialising	5.52	6.35	5.52	3.76		100.712 (0.000)
Having diversity of economic activities	5.49	6.40	5.52	3.46		118.647 (0.000)
F2: Opportunities for living in healthy and quiet environment	**4.86**	**6.00**	**4.37**	**3.97**		104.131 (0.000)
Living in an unpolluted environment	5.00	6.08	4.42	4.46		63.702 (0.000)
Living in a quiet environment	4.67	6.06	4.06	3.61		99.777 (0.000)
Having a healthy life	5.25	6.24	4.92	4.17		66.423 (0.000)

(continued)

Table 7.2 (continued)

Profile of clusters – tourism impacts on residents' QOL domains	Total sample (N = 288) (100%)	Cluster 1 The most benefited (N = 99) (34.4%)	Cluster 2 The quite benefited (N = 143) (49.7%)	Cluster 3 The least benefited (N = 46) (16.0%)	ANOVA F (p-value)	Kruskal-Wallis test Chi-square (p-value)
Feeling safe	5.13	6.19	4.65	4.30		79.604 (0.000)
Living without traffic jams and people	4.26	5.39[b]	3.80[a]	3.282[a]	35.512 (0.000)	
F3: Heritage preservation and psychological benefits	**5.28**	**6.38**	**5.10**	**3.44**		155.016 (0.000)
Having positive feelings	5.19	6.43	4.89	3.43		118.121 (0.000)
Feeling proud to live in this place	5.54	6.55	5.37	3.87		97.912 (0.000)
Preserving natural environment	5.34	6.23	5.36	3.33		104.895 (0.000)
Preserving cultural heritage	5.31	6.22[c]	5.35[b]	3.26[a]	96.586 (0.000)	
Having a meaningful life	5.01	6.49	4.56	3.26		130.498 (0.000)
F4: Opportunities of access to supporting facilities	**5.50**	**6.45**	**5.50**	**3.45**		146.587 (0.000)
Having access to good transport	5.50	6.45	5.56	3.28		109.710 (0.000)
Having facilities to promote mobility/ accessibility	5.39	6.43	5.36	3.22		119.397 (0.000)
Having access to health services	5.19	6.46	5.05	2.93		114.058 (0.000)
Having restaurants and other commercial establishments	5.88	6.45	5.99	4.37		66.734 (0.000)
F5: Changes in cost of living	**5.00**	**6.11**	**4.73**	**3.47**		121.500 (0.000)
Changes in prices of goods and services	4.86	5.99	4.54	3.41		80.241 (0.000)
Occurence of valuation of real estate and land	5.16	6.22[c]	4.98[b]	3.52[a]	77.182 (0.000)	

(continued)

Table 7.2 (continued)

Profile of clusters – tourism impacts on residents' QOL domains	Total sample	Cluster 1 The most benefited	Cluster 2 The quite benefited	Cluster 3 The least benefited	ANOVA	Kruskal-Wallis test
	(N = 288) (100%)	(N = 99) (34.4%)	(N = 143) (49.7%)	(N = 46) (16.0%)	F (p-value)	Chi-square (p-value)
Overall QOL	**5.25**	**6.26**	**5.12**	**3.52**		95.243 (0.000)

Note:
[a]Homogeneous subset 1
[b]Homogeneous subset 2
[c]Homogeneous subset 3

represents 34.4% of the respondents, specifically the residents who consider that tourism has an highest impact on their overall QOL and on each of the domains of this QOL. Conversely, cluster 3 (*The least benefited*), corresponding to only 16% of the sample, includes the residents that recognise the lowest impact of tourism in their QOL (both on QOL in general and on its various domains). The largest cluster, encompassing almost half of the sample (49.7%) is, however, cluster 2 (*The quite benefited*), composed of residents who do not perceive such high impacts of tourism as the residents of cluster 1, but who recognise higher impacts of tourism on their QOL than cluster 3.

7.4.3 Profile of the Clusters

7.4.3.1 Socioeconomic Profile

Comparing the socioeconomic profile of the clusters identified (Table 7.3), no statistical significant differences regarding age, gender, education level and economic status were observed among the clusters. The results obtained also reveal no statistical differences among the clusters identified in terms of having a job related to tourism. However, there is a difference in terms of place of residence. Cluster 1 (*The most benefited*) includes a higher percentage of residents in *Barra* beach while cluster 2 (*The quite benefited*) includes a higher percentage of residents in the *Costa Nova* beach. These results reveal a different impact of tourism in the residents' QOL between *Barra* beach and *Costa Nova* beach, showing that the impacts of tourism on residents' QOL vary between tourism destinations and according to the level of tourism developed.

Table 7.3 Socioeconomic profile of the clusters identified (χ^2 test)

Profile of clusters – socio-demographic characteristics	Total sample (N = 288) (100%) % by column	Cluster 1 The most benefited (N = 99) (34.4%) % by column	Cluster 2 The quite benefited (N = 143) (49.7%) % by column	Cluster 3 The least benefited (N = 46) (16.0%) % by column	Chi-square Chi-square (p-value)
Place of residence					
Barra	44.8%	**53.5%**	45.5%	23.9%	11.195 (0.004)
Costa Nova	55.2%	46.5%	**54.5%**	76.1%	
Duration of residence in *Barra* and *Costa Nova*					
Less than 1 year	7.7%	14.1%	4.3%	4.4%	8.999 (0.061)
[1–5 years]	30.3%	26.3%	32.1%	33.3%	
More than 5 years	62.0%	59.6%	63.6%	62.2%	
Age					
[15–24]	17.4%	13.1%	17.5%	26.1%	7.702 (0.103)
[25–64]	66.7%	72.7%	67.8%	50.0%	
65 or older	16.0%	14.1%	14.7%	23.9%	
Gender					
Male	52.1%	46.5%	55.2%	54.3%	1.920 (0.383)
Female	47.9%	53.5%	44.8%	45.7%	
Education level (highest level)					
Basic education	53.5%	55.1%	51.7%	55.6%	1.251 (0.870)
Secondary education	23.4%	22.4%	23.1%	26.7%	
Higher education	23.1%	22.4%	25.2%	17.8%	
Economic activity status					
Employed	49.7%	53.5%	50.4%	39.1%	2.662 (0.264)
Other	50.3%	46.5%	49.6%	60.9%	
Job related to tourism					
Yes	51.7%	58.6%	44.4%	58.8%	2.976 (0.226)
No	48.3%	41.4%	55.6%	41.2%	

7.4.3.2 Interaction with Visitors

In order to facilitate the comparison and the characterization of the clusters identified regarding social contact with visitors, a PCA with varimax rotation of the 13 items used to measure the frequency of host-tourist interactions in several contexts was carried out (Table 7.4). Three factors emerged from this analysis: (i) F1: *close informal contacts*, contributing to a deeper mutual knowledge (e.g. sharing meals

Table 7.4 PCA of frequency of interaction with visitors

Social contact with visitors	Mean	Communality	F1: Close informal contacts	F2: Contacts in tourism attractions and facilities	F3: Formal contacts
Sharing meals with visitors	2.11	0.767	0.846		
Exchanging gifts with visitors	1.75	0.740	0.844		
Inviting visitors to one's home	2.03	0.739	0.836		
Practising sports with visitors	1.98	0.603	0.688		
Participating in parties with visitors	2.68	0.668	0.676		
Contact with visitors in other commercial establishments	4.09	0.630		0.773	
Contact with visitors on the beach	4.16	0.637		0.761	
Contact with visitors in discos, clubs and bars	3.31	0.586		0.718	
Contact with visitors in food and beverage establishments	4.71	0.598		0.654	
Contact with visitors in events	3.30	0.473		0.653	
Contact with visitors in the workplace	3.52	0.702			0.823
Interacting with visitors when providing goods and services	3.45	0.722			0.809
Providing visitors with information about the municipality	4.74	0.524			0.701
Eigenvalue			3.313	2.931	2.146
Cumulative variance explained (%)			25.487	48.035	64.545
Cronbach's alpha			0.880	0.806	0.737
KMO = 0.855 Bartlett's test of sphericity = 1701.979 (p = 0.000)					

with visitors, participating in parties with visitors); (ii) F2: *contacts in tourism attractions and facilities*, when visitors and hosts use the same places; and (iii) F3: *formal contacts,* when hosts interact with visitors due their professional activities and when residents provide information about the tourism destination. Results of this PCA show its appropriateness, given the *Kaiser-Meyer-Olkin* (KMO), communalities, total variance explained and Bartlett's test values as well as Cronbach's Alpha values, which indicate a suitable internal consistency of the three factors found.

The results presented in Table 7.5 show that close informal contacts occur with a very low frequency (2.14 in average on a scale from 1 "never" to 7 "very frequently") when compared to contact with visitors in tourism attractions and facilities (3.99) and formal contact (3.93). These results corroborate other studies, revealing that

Table 7.5 Cluster profile regarding frequency of interaction with visitors (ANOVA and Kruskal-Wallis tests)

Profile of clusters – Social contact with visitors	Total sample (N = 288) (100%)	Cluster 1 The most benefited (N = 99) (34.4%)	Cluster 2 The quite benefited (N = 143) (49.7%)	Cluster 3 The least benefited (N = 46) (16.0%)	ANOVA F (p-value)	Kruskal-Wallis test Chi-square (p-value)
F1: Close informal contacts	**2.14**	**2.55**	**1.90**	**1.99**		6.782 (0.034)
Sharing meals with visitors	2.13	2.45	1.89	2.17		3.016 (0.221)
Exchanging gifts with visitors	1.77	2.37	1.42	1.61		23.708 (0.000)
Inviting visitors to one's home	2.07	2.61	1.72	1.98		11.148 (0.004)
Practising sports with visitors	2.01	2.18	1.94	1.85		0.788 (0.674)
Participating in parties with visitors	2.72	3.15[b]	2.54[a,b]	2.35[a]	4.463 (0.012)	
F2: Contacts in tourism attractions and facilities	**3.99**	**4.32[b]**	**3.89[a]**	**3.58[a]**	5.346 (0.005)	
Contact with visitors in other commercial establishments	4.15	4.52	3.97	3.96		7.322 (0.026)
Contact with visitors on the beach	4.20	4.58	4.03	3.96	2.857 (0.059)	
Contact with visitors in discos, clubs and bars	3.41	3.72	3.38	2.83	3.011 (0.051)	
Contact with visitors in food and beverage establishments	4.82	5.13[b]	4.76[a,b]	4.33[a]	3.844 (0.023)	
Contact with visitors in events	3.34	3.64	3.30	2.80		5.902 (0.052)
F3: Formal contacts	**3.93**	**4.72[b]**	**3.57[a]**	**3.36[a]**	17.611 (0.000)	
Contact with visitors in the workplace	3.58	4.55[b]	3.15[a]	2.82[a]	13.069 (0.000)	

(continued)

Table 7.5 (continued)

		Cluster 1	Cluster 2	Cluster 3		
	Total sample	The most benefited	The quite benefited	The least benefited	ANOVA	Kruskal-Wallis test
Profile of clusters – Social contact with visitors	(N = 288) (100%)	(N = 99) (34.4%)	(N = 143) (49.7%)	(N = 46) (16.0%)	F (p-value)	Chi-square (p-value)
Interacting with visitors when providing goods and services	3.50	4.24[b]	3.18[a]	2.96[a]	8.605 (0.000)	
Providing visitors with information about the municipality	4.72	5.40[b]	4.37[a]	4.33[a]	12.486 (0.000)	

Note:
[a]Homogeneous subset 1
[b]Homogeneous subset 2

host-tourist interaction is frequently brief and superficial (e.g. Eusébio and Carneiro 2012; Kastenholz et al. 2013, Kastenholz et al. 2015; Reisinger 2009).

The results of the ANOVA and Kruskal-Wallis tests (Table 7.5) display statistical differences among the clusters identified regarding host-tourist interactions. The residents belonging to cluster 1 (*The most benefited*) interact more with visitors when compared with residents belonging to the other clusters, while residents of cluster 3 (the least benefited) revealed to have less interaction with visitors. These results clearly show the relevance of host-tourist interaction in the residents' perception of tourism impacts on their QOL. As Andereck and Nyaupane (2011) observed, the amount of interaction between residents and tourists influences the perception of residents regarding the impact of tourism on their QOL. Then, the residents who have more contact with tourists view tourism in a much more positive way than those who have less contact with tourists.

7.4.3.3 Satisfaction

Satisfaction and QOL are two strongly related constructs, as highlighted in the literature (e.g. Kim et al. 2013; Nawijn and Mitas 2012; Woo et al. 2015). Nawijn and Mitas' (2012) study reveals that perceived tourism impacts are associated with life satisfaction. Moreover, as aforementioned, a positive relationship between host-tourist interaction and the residents' perception of tourism impacts on their QOL is expectable (Andereck and Nyaupane 2011). In this line of thought a positive association is expected between residents' satisfaction with their place of residence, their QOL and their interaction with visitors and the perceptions of tourism impacts on their QOL. Results presented in Table 7.6 clearly reveal that the residents interviewed in this research are highly satisfied with their place of residence (M = 5.98,

Table 7.6 Cluster profile regarding satisfaction with several issues (ANOVA and Kruskal-Wallis tests)

Profile of clusters – Satisfaction with several issues	Total sample	Cluster 1 The most benefited	Cluster 2 The quite benefited	Cluster 3 The least benefited	ANOVA	Kruskal-Wallis test
	(N = 288) (100%)	(N = 99) (34.4%)	(N = 143) (49.7%)	(N = 46) (16.0%)	F (p-value)	Chi-square (p-value)
Satisfaction with their place of residence	5.98	6.24	5.93	5.54		10.673 (0.005)
Satisfaction with contact with tourists	5.34	6.00	5.06	4.83		36.786 (0.000)
Satisfaction with their QOL	5.81	6.21[b]	5.61[a]	5.58[a]	10.687 (0.000)	

Note:
[a]Homogeneous subset 1
[b]Homogeneous subset 2

on a scale from 1 "very unsatisfied" to 7 "very satisfied"), with their QOL (M = 5.81) and with their contact with tourists (M = 5.34). However, although globally all residents interviewed are very satisfied with their place of residence, their QOL and their contact with tourists, statistical differences among the clusters are observable. *The most benefited* residents (cluster 1) are also the most satisfied with all issues (place of residence, QOL and contact with tourists), while *the least benefited* residents (cluster 3) are the least satisfied with all issues analysed, the differences being higher regarding contact with tourists. These results reinforce the relevance of promoting satisfactory encounters between hosts and tourists in order to increase the positive impacts of tourism on residents' QOL.

7.5 Conclusions and Implications

This study highlights the relevance of tourism in improving residents' QOL, corroborating previous research (e.g. Andereck and Nyaupane 2011; Kim 2002; Kim et al. 2013; Liu 2015; Usher and Kerstetter 2014). Moreover, it also shows that tourism may have different impacts on the various QOL domains. Results reveal that in the coastal tourism destinations under analysis, tourism has a particularly important contribution to increasing access to supporting facilities and to improving economic and sociocultural conditions, reinforcing the findings of other studies (e.g. Andereck and Nyaupane 2011; Liu 2015; Usher and Kerstetter 2014). Furthermore, some heterogeneity regarding the perception of tourism impacts was observed in the communities analysed. Two of the three clusters identified recognise considerable positive effects of tourism on all the domains of QOL, while the other perceives very low impacts of tourism on overall QOL and on its various domains. However, this last cluster represents only a minority (16% of the sample). In the present study, in contrast to what happened in other studies (e.g. Andereck and Nyaupane 2011; Roehl 1999) no statistical significant differences were found regarding socioeconomic characteristics, with the exception of place of residence, corroborating the studies of Chancellor et al. (2011), Kim et al. (2013), Meng et al. (2010) and Roehl (1999), which show differences in the impact of tourism on the residents' QOL according to the place of residence. In line with previous research (e.g. Andereck and Nyaupane 2011; Moscardo et al. 2013) this chapter also points out the important influence of host-tourist interaction on residents' perception of tourism impact on their QOL.

Several theoretical and practical contributions of this research may be identified. Theoretically, this study has an important role in the QOL and tourism marketing literature through the following contributions: (i) the scale adopted in this research to measure the impact of tourism on residents' QOL of two Portuguese coastal tourism destinations may be used in other studies in this field; (ii) it adopts the residents' perceptions of tourism impact on several domains of QOL as a segmentation basis, showing the usefulness of this segmentation approach to design tourism development strategies; and (iii) it improves the knowledge concerning the relationship between two important constructs in the field of tourism marketing – host-tourist interaction and impact of tourism on residents' QOL. Additionally, this chapter also provides relevant practical contributions. First, it points out the need to develop specific marketing approaches to each of the clusters identified in the communities analysed. The managers of these tourism destinations should also involve local residents in the development of tourism policies and strategies. It is of utmost importance to promote awareness concerning the potential benefits of tourism to QOL among residents, especially among hosts who still perceive low impacts of tourism on their QOL (cluster 3 – *The least benefited*). Moreover, considering the central role of host-tourist interaction in improving residents' perceptions of tourism impacts on their QOL, marketing strategies should be developed in order to promote more frequent and rewarding encounters between residents and tourists, namely involving the host community in the supply of tourism products and promoting events designed for both residents and tourists, such as gastronomic and music festivals, where local community may have an active role.

The present study is limited to two Portuguese coastal communities. In order to extend research in this field, it would be important to replicate this kind of research in other coastal communities and in other kinds of tourism destinations. Moreover, as tourism development is a dynamic process and the residents' perception of tourism impacts varies across the time, it would be desirable to carry out longitudinal studies to assess changes in this kind of perceptions in the two coastal communities analysed. Furthermore, although host-tourist interaction has an important role in this field of research, studies that examine the role of other factors that may influence residents' perceptions of tourism impacts on their QOL (e.g. place attachment, tourism experience) should be undertaken. Finally, qualitative research should be stimulated in order to have a deeper knowledge of the residents' perceptions of tourism impacts on their QOL.

References

Andereck, K. L., & Nyaupane, G. P. (2011). Exploring the nature of tourism and quality of life perceptions among residents. *Journal of Travel Research, 50*(3), 248–260.

Andereck, K. L., Valentine, K. M., Knopf, R. C., & Vogt, C. A. (2005). Residents' perceptions of community tourism impacts. *Annals of Tourism Research, 32*(4), 1056–1076.

Andereck, K. L., Valentine, K. M., Vogt, C. A., & Knopf, R. C. (2007). A cross-cultural analysis of tourism and quality of life perceptions. *Journal of Sustainable Tourism, 15*(5), 483–502.

Andriotis, K. (2005). Community groups' perceptions of and preferences for tourism development: Evidence from Crete. *Journal of Hospitality and Tourism Research, 29*(1), 67–90.

Aref, F. (2011). The effects of tourism on quality of life: A case study of Shiraz, Iran. *Life Science Journal, 8*(2), 26–30.

Benckendorff, P., Edwards, D., Jurowski, C., Liburd, J. J., Miller, G., & Moscardo, G. (2009). Exploring the future of tourism and quality of life. *Tourism and Hospitality Research, 9*, 171–183.

Brida, J. G., Osti, L., & Barquet, A. (2010). Segmenting resident perceptions towards tourism – A cluster analysis with a multinomial logit model of a mountain community. *International Journal of Tourism Research, 12*(5), 591–602.

Brunt, P., & Courtney, P. (1999). Host perceptions of socio-cultural impacts. *Annals of Tourism Research, 26*(3), 493–515.

Butler, R. W. (2006). The concept of a tourist area cycle of evolution: Implications for management of resources. In R. W. Butler (Ed.), *The tourism area life cycle vol. 1: Applications and modifications* (pp. 3–12). Clevedon: Channel View publications.

Carneiro, M. J., & Eusébio, C. (2011). Hosts' perceptions of tourism impact in an urban area – A cluster analysis. In M. Kozak & N. Kozak (Eds.), *Sustainability of tourism: Cultural and environmental perspectives* (pp. 290–313). Newcastle: Cambridge Scholars Publisher.

Chancellor, C., Yu, C.-P. S., & Cole, S. T. (2011). Exploring quality of life perceptions in rural Midwestern (USA) communities: An application of the core–periphery concept in a tourism development context. *International Journal of Tourism Research, 13*, 496–507.

Chhabra, D., & Gursoy, D. (2009). Life dynamism explorations on perceived quality of life and social exchange paradigms in casino settings. *Leisure Sciences, 31*, 136–157.

De Kadt, E. (1979). *Tourism: Passport to development? Perspectives on the social and cultural effects of tourism in developing countries*. New York: Oxford University Press.

Dolnicar, S., Lazarevski, K., & Yanamandram, V. (2013). Quality of life and tourism: A conceptual framework and novel segmentation base. *Journal of Business Research., 66*, 724–729.

Eusébio, C. A., & Carneiro, M. J. A. (2012). Determinants of tourist–host interactions: An analysis of the university student market. *Journal of Quality Assurance in Hospitality & Tourism, 13*(2), 123–151.

Eusébio, C., & Carneiro, M. J. (2014). The impact of tourism on quality of life: A segmentation analysis of the youth market. *Tourism Analysis, 19*(6), 741–757.

Fredline, L., Deery, M., & Jago, L. (2013). A longitudinal study of the impacts of an annual event on local residents. *Tourism Planning and Development, 10*(4), 416–432.

Gu, M., & Wong, P. P. (2016). Residents' perception of tourism impacts: a case study of homestay operators in Dachangshan Dao, North-East China. Tourism Geographies, 8(3), 253–273.

Guo, Y., Kim, S., & Chen, Y. (2014). Shanghai residents' perceptions of tourism impacts and quality of life. *Journal of China Tourism Research, 10*(2), 142–164.

Haley, A., Snaith, T., & Miller, G. (2005). The social impacts of tourism: A case study of Bath UK. *Annals of Tourism Research, 32*(3), 503–668.

INE. (2012). *Censos 2011 – Resultados Definitivos – Centro*. Lisbon: INE.

INE. (2014). *Anuário Estatístico da Região Centro – 2013*. Lisbon: INE.

Jeon, M. M., Kang, M., & Desmarais, E. (2016). Residents' perceived quality of life in a cultural-heritage tourism destination. *Applied Research Quality Life, 11*, 105–123. https://doi.org/10.1007/s11482-014-9357-8.

Jurowski, C., & Brown, D. O. (2001). A comparison of the views of involved versus noninvolved citizens on quality of life and tourism development issues. *Journal of Hospitality & Tourism Research, 25*(4), 355–370.

Kastenholz, E., Carneiro, M. J., Eusébio, C., & Figueiredo, E. (2013). Host-guest relationships in rural tourism: Evidence from two Portuguese villages. *Anatolia, 24*(3), 367–380.

Kastenholz, E., Carneiro, M. J., & Eusébio, C. (2015). Diverse socializing patterns in rural tourist experiences – A segmentation analysis. *Current Issues in Tourism., 21*, 401–421. https://doi.org/10.1080/13683500.2015.1087477.

Khizindar, T. M. (2012). Effects of tourism on residents' quality of life in Saudi Arabia: An empirical study. *Journal of Hospitality Marketing and Management, 21*, 617–637.

Kim, K. (2002). *The effects of tourism impacts upon quality of life of residents in the community.* Dissertation submitted to the Faculty of the Virginia Polytechnic Institute and State University.

Kim, K., Uysal, M., & Sirgy, M. J. (2013). How does tourism in a community impact the quality of life of community residents? *Tourism Management, 36*, 527–540.

Kotler, P., Armstrong, G., Saunders, J., & Wong, V. (1999). *Principles of marketing* (2nd European edition). London: Prentice Hall.

Liu, Y.-D. (2015). Event and quality of life: A case study of Liverpool as the 2008 European capital of culture. *Applied Research Quality Life., 11*, 707–721. https://doi.org/10.1007/s11482-015-9391-1.

Mai, N. T. T., Rahtz, D. R., & Shultz, C. J., II. (2014). Tourism as catalyst for quality of life in transitioning subsistence market places: Perspectives from Ha Long, Vietnam. *Journal of Macromarketing, 34*(1), 28–44.

Matarrita-Cascante, D. (2010). Changing communities, community satisfaction, and quality of life: A view of multiple perceived indicators. *Social Indicators Research, 98*, 105–127.

Meng, F., Li, X., & Uysal, M. (2010). Tourism development and regional quality of life: The case of China. *Journal of China Tourism Research, 6*(2), 164–182.

Moscardo, G. (2009). Tourism and quality of life: Towards a more critical approach. *Tourism and Hospitality Research, 9*(2), 159–170.

Moscardo, G., Konovalov, E., Murphy, L., & McGehee, N. (2013). Mobilities, community well-being and sustainable tourism. *Journal of Sustainable Tourism, 21*(4), 532–556.

Nawijn, J., & Mitas, O. (2012). Resident attitudes to tourism and their effect on subjective well-being: The case of Palma de Mallorca. *Journal of Travel Research, 51*(5), 531–541.

Polonsky, M., Hall, J., Vieceli, J., Atay, L., Akdemir, A., & Marangoz, M. (2013). Using strategic philanthropy to improve heritage tourist sites on the Gallipoli Peninsula, Turkey: Community perceptions of changing quality of life and of the sponsoring organization. *Journal of Sustainable Tourism, 21*(3), 376–395.

Reisinger, Y. (2009). *International tourism: Cultures and behavior.* Oxford: Butterworth Heinemann.

Reisinger, Y., & Turner, L. (1998). Cultural differences between Mandarin-speaking tourists and Australian hosts and their impact on cross-cultural tourist-host interaction. *Journal of Business Research, 42*(2), 175–187.

Reisinger, Y., & Turner, L. W. (2002). Cultural differences between Asian tourist markets and Australian hosts: Part 2. *Journal of Travel Research, 40*(4), 374–384.

Roehl, W. S. (1999). Quality of life issues in a casino destination. *Journal of Business Research, 44*(3), 223–229.

Sharpley, R. (2014). Host perceptions of tourism: A review of the research. *Tourism Management, 42*, 37–49.

Sinclair-Maragh, G., Gursoy, D., & Vieregge, M. (2015). Residents' perceptions toward tourism development: A factor-cluster approach. *Journal of Destination Marketing and Management, 4*(1), 36–45.

Tucker, H. (2003). Host-guest relationship and its implications in rural tourism. In D. L. Roberts & M. Mitchell (Eds.), *New directions in rural tourism* (pp. 80–89). Aldershot: Ashgate.

Turismo Centro de Portugal. (2014). http://www.visitcentrodeportugal.com.pt/costa-nova/

Usher, L. E., & Kerstetter, D. (2014). Residents' perceptions of quality of life in a surf tourism destination: A case study of Las Salinas, Nicaragua. *Progress in Development Studies, 14*(4), 321–333.

Uysal, M., Sirgy, M. J., Woo, E., & Kim, H. (2015). Quality of life (QOL) and well-being research in tourism. *Tourism Management, 53*, 244–261. https://doi.org/10.1016/j.tourman.2015.07.013.

Woo, E., Kim, H., & Uysal, M. (2015). Life satisfaction and support for tourism development. *Annals of Tourism Research, 50*, 84–97.

Yu, C.-P., Cole, S. T., & Chancellor, C. (2014). Assessing community quality of life in the context of tourism development. *Applied Research Quality Life, 11*, 147–162. https://doi.org/10.1007/s11482-014-9359-6.

Chapter 8
Can Personal Values Modulate the Perception of Tourism Impacts by Local Population?: Testing for the Role of Product Identity in a Mining Tourism Destination

Andrés Artal-Tur, Pilar Jiménez-Medina, and Noelia Sánchez-Casado

Abstract Tourism industry presents a remarkable development, with more than 1185 million international travels in 2016. This situation poses enormous pressure on world tourism destinations. The impact of tourist activities is increasingly perceived as a negative question by local residents, affecting their quality of life. In this context, the present chapter investigates how linkages between personal values and tourism development can modulate the perception of tourism impacts by local residents. Social and physical attributes of a given place help to conform the sense of being of the local population. This sense is known as place identity in literature. Mining heritage destinations deeply root on that sense while developing their tourism activities. In the analysis of the mining heritage destination of La Unión in Spain, we employ structural equations modelling in testing for this main research hypothesis. Results of the investigation show that place/product identity helps to modulate the perceptions of tourism impacts by residents. Main effects are found to arise on attitudes toward socio-cultural impacts, where identity issues seem to exert the highest influence, increasing the quality of life standards of local population. In this regard, research findings recommend building on local identity issues to increase the level of sustainability of tourism destinations.

Keywords Product identity · Mining destination · Tourism impacts · Socio-cultural dimension · SEM modelling

A. Artal-Tur (✉) · P. Jiménez-Medina · N. Sánchez-Casado
Technical University of Cartagena (UPCT), Cartagena, Spain
e-mail: Andres.artal@upct.es

A. M. Campón-Cerro et al. (eds.), *Best Practices in Hospitality and Tourism Marketing and Management*, Applying Quality of Life Research,
https://doi.org/10.1007/978-3-319-91692-7_8

8.1 Introduction

At the edge of the twenty-first century tourism has become a global industry. More than 1185 million people travelled in 2016, and 43 million people are expected to enter the market every year in 2015–2030 (UNWTO 2016). This situation leads to a boost of new destinations all around the world. Given the global scale reached by the industry, the literature has started to explore the effects of tourism on local population, as a pivotal dimension conforming the sustainability of destinations (Boley and McGehee 2014; Eligh et al. 2002). The impact of tourism at destinations is undeniable, either on natural resources, level of prices, or quality of life standards (Uysal et al. 2016). In the initial stages of the destination life cycle, tourism is perceived as a desirable activity, providing new incomes, jobs and welfare (Butler 2006). However, while tourism develops, life conditions of local population change, and some negative externalities arise (Kim et al. 2013).

Inside this research field, some authors analyse how local population perceives the impact of tourism, hence influencing their support for such activities (Andereck et al. 2005). Departing from the traditional cost-benefit analysis in Social Exchange Theory, new contributions investigate how personal values of people arising from ties with geographical places could influence their perceptions and attitudes toward tourism (Nunkoo and Gursoy 2012). Three main concepts emerge in this area: place attachment, place image and place identity. Original contributions focused on place attachment. The concept was primarily investigated in terms of how it affects the experience of visitors at destinations. In particular, the literature focused on the emotional bonds developed by tourists with a particular destination after a repeating pattern of holidays (Lewicka 2011). Further, the focus moved towards the resident population and related perceptions of tourism impacts. In both cases, place attachment was found to be conforming personal perceptions regarding tourism activities (Cui and Ryan 2011). Literature then moved to study the more general concept of place image.

Place image is another important construct usually defined in the literature as "destination image". Definition of place image includes the beliefs, ideas and impressions that people hold of a place, the individual's perception of particular place attributes (hospitality, quality of supplies, landscape, branding, accessibility), further from their psychological involvement linked to the place attachment (Gallarza et al. 2002). Tourists rely on place image when choosing a destination, while residents evaluate impacts of tourism according to how it is affecting the image of the place they live in (Henkel et al. 2006). Place image usually evolves with time, given image rebuilding and rebranding processes developed by stakeholders to renew tourism destinations (Reiser and Crispin 2009). General findings have been showing that place/destination image influences both the perception of visitors and those of residents on the impacts and support for tourism (Ramkissoon and Nunkoo 2011; Stylidis et al. 2014).

Finally, more recent studies focus on the role of place identity in shaping the perception of tourism by residents (Gu and Ryan 2008; Wang and Chen 2015). The development of a tourism destination not always implies an improvement of the social welfare. In fact both issues can be in contradiction in early stages of development, affecting the life-style of local residents (Andereck and Vogt 2000). Nowadays, with the spread of sustainable practices, some destinations start to build on local identity issues when promoting tourism development. This strategy helps to align the interest of entrepreneurs with those of the population, providing higher levels of support for tourism (Korpela 1989; Nunkoo and Gursoy 2012).

In this setting, the case of mining tourism provides a good laboratory for testing the role of personal values and identity issues in influencing attitudes and behaviour regarding tourism activities. Locations where mining industry has been settled for a long times how good memories of this process (Vargas-Sánchez et al. 2009). When building mining heritage destinations, the linkages between local identity and tourism development could ensure higher levels of sustainability and support for tourism. In these places, identity issues are expected to modulate the perception of tourism impacts by residents too (Ruiz-Ballesteros and Hernández-Ramírez 2007).

The present chapter aims to explore those issues by focusing in the case of La Unión, Spain. This is a mining heritage tourism destination historically linked to the mining industry. Building on survey data, we conduct a Structural Equation Modelling(SEM) exercise testing if the heritage cultural setting, where identity issues are very present, exert a modulating effect on perceptions and attitudes of residents towards tourism impacts as a mediating effect between personal values and support for tourism at destination. In particular we are interested in better understanding how social and local identity in specific contexts drive the linkages between personal values, local attitudes and behavioural intents on tourism developments, given the lack of a clear result in previous literature regarding this issue. The rest of the chapter is organised as follows: In Sect. 8.2, we review the literature relating identity issues, tourism impacts and support. In Sect. 8.3 we analyse the surge of identity issues at mining destinations. In Sect. 8.4 we implement the SEM model and discuss main findings of the investigation. Section 8.5 concludes and provides some policy recommendations.

8.2 Place Identity, Tourism Impacts and Support for Tourism

Social identity has a symbolic dimension of representing reality. It helps to guide and stimulate social action (Bauman 2004). Strong collective identities linked to life spaces give rise to a solid sense of belonging, conforming what is known as place identity (Augé 1992; Gu and Ryan 2008). This is a complex concept including several dimensions of identity as self-steem, continuity, distinctiveness, or self-efficacy as shown by Breakwell (1992). Sometimes, the meaning of community becomes a decisive factor for local development, as in the case of heritage tourism projects (Bessière 1998).

In the case of the mining tourism, several authors have explored the role played by identity issues. Cohen (1988) studies how tourism reinforces the local identity, while Balcar and Pearce (1996) describe the exploitation of mining resources and heritage in New Zealand as a tourism product. They observe that mining tourism is closely related to preserve the historical richness and identity of local populations, with less relevance of the economic dimension. The strong role of local identities in the surge of mining and industrial tourism heritage is widely discussed in Edwards and Llurdés (1996). Ruiz-Ballesteros and Hernández-Ramírez (2007) also show how heritage tourism builds on identity as a central element.

8.2.1 Place Identity, Tourism Impacts and Host Perceptions

The impact of tourism activities on destinations has been extensively reviewed since the early contributions of Turner and Ash (1975) and Young (1973). The cost-benefit method has been the usual framework in this type of analysis (Telfer and Sharpley 2008). Residents will support tourism if economic benefits compensate for their social and environmental impacts (Nepal 2008). This is the central hypothesis in the Social Exchange Theory (SET) (Andereck et al. 2005).

Following the literature, the type of tourism impacts can be categorized as economic, social and environmental (Almeida-García et al. 2016; Wall and Mathieson 2006). Other authors introduce the positive or negative character of impacts (Gursoy and Rutherford 2004; Lee et al. 2010). In this framework, the type of destination (urban or rural), visitors (involved or not with the destination), and tourism offer (seaside or cultural) appear to be important in conforming the perception or attitudes of residents regarding tourism (Lundberg 2017; Rasoolimanesh et al. 2017; Stoeckl et al. 2006).

Sharpley (2014) surveys the advances in host perception of tourism impacts, arriving to several conclusions: First, he states the limited scope of this type of analysis out of some well-known developed destinations. Second, he finds that perception of impacts depend at some extent on the relationship of residents with tourism activities (engaged or not in tourism business), the profile of the resident (level of income, education) and their location inside the town (close or away from the city centre) (Andriotis and Vaughan 2003). Third, the author also points to recent efforts in developing new tools when dealing with impact perceptions, including larger sets of indicators for measuring impacts (Vargas-Sánchez et al. 2011).

As Choi and Murray (2010) point out, what is important in the case of tourism is that residents' attitudes appear to be influenced by whether the benefits reach the community. In this way, when tourism development relies on place identity, personal values get involved in the process, and local population can more directly feel the social benefits provided by tourism(McCool and Martin 1994). As a result, the imaginary of residents is reinforced by the development of new products building on identity issues, and the making of a destination becomes a singular process (Bott et al. 2003). Developing tourism experiences that build on place identity components could then improve the local support on those activities, increasing the sustainability of destinations (McGehee and Andereck 2004). In this case, identity would be acting as a reference to guide personal behaviour of people, with identity theory helping to explain how individuals make choices and conduct their behaviour (Stets and Biga 2003).

In this context, place identity could have an influence in the perceptions and attitudes of residents regarding tourism impacts. Positive place identity occurs when the social and physical resources within a local environment are convenient to satisfy the needs and aspirations of residents (Shumaker and Taylor 1983). If self-verification exists, place identity would be driving attitudes of residents, leading to actions that reinforce their connection to social life and coexistence (McCool and Martin 1994). Place identity is then determined at first stage by physical matters and more deeply by the linkages and meaning between people and places (Bott et al. 2003).

Literature on the relationship between place identity and tourism impacts is still scarce, including the following contributions. The pioneer investigation by Gu and Ryan (2008) observe that the extension of tourism leads to a negative impact on the conservation of heritage when studying a particular cultural place in Beijing, China. Development could even restrain traditional activities on the street because of the extension of tourism itself. However, these findings appear to be dependent on the age of the respondent and his engagement with tourism business, as well as on the role played by the state in promoting new tourism activities. Further, Nunkoo and Gursoy (2012) find empirical support of three types of identity, namely environmental, occupational and gender identity, on support for tourism, but limited capacity in shaping perceptions of tourism impacts by residents in an island context (Mauritius Island). In fact, occupational identity, that is, people working in traditional jobs, appear to be more afraid of the negative impacts of tourism, and how this industry can change their traditional life. Gender identity not appears to be shaping perception of positive impacts, but of negative ones, while environmental identity remains non-significant in influencing positive or negative attitudes towards tourism impacts. One interesting result of this research is that attitudes towards tourism impacts appear not to be sufficient in conforming resident's support for tourism (behaviour), although this could be a particular outcome depending on the specific conditions of the case study. In general, these authors find that more salient and prominent identities influence behaviour to a larger extent than second-order identity treats. As a result, identity seems to influence local behaviour in particular contexts where both issues reinforce each other. The link between attitudes towards tourism impact and support is not always a direct one, with identity issues playing the prominent role in this setting. Research findings would be pointing to a good complementarity between Social Exchange and Identity theories in explaining attitudes towards tourism impacts by local population.

In sum, destinations are always complex environments, with many dimensions at play in terms of identity issues and attitudes towards tourism. Different environments could provide dissimilar results on the link between place identity and impact perceptions. This type of studies would then require controlled environments where hypotheses of the model can be better tested. A mining heritage destination provides a suitable scenario where social and place identity would be susceptible to influence local perceptions of tourism development and related impacts (Ruiz-Ballesteros and Hernández-Ramírez 2007).

8.2.2 Place Identity and Local Support for Tourism

As we have seen, place identity not always influences the perception of tourism impacts by local residents. This outcome will depend on the specific features of the destination and tourism product themselves. One step beyond, some authors investigate the mediating effect that local perception of tourism impacts could exert on the relationship between place identity and support for tourism. Wang and Chen (2015) provide updated evidence on this issue for the case of Indianapolis (USA). They find a mediating effect of modulated perceptions on support for tourism of residents. However, this effect appears to be significant only for two components of place identity, self-steem and self-efficacy, and not for the remaining two, distinctiveness and continuity. In an urban setting, local attitudes on tourism impact would be mediating between place identity sense and support for tourism. However, the relationship between attitudes to impacts and identity issues appear to be significant only partially. In the case of (Mauritius) Island, Nunkoo and Gursoy (2012) find identity to promote support for tourism, although mainly for the dimensions strictly linked and affected by tourism development, such as occupational identity. An interesting finding shows however that identity not always affects attitudes towards tourism impacts.

Additional studies find an influence of a number of variables on the local support for tourism, including the level of development, or position in the life-cycle, of the destination (Vargas-Sánchez et al. 2015), perceived personal benefits and general economic conditions promoted by tourism activities (Alector-Ribeiro et al. 2017), capacity of tourism in preserving local culture (Besculides et al. 2002), relationship with quality of life standards (Liang and Hui 2016), and the rural vs urban character of the destination (Rasoolimanesh et al. 2017).

After this literature review, the next section of the chapter conducts an empirical exercise for a mining heritage destination with deep local identity issues. The main objective is testing for the role that personal values could exert in modulating people attitudes and behaviour towards tourism in line with this emerging literature.

8.3 Mining Heritage Tourism and Place Identity

The mining activity is present in Europe since times of the Roman Empire. Mining heritage tourism is a recent concept appearing in former industrial locations where the mining industry was abandoned, receiving around 30 million visits in 2014 in the European Union. The development of a tourism product based in the past mining history implies the interpretation, restoration and commoditisation of the mining resources (Edwards and Llurdés 1996).

Nowadays, heritage sites exploiting mining tourism show a great number of attractions, including museums, underground mining tours, or theme parks among others (Conllin and Jonliffe 2011). This type of heritage tourism and recreations connects with the idiosyncrasy of the local community. More than five hundred old mining exploitations have become mining museums, natural protected areas, and geoparks at the EU level, with some mining landscapes being considered as part of the human heritage, joining the list of the UNESCO World Heritage sites (Peña 2002).

In Spain, the mining heritage tourism has traditionally received little consideration by institutions, more interested in sun-and-sand tourism. The development of mining tourism has usually faced a number of impediments linked to the idiosyncrasy of the product and those of the surrounding locations. Because of the economic crisis of the 1970s, many mining areas in Spain were closing their industrial facilities, with an impact in the economy of the traditional mining regions. However, a variety of elements, tangible and intangible, remained in these locations, showing a strong link to the mining history of the place, and helping to develop cultural and heritage tourism products (Ruiz-Ballesteros and Hernández-Ramírez 2007).

8.3.1 Developing a Mining Heritage Tourism Product in La Unión, Spain

The municipality of La Unión is located at the Southeast of Spain in the Region of Murcia, in the Mediterranean coast. The local history in terms of mining resources and industry goes back to the Iberian period, reaching a significant development in times of the Roman Empire with the silver mines that brought great prosperity to the area. More recently, the mid-nineteenth century assisted to a rebirth of the mining industry, gaining ascendancy along the next century with the introduction of new techniques of mineral extraction and the foreign capital entrances (Conesa 2010). The development of La Unión as a mining tourism destination started in the 1990s with new regulations seeking to protect the mining heritage. The whole mountain-range area was declared a Cultural Interest Resource named as an Heritage Site. Mining machinery, underground galleries, open pits, refining centres, and smelters were present in more than the one hundred sites (Manteca and Berrocal 1997). The construction of the Mining Park of La Unión, with more than 50,000 $m^2$of extension, shows the whole process of the mining industry, since the extraction of the mineral to the final melting process. It also includes a restored mine with more than 4000 $m^2$of galleries open to tourists, a mining-train taking people around heritage sites surrounding, and an interpretation centre (see Fig. 8.1).

The Mining Park of La Unión was launched on July 2011, managed by the Sierra Minera Foundation including the local society, business sector, and local government. The Mining Park is present on the Internet, resulting in a considerable increase

Fig. 8.1 Map of the Mining Park in La Unión, Murcia, Spain. (Source: Mining Park, La Unión, Spain)

in visitors from 10,000 visitors in 2011, to more than 50,000 in 2014. In 2015, new mine sites, some of them containing well-conserved rests of the pre-historical civilizations in the area, are being explored as additional tourism resources in La Unión.

Other events and tourism resources integrate this monographic tourism product. The city exhibits a mining heritage museum, and the Festival del Cante de Las Minas, a flamenco music event receiving more than 50,000 international visits in 2014. The highly renowned tradition of this festival as a flamenco show, dating from 1961, and the fact that some of the concerts take place inside the mining environment, reinforces the mining product identity of La Unión.

8.3.2 *Hypotheses Development and Measures of Constructs in the Model*

In order to test the relationships between place identity, attitudes on tourism impacts, and support, in this section we develop the hypotheses of the model. According to literature, tourism impacts can be classified into economic, socio-cultural and environmental ones (see Almeida-García et al. 2016 for a review). In our questionnaire we employ measures of all three type of impacts following the literature. Economic impacts include measures of the perceptions of residents on the capacity of Mining Heritage Tourism (MHT) in generating economic revenues, employment, attracting investments and generate new expenditures in the tourism related and other local services. These are traditional measures in the literature (Almeida-García et al. 2016; Andereck and Vogt 2000; Andriotis and Vaughan 2003). Regarding socio-cultural impacts we include measures capturing infrastructure, socio-cultural spirit, and contribution of tourism to improve educational endowments of residents, widening the local offer, as well as the heritage and cultural supplies. Measures are similar to those of previous studies in literature (Aguiló et al. 2004; Besculides et al. 2002; Bujosa and Rosselló 2007). Environmental impacts include measures of conservation of plants and wildlife, recovering degraded areas and reducing levels of pollution in the area. Measures are also from literature (Andereck and Nyaupane 2011; Dyer et al. 2007; Jurowski and Gursoy 2004). Tourism impacts are measured in positive terms, given that La Unión is still an emerging destination, and we do not expect to find local perceptions of negative impacts in such an initial stage of the destination life-cycle (Almeida-García et al. 2016; Nunkoo and Gursoy 2012; Vargas-Sánchez et al. 2009, 2011).

The study seeks to analyse the relationship between place identity issues and attitudes of local population towards tourism impacts. However, we focus on an identity concept that we define as "product identity", that mainly seeks to test for the capacity of Mining Heritage Tourism to preserve the mining tradition in the city, revitalise the mining culture and heritage and, in general, to represent, show and share the mining spirit of the village with tourists and visitors. In our case, the construct of product identity we employ in the investigation is closely related to those of previous studies showing the concerns of local population in regards to tourism being able of preserving the local culture (Gu and Ryan 2008; Nunkoo and Gursoy 2012), reinforcing that (Besculides et al. 2002), and showing that cultural and historical richness to visitors from all over the world. In this way, our identity measure would be closer to the treats of self-esteem (Korpela 1989; Uzzell 1995) and continuity (Taylor 2010; Ujang 2010) in Breakwell's terminology. The three first hypotheses of the model would be testing for the capacity of product identity to influence local attitudes towards the three types of tourism impacts in the mining heritage city of La Unión, Spain. Hypotheses 1, 2 and 3 then are defined as follows:

H1: Product identity influences the perception and attitudes of residents toward economic tourism impacts.

H2: Product identity influences the perception and attitudes of residents toward socio-cultural tourism impacts.

H3: Product identity influences the perception and attitudes of residents toward environmental tourism impacts.

Further on, the model will test for the effects of modulated impacts on support for tourism in a product identity framework. As shown by literature review, this is not a straightforward result in this type of exercises. Characteristics of the context and type of identity issues use to drive these relationships, as noted in Sect. 8.2. In the mining heritage tourism context we expect to find a positive relationship between these constructs of the model. Particularly, support for tourism is measured in our model as a positive view of local population on the use of land and resources for a miming heritage tourism development taking place in the city, as well as a positive effect of tourism on increasing the quality of life of resident population as noted in the questionnaire. These will be the main dimensions that results on support for tourism will provide in our analysis. Contextual framework on the expected relationships between local attitudes and support for tourism are widely reviewed in Sect. 8.2, as well as for the linkages between place/product identity and behavioural actions (support) on tourism from resident population. In this setting, we propose the following hypotheses of the model, namely H4, H5 and H6:

H4: Attitudes of residents toward economic tourism impact influences their support for tourism.

H5: Attitudes of residents toward socio-cultural tourism impact influences their behavioural intent on supporting tourism.

H6: Attitudes of residents toward environmental tourism impact influences their behavioural intent on supporting tourism.

Finally, following pioneer study of Wang and Chen (2015), we will test for the linkage between product identity on support for tourism mediated by local attitudes or perceptions on tourism impacts. This is an important hypothesis of the model, given that should hardly rely on the contextual framework defined for social and place identity. In fact, identity issues arising in the model become pivotal for the significance of such mediating effects, as shown by literature (see for example Nunkoo and Gursoy 2012). In this way H7 becomes:

H7: Product identity influences the support for tourism of residents through the mediating effect of the perception and attitudes of residents toward tourism impacts.[1]

The conceptual model is then defined in Fig. 8.2.

In the following sections we test for the significance of these seven research hypotheses.

[1] See Sect. 8.5.3 for results and discussion of test on H7.

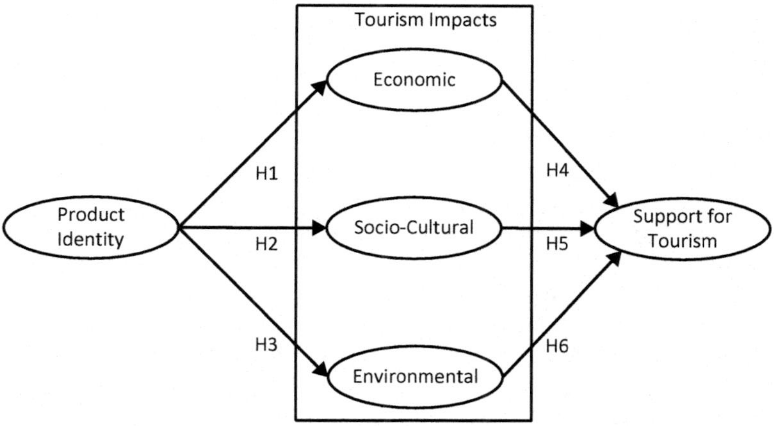

Fig. 8.2 Conceptual model

8.4 Method

As shown in questionnaire in the Appendix, we employ a number of 21 indicators in order to approach the constructs of the model, including product identity, perception of impact of tourism activities, and support for tourism development. Indicators were collected through a questionnaire with a seven-point scale as usual in the literature, ranging from strongly disagree (1) to strongly agree (7) (see Appendix).

8.4.1 Data Collection and Sample

The surveying fieldwork was carried out along May and June 2014, when tourism activity was more intense, as a way of ensuring that residents were more conscious of the impact of tourism in their daily lives, given that La Unión is close to the seaside and the bulk of visits are concentrated in spring and summertime. Student research assistants from the Technical University of Cartagena, a neighbouring town of La Unión, collected survey data, and after depuration we count on a number of 222 usable instruments. It was a random data collection process where residents were surveyed all along the town. Profile of respondents include a share of 46% of females in the full sample, with a mean age of 45 years old (17% up to 25 years old, 46% between 25 and 50 years old, and 34% older than 50 years), level of studies of secondary (40%) and post-secondary education (20%), income level of up to €1000 per month (50%), €1000–1500 per month (30%), and higher than €1500 per month (20%), and a direct relationship to tourism-related business for the 15% of the sample. The sample reflects consistently the characteristics of the whole population in La Unión, making 19,000 inhabitants, according to the last 2011 National Population Census (INE 2012). Level of income of the town is under the average of the whole

Region of Murcia, where it is located, and level of studies of residents is slightly below that average too.

8.4.2 Data Analysis

Data analysis is conducted with Partial Least Squares (PLS) in the framework of the Structural Equations Modeling (SEM) by using Smart PLS software (Ringle et al. 2014). PLS was chosen because is a less demanding method in terms of normality of distributions and the unlikelihood of non-convergent solutions (Chin et al. 2003). We decide to follow a two-step procedure in the empirical analysis. The first step includes the assessment of the measurement model, allowing the relationships between the observable variables and theoretical concepts to be specified. In the second step, the structural model is evaluated, testing for the significance of the research hypotheses (Hair et al. 2013).

8.5 Results

8.5.1 Measurement Model

The assessment of the measurement model is performed through the analysis of reliability and validity for reflective constructs (Henseler et al. 2009). First, individual item reliability is assessed by examining the factor loadings with their respective construct (λ). Second, construct reliability is assessed using the composite reliability score (CR) and Cronbach's Alpha (α). Results in Table 8.1 indicate that all items are reliable, with all factor loadings higher than 0.70 (Hair et al. 2013). Moreover, constructs are reliable because their CR and CA values are also above 0.70 levels. Convergent validity of the scales is evaluated by average variance extracted (AVE), exceeding 0.50 for all constructs (Table 8.1).

To assess the discriminant validity according to Fornell and Larcker (1981), the square root of the AVE (diagonal in Table 8.2) must be compared with the squared correlations between paired constructs (the off-diagonal elements). All constructs appear to be statistically different from the other, according to Table 8.2.

According to Henseler et al. (2015), discriminant validity is accepted, as HTMT ratio not exceeds 0.85–1 (Table 8.3).

However, reliability and validity check is not appropriate to assess formative constructs as we have approached *support for tourism* (Peng and Lai 2012). This construct is defined as a joint measure of the Mining Heritage Tourism product to be a good use of land and territory from the resident's point of view, and a product that significantly improves their quality of life. We have to check for multi-collinearity, weights, loadings, and their corresponding level of significance for the formative

Table 8.1 Properties of measurement reflective constructs: reliability and convergent validity

Construct	Items	Factor Loading	CR	CA	AVE
Product Identity (PI)	PI_1	0.867	0.864	0.767	0.681
	PI_2	0.765			
	PI_3	0.840			
Economic Tourism Impacts (ECTI)	ECTI_1	0.717	0.925	0.905	0.639
	ECTI_2	0.747			
	ECTI_3	0.742			
	ECTI_4	0.809			
	ECTI_5	0.848			
	ECTI_6	0.843			
	ECTI_7	0.876			
Sociocultural Tourism Impacts (STI)	STI_1	0.801	0.901	0.862	0.647
	STI_2	0.794			
	STI_3	0.867			
	STI_4	0.843			
	STI_5	0.708			
Environmental Tourism Impacts (ENTI)	ENTI_1	0.872	0.889	0.833	0.669
	ENTI_2	0.841			
	ENTI_3	0.728			
	ENTI_4	0.822			

CA Cronbach's Alpha, *CR* composite reliability, *AVE* average variance extracted

Table 8.2 Correlation matrix

	PI	ECTI	STI	ENTI
Product Identity (PI)	**0.825**			
Economic Tourism Impacts (ECTI)	0.398	**0.800**		
Sociocultural Tourism Impacts (STI)	0.523	0.719	**0.804**	
Environmental Tourism Impacts (ENTI)	0.490	0.331	0.489	**0.818**

Table 8.3 HTMT matrix

	PI	ECTI	STI	ENTI
Product Identity (PI)				
Economic Tourism Impacts (ECTI)	0.457			
Sociocultural Tourism Impacts (STI)	0.629	0.809		
Environmental Tourism Impacts (ENTI)	0.607	0.369	0.575	

construct (Hair et al. 2013). We observe no multi-collinearity problems, as the VIF test for the dimensions of each formative construct in the model is below a value of 10 in Table 8.4 (Petter et al. 2007). A formative dimension should be retained if weight and/or loading are significant. In the bootstrap analysis all weights and loadings also appear to be significant (Table 8.4).

Table 8.4 Properties for formative constructs

Construct	Items	VIF	Weight	t-value	Loading	t-value
Support for tourism	ST_1	1.001	0.452***	4.719	0.473***	4.157
	ST_2	1.001	0.881***	14.143	0.892***	17.706

*p < 0.05; **p < 0.01; ***p < 0.001

Table 8.5 Summary of the hypotheses testing results

Hypothesis	Path coefficients (β)	t-value	R^2	f^2	Q^2	SRMR
H1: Product Identity ➔ Economic	0.398***	7.285	0.158	0.188	0.099	0.069
H2: Product Identity ➔ Sociocultural	0.523***	10.738	0.273	0.376	0.172	
H3: Product Identity ➔ Environmental	0.490***	8.932	0.240	0.315	0.158	
H4: Economic ➔ Support	0.290***	3.410	0.446	0.073	–	
H5: Sociocultural ➔ Support	0.275***	3.625		0.056		
H6: Environmental ➔ Support	0.243**	3.202		0.081		

*p < 0.05; **p < 0.01; ***p < 0.001

8.5.2 Structural Model

The assessment of the structural model is based on the algebraic sign, magnitude and significance of the structural path coefficients, the R^2 values, the effect size f^2, and the Q^2 test for predictive relevance. The SRMR index is also included as a quality criteria (Henseler et al. 2014). Consistent with Hair et al. (2013), bootstrapping analysis (5000 subsamples) is used to generate t-statistics in assessing significance of the path coefficients. Table 8.5 presents the path coefficients of each hypothesized association in the research model, with t-values confirming the significance of all six hypotheses.

The structural model shows good predictive capacity, as the variances explained (R^2) in the endogenous constructs are in the range shown by Chin (1998a), with 0.19, 0.33 and 0.67 as weak, moderate and substantial capacity, respectively. In sum, the model shows a substantial predictive capacity of local attitudes towards economic, socio-cultural, and environmental impacts(0.446) on "support for tourism", and moderate-to-medium capacity of product identity in predicting tourism impacts, economic (0.158), sociocultural (0.273), and environmental (0.240) (Fig. 8.3).

The f^2 value provides the relative size of each incremental effect introduced in the model. The f^2 values of 0.02, 0.15 and 0.35 indicate a small, medium and large effect size, respectively. As shown in Table 8.5, the proposed model has a very good explanatory power. Furthermore, the blind folfing approach was followed to calculate the construct cross-validated redundancy index or Stone-Geiser's Q^2 statistic to evaluate the predictive relevance of the model. All endogenous reflective values being positive are considered predictive. Results in Table 8.5 show all values of Q^2

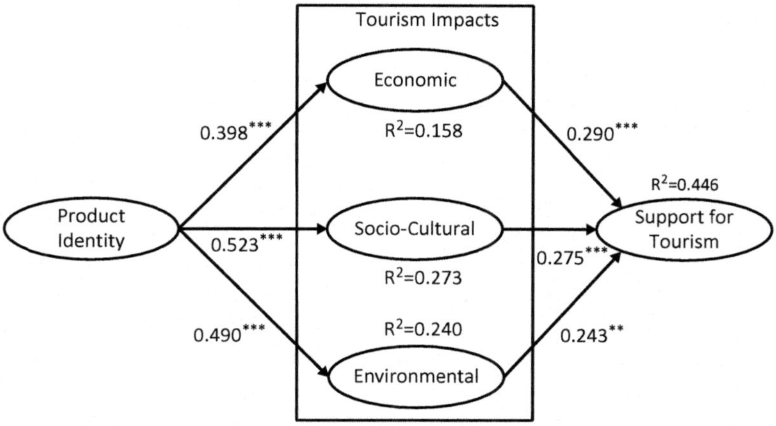

Fig. 8.3 Main effects in the model

Table 8.6 Summary of the hypotheses testing results including H7

Hypothesis	Path coefficients (β)	t-value	R^2	f^2	Q^2	SRMR
H1: Product Identity ➔ Economic	0.398***	7.324	0.159	0.188	0.099	0.069
H2: Product Identity ➔ Sociocultural	0.523***	10.69	0.273	0.376	0.172	
H3: Product Identity ➔ Environmental	0.490***	9.089	0.240	0.315	0.158	
H4: Economic ➔ Support	0.284**	2.957	0.447	0.070	–	
H5: Sociocultural ➔ Support	0.268***	3.344		0.050		
H6: Environmental ➔ Support	0.239***	3.479		0.071		
H7: Product Identity ➔ Support	0.026ns	0.439		0.001	–	

*$p < 0.05$; **$p < 0.01$; ***$p < 0.001$

to be positive (Chin 1998b), so the relations in the model show predictive relevance. Finally, the level of SRMR is lower than 0.1, meaning there is a good fit between theory and data (Henseler et al. 2014).

8.5.3 *Post-hoc Mediation Analysis*

Finally, we perform a post-hoc mediation analysis, computing if an indirect effect of *product identity* on *support for tourism* arises in the model mediated by *tourism impacts*. Specifically, we add a link between *product identity* and *support for tourism* to the base model (H7), not appearing to be significant (Table 8.6). According to Zhao et al. (2010) results in Table 8.7 confirm that *product identity* exerts a positive and significant effect on *support for tourism* through the set of *perceived* tourism impacts or *local attitudes*.

Table 8.7 Post-hoc indirect effect analysis

Indirect effects	Path coefficients (β)	Lower confidence interval	Upper confidence interval
Support for tourism	0.370^{***}	0.294	0.447
Identity➔Impacts ➔Support			

$^{*}p < 0.05$; $^{**}p < 0.01$; $^{***}p < 0.001$

Results in the model clearly show that product identity influence the attitude of residents towards economic, socio-cultural and economic impacts of tourism, with higher effects on the socio-cultural and environmental side. Moreover, and indirect effect of product identity arises on support for tourism of residents, mediated by perceptions on tourism impacts. Both results are important in the literature. First, mediation effects are not usually arising in this framework for previous contributions. Island and urban contexts do not find a clear effect of identity on impact perceptions of residents (Nunkoo and Gursoy 2012; Wang and Chen 2015). In the urban heritage setting, identity issues are more clearly present in tourism developments, so residents become so much more aware of them, what in fact modulates their perceptions of tourism impacts and then their behaviour on support for tourism. The relevance of accurately define the contextual framework when analysing effects of place identity on local attitudes and corresponding behaviour is clearly shown in our modeling exercise. Moreover, the outstanding predominance of the socio-cultural dimension in tourism developments based on local identity, and its perception by local residents, provides an important complement to the traditional predominance of economic issues in the cost-benefit analysis of tourism in literature and destination planning. Both are key results of the investigation adding new evidence to this still scarce literature, mainly in what regards the socio-cultural dimension of tourism (Besculides et al. 2002).

8.6 Conclusions and Policy Issues

The analysis of tourism impacts and local attitudes towards tourism has arised as a hot topic in academic literature. The international extension of the tourism industry has made this to be a relevant issue, with the increasing impact of tourism at destinations and the need of making this process more sustainable from a resident's point of view. In this framework, the study of how personal values can modulate the perception of such impacts by local population emerges as a key issue. Place image, attachment and identity are people's values increasingly analysed here.

The recent literature has been showing the relationship between values and impact perceptions of residents to be dependent on the own characteristics of the residents, on those of the destinations and their specialization, and on the salient dimensions of the identity issues at play. Direct linkages between local attitudes on tourism impacts and further support to tourism development not always arise in empirical studies. In fact, identity issues seems to exert a direct influence on tourism support, but not necessarily mediated by perceptions of residents on tourism impacts.

In this chapter we have tested for all these relationships in a mining tourism environment. Closer ties between local population and mining identity issues let us expect this to be a good setting for getting deeper insights in the role of identity theory as a complement of the social exchange paradigm. We have built on the product identity concept in testing this theory. Product identity, a concept closely related to the place identity construct has been defined as the way in which local identity becomes endorsed in tourism products. In particular product identity helps to approach the capacity of the Mining Heritage Tourism in preserving the mining tradition in the locality, revitalizing the mining culture and heritage in the area, and remarkably representing the mining tradition of the tourist place of La Unión in Spain.

In general, results have shown higher average effects of identity on local attitudes towards socio-cultural and environmental impacts in comparison with urban and seaside contexts. On the contrary, identity has shown less influence in modulating perceptions of economic impacts of tourism for the mining heritage destination. Our measure of product identity mainly includes attributes of continuity and self-steem for local inhabitants, with tourism being able to maintain, preserve and valuing local mining history and heritage. In this way, identity treats underlying tourism developments in the village show positive impacts on community life, in line with literature, and in particular all along the cultural and social dimension of life for residents. Additionally, results of the model have shown that local attitudes (impacts) appear to influence corresponding behaviour (support) regarding tourism development for residents in a stronger and highly significant way than other cases in literature. In this way, the mining heritage setting appears to be well suited for testing between the linkages of all constructs in the model, and particularly for understanding the role of identity and values as a central factor in modulating the impact of tourism at destinations.

In policy terms, results would be showing that destinations where identity issues drive tourism developments could help to reduce negative impacts on residents, as well as amplifying positive perceptions of local population on tourism, as shown by descriptive findings in our case study. For cultural-and-heritage based destinations, social and cultural impacts come to the forefront of the positive impacts noted by residents. This is an important result in contrast with the social exchange theory and traditional cost-benefit analysis, where the economic dimension nearly stays as the only real concern of local authorities and businessmen. Moreover, local attitudes towards tourism impacts appear to mediate between identity and support for tourism, an important result in the literature reinforcing the straight link between the heritage destination, place identity and behavioural intentions of local population. Residents feel socio-cultural impacts to be the leading dimension involved in the valuing of local identity. Further, destination sustainability increases because of this direct effect of identity on support and indirect effect through the modulation of tourism impacts. It is important to note that this result points towards a strong link between product identity (personal self-steem, continuity of traditions, plus the valuing of local history) and a good usage of the local territory with a clear improvement of quality of life of the population. A striking result of the chapter is that cultural and heritage developments at a local level building on social and personal values, including local identity, remembrance of the local history and memories and other valuing experiences are felt by residents as clearly increasing their levels of life quality.

Managerial recommendations, in times where tourism clearly impact the quality of daily life of people at destinations, point towards the opportunity of counterbalancing such situation by valuing social and place identity issues of residents. Destination management organizations (DMOs) should then view cultural identity-based interventions as a way of improving self-steem and positive perceptions of local people on the path of development followed by the destination they live in. In the end, this has been notably recognised by residents as a way of significantly improving their quality of life, an outstanding objective to be pursued by DMOs as shown by the most recent literature on Quality of Life and Well-Being in Tourism (Uysal et al. 2016).

In sum, focusing on personal values appears as a relevant and suitable strategy to modulate the impact of tourism on local population, increasing support for tourism in the future. This emerges as the main policy recommendation of the investigation, with place identity becoming a strong tool in the management and marketing of destinations, with capacity in modulating or even reducing the undesired negative externalities of tourism and increasing their sustainability levels by increasing their quality of life.

Acknowledgements Dr. Andres Artal-Tur wants to acknowledge financial support from Groups of Excellence Program of Fundación Séneca, Science and Technology Agency of the Region of Murcia, project 19884/GERM/15.

Appendix: Questionnaire Items

	Product Identity (PI)
PI_1	*The Mining Heritage Tourism (MHT) is key to preserve the mining tradition*
PI_2	*MHT helps to revitalize the mining culture and heritage in the area*
PI_3	*MHT remarkably represents the mining tradition in the area*
	Economic Tourism Impacts (ECTI)
ECTI_1	*MHT generates economic revenues*
ECTI_2	*MHT makes an impact in the regional economy*
ECTI_3	*MHT creates local employment*
ECTI_4	*MHT creates employment in the local tourism sector*

(continued)

ECTI_5	*MHT attracts new investments*
ECTI_6	*MHT generates new expenditures in the local hospitality industry*
ECTI_7	*MHT generates new expenditures in the local retailing sector*
	Socio-cultural Tourism Impacts (STI)
STI_1	*MHT improves socio-cultural infrastructure*
STI_2	*MHT improves the cultural spirit*
STI_3	*MHT improves the leisure activities and entertainment*
STI_4	*MHT improves educational level of people*
STI_5	*MHT helps to recover the cultural and industrial heritage*
	Environmental Tourism Impacts (ENTI)
ENTI_1	*MHT improves the wildlife state of conservation*
ENTI_2	*MHTimproves the indigenous plants*
ENTI_3	*MHT recovers the environmentally degraded areas*
ENTI_4	*MHTreduces pollution level*
	Support for Tourism (ST)
ST_1	*MHT is considered a good use of the land and territory*
ST_2	*MHT has significantly improved the quality of life of residents*

References

Aguiló, E., Barros, V., García, M. A., & Roselló, J. (2004). *Las actitudes de los residentes en Baleares frente al turismo*. Palma: Universidad de las Islas Baleares.

Alector-Ribeiro, M., Pinto, P., Albino-Silva, J., & Woosman, K. M. (2017). Resident's attitudes and the adoption of pro-tourism behaviour: The case of developing islands countries. *Tourism Management, 61*, 523–537.

Almeida-García, F., Peláez-Fernández, M. A., Balbuena-Vázquez, A., & Cortés-Macías, R. (2016). Resident's perception of tourism development in Benalmádena (Málaga). *Tourism Management, 54*, 259–274.

Andereck, K. L., & Nyaupane, G. P. (2011). Exploring the nature of tourism and quality of life perceptions among residents. *Journal of Travel Research, 50*(3), 248–260.

Andereck, K. L., & Vogt, C. A. (2000). The relationship between residents' attitudes toward tourism and tourism development options. *Journal of Travel Research, 39*(1), 27–36.

Andereck, K., Valentine, K., Knopf, R. C., & Vogt, C. A. (2005). Residents' perceptions of community tourism impacts. *Annals of Tourism Research, 32*(4), 1056–1076.

Andriotis, K., & Vaughan, R. D. (2003). Urban residents' attitudes toward tourism development: The case of Crete. *Journal of Travel Research, 42*(2), 172–185.

Augé, M. (1992). *Non-lieux. Introduction a 'une antrhropologie de la surmodernite'*. Paris: Editions du Senil.

Balcar, M. J., & Pearce, D. G. (1996). Heritage tourism on the west coast of New Zealand. *Tourism Management, 17*, 203–212.

Bauman, Z. (2004). *Identity: Conversations with Benedetto Vecchi*. Cambridge: Polity Press.

Besculides, A., Lee, M. E., & McCormick, P. J. (2002). Residents' perceptions of the cultural benefits of tourism. *Annals of Tourism Research, 29*(2), 303–319.

Bessière, J. (1998). Local development and heritage: Traditional food and cuisine as tourist attractions in rural areas. *Sociologia Ruralis, 38*(1), 21–34.

Boley, B. B., & McGehee, N. G. (2014). Measuring empowerment: Developing and validating the resident empowerment through tourism scale (RETS). *Tourism Management, 45*(0), 85–94.
Bott, S., Cantrill, J. G., & Myers, O. E. (2003). Place and promise of conservatory psychology. *Human Ecology Review, 10*(2), 100–112.
Breakwell, G. M. (1992). *Social psychology of identity and the self concept*. Guildford: Surrey University Press.
Bujosa, A., & Rosselló, J. (2007). Modelling environmental attitudes toward tourism. *Tourism Management, 28*, 688–695.
Butler, R. W. (2006). *The tourism area life cycle volume 2: Conceptual and theoretical issues*. Clevedon: Channelview Publications.
Chin, W. W. (1998a). Commentary: Issues and opinion on structural equation modeling. *MIS Quarterly, 22*(1), 7–16.
Chin, W. W. (1998b). *The partial least squares approach to structural equation modeling*. Mahwah: Lawrence Erlbaum Associate.
Chin, W. W., Marcolin, B. L., & Newsted, P. R. (2003). A partial least squares latent variable modeling approach for measuring interaction effects: Results from a Monte Carlo simulation study and an electronic-mail emotion/adoption study. *Information Systems Research, 14*(2), 189–217.
Choi, H. C., & Murray, I. (2010). Resident attitudes toward sustainable community tourism. *Journal of Sustainable Tourism, 18*(4), 575–594.
Cohen, E. (1988). Traditions in the qualitative sociology of tourism. *Annals of Tourism Research, 15*, 29–46.
Conesa, H. M. (2010). The difficulties in the development of mining tourism projects: The case of La Unión Mining District (SE Spain). *Pasos, 8*(4), 653–660.
Conllin, M. V., & Jonliffe, L. (2011). *Mining heritage and tourism: A global synthesis*. New York: Routledge Advances in Tourism.
Cui, X., & Ryan, C. (2011). Perceptions of place, modernity and the impacts of tourism differences among rural and urban residents of Ankang, China: A likelihood ratio analysis. *Tourism Management, 32*(3), 604–615.
Dyer, P., Gursoy, D., Sharma, B., & Carter, J. (2007). Structural modeling of resident perceptions of tourism and associated development on the Sunshine Coast, Australia. *Tourism Management, 28*, 409–422.
Edwards, J. A., & Llurdés, J. C. (1996). Mines and quarries. Industrial heritage tourism. *Annals of Tourism Research, 23*(2), 341–363.
Eligh, J., Welford, R., & Ytterhus, B. (2002). The production of sustainable tourism: Concepts and examples from Norway. *Sustainable Development, 10*(4), 223–234.
Fornell, C., & Larcker, D. F. (1981). Evaluating structural equation models with unobservable variables and measurement error. *Journal of Marketing Research, 18*(1), 39–50.
Gallarza, M. G., Saura, L. G., & García, H. C. (2002). Destination image: Towards a conceptual framework. *Annals of Tourism Research, 29*(1), 56–78.
Gu, H., & Ryan, C. (2008). Place attachment, identity and community impacts of tourism – The case of a Beijing Hutong. *Tourism Management, 29*, 637–647.
Gursoy, D., & Rutherford, D. G. (2004). Host attitudes toward tourism: An improved structural model. *Annals of Tourism Research, 31*(3), 495–516.
Hair, J. F., Hult, G. T. M., Ringle, C. M., & Sarstedt, M. (2013). *A primer on partial least squares structural equation modeling (PLS-SEM)*. Thousand Oaks: SAGE Publications Incorporated.
Henkel, R., Henkel, P., Agrusa, W., Agrusa, J., & Tanner, J. (2006). Thailand as a tourist destination: Perceptions of international visitors and Thai residents. *Journal of Tourism Research, 11*(3), 269–287.
Henseler, J., Ringle, C. M., & Sinkovics, R. R. (2009). The use of partial least squares path modeling in international marketing. *Advances in International Marketing, 20*, 277–320.

Henseler, J., Dijkstra, T. K., Sarstedt, M., Ringle, C. M., Diamantopoulos, A., Straub, D. W., Ketchen, D. J., Hair, J. F., Hult, G. T. M., & Calantone, R. J. (2014). Common beliefs and reality about PLS: Comments on Ronkko and Evermann (2013). *Organizational Research Methods, 17*(2), 182–209.

Henseler, J., Ringle, C. M., & Sarsted, M. (2015). A new criterion for assessing discriminant validity in variance-based structural equation modeling. *Journal of the Academy of Marketing Science, 43*, 115–135.

INE Annual Report. (2012). http://www.ine.es/ine/planine/informe_anual_2012.pdf

Jurowski, C., & Gursoy, D. (2004). Distance effects on residents' attitudes toward tourism. *Annals of Tourism Research, 31*(2), 296–312.

Kim, K., Uysal, M., & Sirgy, M. (2013). How does tourism in a community impact the quality of life of community residents? *Tourism Management, 36*, 527–540.

Korpela, K. M. (1989). Place identity as a product of environmental self-regulation. *Journal of Environmental Psychology, 9*, 241–256.

Lee, C., Kang, S., Long, P., & Reisinger, Y. (2010). Residents' perceptions of casino impacts: A comparative study. *Tourism Management, 31*(2), 189–201.

Lewicka, M. (2011). Place attachment: How far have we come in the last 40 years? *Journal of Environmental Psychology, 31*(3), 207–230.

Liang, Z. X., & Hui, T. K. (2016). Residents' quality of life and attitudes toward tourism development in China. *Tourism Management, 57*, 56–67.

Lundberg, E. (2017). The importance of tourism impacts for different local resident groups: A case study of a Swedish seaside destination. *Journal of Destination Marketing & Management, 6*, 46–55.

Manteca, J. I., & Berrocal, M. C. (1997). Sobre la creación de un parque geo-minero y arqueo-industrial en La Unión como medida de protección y puesta en valor del patrimonio histórico-minero. *II Congreso Empresarial COEC. Desarrollo turístico y económico de la Comarca de Cartagena*. Cartagena, 20–21 February, pp. 181–199.

McCool, S. F., & Martin, S. R. (1994). Community attachment and attitudes toward tourism development. *Journal of Travel Research, 32*(2), 29–34.

McGehee, N. G., & Andereck, K. L. (2004). Factors predicting rural residents' support of tourism. *Journal of Travel Research*, 43(2), 131-140.

Nepal, S. (2008). Residents' attitudes to tourism in central Bristyih Columbia, Canada. *Tourism Geographies, 10*(1), 42–65.

Nunkoo, R., & Gursoy, D. (2012). Residents' support for tourism: An identity perspective. *Annals of Tourism Research, 39*(1), 243–268.

Peña, D. G. (2002). Endangered landscapes and disappearing peoples? Identity, place, and community in ecological politics. In J. Adamson, M. M. Evans, & R. Stein (Eds.), *The environmental justice reader: Politics, poetics, and pedagogy* (pp. 58–81). Tucson: University of Arizona Press.

Peng, D. X., & Lai, F. (2012). Using partial least squares in operations management research: A practical guideline and summary of past research. *Journal of Operations Management, 30*(6), 467–480.

Petter, S., Straub, D., & Rai, A. (2007). Specifying formative constructs in information systems research. *MIS Quarterly, 31*(4), 623–656.

Ramkissoon, H., & Nunkoo, R. (2011). City image and perceived tourism impact: Evidence from Port Louis, Mauritius. *International Journal of Hospitality and Tourism Administration, 12*(2), 123–143.

Rasoolimanesh, S. M., Ringle, C. M., Jaafar, M., & Ramayah, T. (2017). Urban vs rural destinations: Residents' perceptions, community participation and support for tourism development. *Tourism Management, 60*, 147–158.

Reiser, D., & Crispin, S. (2009). Local perception of the reimagining process. *Journal of Place Management and Development, 2*(2), 109–124.

Ringle, C. M., Wende, S., & Becker, J. M. (2014). *SmartPLS 3*. Hamburg: SmartPLS.
Ruíz-Ballesteros, E., & Hernández-Ramírez, M. (2007). Identity and community-reflections on the development of mining heritage tourism in Southern Spain. *Tourism Management, 28*, 677–687.
Sharpley, R. (2014). Host perceptions of tourism: A review of the research. *Tourism Management, 42*, 37–49.
Shumaker, S. A., & Taylor, R. B. (1983). Toward a clarification of people-place relationships: A model of attachment to place. In N. R. Feimer & E. S. Geller (Eds.), *Environmental psychology: Directions and perspectives* (pp. 219-256). New York: Praeger.
Stets, J. E., & Biga, C. F. (2003). Bringing identity theory into environmental sociology. *Sociological Theory*, 21(4), 398-423.
Stoeckl, N., Greinerb, R., & Mayocchib, C. (2006). The community impacts of different types of visitors: An empirical investigation of tourism in North-West Queensland. *Tourism Management, 27*, 97–112.
Stylidis, D., Biran, A., Sit, J., & Szivas, E. M. (2014). Residents' support for tourism development: The role of residents' place image and perceived tourism impacts. *Tourism Management, 45*, 260–274.
Taylor, S. (2010). *Narratives of identity and place*. London: Routledge.
Telfer, D., & Sharpley, R. (2008). *Tourism and development in the developing world*. Abingdon: Routledge.
Turner, L., & Ash, J. (1975). *The golden hordes: International tourism and the pleasure periphery*. London: Constable.
Ujang, N. (2010). Place attachment and continuity of urban place identity. *Asian Journal of Environment-Behavior Studies, 1*(2), 61–76.
UNWTO. (2016). *UNWTO tourism highlights 2016*. Madrid: World Tourism Organization.
Uysal, M., Sirgy, M. J., Woo, E., & Kim, L. (2016). Quality-of-Life (QoL) and well-being research in tourism. *Tourism Management, 53*, 244–261.
Uzzell, D. L. (1995). Conferring a sense of place identity: The role of museums. *The International Journal of Heritage Studies, 1*, 4.
Vargas-Sánchez, A., Plaza-Mejía, M. A., & Porras-Bueno, N. (2009). Understanding residents' attitudes toward the development of industrial tourism in a former mining community. *Journal of Travel Research, 47*(3), 373–387.
Vargas-Sánchez, A., Porras-Bueno, N., & Plaza-Mejía, M. (2011). Explaining residents attitudes to tourism: Is a universal model possible? *Annals of Tourism Research, 38*(2), 460–480.
Vargas-Sánchez, A., Valle, P. O., Mendes, J. C., & Silva, J. A. (2015). Residents'attitude and level of destination development: An international comparison. *Tourism Management, 48*, 199–210.
Wall, G., & Mathieson, A. (2006). *Tourism: Change, impacts, and opportunities*. New York: Pearson Education.
Wang, S., & Chen, J. S. (2015). The influence of place identity on perceived tourism impacts. *Annals of Tourism Research, 52*, 16–28.
Young, G. (1973). *Tourism: Blessing or blight?* Harmondsworth: Penguin.
Zhao, X., Lynch, J. G., Jr., & Chen, Q. (2010). Reconsidering Baron and Kenny: Myths and truths about mediation analysis. *Journal of Consumer Research, 37*(2), 197–206.

Chapter 9
Film Tourism and Its Impact on Residents Quality of Life: A Multi Logit Analysis

Subhash Kizhakanveatil Bhaskaran Pillai, Kaustubh Kamat, Miriam Scaglione, Carmelita D'Mello, and Klaus Weiermair

Abstract Past research has confirmed film tourism emerging as a major growth sector for research in tourism and a driver of tourism development for many destinations. To date, there has been relatively substantial literature on the subject, yet this paper tries to shed some light on the quality of life perception with respect to the International Film Festival of India (IFFI). Earlier research results have shown different impacts of film tourism on the quality of life of the local community, and the perceptions and attitudes of residents towards tourism, but no research has shown neither how nor how much these perceptions and attitudes change according to a change in the demographic profile of the local community. The empirical findings show that: age, income, education and marital status have a significant impact on residents' attitude towards film tourism. Factor analysis resulted in 4 latent factors which drive residents' perception about quality of life, viz., Community Pride, Personal Benefits, Negative Environmental effect and Negative Social effect. The results have shown that a varia-

S. K. B. Pillai (✉)
Department of Commerce, Goa University, Goa, India
e-mail: subhash@unigoa.ac.in

K. Kamat
Department of Business Administration, Goa Multi-Faculty College, Goa, India
e-mail: kamatkau@gmail.com

M. Scaglione
Institute of Tourism, University of Applied Sciences and Arts Western Switzerland, HES-SO Valais, Sierre, Switzerland
e-mail: miriam.scaglione@hevs.ch

C. D'Mello
Department of Commerce, St. Xavier's College of Arts, Science & Commerce, Goa, India
e-mail: litad@rediffmail.com

K. Weiermair
Schulich School of Business, York University Toronto, York, Canada

Department of Tourism and Service Management, Institute of Strategic Management, Marketing and Tourism, University of Innsbruck, Innsbruck, Austria
e-mail: Klaus.Weiermair@uibk.ac.at

A. M. Campón-Cerro et al. (eds.), *Best Practices in Hospitality and Tourism Marketing and Management*, Applying Quality of Life Research,
https://doi.org/10.1007/978-3-319-91692-7_9

tion in the demographic profile of the resident community determines a variation in the attitudes towards tourism impacts. In a time of mass movement of people, man power and immigration, changes in the demographic profile of residents are very likely and this research shows that it should be taken into consideration when managing tourism destinations and planning new tourism policies.

Keywords Film tourism · Residents perception · Quality of life · Indian cinema · International film festival of india · Goa · Multinomial logit

9.1 Introduction

Film festivals represent one of the most rapidly expanding areas of cultural events worldwide (Getz and Page 2016; Mueller 2006). International film festivals draw film professionals such as directors, actors/actresses, critics, producers, and buyers as well as multitudes of cultural tourists who travel to attend diverse national and/or international film festivals. These cultural travelers come to the venue of the festival and support the local economy through expenditures on lodging, meals, local products, and other cultural consumption in the region. With anticipated economic benefits generated by visitor spending at film festivals, public and private agencies are embracing film festival tourism as a new source of income for local business and taxation. In addition to the economic benefits, film festivals are also perceived to benefit local residents in the communities by providing more cultural events, improved infrastructural facilities in terms of world class accommodation and food availability, efficient transportation, excellent sanitation and garbage management, and also hassle free parking facilities, which are considered as part of improving the quality of life at the film tourism destination. At the same time, strict and efficient mechanisms for minimising the negative impact of social evils like crime, drugs, and human trafficking. Garnering support for film festivals is an appealing activity among policy makers as a way to develop a reputation for promoting arts and culture. With economic and political benefits derived from investing in film festivals and cultural events, financial support by public authorities continues to expand in many places worldwide which also improve the quality of life at the destination.

Though the history of cinema/films in India dates back to 1896, recognizing the catalytic nature of film tourism and immediately after independence, the then Indian government headed by the first prime minister Pandit Jawaharlal Nehru initiated the International Film Festival of India (IFFI) in 1952. During the last 6 decades IFFI has been inaugurated in most of the metropolitan cities, viz., Mumbai, Delhi, Kolkata, Chennai, Hyderabad, Bengaluru, and Thiruvananthapuram. In 2004, the then government Bharatiya Janatha Party (BJP) at the centre and also in Goa unanimously decided to make Goa the permanent venue for IFFI and inaugurated the 35th International Film Festival of India (IFFI-2004) in Panaji, Goa on November 29, 2004. This initiative was based on the unique blend of Indo-Portuguese culture, cuisine and lifestyle but most importantly, Goa's unique selling proposition (USP), her friendly, warm hearted and hospitable people (D'Mello et al. 2015). Historically ancient Goa was self-ruled by Gaonkaris (1000 BC–500 BC), Hindu Dynasties (500 BC–1330 AD), Islamic dynasties (1326–1510), Portuguese (1510–1961), until it became liberated in 1961 (Wiki 2015a, b). This being the case, coupled with the mythological spiritual cleansing power, traditional adithi-devo-bhava culture, and 450 year long Portuguese colonial rule molded the very Goan culture in to one of the best in the world.

Even after 13 years of hosting IFFI in Goa (IFFI 2015), no studies were carried out by the government nor by any private researchers on assessing the factors which drive local residents' perceptions about film tourism and the impact of film tourism on the quality of life of the residents, hence the present study was conducted to identify underlying structures of residents' attitudes toward Film tourism in terms of social, economic, and environmental impacts and to examine causal relationships between the impact variables and benefits and costs which provides some insight on the quality of life of the residents. This study further identifies the effect of demographic variation of the residents' support for Film tourism, contributing to the debate on Film tourism development, and also provides a base for successful tourism policies. Past research has shown the different impacts of tourism on the local community, and the perceptions and attitudes of residents towards tourism, however no research has shown neither how nor how much these perceptions and attitudes change according to a change in the demographic profile of the local community. Therefore, the present study fills this gap by adding valuable knowledge, new perspectives, and presents possibilities for consideration. The paper offers valuable inputs for different stakeholders of the film tourism industry; especially the event organizers, film producers, movie lovers, academicians, academic institutions, government, and NGO's in the region under study.

9.2 Literature Review

To some, the idea of traveling to a distant locale to see movies makes no sense; after all, you can see movies in your own city or town. But for others, combining travel with movie-going offers a happy partnership in which the rigors of sightseeing or the indulgence of sunbathing are leavened by taking time out each day to see films. International film festivals offer the latest and best of what is available in the global marketplace. Film tourism can take a number of different forms and activities as identified and discussed by a number of authors (Beeton 2005; Busby and Klug 2001; Connell 2012; Couldry 2005; Croy 2010, 2011; Croy and Heitmann 2011; Li et al. 2017; Lin et al. 2007; Lin and Huang 2008).

9.2.1 Residents Perception About Film Tourism and Quality of Life

"Special events; like music festivals, film festivals; have economic impacts which are estimated from the expenditures made by attendees, performers, and sponsors, either directly or indirectly associated with the event (Murphy and Carmichael 1991)".

They supplement the traditional financial balance sheets provided to the government (Crompton et al. 2001), since they address the broader issue of what community residents receive in return of their investment of tax funds.

Studies (Riley and van Doren 1992; Riley et al. 1998) identified that the benefits of film tourism are three-fold: first, raising tourist awareness; second, increasing destination appeal, and: third, contributing to the viability of tourism, which ultimately leads to improvement of quality of life at the destination. Film and literary induced tourism typify the values of post modernity where the symbolic values of a product (in this case, a landscape, place or setting) often have greater appeal to the consumer than the product itself (Rojek 1995). However, film induced tourism, like any other form of tourism, also bring negative impacts to a destination (Mordue 2001, 2009) in the form of traffic congestion, high cost of living, garbage and waste management, drugs and prostitution, insufficient infrastructure, and also law and order problems, which the residents consider as negative impacts on their quality of life. Moreover, some of the sites are not prepared for the sudden increase in tourist volume. The insufficient infrastructure and developing film tourism not only diminish tourists' experiences, but also compromise the local environment. This fact makes film tourism an important issue that requires more study.

In the field of tourism, residents' perceptions and attitudes to tourism development of a destination is a frequently studied topic (Lee et al. 2010). Earlier works show improvement in various areas, i.e., employment opportunities, tax revenues, economic diversity, festivals, restaurants, natural and cultural attractions, and outdoor recreation opportunities have improved quality of life perception of residents. Past studies have indicated that the support of local residents is a vital element in the tourism development of a destination (Andereck and Vogt 2000). Further research in tourism planning and development suggested that egions must involve various stakeholders including the local community (Ap 1992; Ap and Crompton 1993; Brayley et al. 1990). Resident's attitude plays a crucial role in sustainability of any tourism; moreover Destination Management Office (DMO) should identify what the real drivers behind resident's attitudes are. A review of the literature suggests commonly used theoretical frameworks explaining resident perceptions toward impacts of tourism; viz.; social exchange theory (SET). SET has been advocated as the most appropriate framework for explaining residents' perceptions on the impact of gambling tourism (Giacopassi and Stitt 1994; Jurowski 1994; Jurowski et al. 1997; Pizam and Pokela 1985; Stitt et al. 2003); which suggests that residents would evaluate benefits and costs associated with a tourism avenue and then decide whether they should support it or not, i.e., in other words residents becomes supporters if their quality of life is improved, opposers if their quality of life is hampered, or become neutral if no change takes place. The more the benefits, the more residents will become supportive and vice versa, depending on their demographic characteristics (D'Mello et al. 2015, 2016a, b; Kamat et al. 2016). Film induced tourism, like other forms of tourism, introduced both positive and negative impacts on a destination (Heitmann 2010). Many of the impacts are extensions of those witnessed in tourism destinations generally, although some are more emphasized in film locations. This leads to the first and second research questions and related hypothesis.

RQ1: Is it possible to identify the effect of demographic variables on resident's perception about film tourism in Goa, and also to describe the main characteristics of each of the groups; viz.; Supporters, Neutral, or Opposers?

H_1: No significant difference exists between residents attitudes towards Film Tourism (Supporters /Neutral /Opposers) with respect to age, gender, income, marital status, education, length of stay.

RQ2: Is it possible to identify the effect of variations of population characteristics on each of the groups, viz., Supporters, Neutral, or Opposer?

The problems and issues that have emerged from the increased flow of film tourists usually leads to carrying capacity problems with respect to the four A's of tourism; viz.; attraction (overcrowding, misuse of resources, pollution, etc); amenities (improper accommodation facility, poor quality food, bad sanitation facility, shortage of water and electricity, etc); accessibility (inadequate transportation, traffic congestion, parking difficulty, etc); and *ancillary services* (lack of additional / supplementary attractions, inadequate peripheral tourism development, etc). This may lead to a situation where conflict between guest-host takes place (Beeton 2001, 2004a, b, 2005; Connell 2005a, b; Croy and Walker 2003; Hudson and Ritchie 2006a, b; Mordue, 2001, 2009; O'Neill et al. 2005; Riley and van Doren 1992; Riley et al. 1998; Tooke and Baker 1996). A common thread can be drawn which highlights that conflicts occur if locals are not taken into consideration while planning events of this nature. Furthermore, to determine the perspectives of the community and to understand the aspirations and concerns of those who will be impacted by the film's development and tourism potential, individual responses should be considered. Therefore, it is important to understand how residents perceive the impacts of Film based Tourism on their quality of life (Busby and Klug 2001; Busby et al. 2013; Connell 2012; Kim et al. 2013; Kim et al. 2017; Li et al. 2017; Sine 2010; Zhang et al. 2016). This leads to the third and fourth research questions and the related hypothesis.

RQ 3: Is it possible to identify important factors which drive Quality of Life perception of residents due to Film tourism in Goa?

RQ 4: Is there any difference in perception with regards to Quality of life factors across demographic profiles?

H_2: No significant difference exists between perceived factors which drives Quality of life perception with respect to age, gender, income, marital status, education, length of stay.

9.2.2 Historical Perspective of Indian Cinema and the Final Destination of IFFI

Films in India have a long history; divided in to pre-independence era (1896–1946) and post-independence era (1947–2015). The pre-independence movie era began with the screening of moving picture in 1896 in Mumbai. Slowly, interest towards films started taking place in the form of talkies in cities like Kolkata and Andhra Pradesh. In the year 1913, the first ever movie was released by Dadasaheb Phalke whose contributions to Indian Cinema went on to be recognized as the highest national recognition award in Cinema. During 1943, Information Films of India and the Indian New Parade were set up to cover the World War. With movement for independence gaining pace in India movies which were related to encouraging and making society aware of their right to be independent, British regulated and started banning such movies namely Wrath and Raithu Bidda. Subsequently, Statutory Bodies were formed (Information Films of India and Indian new Parade) to produce documentaries with the prime objective to censor the information communicated through movies and documentaries.

With India getting independence in 1947, there was a division of national assets and the merging of two prominent film associations namely, Information Films of India and the Indian New Parade into the Film Division of India in 1948 by the then prime minister Jawaharlal Nehru, mainly for the purpose of production and distribution of information films, enlisting documentary cinema (news based or animation film in 15 national languages to be shown in theaters throughout the country) for the larger project of nation building, integration, and development (Deprez 2013). On March 21, 1952, The Cinematograph Act was passed by Indianising the earlier The Cinematograph Act of 1918 making the screening of the documentaries by the Film Division compulsory throughout the country. The Division also aims at fostering the growth of the documentary film movement, which is of immense significance to India in the field of national information, communication and integration (Knowindia 2015). Just before passing The Cinematograph Act on March 21, 1952, 1st edition of International Film Festival of India (IFFI) was organised by Film Division in Mumbai (New Empire cinema) from January 24 to February 1, 1952.

The fundamental philosophical theme on which the IFFI was started is: "Ayam bandhurayam neti gananā laghuchetasām, Udāracharitānām tu vasudhaiva kutumbakam", The English translation of this ancient Vedic period Indian philosophical thought is "One is my brother and the other is not – is the thinking of a narrow-minded person. For those who are broad-minded, liberals, or noble people, the entire world is one big family". This ancient Indian philosophical thought is considered as the origin of globalization with a heart, in contrast with the present globalization (without a heart) propagated by the western and European economies (Subhash and Chen 2012). *Nothing exemplifies the Indian no*tion of non-violence and peaceful coexistence as 'Vasudhaiva Kutumbakam', the phrase on which the IFFI and its theme are rooted (IFFI 2015). The 1st edition of IFFI saw entries from 23 countries with around 40 feature and 100 short films, of which the 4 Indian entries were Awara (Hindi), Patala Bhairavi (Telegu), Amar Bhoopali (Marathi), and Babla (Bengali) and other notable films were Bicycle Heives, Miracle of Milan & Open City (Italy). Yukiwarisoo (Japan), Dancing Fleese (UK), The River (USA) and Fall of Berlin (USSR). It was the first time that the Indian Film Industry was exposed to a vast range of outstanding post–war era films, and the festival was non-competitive in nature (DFF 2015). The festival was subsequently taken to Chennai, Delhi, and Kolkata, but it was not organized on an annual basis. The 2nd edition of IFFI held in

New Delhi from October 27 to November 2, 1962 was also non-competitive; and the 3rd edition held in New Delhi from January 3 to 21, 1965, competition was introduced and continued for the next 7 years, all held in New Delhi.

From 1965 to 2004 IFFI was held in different states of India and during 2004 Goa was identified as the permanent venue with the inauguration of the 35th International Film Festival of India (IFFI-2004) in Panaji, Goa on November 29, 2004. Now, and for the last decade, film tourism is being promoted during the month of November every year and it has resulted in many changes in the social setup of Goa, which directly and indirectly influences the quality of life of the residents of Goa.

9.3 Methodology

Since there were very few studies carried out on film tourism and its impact on the residents quality of life, and also no similar studies were carried out on IFFI and its impact on the quality of life of the residents in the state of Goa, the present study was carried out with the aim of identifying the perception of residents about the impact of IFFI on their life. IFFI is an annual event, usually taking place during November every year, data were hence collected during the 45th IFFI from November 2014 to April 2015 from residents who has been living in Goa for more than 6 months, because any lesser stay period may not allow the residents to assess the impact on their quality of life from such events. The selection of respondents was based on convenience because, in general, the residents who were approached by the investigator were reluctant to participate in the survey as most of them were not happy with the way the event IFFI was organized by the authorities. Those residents who were willing to participate after convincing the purpose of the present research were given the questionnaire. Based on the existing literature review on event tourism, especially focusing on film tourism and its impact on quality of life of various stakeholders, a structured questionnaire was developed. Around 200 questionnaires were distributed, of which 190 questionnaires were returned by the respondents, of which 4 were incomplete, and thus, only 186 useable questionnaires were received with a response rate of 93%.

The survey questionnaire consisted of three parts. The first part included 35 statements on residents' perceptions of the film tourism and how it affects their quality of life. These statements were derived from the previous literature review on resident reactions to tourism and various events including film tourism (Beeton 2001, 2004a, b, 2005; Connell 2005a, b; Croy and Walker 2003; Hudson and Ritchie 2006a, b; Hudson and Tung 2010; Hudson et al. 2010; Getz and Page 2016, Mordue 2001, 2009; Riley and van Doren 1992; Riley et al. 1998; Tooke and Baker 1996). All 35 statements came under the four subsets of quality of life, viz., Community Pride, Personal Benefits, Negative Environmental effect and Negative Social effect. Both positive and negative aspects of quality of life were included. The participants were asked to rate the extent to which they agreed or disagreed with each statement on a 7-point Likert scale ranging from 1 (strongly disagree) to 7 (strongly agree).

The second part of the questionnaire tried to identify the residents general perception about IFFI; viz.; "I support IFFI Tourism", "I am Neutral", and "I oppose IFFI Tourism". Options were given to respondents to identify themselves as a Supporter/Neutral/Opposer of film tourism during the survey. They were informed that after answering the 35 statements which reflects on improvement of quality of life as a result of IFFI, they may identify themselves as a supporter if they feel that their quality of life is improved, as an opposer if they feel that their quality of life is adversely affected and neutral if no change had taken place in their quality of life. Based on their opinion, analysis was carried out by classifying respondents as supporter/neutral/opposer of film tourism. The respondent's basic demographic information, viz., age, gender, education, marital status, monthly income, and occupation were collected using the third part of the questionnaire.

A chi-square test is applied to find the answer to RQ1 and a multi-logit analysis is applied to study the effects of variations in demographic characteristics of residents with respect to their attitude towards film tourism to find the answer to RQ2. Change in demographic variables seems to be relevant in defining the community opinion toward tourism aspects. Demographic resident tendency related with host's attitude could be useful tool for tourism developers. To achieve this, a multi-logit model was run. If any demographic characteristic showed a significant difference between the clusters, logit analysis permits the deviation of predictive parameters on the significant variables. In this multi-logit analysis, the variable of three groups (CL_3i; Supporters/Neutral/Opposers) was treated as the dependent variable and demographic characteristics as independent variables and multi-logit regression is applied to determine the factor that explains the pertinence of a concrete type of cluster. In multinomial logit notation, the model was written as:

$$\text{Multinomial Logit} \qquad \text{CL\_3i} = \alpha + \beta\, j\, xk,$$

Where CL_3i is the odds of occurrence on cluster i over the other clusters 2; α = the intercept parameter; βj = the vector of slope parameter and xk = the explanatory demographic variables (Age, Education, Gender, Income, Length of Stay, Marital Status). Finally Factor Analysis is applied to find the answer for RQ3 and a Mean test is used to answer RQ 4.

9.4 Analysis and Discussion

9.4.1 Demographic Profiling of Residents

Change in demographic variables seems to be relevant in defining the community opinion towards tourism development, in this case, the impact of film tourism. With the exception of gender and length of stay, all other demographic characteristics of residents have statistical significance when it comes to impact of IFFI on the quality of life. Exhibit 9.1 shows general demographic profiling of residents gives age

Exhibit 9.1 Demographi profiling of residents and attitude towards film tourism

Demographic characteristic (N = 186)		Residents Attitude				
		Supporter	Neutral	Opposer	Total (%)	$\chi2$
Age	**20–29**	25	48	7	**43.0**	57.33*
	30–39	9	20	5	18.3	
	40–49	3	26	8	19.9	
	50 and above	2	9	24	18.8	
Education	Up to 12 years study	11	22	23	30.1	15.16*
	Graduation	11	29	5	24.2	
	Post graduation	17	52	16	**45.7**	
Gender	**Male**	19	53	26	**52.7**	1.033
	Female	20	50	18	47.3	
Income	**Less than 2000 USD**	28	50	25	**55.4**	11.75*
	2000–20,000 USD	6	47	15	26.6	
	Above 20,000 USD	5	6	4**	8.1	
Length of stay	Less than a year	5	7	1**	7.0	5.451
	1–10 years	22	65	24	**59.7**	
	10 years ad above	12	31	19	33.3	
Marital status	Unmarried	18	46	21	45.7	15.16*
	Married	21	57	23	**54.3**	

*$p < 0.05$
**The authors acknowledge that the number of observations in those cases are low (the expected value under the hypothesis of independences is less than 5) but they leave this analysis for the sake of explanation

distribution as follows Age 20–29 (43%), 30–39 (18.3%), 40–49 (19.9%), 50 and above (18.8%), it clearly shows that there was a significant age difference between supporters, neutral and opposers of film tourism with regards to age ($\chi2 = 57.33$, $p < 0.05$), with older people opposing IFFI, while younger people were more supportive to film based tourism. Significant difference was found between education groups ($\chi2 = 15.16$, $p < 0.05$), as more educated people were neutral towards IFFI and less educated group opposed IFFI. Educational levels were distributed as follows, up to 12 years of schooling (30.1%), graduation (24.2%) and post-graduation (45.7%). It was found to have significant difference ($\chi2 = 15.16$, $p > 0.05$). Income levels were distributed as follows, less than 2000 USD (55.4%), 2000 USD – 20000 USD (26.6%), and above 20000 USD (8.1%). Significant difference was found with more middle income group being neutral towards Film based tourism ($\chi2 = 11.75$, $p < 0.05$). Significant difference existed with respect to marital status among opposers, neutral and supporters. With respect to marital status, married people were more neutral in attitude towards film tourism ($\chi2 = 15.16$, $p < 0.05$).

With respect to gender and length of stay, no statistical significance was observed among the three categories of respondents. There was a roughly even distribution of male and female with 52.2% for male and 47.3% for female in responses with significant difference found with gender ($\chi2 = 1.033$, $p > 0.05$). Respondents' length of residence ranged from less than 1 years (7%), 1–10 years (59.7%), and 10 years and above (33.3%), with no statistical significance($\chi2 = 5.451$, $p > 0.05$). Hence, based on the above, the formulated hypothesis (H_1) of RQ1 that "no significant difference between Film Tourism (Supporters/Neutral/Opposers) with respect to age, gender, marital status, income, education, and length of stay" is rejected with an exception of gender, and length of stay.

9.4.2 Marginal Coefficient

Multi Logit Regression and Marginal effects were to answer RQ2: Is it possible to identify the effect of variations of population characteristics on each of the groups viz.; Supporters, Neutral, or Opposer?; which investigates the effects of the demographic variables over the dependent variable for each group significantly different between the clusters. As shown by the result in Exhibit 9.2, the marginal effect for variable age and income is significant at 95% level of confidence for group of Supporters, meaning that if a resident belonging to the age group (50 and above), the probability of being a supporter will be decreased by 25.2% as compared to the age group 20–29, also a resident belonging to the age group (40–49 years), the probability of being a supporter will be decreased by 21.9% as compared to age group (20–29 years). Similarly, a resident belonging to Income group (2000–20,000 USD), the probability of being a supporter will be decreased by 14.3% as compared to a resident belonging to the income group of less than 2000USD.

Exhibit 9.2 Residents classification based on their different attitudes towards film tourism (supporters, neutral and opposers)

Demographic characteristic		Residents attitude		
		Supporter	Neutral	Opposer
Age	20–29	**BC**	**BC**	**BC**
	30–39	−0.0743	−0.0009	0.0752
	40–49	−0.219*	0.0922	0.1268
	50 and above	−0.252*	−0.2831*	0.5355*
Education	Up to 12 years study	**BC**	**BC**	**BC**
	Graduation	−0.0143	0.213*	−0.1999*
	Post graduation	−0.0005	0.204*	−0.2043*
Gender	Male	−0.0492	0.0217	0.0274
	Female	**BC**	**BC**	**BC**
Income	Less than 2000USD	**BC**	**BC**	**BC**
	2000–20,000 USD	−0.143*	0.188*	−0.0447
	Above 20,000 USD	0.1621	−0.104	−0.0579
Length of stay	Less than a year	**BC**	**BC**	**BC**
	1–10 years	−0.1537	0.115	0.0379
	10 years and above	−0.1486	−0.004	0.1531
Marital status	Unmarried	−0.0782	0.0338	0.0443
	Married	**BC**	**BC**	**BC**

*$p < 0.05$; ***BC*** base category

Residents showing Neutral attitude towards Film Tourism had a marginal effect for variable age, education and income significant at 95% level of confidence, meaning that for a resident in the age group (50 and above), the probability of having a neutral opinion will decrease by 28.3% as compared to age group 20–29. Similarly a resident with the education qualification of Post-Graduation, the probability of them having a neutral opinion will increase by 20.4% as compared to a resident with education qualification of up to 12 years of schooling, also a resident with the education qualification of Graduation, probability of them having neutral opinion will increase by 21.3% as compared to a resident with education qualification of up to 12 years of schooling. Also residents belonging to Income group (2000–20,000 USD), the probability of them having a neutral opinion will increase by 18.8% as compared to a resident with income of less than 2000 USD.

The variable age and education is significant at 95% confidence interval for *Opposer*, meaning a resident belonging to the age group (50 and above), the probability of them being an Opposer will be increase by 53.5% as compared to residents in the age group 20–29. Similarly a resident with education qualification of post-graduation, the probability of them opposing film tourism will decrease by 19.9% as compared to a resident with an education qualification of up to 12 years of school education, also a resident with education qualification of Graduation, the probability of Opposing Film Tourism will decrease by 20.43% as compared to a resident with education qualification of up to 12 years of school education.

9.4.3 Factor Analysis of Residents Perception

Exploratory factor analysis is used in order to answer RQ3: Is it possible to identify important factors which drive Quality of Life perception of residents due to Film tourism in Goa?; i.e.; to identify factors driving resident's perception; this analysis was conducted to assess the dimensionality of the 38 items (refer Exhibit 9.3). Kaiser's (1974) overall measure of sampling adequacy is 0.85, indicating that the data are appropriate for the principal components model. Values of 0.6 and above are required for a good factor analysis (Tabachnick and Fidell 1989). An examination of the screen plots derived from principal component analysis with varimax rotation indicated that a four-factor solution was appropriate for these data.

These four factors explained 57.43% of the variance in attitudes toward tourism. Although this percentage is a little less than the 58% found by Lankford and Howard (1994). Of all 38 perception related items based upon the post-survey data were initially factor analyzed; 4 items was removed due to factor loading lower than 0.4. Thirty-four items were factor analyzed again, resulting in the following four underlying dimensions. All factors had reliability coefficients from a low of 0.90 to the high of 0.94. These factors were labelled as: (F1) Community Pride, (F2) Personal gains, (F3) Negative Environmental impact, and (F4) Negative social impact. F1 and F2 deal with the positive aspects of quality of life where as F3 and F4 represents negative aspects. This clearly shows that film tourism in Goa does have positive and negative

Exhibit 9.3 Factors driving residents quality of life

	Quality of life perception statements	Factor loading			
		F1	F2	F3	F4
	COMMUNITY PRIDE (F1)				
1	They have improved the city's tourism image	0.522			
2	I've gained a sense of pride through these events	0.677			
3	They have made the city more international	0.780			
4	They have contributed to the city's tourism	0.739			
5	They have created more network opportunities for residents	0.838			
6	They have promoted economic development	0.844			
8	I've had lots of enjoyment through IFFI	0.646			
9	They have raised the employment rate	0.743			
10	They have created profits for the government	0.652			
11	They have improved shopping opportunities	0.625			
12	They have created profits for private enterprise	0.543			
13	They have led to the creation of new facilities	0.679			
14	They have improved overall living standards of the residents	0.763			
15	They have created many leisure & entertainment opportunities	0.811			
16	They have created new family-based leisure opportunities	0.739			
17	They have provided opportunities to learn about their own community	0.637			
18	These events expose local artists to expertise	0.784			
19	These events provide local artists with an opportunity to show case their talents	0.835			
	PERSONAL GAINS (F2)				
20	They have enriched my life		0.734		
21	They have brought excitement to my life		0.704		
22	They have brought emotional experience to my life		0.759		
	NEGATIVE ENVIRONMENTAL EFFECT (F3)				
23	They have created air pollution			0.798	
24	They have destroyed the natural environment			0.832	
25	They have damaged heritage sites			0.702	
26	They have disrupted normal life			0.766	
27	They have created traffic jams			0.710	
28	They have put pressure on urban services			0.784	
29	Parking space has reduced			0.727	
30	Sewage problems has increased			0.813	
31	They have made the place more dirty (littering)			0.805	
32	These have led to increase in alcohol and drug abuse			0.627	
	NEGATIVE SOCIAL EFFECT (F4)				
33	These have led to increase in prostitution				0.88
34	These have led to increase in crime rate				0.88
	ITEMS	19	3	10	2
	EIGEN VALUE	11.5	6.01	2.05	1.67
	VARIANCE EXPLAINED	31.1	16.2	5.56	4.51
	TOTAL VARIANCE EXPLAINED	57.43%			
	KMO MEASURE OF SAMPLING ADEQUACY	0.861			
	CRONBACH'S ALPHA	0.94	0.94	0.94	0.94

impacts on the quality of life of residents. Respondents are very well aware that the DMOs are not managing the event IFFI in the best possible manner, but rather as a stop gap arrangement. Furthermore, the majority of residents were of the opinion (based on the informal conversations) that other stakeholders of film tourism (DMOs, producers, tourists, entrepreneurs) are not bothered about making IFFI a sustainable event for the betterment of Goa as an international film tourism destination.

9.4.4 Mean Test of Factors Across Demographic Profile

In order to answer RQ 4: Is there any difference in perception with regards to Quality of life factors across demographic profiles; a mean test was done to analyze difference in perceived Quality of Life factors identified in the preceding section across demographic profiles. Results as per Exhibit 9.4 showed that Factor 1 (Community pride) was not found to be different across various demographic profiles. Factor 2 (Personal Gain) was perceived differently across variable length of stay, implying people who are residents of Goa for more than 10 years found more

Exhibit 9.4 Factors driving residents quality of life and demographic profiling)

		Factors driving resident perception			
Demographic characteristic		F1	F2	F3	F4
Age	20–29	4.28	3.12	4.49	3.56
	30–39	4.84	3.57	4.83	3.86
	40–49	4.25	3.11	4.88	4.29
	50 and above	4.57	3.21	5.73	4.75
	F-value	**0.67**	**0.50**	**7.31***	**3.44***
Education	Up to 12 years study	4.49	2.96	5.00	3.58
	Graduation	4.38	3.72	4.38	3.97
	Post graduation	4.27	3.11	5.03	4.25
	F-value	**0.558**	**2.26**	**3.33***	**1.93**
Gender	Male	4.44	3.09	5.07	4.20
	Female	4.28	3.36	4.65	3.75
	t-value	**−0.886**	**0.947**	**−2.112***	**−1.563**
Income	Less than 2000USD	4.48	3.36	4.75	3.58
	2000–20,000 USD	4.26	3.07	5.04	4.63
	Above 20,000 USD	4.00	2.84	4.80	3.83
	F-value	**1.38**	**0.76**	**0.92**	**6.02***
Length of stay	Less than a year	4.67	2.94	4.09	2.15
	1–10 years	4.28	2.75	4.71	3.76
	10 years and above	4.45	4.09	5.31	4.78
	F-value	**0.85**	**10.79***	**6.37***	**12.63***
Marital status	Unmarried	4.48	3.24	4.80	4.05
	Married	4.26	3.19	4.91	3.93
	t-value	**1.201**	**0.198**	**−0.531**	**0.437**

*$p < 0.05$

personal benefits with Film based Tourism activity ($F = 10.79$, $p < 0.05$). Factor 3 (Negative environmental effect) was perceived significantly different across Age ($F = 7.31$, $p < 0.05$), Education ($F = 3.33$, $p < 0.05$), Gender ($t = -2.121$, $p < 0.05$), Length of stay ($F = 6.37$, $p < 0.05$).

Residents in the age group 50, Post graduates, males and residing in Goa for more than 10 years perceived that Film tourism has brought negative environmental effects such as increased air pollution, heritage sites getting damaged, an increase in drug abuse, parking space, sewage problems as well as putting enormous pressure on facilities meant for locals. Factor 4 (Negative social effect) was perceived across Age ($F = 3.44$, $p < 0.05$), Income ($F = 6.02$, $p < 0.05$) and Length of stay ($F = 12.63$, $p < 0.05$). Residents in the age group 50, belonging to the income group (2000–20,000 USD) and residing in Goa for more than 10 years highly agreed that Film Tourism has brought with it negative social effects such as an increase in crime rate, drug mafia and prostitution.

Hence, based on the above, the formulated hypothesis (H_2) of RQ 3, that "no significant difference exists between perceived Quality of life factors which drives resident's perception with respect to age, gender, income, marital status, education, length of stay" is rejected with an exception of F1 (Community pride) which was not perceived differently, and which clearly corroborates with similar studies previously carried out, that age, education and income influences residents perception towards Film tourism.

9.5 Conclusion

It has been observed that resident's perception is driven by the benefits they perceive about tourism. If cost outweighs benefits, opposition happens for a tourism venture and vice versa. Findings of this paper are in line with SET (Social Exchange Theory), as the majority of the respondents feels that the benefits are not completely passed on to the residents, hence they feel that being in a position to manage and control the event like EFFI, DMOs are not really taking interest in improving the quality of life at the destination. The majority of studies carried out in Film tourism measured resident attitude but failed to analyze the possibility of predicting the change in perception with variations of demographic factors. With this background, the present study tried to find out whether any relation exists between demographic variables and residents attitude towards Film tourism as well as the effect a change in demographic variables will have on resident's attitude and to what extent. Also this study sheds light on factors which drive resident's perception about Film tourism. The present study is unique in the sense that no similar study combining film tourism and its impact on residents quality of life has been carried out so far, this adds to the existing literature, and is hence relevant in the present tourism literature.

The importance of assessing the demographic characteristics of residents will help the DMOs to plan and manage film tourism as an important event. The result of the study showed that age, income and education of residents has a significant impact on resident's attitude towards film tourism, implying highly educated and younger people support Film based tourism. Senior residents were the prime opposers. Furthermore, this research shows that any increase in age leads to an increase in the probability of being opposer primarily due to negative environmental and social effect it has on society. Moreover, the increase in Education level showed a sharp increase in attitudes towards supporting these activities mainly because of new job opportunities which these kinds of tourism activities bring to the society at large.

Assessing factors driving resident's quality of life revealed four distinct groups of variables, viz.; Community pride, Personal Benefits, Negative Environmental effect and Negative Social Effect. These four factors are essentially the very basic factors studied when it comes to assessing the quality of life of residents in a particular region, both positive and negative aspects. Residents staying in a destination for more than 10 years showed a high rating for Personal benefits implying that they feel it has helped them with employment and monetary terms, which again corroborates with the SET, i.e., residents will be more supportive when the benefits are more, oppose when the cost is more than benefits, and be neutral when no change is perceived. Senior Residents, Post-graduates, Males and residing in Goa for more than 10 years perceived that Film tourism has brought negative environmental effects such as increased air pollution, heritage sites are getting damaged, an increase in drug abuse, parking and sewage problems, as well as putting enormous pressure on facilities meant for locals. These are the negative aspects on quality of life which needs to be taken care of before the destination ceases to attract tourists in the future. Event organizers can address this problem which might reduce the resistance of locals for these kinds of events. In essence, one can see that residents are very much concerned about negative environmental and social effects which directly impact the quality of life due to film tourism.

As stated in the literature, local support is essential for the creation of an enjoyable tourism product and therefore, this research provides a base for successful tourism policies. Past research has shown the different impacts of tourism on the local community, and the perceptions and attitudes of residents towards tourism, however no research has shown nor how much these perceptions and attitudes change according to a change in the demographic profile of the local community. This research limits to the prediction of purely film based tourism activity in Goa which is comparatively in a nascent stage as compared to other developed countries where film tourism has been developed in the most sustainable manner. The DMOs [Entertainment Society of Goa (ESG) as well as Goa Tourism Development Corporation (GTDC)] must consider the residents' perceptions and opinions into consideration and improve the essential four A's of tourism. Currently, Goa as an attraction is getting negatively affected due to overcrowding, increased pollution especially due to inefficient garbage disposal policy, and misuse of resources. Similarly the amenities are also not in good condition, viz., accommodation issues, poor sanitation facilities, inferior food quality, as well as shortage of water and electricity. The most difficult issue is accessibility, viz., inefficient transportation facilities especially the private taxi operations, regular traffic congestion during season time, and inadequate parking facilities. Finally, absence of ancillary services (for example lack of additional or supplementary attractions and also inadequate peripheral tourism development) resulted in Goa as being the least sought after film tourism destination. Hence DMOs must take reactive (since not taken any proactive action, resulted in the existing pathetic condition) strategic initiatives for improving all the above mentioned conditions and issues so as to ensure that Goa becomes one of the top ten film tourism destinations in the world by 2020. Furthermore, finding a core reason for opinion and then applying logit model to predict the change could have a wider application in policy formulation and the development of film based tourism in Goa. If the DMOs take the necessary measures for improving the overall infrastructure and allow and enable the benefits to be passed on to the residents, residents attitude towards film tourism will improve considerably in a positive manner. Being one of the smallest states in India, DMOs of the state of Goa have the advantage of formulating and implementing efficient and sustainable strategic initiatives for developing and improving the film tourism segment as one of the most sought after annual events in India in the coming years.

Further research may reveal more information on the impact of IFFI. Assessing film tourists' perceptions and motivations may reveal the much required information about the potential future demand for IFFI that can be used by the DMOs to segment the film tourists and market the IFFI in a better way to both domestic and international markets. Another aspect which needs attention concerns the hospitality industry, which will provide the information about carrying capacity and subsequently allow the stakeholders to improve the quality and standard of their operations to be on par with any other international destination. Along with this, a serious effort is to be done to study the role and importance of transportation facilities available for providing better, efficient and cheaper transport for the tourists that are on par with any other tourist destinations around the world.

Note:
Earlier version the paper titles "Residents Perception Towards Film Tourism in Goa: A Multi-Logit Analysis", was presented at the 3rd World Research Summit for Tourism and Hospitality & 1st USA-China Tourism Research Summit; Florida, USA, 15–19 December 2015 (jointly organized by UCF Rosen College of Hospitality Management, Orlando, FL, USA and Elsevier).

Acknowledgement Authors acknowledge the constructive criticism received from two anonymous referees, which helped in bringing the paper in its present form. Authors also acknowledge the English proofreading and editing support by Simone Dimitriou, Assistant of Research, Institute of Tourism, University of Applied Sciences and Arts Western Switzerland, Valais.

References

Andereck, K. L., & Vogt, C. A. (2000). The relationship between residents' attitudes toward tourism and tourism development options. *Journal of Travel Research, 39*(1), 27–36.

Ap, J. (1992). Residents' perceptions on tourism impacts. *Annals of Tourism Research, 19*(4), 665–690.

Ap, J., & Crompton, J. L. (1993). Residents' strategies in responding to tourism impacts. *Journal of Travel Research, 17*(4), 610–616.

Beeton, S. (2001). Smiling for the camera: The influence of film audiences on a budget tourism destination. *Tourism, Culture and Communication, 3*, 15–25.

Beeton, S. (2004a). The more things change. A legacy of film-induced tourism. In W. Frost, W. G. Croy, & S. Beeton (Eds.), *Proceedings of the international tourism and media conference* (pp. 4–14). Melbourne: Australia, Tourism Research Unit, Monash University.

Beeton, S. (2004b). Rural tourism in Australia: Has the gaze altered? Tracking rural images though film and tourism promotion. *International Journal of Tourism Research, 6*(3), 125–135.

Beeton, S. (2005). *Film-induced tourism*. Clevedon: Channel View Publications.

Brayley, R., Var, T., & Sheldon, P. (1990). Perceived influence of tourism on social issues. *Annals of Tourism Research, 17*(2), 284–289.

Busby, G., & Klug, J. (2001). Movie-induced tourism: The challenge of measurement and other issues. *Journal of Vacation Marketing, 7*(4), 316–332.

Busby, G., Ergul, M., & Eng, J. (2013). Film tourism and the lead actor: An exploratory study of the influence on destination image and branding. *Anatolia: An International Journal of Tourism and Hospitality Research, 24*, 395–404.

Connell, J. (2005a). Toddlers, tourism and Tobermory: Destination marketing issues and TV-induced tourism. *Tourism Management, 26*, 763–776.

Connell, J. (2005b). What's the story in Balamory? The impacts of a children's TV programme on small tourism enterprises on the Isle of Mull, Scotland. *Journal of Sustainable Tourism, 13*, 228–255.

Connell, J. (2012). Film tourism: Evolution, progress and prospects. *Tourism Management, 33*(5), 1007–1029.

Couldry, N. (2005). On the actual street. In D. Crouch, R. Jackson, & F. Thompson (Eds.), *The media and the tourist imagination. Converging cultures* (pp. 60–75). London: Routledge.

Crompton, J. L., Lee, S., & Shuster, T. J. (2001). A guide for undertaking economic impact studies: The Springfest example. *Journal of Travel Research, 40*(1), 79–87.

Croy, W. G. (2010). Planning for film tourism: Active destination image management. *Tourism and Hospitality Planning & Development, 7*(1), 21–30.

Croy, W. G. (2011). Film tourism: Sustained economic contributions to destinations. *Worldwide Hospitality and Tourism Themes, 3*(2), 159–164.

Croy, W. G., & Heitmann, S. (2011). Tourism and film. In P. Robinson, S. Heitmann, & P. Dieke (Eds.), *Research themes in tourism* (pp. 188–204). Wallingford: CABI.

Croy, G., & Walker, R. D. (2003). Rural tourism and film e issues for strategic rural development. In D. Hall, L. Roberts, & M. Mitchell (Eds.), *New directions in rural tourism* (pp. 115–133). Aldershot: Ashgate.

Deprez, C. (2013). The film division of India, 1948–1964: The early days and the influence of the British documentary film tradition. *Film History, 25*(3), 149–173.

DFF. (2015). International Film Festival of India. Directorate of Film Festivals. http://www.dff.nic.in/iffi.asp. Accessed 9 June 2015.

D'Mello, C., Chang, L., Kamat, K., Scaglione, M., Weiermair, K., & Subhash, K. B. (2015). An examination of factors influencing tourists attitude towards tourism in Goa. *International Journal of Tourism and Hospitality Systems, 8*(2), 1–11.

D'Mello, C., Fernandes, S., Zimmermann, F. M., Subhash, K. B., & Ganef, J. P. (2016a). Multi-stakeholder perceptions about sustainable tourism in Goa: A structural equation modeling. *International Journal of Tourism and Travel, 9*(1–2), 21–39.

D'Mello, C., Chang, L., Subhash, K. B., Kamat, K., Zimmermann, F. M., & Weiermair, K. (2016b). Comparison of multi-stakeholder perception of tourism sustainability in Goa. *International Journal of Tourism and Hospitality Systems, 11*(2), 1–13.

Getz, D., & Page, S. J. (2016). Progress and prospects for event tourism research. *Tourism Management, 52*, 593–631.

Giacopassi, D., & Stitt, B. G. (1994). Assessing the impact of casino gambling on crime in Mississippi. *American Journal of Criminal Justice, 18*(1), 117–131.

Heitmann, S. (2010). Film tourism planning and development - questioning the role of stakeholders and sustainability. *Tourism and Hospitality Planning & Development, 7*(1), 31–46.

Hudson, S., & Ritchie, J. R. B. (2006a). Promoting destinations via film tourism: An empirical identification of supporting marketing initiatives. *Journal of Travel Research, 44*, 387–396.

Hudson, S., & Ritchie, J. R. B. (2006b). Film tourism and destination marketing: The case of Captain Corelli's Mandolin. *Journal of Vacation Marketing, 12*(3), 256–268.

Hudson, S., & Tung, V. W. T. (2010). "Lights, camera, action...!" Marketing film locations to Hollywood. *Marketing Intelligence and Planning, 28*(2), 188–205.

Hudson, S., Wang, Y., & Gil, S. M. (2010). The influence of a film on destination image and the desire to travel: A cross-cultural comparison. *International Journal of Tourism Research, 13*, 177–190.

IFFI. (2015). International Film Festival of India. http://www.iffi.nic.in/aboutus.asp. Accessed 9 June 2015.

Jurowski, C. (1994). *The interplay of elements affecting host communityresident attitudes toward tourism: A path analytic approach.* Unpublished Ph.D.dissertation, Department of Hospitality and Tourism Management, VirginiaPolytechnic Institute and State University.

Jurowski, C., Uysal, M., & Williams, D. R. (1997). A theoretical analysis of host community resident reactions to tourism. *Journal of Travel Research, 34*(2), 3–11.

Kaiser, H. F. (1974). An index of factorial simplicity. *Psychometrika, 39*, 31–36.

Kamat, K., Chen, R. F., D'Mello, C., Scaglione, M., Weiermair, K., & Subhash, K. B. (2016). The social, economic, and environmental impacts of Casino tourism on the residents of Goa. *Latin American Tourismology Review* [Revista Latino-Americana De Tourismologia], *2*(1), 44–54.

Kim, K., Uysal, M., & Sirgy, M. J. (2013). How does tourism in a community impact the quality of life of community residents? *Tourism Management, 36*, 527–540.

Kim, S. (sean), Kim, S. (San), & Oh, M. (2017). Film tourism town and its local community. *International Journal of Hospitality & Tourism Administration*. https://doi.org/10.1080/15256480.2016.1276005. Accessed 9 June 2017.

Knowindia. (2015). *Cinema in India: Film Division*. http://knowindia.gov.in/knowindia/cinema.php. Accessed 9 June 2015.

Lankford, S. V., & Howard, D. (1994). Revising TIAS. *Annals of Tourism Research, 21*(4), 829–831.

Lee, C. K., Kang, S. K., Long, P., & Reisinger, Y. (2010). Residents' perceptions of casino impacts: A comparative study. *Tourism Management, 31*(2), 189–201.

Li, S., Li, H., Song, H., Lundberg, C., & Shen, S. (2017). The economic impact of on-screen tourism: The case of The Lord of the Rings and the Hobbit. *Tourism Management, 60*, 177–187.

Lin, Y. S., & Huang, J. Y. (2008). Analyzing the use of TV mini-series for Korea tourism marketing. *Journal of Travel & Tourism Marketing, 24*(2–3), 223–227.

Lin, Y. S., Lin, P. L., & Huang, H. L. (2007). Study on correlation among tourists' travel behavior, service quality, satisfaction and loyalty – Using Jian Hu Shan Theme Park as an example. *Journal of Sport, Leisure and Hospitality Research, 2*(2), 67–83.

Mordue, T. (2001). Performing and directing resident/tourist cultures in heartbeat country. *Tourist Studies, 1*, 233–252.

Mordue, T. (2009). Television, tourism and rural life. *Journal of Travel Research, 47*(3), 332–345.

Mueller, C. (2006). *Film festival tourism*. http://www.filmfestivals.com/cgi-bin/shownews.pl. Accessed 15 Sept 2008.

Murphy, P. E., & Carmichael, B. A. (1991). Assessing the tourism benefits of an open access sports tournament: The 1989 B.C. winter games. *Journal of Travel Research, 29*, 32–36.

O'Neill, K., Butts, S., & Busby, G. (2005). The corellification of Cephallonian tourism. *Anatolia, 16*(2), 207–226.

Pizam, A., & Pokela, J. (1985). The perceived impacts of casino gambling on the community. *Annals of Tourism Research, 12*(2), 147–165.

Riley, R., & van Doren, C. (1992). Movies as tourism promotion: A push factor in a pull location. *Tourism Management, 13*, 267–274.

Riley, R., Baker, D., & van Doren, C. (1998). Movie-induced tourism. *Annals of Tourism Research, 25*, 919–935.

Rojek, C. (1995). *Decentring leisure. Rethinking leisure theory*. London: Sage.

Sine, H. (2010). Film tourism planning and developments – Questioning the role of stakeholders and sustainability. *Tourism and Hospitality Planning & Development, 7*(1), 31–46.

Stitt, B. G., Nicholas, M., & Giacopassi, D. (2003). Does the presence of casinos increase crime? An examination of casino and control communities. *Crime & Dilinquency, 49*, 253–283.

Subhash, K. B., & Chen, R. (2012). Geography of transnational terrorism: An Indian perspective. In S. Sharma, D. Das, R. Jain, & P. S. Sangwan (Eds.), *India emerging: Opportunities and challenges* (pp. 106–124). New Delhi: Pragun Publication.

Tabachnick, B. G., & Fidell, L. S. (1989). *Using multivariale statistics* (2nd ed.). Cambridge: Harper & Row.

Tooke, N., & Baker, M. (1996). Seeing is believing: The effect of film on visitor numbers to screened locations. *Tourism Management, 17*, 87–94.

Wiki. (2015a). *History of Goa*. https://en.wikipedia.org/wiki/History_of_Goa. Accessed 18 June 2015.

Wiki. (2015b). *Timeline of Goan History*. https://en.wikipedia.org/wiki/Timeline_of_Goan_history. Accessed 18 June 2015.

Zhang, X., Ryan, C., & Cave, J. (2016). Residents, their use of a tourist facility and contribution to tourist ambience: Narratives from a film tourism site in Beijing. *Tourism Management, 52*, 416–429.

Chapter 10
Sustainable Practices in Spanish Hotels: A Response to Concerns on Quality of Life in Highly Visited Tourism Areas

Irene Gil-Saura and María-Eugenia Ruiz-Molina

Abstract The intense tourism activity may involve significant negative impacts on the quality of life in tourism destinations with a high number of tourist arrivals. The objective of this chapter is to explore the available tools and measures that hotels may implement to mitigate or cope with these negative economic, social and environmental impacts. An example of hotel managers' perceptions of the importance of the main environmentally sustainable practices in hospitality to mitigate the negative impact of the tourist industry on the quality of life of residents in highly visited tourism destinations in the Mediterranean coast of Spain is provided, with the purpose of stimulating further research in this topic.

Keywords Sustainable practices · Hotels · Quality of life · Consolidated tourism destinations

10.1 Introduction

It is widely accepted that quality of life, tourism activities, and sustainability are all interrelated (Mathew and Sreejesh 2017; Scheyvens 1999; Tsaur et al. 2006; Uysal et al. 2016). As tourism grows, an important challenge should be to conciliate sustainability and development, with quality of life of all stakeholders. In this context, tourism companies should contribute to improving the quality of life not only of tourists but also residents in host communities and employees of tourism services. In this vein, it has been highlighted the contribution of the hospitality industry to

The authors are grateful for the support of the projects ECO2013–43353-R and ECO2016–76553-R of the Spanish Ministry of Education and Science, as well as to Mr. Pablo Pintado and the "Pioneers into Practice" Program 2015 financed by the EIT-Climate KIC.

I. Gil-Saura · M.-E. Ruiz-Molina (✉)
Departamento de Comercialización e Investigación de Mercados, Universitat de València, Valencia, Spain
e-mail: M.Eugenia.Ruiz@uv.es

A. M. Campón-Cerro et al. (eds.), *Best Practices in Hospitality and Tourism Marketing and Management*, Applying Quality of Life Research,
https://doi.org/10.1007/978-3-319-91692-7_10

improve the quality of life in host communities through ensuring high labour standards, supporting local communities or promoting environmental sustainability (Bohdanowicz and Zientara 2009). Focusing on the latter, when hotels are highly committed to environmental management, they enhance the quality of life of destination residents, thus improving the local community's predisposition to accept tourism-related initiatives (Claver et al. 2007).

In highly developed tourism destinations, locals have generally informed positive attitudes in terms of improved economic quality of life (Teye et al. 2002). But in many cases, tourism destinations develop to meet tourists' needs and wants without caring about environmental impact (Andereck et al. 2005). Among the potential environmental consequences of tourism development, Andereck (1995) mentions air pollution related to traffic congestion, water pollution, plant destruction and deforestation.

In view of all this, tourism destinations' challenge is to minimize the negative impacts of tourism while maintaining the quality of life of residents, and maximize the positive impacts of tourism through "sustaining resources that provide quality experience and services for both tourists and locals" (Uysal et al. 2012).

The objective of this paper is to present the hotel managers' perceptions of the main environmentally sustainable practices in hospitality to mitigate the negative impact of the tourist industry on the quality of life of residents in highly visited tourism destinations. Since many areas in Spain receive millions of visitors year after year, assuming a Triple-Bottom-Line (TBL) approach, that considers economic, social and environmental issues, we aim at providing an overview about the assessment of the importance of several practices by the main hotel chains with 4 and 5-star hotels in the Spanish Mediterranean coast.

As one of the top-five tourism destinations in the world (UNWTO 2017), there is a trade-off between the contribution of Tourism to GDP and job creation, and the economic, social and environmental impact of this activity. Sustainable practices may allow to conciliate the economic benefits and the mitigation of the negative impact on the quality of life of residents and visitors. But the perceived importance of these practices by hotel managers may strongly influence their actual implementation.

10.2 Sustainable Practices in Hospitality

Three-pillar sustainability has been pointed out as a source of benefits for hotels, the local communities and the natural environment (Cvelbar and Dwyer 2013; Ryan 2003), being compatible with firm financial goals and competitiveness (Zink and Fischer 2013; Bryson and Lombardi 2009). Notwithstanding, there are still many companies in the tourism industry whose decisions are based on short-term economic benefits, thus neglecting social and environmental sustainability (Bach et al. 2014). In this sense, a heavy intensive usage of natural resources in search of short-term financial turnover may lead to overcrowding and the destruction of natural resources that could damage the company's long-term financial performance as well as the local economy (Clayton 2002) and threatening quality of life in the community (Bansal 2002).

Tourism development is considered as a way of improving a country's economy and social well-being, but if this development is not driven by sustainability principles, tourists may choose alternative destinations or attractions, thus resulting in limited business and economic results for the tourism companies in this region (De Sausmarez 2004).

Moreover, tourism is an industry that very much depends on the natural environment (Weaver 2012). Recent research has emphasized the importance of the environment for tourism activity and development (Butler 2008). It has also been concerned with the impacts that tourism has on natural resources (Claver et al. 2007). In the United Nations Climate Change Conference held in Copenhagen in December 2009, it has been highlighted that the role of tourism in the generation or control of greenhouse gases is highly relevant. If global warming process evolves according to forecasts, winter sports, island holidays and sun and sand holiday destinations will be under massive pressure. Certainly, it will mean that the geography of the tourism industry will change dramatically (UNFCCC 2010). In this context, environmental factors have gained major importance. The hotel industry has been traditionally considered one that does not have a great impact on the natural environment compared to manufacturing industry. However, it generates much more negative environmental impacts that the public opinion perceives, consuming a vast amount of local and imported nondurable goods, energy and water, as well as emitting a large amount of carbon dioxide (Bohdanowicz 2006).

Since the early 1990s, tourism companies, mostly hotel facilities, have undertaken different initiatives to both, provide evidence of their commitment to sustainable tourism, and in particular for the mitigation and adaptation to the increasing threats of Climate Change. For instance, large corporations, such as TUI, try to promote "environmentally-compatible management" as well as socioeconomic viability, by publicizing and awarding the best practices of tourism services suppliers within its business network (Sigala 2008). Similarly, in Nordic countries, an innovative corporate social responsibility program has been implemented, contributing greatly to increased satisfaction amongst managers, employees and customers (Bohdanowicz and Zientara 2008).

Tools and practices to measure economic sustainability include business ratios and formulas (Bragg 2006), as well marketing metrics (Farris et al. 2006). Concerning social sustainability, a reference in assessing tools and measures is the CSR Europe's Toolbox (CSR Europe 2012) report, that covers personnel policies, human rights, and local community impact and activities.

In terms of environmental sustainability, the most common tools and mechanisms applied by the hotel industry are codes of conduct, best environmental practices, eco-labels, environmental management systems (EMS) and environmental performance indicators.

As indicators of hotel Environmental Management Standards (EMS), items included in the ISO14000 standards are considered. Some representative foreign green hotel assessment systems are also commonly considered as a reference in this industry, e.g. the Green Hotels Association, the State Economic and Trade

Commission, the Caribbean Hotel Association, Grecotels, the Coalition for Environmental Responsible Economies (CERES), the South Pacific Tourism Organization (SPTO), the Global Stewards and the Bench-markhotel.com website.

These systems commonly undertake hotel and tourism environmental cooperation programs and activities. They are committed to promote the effective management of natural resource and to achieve sustainable tourism. These indicators consider the impact on the environment of both the internal management (services, operations, personnel, administration, marketing, and finance) and to the external environment (economics, technology, social trends, ecological environment, customers, competitors, and suppliers). In addition, the primary management issues of hotels (Webster 2000) were also given while auditing the environment.

When implementing an environmental policy, hotels are mainly focusing on technical efficiency (Hathroubi et al. 2014) and cost efficiency (Shieh 2012). In these sense, there is evidence in the hospitality industry about the importance of the savings arising from efficient water management (e.g. Kasim et al. 2014), measuring and implementing practices to reduce energy consumption (e.g. Abdi et al. 2013; Araki et al. 2013; Day and Cai 2012; Sheivachman 2011), and the benefits of recycling solid waste (Singh et al. 2014). Examples of sustainable practices related to the creation of a healthy and safe indoor environment in hotels are also provided in the literature, e.g. hotel management of construction (Cui and Hui 2011), LEED certification for buildings (De Lima et al. 2012), design (Brody 2014) and green renovation schedule requirements (Dienes and Wang 2010).

The hotel sustainable practices usually involve several stakeholders. First, regarding the corporate management, a relationship is found between managers' environmental perceptions, environmental management and firm performance in Spanish hotels (López et al. 2011).

Second, hotel sustainable practices often involve staff education. Indeed, according to Stalcup et al. (2014), sustainable programs in hotels should start with staff. In this vein, there is wide evidence about human resources practices for environmental sustainability in hotels (Chan et al. 2014; Chou 2014; Kim and Choi 2013; Park and Levy 2014; Stalcup et al. 2014; Yen et al. 2013).

Last, regarding consumers, as green practices are becoming more commonly used by hotels, guests are supporting these initiatives (Withiam 2015). When educating customers about sustainability, it has been highlighted the importance of developing effective communication strategies to encourage hotel guests' green behavior (Lee and Oh 2014), being credibility on green messages in hotels a major concern (Kim and Kim 2014). Recent research has found support to the relation between environmental friendly programs in hotels and customers intention to stay (Kim et al. 2012) as well as between sustainability and customer loyalty (Chen 2015).

All in all, we enunciate the following research questions:

RQ1: *What is the perceived importance of practices for economic, social and environmental sustainability by hotel managers?*

RQ2: *What is the perceived importance of measures for environmental sustainability for different stakeholders by hotel managers?*

10.3 Method

The present paper aims at providing an overview about the assessment of the importance of several practices for economic, social and environmental sustainability by the managers of the main hotel chains with 4 and 5-star hotels in the Spanish Mediterranean coast of Spain. Hotel chains are prone to standardize their procedures and manuals (Kasim 2007), while upscale hotels are a reference in this industry (Stylos and Vassiliadis 2015).

Following the Triple-Bottom-Line approach suggested by Elkington (1994), we have included items for measuring the level of development or implementation of practices for the economic, social and environmental sustainability of the hotel. The items were adapted from Stylos and Vassiliadis (2015), excepting those regarding consumer education about green mobility, that were proposed by the authors. All items were measured in a 5-point Likert scale (1 = not at all important; 5 = totally important).

In order to perform the study, a census of 4 and 5-star hotels in two main Spanish cities in the Mediterranean in terms of tourist arrivals – i.e. Valencia and Gandía – was elaborated based on the secondary information available in the Official guide of hotels in Spain and the hotel directory of the Valencian Tourism Agency. Hotel managers of 39 hotel chains with 4 and 5-star hotels in the Mediterranean coast of Spain were invited to participate in the survey by phone and then the link to the structured questionnaire was sent by e-mail in the last week of May and the months of June and September 2015. The online questionnaire was generated through Google Forms, and the link to the survey was sent to the e-mail address provided by hotel managers who accepted to participate in the study. After several reminders by phone and e-mail, 12 valid questionnaires were finally received, representing a response rate of 30.77%. With the quantitative information collected through the valid questionnaires received, descriptive analyses are performed to provide an overview regarding the importance of these practices from the point of view of the hotel chain.

10.4 Results

First, regarding the importance of measures for economic viability, means values for responses are shown in Table 10.1.

Measuring customer satisfaction is considered as totally important by all hotels. Market share evaluation and measuring customer loyalty follow, being considered as totally important for almost all hotel managers interviewed. Scores are higher or near to 4 for the rest of items measuring the importance of the rest of issues regarding economic viability and innovation for the hotel manager.

Table 10.1 Means and standard deviations of items of importance measures for economic viability and innovation

	Mean	St. dev.
Hotel economic feasibility		
Market share evaluation	4.75	0.45
Brand development index	4.25	0.75
Evaluate brand penetration	4.42	0.67
Evaluate customer loyalty	4.75	0.45
Evaluate customer satisfaction	5.00	0.00
Calculate profit margins	4.73	0.47
Determine break-even sales	4.08	0.79
Estimate optimal prices of hotel services	4.58	0.67
Calculate promotional costs	4.25	0.75
Calculate advertising costs per medium	4.17	0.83
Count customers/customer visits	4.25	0.62
Implement SWOT analysis	4.08	1.16
Implement customer relationship management system	4.67	0.65
Innovation		
Support, analyze, record, and assess proposed and innovative ideas, processes, and services on behalf of personnel	3.83	0.94
Evaluate degree of innovation	3.92	0.79
Make use of models for planning, implementation, and control of investments and relevant budgets	4.25	1.22
Use of perceptual analysis for depicting the position of our hotel in relation to competitors in customers' minds	4.45	1.19

Next, respondents were asked about the importance placed by the hotel chain on social sustainability issues such as personnel policies, human rights and local community impact and activities (Table 10.2).

Regarding personnel policies, according to the scores provided by hotel managers, the hotel chains they represent consider as totally important or important (scores above 4) avoiding discrimination in staff recruitment, employing personnel with special skills and evaluating the impact of human resource decisions. In contrast, absenteeism does not seem to be a great problem for these companies.

Concerning human rights and impact assessment on the hotel chain activities on the local community, average scores are near to the midpoint of the scale. Therefore, in general, hotel chains put more interest on their internal stakeholders than in the external groups of interest.

The importance of the environmental policy for the hotel is also assessed (Table 10.3). Widely promoting the hotel's environmental policy to all employees, customers, and suppliers is important for most hotels. The rest of items show also values higher than the midpoint of the scale (i.e. 3).

Respondents are asked about the importance of some specific topics addressed by the environmental policy of the hotel, i.e. water management, energy, solid waste

Table 10.2 Means and standard deviations of items of importance measures for social sustainability

	Mean	St. dev.
Personnel policies		
Workers and managers are hired without an age, gender or nationality criterion	4.33	0.65
Hotel employs people with special skills	4.33	0.78
Absenteeism is a quite often phenomenon among the employees	2.33	1.44
The hotel tries to avoid high staff turnover	3.92	1.24
Salaries and working conditions are above average within local market	3.25	0.62
Hotel budget includes expenses for educational sessions and training	4.00	0.74
In case of important decisions such as personnel downsizing, training, etc., an evaluation of relevant impacts takes place	4.17	0.72
Hotelier is interested in a balanced relationship between work and personal life of personnel	4.00	0.74
Human rights		
Hotel supports local community's activities with money as a percentage of profits before taxes	3.08	0.67
Evaluation of unified value of salaries, bonuses, and other benefits directed to the families of local community	3.17	0.94
There are positive/negative comments or news concerning the actions taken by the hotel in respect of local community	3.50	0.67
Local community impact and activities		
Existence of an annual program for organizing events or supporting public infrastructure for the local community	3.00	0.74
Impact assessment of the support provided to local community organizations	2.92	0.67
Impact assessment of the support provided to environmental organizations	3.17	0.83
Impact assessment of the support provided to training social initiatives	3.33	0.98

Table 10.3 Means and standard deviations of items of importance measures for environmental sustainability: Hotel environmental policy

	Mean	St. dev.
Publicly declare the hotel's specific environmental policy	3.92	0.67
Widely promote the hotel's environmental policy to all employees, customers, and suppliers	4.08	0.67
Environmental policy possesses clear goals (short, medium, and long terms)	3.67	1.07
Hotel has already established action plan for potential environmental problems	3.75	0.62

management, health and safety in indoor environment and green purchasing (Table 10.4).

The average values of all items related to energy are higher than 4, evidencing the importance of measuring and saving energy for these hotels. In general, the importance of these environmental practices is high (i.e. above 3.5), excepting for converting kitchen or organic wastes into compost, that shows an average value below the midpoint of the scale. Figure 10.1 shows the average values for each aspect of sustainability under consideration.

Table 10.4 Means and standard deviations of items of importance measures for environmental sustainability: Topi

	Mean	St. dev.
Water resource		
Install low-flow showerheads and faucet	4.08	0.51
Install water consumption monitoring system to record the tracking	4.25	0.45
In areas where water usage is higher, install metering equipments to track and management	4.17	0.58
Install leak detection system, and provide for quick leak repair	4.25	0.62
Install water recycling system (e.g., reclaimed water or rain water collection and reuse)	4.08	0.51
Install sewage disposal and/or monitoring system	3.75	0.62
Provide customers the choice not to change towels daily	4.50	0.52
Provide customers the choice not to change bed linens daily	4.17	0.94
Energy		
Install energy management system in carrying capacity of electricity (e.g., lighting and air conditioning) of departments	4.50	0.52
For intermittently used areas (e.g., lighting equipment), use timers or sensors	4.33	0.65
Try to use natural lighting	4.17	0.58
Use natural ventilation as much as possible	4.00	0.60
Regularly maintain and clean ventilation, air conditioning, heating, and ice making equipments	4.42	0.67
Check at any time to make sure that all the freezers and windows are closed tightly	4.25	0.62
Actively adopt new energy-saving technologies, such as solar heating devices or wind power, etc.	4.00	0.74
Solid waste		
Avoid using disposable items (e.g., disposable tableware…)	4.17	0.58
Minimize food wasting through appropriate distribution, storage, and management systems	4.42	0.51
Convert kitchen or organic wastes into compost	2.83	1.19
Use refillable containers such as shower bottles	3.42	1.08
Establish two-side photocopy systems in the office, and reuse scraps, envelopes, and paper	4.25	0.75
Use electronic versions to transfer and save data in order to decrease paper consumption and waste	4.50	0.67
Provide recycling bins in public areas, kitchen and back office	4.25	1.06
Indoor environment (health and safety)		
Install air filter cleaning equipment in air conditioning system	4.33	0.78
Use low-vitality organic materials on building and decoration	4.00	0.43
Avoid using toxic and dangerous chemicals	4.42	0.51
Various places inside the hotel (lobby, rooms, corridors, etc.) have moderate lighting	4.42	0.51
Healthy and comfortable indoor environment (temperature, humidity, wind speed) with regular monitoring	4.42	0.51

(continued)

Table 10.4 (continued)

	Mean	St. dev.
Noise volume controls within the statutory standards	4.00	1.04
Should regularly monitor noise levels generated by air-conditioning, bathroom, water supply, and drainage	4.33	0.49
Guest rooms set up with independent air-conditioning systems to reduce the chances of pathogens spreading	3.92	1.31
Green purchasing		
Procure durable goods that can be reused and recycled	3.75	0.97
Only work with suppliers who have a clearly declared environmental policy	3.58	0.67
Purchase local goods (e.g., food and materials)	4.08	0.67
Use minimum amounts of chemicals (e.g., cleaning agents, disinfectants, etc.)	3.83	0.58
Purchase goods that have national certification mark (of environmental protection or health)	4.00	0.60

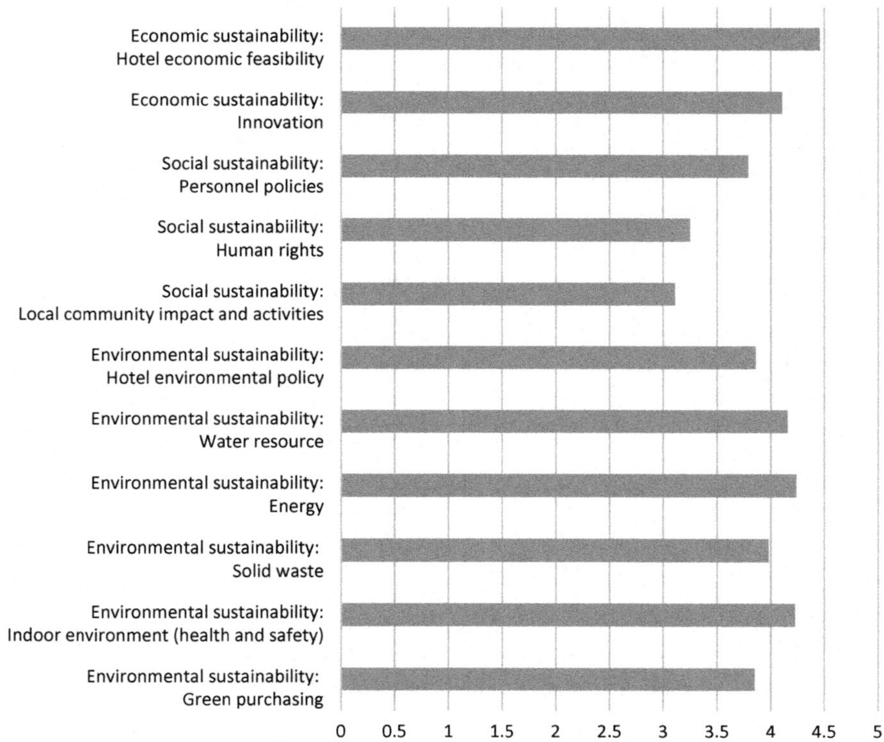

Fig. 10.1 Means of items of importance measures for each category of sustainability

Table 10.5 Means and standard deviations of items of importance measures for environmental sustainability: Stakeholders

	Mean	St. dev.
Corporate management		
Environmental policy can be successfully implemented under corporate management systems	3.42	0.67
All employees are aware of the appointed objectives and are assigned environmental responsibilities	4.08	0.67
Under the principle of introducing minimum impact to the environment, reduce operating costs	4.25	0.45
Hotel provides concept of green consumption and actively implements it	4.42	0.51
Customer satisfaction with hotels' implementation of environmental policies is more than 80%	4.10	0.57
Service quality of the hotel has obtained relevant certification mark (e.g., ISO14000)	4.25	0.75
Company has related insurance (accidental insurance, environmental damage insurance)	4.40	0.70
Staff education		
Provide training courses and environmental education workshop	3.58	1.08
Employees fully understand the extent of corporate environmental policy	3.67	0.98
Employees develop habits for effective use of resources (e.g., turning off the lights, exhaust fans, and air conditioning when vacating areas)	4.42	0.51
Actively reward employees who provide suggestions on environmental improvement	3.42	0.79
Encourage employees to use public transportation	3.10	1.10
Public community relationship		
Promote the green hotel concept	3.58	0.51
Actively involved in green and environmental protection-related activities	3.00	0.95
Donate surplus materials to local non-profit organizations	3.83	0.72
Actively participate in public affairs of local community	3.58	0.67
Provide green messages in public areas, rooms, and websites	3.75	0.97
Consumer education		
Provide signs to remind customers whenever to save resources	3.58	1.24
Provide customers with ways to participate in recycling and re-utilizing	3.75	0.87
Provide customers with public transportation information (MRT, bus, shuttle, etc.)	4.09	1.04
Bikes rental available at the hotel	2.75	0.62
Car sharing available at the hotel	1.42	0.79
Charging facilities for e-vehicles (bikes; scooters; cars) available at the hotels	1.75	0.87
Free public transport tickets for guests	1.08	0.20

The importance of the environmentally sustainable practices in relation to the hotel stakeholders is also assessed (Table 10.5).

In general, hotel managers consider the involvement of corporate management in the hotel environmental practices as very important. The items with the highest scores are those related to the hotel active implementation of the concept of green consumption and the existence of an insurance policy covering potential hotel environmental damage.

Concerning staff education, hotel managers consider as very important or totally important developing habits for efficient use of resources among their employees. The rest of environmental practices related with the staff are also considered as important (i.e. average values above 3).

Regarding the importance of the relationship of the hotel with the public community, average scores are near to 4 in donating surplus materials to non-profit organizations and providing green messages. In contrast, hotel managers seem to be indifferent regarding the hotel being actively involved in environmental protection activities.

Last, hotels state they make an effort to educate customers about saving resources and the use of public transport services. Notwithstanding, it is still reduced the perceived importance of providing customers with services for low carbon mobility – bikes rental, car sharing, charging facilities for electrical vehicles, or free public transport tickets for hotel guests. Figure 10.2 summarizes the averages of the items for environmental sustainability for each stakeholder.

In order to test the existence of significant differences in the importance measures for sustainability and stakeholders depending on hotel category (4 vs. 5 stars) and location (city vs. seaside), due to the small sample size, we calculate the non-parametric Mann-Whitney U test. This test can be used to analyse the existence of differences between groups, being suitable for small samples (5–20 individuals) and for variables measured in an ordinal scale (Nachar 2008) (Table 10.6).

As a result of this analysis, only significant differences are obtained in the importance of measures for hotel economic feasibility between 4 and 5 star hotels, whereas differences are observed between city and seaside hotels for human rights, solid waste management and consumer education, being more important for city hotels in comparison to those located in coastal areas.

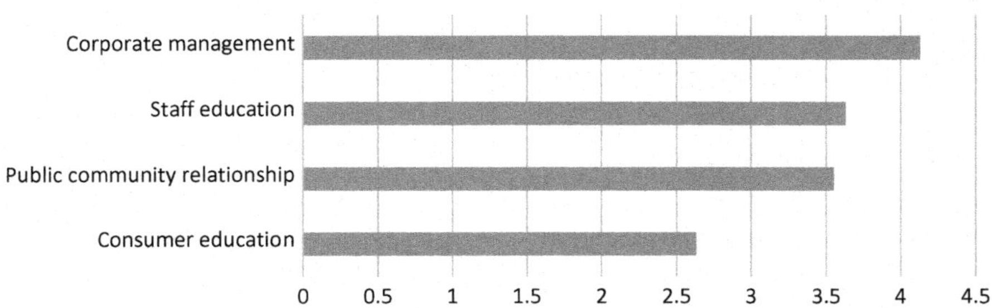

Fig. 10.2 Means of items of importance measures for environmental sustainability for each stakeholder

Table 10.6 Differences in means of importance measures for environmental sustainability and stakeholders depending on hotel category and location

	Ave. rank 4 stars N = 9	Ave. rank 5 stars N = 3	Mann-Whitney U test	Ave. rank City N = 7	Ave. rank Seaside N = 5	Mann-Whitney U test
Sustainability measures						
Economic sustainability						
Hotel economic feasibility	7.72	2.83	2.50[b]	5.71	7.60	12.00
Innovation	6.94	5.17	9.50	6.50	6.50	17.50
Social sustainability						
Personnel policies	6.61	6.17	12.50	6.50	6.50	17.50
Human rights	6.22	7.33	11.00	8.21	4.10	5.50[a]
Local community impact and activ.	6.33	7.00	12.00	7.36	5.30	11.50
Environmental sustainability						
Hotel environmental policy	6.28	7.17	11.50	6.36	6.70	16.50
Water resource	6.39	6.83	12.50	7.79	4.70	8.50
Energy	6.67	6.00	12.00	6.64	6.30	16.50
Solid waste	6.44	6.67	13.00	8.14	4.20	6.00[b]
Indoor environment	6.72	5.83	11.50	6.71	6.20	16.00
Green purchasing	6.11	7.67	10.00	7.21	5.50	12.50
Stakeholders						
Corporate management	6.28	7.17	11.50	6.86	6.00	15.00
Staff education	6.00	8.00	9.00	8.00	4.40	7.00
Public community relationship	6.17	7.50	10.50	6.93	5.90	14.50
Consumer education	6.06	7.83	9.50	8.43	3.80	4.00[a]

[a, b] Statistically significant at $p < 0.01$, $p < 0.05$, $p < 0.10$, respectively

10.5 Conclusions

The policies implemented by hotels to guarantee economic, social and environmental sustainability are expected to contribute to the quality of life of residents in tourism destinations, being generally accepted that sustainability is an important driver for the future success of the hotel industry (Boley and Uysal 2013). The perceptions about the importance of sustainable practices by hotel managers may be considered as a determinant of their actual implementation (Carmona et al. 2004).

Although hotel managers of upscale hotel chains interviewed declare considering as very important or totally important most of items used to assess economic, social and environmental sustainability, the TBL pillar related to economic viability is the one with the highest scores, in the line of previous studies (e.g. Bianchi 2004; Harrison et al. 2003). Environmentally sustainable practices are also prioritized by hotel chains, specially those increasing efficiency and reducing costs in the use of resources. In comparison to practices oriented towards economic and environmental sustainability, social sustainability issues as not considered as important. Therefore, hotel managers seem to be specially concerned on the factors with a direct impact on hotel financial performance, as well as those environmental measures contributing to increase efficiency and reduce costs, i.e. water and energy management. Although many researchers have underlined the importance of social sustainability for the hotel industry (Kang et al. 2010; Tsai et al. 2014), in the case of Spanish hotels in the Mediterranean coast, measures addressing economic and environmental sustainability are more appreciated.

Concerning stakeholders, more attention is paid to practices related to sustainability for internal groups of interest (i.e. corporate management and staff education) in comparison to external stakeholders (e.g. local community), even if they may experience a strong impact of the hotel activity on their quality of life (Uysal et al. 2012). In particular, corporate management followed by staff and public community, are the stakeholders on which measures for environmental sustainability should be mainly focused, while investing in environmentally sustainable measures targeting customers are perceived as much less important. Therefore, there is the need for hotels to consider all stakeholders in order to bring a holistic sustainable strategy into the hospitality industry.

Notwithstanding, the present research is not free from limitations. First, due to the reduced sample size, our findings can not be considered as conclusive, since ANOVA and multigroup analyses cannot be performed. Extending the geographical scope and including also other hotel categories may help to increase the number of respondents. This may also allow to perform comparisons to test if hotel location is a determinant of the implementation of sustainable practices, as some researchers suggest (e.g. Erdogan and Baris 2007; Le et al. 2006).

Second, only one respondent was interviewed in each organization. Additional responses of other members of the hotel staff, and other hotels in the same hotel chain may provide a more objective overview of the perceived importance of the sustainable practices for each organization. In this sense, it would be interesting to analyse if the importance of sustainable practices differs across hotel category or hotel chain characteristics. Qualitative research could be employed in order to gain insight about the reasons for prioritizing the economic and environmental dimensions of sustainability in comparison to the social one. In addition to this, managers could be asked about the real implementation of sustainable practices. And not only managers but also employees, customers or specialists could be interviewed for obtaining objective information as the managers' opinion could be biased.

Last, policy makers may find useful to analyse if changes in some interventions may modify hotel managers' perceptions on their relative importance of the practices for economic, social and environmental sustainability. In this way, the use of longitudinal analysis through panel data, i.e. replicating the survey in a future moment of time, may be a further research avenue with practical implications.

References

Abdi, H., Creighton, D., & Nahavandi, S. (2013). A sustainable energy saving method for hotels by green hotel deals. In A. Håkansson, M. Höjer, R. J. Howlett, & L. C. Jain (Eds.), *Sustainability in energy and buildings, smart innovation, systems and technologies* (pp. 669–677). Berlin/Heidelberg: Springer.

Andereck, K. L. (1995). Environmental consequences of tourism: A review of recent research. In Linking tourism, the environment, and sustainability. *Annual meeting of the national recreation and park association* (General Technical Report INT-GTR-323, pp. 77–81).

Andereck, K. L., Valentine, K. M., Knopf, R. C., & Vogt, C. A. (2005). Residents' perceptions of community tourism impacts. *Annals of Tourism Research, 32*(4), 1056–1076.

Araki, H., Fujiwara, S., Jishi, T., Fujii, M., Yokota, T., & Nishida, T. (2013). Winter production of green asparagus by using surplus heat from machinery room and used hot water from hotel's spa. In *International symposium on new technologies for environment control, energy-saving and crop production in greenhouse and plant* 1037 (pp. 155–161).

Bach, M. P., Zoroja, J., & Merkac-Skok, M. (2014). Social responsibility in tourism: System archetypes approach. *Kybernetes, 43*(3/4), 17–17.

Bansal, P. (2002). The corporate challenges of sustainable development. *The Academy of Management Executive, 16*(2), 122–131.

Bianchi, R. V. (2004). Tourism restructuring and the politics of sustainability: A critical view from the European periphery (The Canary Islands). *Journal of Sustainable Tourism, 12*(6), 495–529.

Bohdanowicz, P. (2006). Environmental awareness and initiatives in the Swedish and polish hotel industries—Survey results. *International Journal of Hospitality Management, 25*(4), 662–682.

Bohdanowicz, P., & Zientara, P. (2008). Corporate social responsibility in hospitality: Issues and implications. A case study of Scandic. *Scandinavian Journal of Hospitality and Tourism, 8*(4), 271–293.

Bohdanowicz, P., & Zientara, P. (2009). Hotel companies' contribution to improving the quality of life of local communities and the well-being of their employees. *Tourism and Hospitality Research, 9*(2), 147–158.

Boley, B. B., & Uysal, M. (2013). Competitive synergy through practicing triple bottom line sustainability: Evidence from three hospitality case studies. *Tourism and Hospitality Research, 13*(4), 226–238.

Bragg, S. M. (2006). *Business ratios and formulas: A comprehensive guide* (2nd ed.). Hoboken: Wiley.

Brody, D. (2014). Go green: Hotels, design, and the sustainability paradox. *Design Issues, 30*(3), 5–15.

Bryson, J. R., & Lombardi, R. (2009). Balancing product and process sustainability against business property development process. *Business Strategy and the Environment, 18*(2), 97–107.

Butler, J. (2008). The compelling 'hard case' for 'green' hotel development. *Cornell Hospitality Quarterly, 49*(3), 234–244.

Carmona, E., Céspedes, J., & De Burgos, J. (2004). Environmental strategies in Spanish hotels: Contextual factors and performance. *The Service Industries Journal, 24*(3), 101–130.

Chan, E. S. W., Hon, A. H. Y., Chan, W., & Okumus, F. (2014). What drives employees' intentions to implement green practices in hotels? The role of knowledge, awareness, concern and ecological behavior. *International Journal of Hospitality Management, 40*(July), 20–28.

Chen, R. J. C. (2015). From sustainability to customer loyalty: A case of full service hotels' guests. *Journal of Retailing and Consumer Services, 22*, 261–265.

Chou, C. J. (2014). Hotels' environmental policies and employee personal environmental beliefs: Interactions and outcomes. *Tourism Management, 40*, 436–446.

Claver, E., Molina, J. F., Pereira, J., & López, M. D. (2007). Environmental strategies and their impact on hotel performance. *Journal of Sustainable Tourism, 15*(6), 663–679.

Clayton, A. (2002). Strategies for sustainable tourism development: The role of the concept of carrying capacity. *Social and Economic Studies, 51*, 61–98.

CSR Europe. (2012). *CSR Europe's toolbox—user manual*. http://www.csreurope.org/pages/en/toolbox.html. Accessed 20 June 2017.

Cui, B., & Hui, Z. (2011). Research on the green hotel management of construction 1. In *ICEIS 2011 Proceedings of the 13th international conference on enterprise information systems* (pp. 453–456). 1 DISI.

Cvelbar, L. K., & Dwyer, L. (2013). An importance–performance analysis of sustainability factors for long-term strategy planning in Slovenian hotels. *Journal of Sustainable Tourism, 21*(3), 487–504.

Day, J., & Cai, L. (2012). Environmental and energy-related challenges to sustainable tourism in the United States and China. *International Journal of Sustainable Development and World Ecology, 19*(5), 379–388.

De Lima, M., Machado, D. F. C., Passador, J. L., & Passador, C. S. (2012). Adopting LEED certification in lodging facilities: Greening the hospitality industry. *RAE Revista de Administracao de Empresas, 52*(2), 179–192.

De Sausmarez, N. (2004). Crisis management for the tourism sector: Preliminary considerations in policy development. *Tourism and Hospitality Planning & Development, 1*(2), 157–172.

Dienes, C. J., & Wang, L. (2010). Using a capacity control model to define optimal green hotel renovation schedule requirements. *International Journal of Operations and Quantitative Management, 16*(3), 255–283.

Elkington, J. (1994). Towards the sustainable corporation: Win-win-win business strategies for sustainable development. *California Management Review, 36*(2), 90–100.

Erdogan, N., & Baris, E. (2007). Environmental protection programs and conservation practices of hotels in Ankara, Turkey. *Tourism Management, 28*(2), 604–614.

Farris, P. W., Bendle, N. T., Pfeifer, P. E., & Reibstein, D. J. (2006). *Marketing metrics: 50+ metrics every executive should master*. Upper Saddle River: Pearson Education.

Harrison, L. C., Jayawardena, C., & Clayton, A. (2003). Sustainable tourism development in the Caribbean: Practical challenges. *International Journal of Contemporary Hospitality Management, 15*(5), 294–298.

Hathroubi, S., Peypoch, N., & Robinot, E. (2014). Technical efficiency and environmental management: The Tunisian case. *Journal of Hospitality and Tourism Management, 21*, 27–33.

Kang, K. H., Lee, S., & Huh, C. (2010). Impacts of positive and negative corporate social responsibility activities on company performance in the hospitality industry. *International Journal of Hospitality Management, 29*(1), 72–82.

Kasim, A. (2007). Towards a wider adoption of environmental responsibility in the hotel sector. *International Journal of Hospitality & Tourism Administration, 8*(2), 25–49.

Kasim, A., Gursoy, D., Okumus, F., & Wong, A. (2014). The importance of water management in hotels: A framework for sustainability through innovation. *Journal of Sustainable Tourism, 22*(7), 1090–1107.

Kim, S. H., & Choi, Y. (2013). Hotel employees' perception of green practices. *International Journal of Hospitality and Tourism Administration, 14*(2), 157–178.

Kim, S. B., & Kim, D. Y. (2014). The effects of message framing and source credibility on green messages in hotels. *Cornell Hospitality Quarterly, 55*(1), 64–75.

Kim, Y. J., Palakurthi, R., & Hancer, M. (2012). The environmentally friendly programs in hotels and customers' intention to stay: An online survey approach. *International Journal of Hospitality and Tourism Administration, 13*(3), 195–214.

Le, Y., Hollenhorst, S., Harris, C., McLaughlin, W., & Shook, S. (2006). Environmental management: A study of Vietnamese hotels. *Annals of Tourism Research, 33*(2), 545–567.

Lee, S., & Oh, H. (2014). Effective communication strategies for hotel guests' green behavior. *Cornell Hospitality Quarterly, 55*(1), 52–63.

López, M. D., Molina, J. F., & Claver, E. (2011). The relationship between managers' environmental perceptions, environmental management and firm performance in Spanish hotels: A whole framework. *International Journal of Tourism Research, 13*(2), 141–163.

Mathew, P. V., & Sreejesh, S. (2017). Impact of responsible tourism on destination sustainability and quality of life of community in tourism destinations. *Journal of Hospitality and Tourism Management, 31*, 83–89.

Nachar, N. (2008). The Mann-Whitney U: A test for assessing whether two independent samples come from the same distribution. *Tutorials in Quantitative Methods for Psychology, 4*(1), 13–20.
Park, S. Y., & Levy, S. E. (2014). Corporate social responsibility: Perspectives of hotel frontline employees. *International Journal of Contemporary Hospitality Management, 26*(3), 332–348.
Ryan, P. (2003). Sustainability partnerships: Eco-strategy theory in practice? *Management of Environmental Quality: An International Journal, 14*(2), 256–278.
Scheyvens, R. (1999). Ecotourism and the empowerment of local communities. *Tourism Management, 20*(2), 245–249.
Sheivachman, A. (2011). Efficiency leads to savings mobility. *Hotel Management, 96.*
Shieh, H. S. (2012). The greener, the more cost efficient? An empirical study of international tourist hotels in Taiwan. *International Journal of Sustainable Development and World Ecology, 19*(6), 536–545.
Sigala, M. (2008). A supply chain management approach for investigating the role of tour operators on sustainable tourism: The case of TUI. *Journal of Cleaner Production, 16*(15), 1589–1599.
Singh, N., Cranage, D., & Lee, S. (2014). Green strategies for hotels: Estimation of recycling benefits. *International Journal of Hospitality Management, 43*, 13–22.
Stalcup, L. D., Deale, C. S., & Todd, S. Y. (2014). Human resources practices for environmental sustainability in lodging operations. *Journal of Human Resources in Hospitality and Tourism, 13*(4), 389–404.
Stylos, N., & Vassiliadis, C. (2015). Differences in sustainable management between four- and five-star hotels regarding the perceptions of three-pillar sustainability. *Journal of Hospitality Marketing and Management*, 1–35.
Teye, V., Sirakaya, E., & Sönmez, S. F. (2002). Residents' attitudes toward tourism development. *Annals of Tourism Research, 29*(3), 668–688.
Tsai, Y. H., Wu, C. T., & Wang, T. M. (2014). Attitude towards green hotel by hoteliers and travel agency managers in Taiwan. *Asia Pacific Journal of Tourism Research, 19*(9), 1091–1109.
Tsaur, S. H., Lin, Y. C., & Lin, J. H. (2006). Evaluating ecotourism sustainability from the integrated perspective of resource, community and tourism. *Tourism Management, 27*(4), 640–653.
UNFCCC – United Nations Framework Convention on Climate Change. (2010). *Report of the conference of the parties at its fifteenth session (COP15)*. http://unfccc.int/resource/docs/2009/cop15/eng/11.pdf. Accessed 20 June 2017.
Uysal, M., Woo, E., & Singal, M. (2012). The tourist area life cycle (TALC) and its effect on the quality of life (QOL) of destination community. In M. Uysal, R. Perdue, & M. J. Sirgy (Eds.), *Handbook of tourism and quality-of-life research: Enhancing the lives of tourists and residents of host communities* (pp. 423–444). Dordrecht: Springer Science & Business Media.
Uysal, M., Sirgy, M. J., Woo, E., & Kim, H.(L.). (2016). Quality of life (QOL) and well-being research in tourism. *Tourism Management, 53*, 244–261.
UNWTO (2017). UNWTO tourism highlights. https://www.e-unwto.org/doi/pdf/10.18111/9789284419029. Accessed 30 April 2018.
Weaver, D. B. (2012). Organic, incremental and induced paths to sustainable mass tourism convergence. *Tourism Management, 33*(5), 1030–1037.
Webster, K. (2000). *Environmental Management in the Hospitality Industry: A guide for students and managers*. London: Cassell.
Withiam, G. (2015). As green practices gain ground, so does guest support. *Hotel Management, 15.*
Yen, C. H., Chen, C. Y., & Teng, H. Y. (2013). Perceptions of environmental management and employee job attitudes in hotel firms. *Journal of Human Resources in Hospitality and Tourism, 12*(2), 155–174.
Zink, K. J., & Fischer, K. (2013). Do we need sustainability as a new approach in human factors and ergonomics? *Ergonomics, 56*(3), 348–356.

Chapter 11
The Impact of Music Festivals on Local Communities and Their Quality of Life: Comparation of Serbia and Hungary

Vanja Pavluković, Tanja Armenski, and Juan Miguel Alcántara-Pilar

Abstract Music festivals are often seen as the key drivers of cities economy, and hence there is an increasing interest in the numerous benefits and costs associated with hosting them. The local governments and event organizers usually focus on the economic benefits, but the social impacts may have an even more profound effect upon the quality of life of local community. Moreover, quality of life research has been well explored in medicine, psychology, and the social sciences, although it has received very little attention within festival studies (Andereck KL, Nyaupane G, Development of a tourism and quality-of-life instrument. In: Budruk M, Phillips R (eds) Quality-of-life community indicators for parks, recreation and tourism management, vol 43. Springer, Dordrecht, pp 95–113, 2011). Therefore, the aim of this paper is to explore the social impacts of two famous European music festivals EXIT in Serbia and SZIGET in Hungary on their communities. The research was inspired by the previous work of Delamere (Development of a scale to measure local resident attitudes toward the social impact of community festivals. Faculty of Physical Education and Recreation, Edmonton, 1998, Event Manag 7:25–38, 2001) who developed the Festival Social Impact Attitude Scale (FSIAS). The results indicate that social impacts have two main dimensions, social benefits and social costs. In addition, residents perceived more social benefits than social costs of the festivals in both countries. The findings have practical implications for the local authority and festival management such as acknowledgement of residents' opinion towards impacts of festivals on their quality of living and, consequently, their willingness to support the organization of the event that, in long term, influence overall sustainability of the festival.

V. Pavluković (✉) · T. Armenski
University of Novi Sad, Faculty of Sciences, Department of Geography, Tourism and Hotel Management, Novi Sad, Serbia
e-mail: vanja.dragicevic@dgt.uns.ac.rs

J. M. Alcántara-Pilar
University of Granada, Granada, Spain

A. M. Campón-Cerro et al. (eds.), *Best Practices in Hospitality and Tourism Marketing and Management*, Applying Quality of Life Research,
https://doi.org/10.1007/978-3-319-91692-7_11

Keywords Social impacts · Music festival · Local community · FSIAS · Serbia · Hungary

11.1 Introduction

Events are one of the fastest growing segments of tourism industry that yield profound impacts on economy, environment and society at the individual level, the community level, and the regional level. (Arcodia and Whitford 2006; Bagiran and Kurgun 2013; Dragićević et al. 2015; Getz 1997; Loots et al. 2011; McDonnell et al. 1999). Since festivals are not dependant on the natural resources and cultural heritage of the destination, they can be developed more easily than other forms of travel and tourism. With the potential for the fast commercialization and, hence, economic revitalisation, the festivals represent "quick wins" for many destinations (Getz 2008) and of urban reconstruction strategies for deindustrialised cities in many countries around Europe (Richards 2000). Events and festivals are often seen as the main feature of modern urban economies (Bole 2008; Montgomery 2007). They are organized for several reasons including preserving local culture and history, providing recreation and leisure opportunities for residents as well as for visitors, enhancing the local tourism industry, changing destination image to make it more appealing and representative of the quality of life etc. (Richards 2000). To gain local support, festivals and events are increasingly used by governments as a platform for economic development, and costs related to event are justified in terms of the economic impacts that the event brings to their host region (Burgan and Mules 2000).

Further, festivals are part of city's creative industry which affects local community's everyday life and provide special experience for visitors as well as local population. They add life to city, give citizens renewed pride and could improve city image (Richards and Wilson 2004; Van den Berg 2012). Also, festivals reinforce social and cultural identity and help to build social cohesion by reinforcing ties within a community (Gursoy et al. 2004). Bowdin et al. (2006) add that social and cultural impacts of festivals may involve shared experience, validation of groups in the community, widening of cultural horizons or creating new and challenging ideas for community development. However, different social issues can emerge from hosting events and affect quality of everyday life of community such as: loss of amenity due to noise or crowds, resentment of inequitable distribution of costs and benefits, risky sexual behaviors, abuse of alcohol and drugs, conflicts with visitors arriving at festival, xenophobia, commodification and exploitation of culture and traditional ways of life, threats to traditional family life in host communities etc. (Saayman 2000).

Since festivals have a wide range of impacts on their hosting communities' everyday life and can provide both tangible (such as additional income, jobs, tax revenues for locals) and intangible benefits (such as community pride, enhanced image of the place), this chapter aimed to reveal the impacts of two famous European music festivals EXIT in Serbia and SZIGET in Hungary on their host communities.

The object of the present work is to examine the social consequences of music festivals experienced by community of Novi Sad (Serbia) and Budapest (Hungary)

and to compare the events' impacts across two countries in order to reveal how these events' impacts locals' well-being and quality of life.

This study is important because it contributes to knowledge of social impacts of events on host communities and their well-being as in many countries, especially in emerging ones such in the case of Serbia and Hungary social impacts of events are empirically still under-researched. More importantly, in planning and organizing festivals and events the role of local community is often marginalized and local governments often make the crucial decision of whether to host the event without adequate community consultation. Bowdin et al. (2006) stated that local communities often value the 'feel-good' aspects of events, and are willing to accept temporary inconvenience and disruption because of the excitement and the opportunities which they generate, as well as long-term expectation of improved facilities.

As local residents' perception toward these (social) impacts and the amount of perceived control residents have over these impacts play a crucial role in community acceptance or rejection of the festival (Delamere 1999) it is of vital importance for the destination practitioners and event managers to acknowledge residents' attitude toward these impacts to maximize benefits and minimize negative unintended festival outcomes on the community (Small and Edwards 2003).

11.2 Literature Review

11.2.1 Impacts of Events on Local Community

Although there are evident changes in community's quality of life specifically during the hosting of a festival, quality of life concept has received very little attention within festival studies. Quality of life is hard to uniformly define (Godfrey 2002), due to the broad conceptualization that imply contribution of some determinants that improve people's social, economic and environmental welfare (Veenhoven 1996). Authors Rahman et al. (2011) argued that eight factors should be considered when measuring the quality of life including family and friends' relations, emotional well-being, health, material well-being, belonging to local community, work and activity, personal safety, and quality of environment.

Slightly simplified measurement tool, the WHO's instrument proposes a four-dimensional structure of well-being impacts including their physical, social, psychological, and environmental domain that can be measured at the individual level, the household level, the community level, and the regional level (Andereck and Nyaupane 2011).

Pfitzner and Koenigstorfer (2016) conducted a study at the individual level to assess the changes in quality of life of host city residents over the course of hosting a mega-sport event until 3 months after the event. They looked at individual changes of quality of life, considering the WHO's dimensions of quality of life. Moreover, they considered perceived atmosphere as one variable that might influence how residents rated their quality of life during the hosting of a mega-sport event referring to the four dimensions abovementioned. The results of the study showed that there was no change in quality of life with respect to physical, social, psychological, and environmental health for all participants during the event. However, residents who perceived a positive atmosphere rated the social and environmental domains of quality of life more positively right after the end of the event.

More generally, the relevant event studies groups festival impact into economic, environmental, socio-cultural and political categories (Arcodia and Whitford 2006). It is important to bear in mind how these impacts are perceived by the local community as it may improve community quality of life and increase support for the festival.

Most literature and studies written on the festivals give special importance to **economic** impacts (Anderson and Solberg 1999; Dwyer et al. 2000, 2006; Herrero et al. 2006; Jackson et al. 2005; Long and Perdue 1990; Mules and Faulkner 1996; Richards 2000). Also, local authorities and festival organizers usually focus on the economic benefits of attracting as many visitors as possible, since festivals play a significant role in local tourism development. On a positive note, economic impacts of a festival reflect in its' capacity to generate increased revenues and job opportunities for residents (Dwyer et al. 2000). Also, they can contribute to development of service, culture and entertainment industry, as well as promotion of the destination which further could encourage investment activities in region and tourism development. But, there are several negative economic impacts of festivals, such as higher prices of basic services, higher costs of communal services (more litter), residents' exoduses and interruption of normal business (Arcodia and Whitford 2006; Dwyer et al. 2000). All these impacts of festivals affect quality of life of hosting community.

There is no doubt that the economic impacts of festivals are important, but the social impacts may have an even more profound effect upon the local community's everyday life (Delamere 1998; Fredline et al. 2003). However, recently there has been growing interest in studying the non-economic impacts of the events on residents in academic circles (Arcodia and Whitford 2006; Bagiran and Kurgun 2013; Dragićević et al. 2015; Loots et al. 2011; Robertson and Wardrop 2012). In this respect, Deery and Jago (2010) stated that understanding the social and environmental impacts of events became both a practitioner and academic priority.

Environmental impacts associated with festivals could be different. In some cases, unique physical characteristics of host destination could be an advantage in (place) marketing festival. For example, EXIT festival is held on the Petrovaradin fortress which is protected cultural heritage and presents the symbol of the city of Novi Sad. But on the other side, those same environmental attributes could be endangered due to substantial number of festival visitors and participants. Environmental damage, degradation of green areas, noise and overcrowding during festivals affects quality of everyday life of residents. In some destinations, specifically industrializing cities, festivals have contributed to urban renewal, through redevelopment of old and unused venues. Also, due to organizing diverse types of events on destination and considerable number of visitors, tourism, communal and traffic infrastructure could be improved, which further enhance quality of life of local community.

Social impacts are mainly related to host community opportunity to get involve with other nations and trough multi-national encounter learn about foreign cultures, customs, heritage, music and language (Gondos 2014). The highest form of interaction between residents and foreign tourists is the creation of a desire to share knowledge and experience, and creating an atmosphere in which local people will be intrigued to visit the country of foreign tourists, and tourists have the desire to re-visit destination or promote it (word of mouth) (Armenski et al. 2011). The quality of interaction between tourists and residents contributes to both tourists experience and perception of the visited destination and acceptance and tolerance of tourist by residents. Furthermore, the acceptance and tolerance of tourists by residents has been acknowledged also to be vital for long-term successful of destination development (Thyne et al. 2006).

The social interaction between host community and festival goers also helps to achieve the mutual understanding, co-operation between host country and countries of festival goers' origin as well as to improve international recognition that might have implication on foreign policy and international relations (Mings 1988). These outcomes of events might have political implications for the community and country in general.

11.2.2 Social Impacts of Events on Local Community

Deery and Jago (2010) in their paper on social impacts of events pointed out that examining the social impacts of events on communities is significant for numerous reasons and these effects either positive or negative have much more potential to interrupt the everyday life of a community than does "normal" tourism for a brief period. They grouped positive impacts of events on communities into two categories: "social and economic impacts" (such as increased employment and standard of living, economic and entertainment benefits of events) and "longer term impacts" (such as enhanced community image and pride, preservation of local culture, increased skill base, new facilities). They add that the most successful long-term events are seen to promote the host destination and enhance community pride; therefore, community pride should not be overlooked. Dwyer et al. (2000, 185) write about "psychic income", as a positive impact of events, which refers to civic pride which entails opportunities of home hosting and socio-cultural interaction.

In contrast, two groups of negative impacts of events are formed: "inconvenient" dimensions of the event which usually contribute to short-term irritation (noise, crowd, traffic and parking problems, disruption of normal life) and "ASB" group or anti-social behaviour, which is very common on events such as music festivals, and includes drunken, rowdy and delinquent behaviour (Deery and Jago 2010; Lundberg 2015; Van Wynsberghe et al. 2012; Ziakas 2016).

In literature, the range of impacts generated by the event on a host community could be found, but there is still little research about some aspects of negative impacts on the community's attitude towards the event itself, particularly about anti-social behaviour. Deery and Jago (2010) highlighted that anti-social behaviour (ASB) has the potential to threaten the positive impacts of events on a host community and that the consequences of the ASB impact could seriously damage the image of an event in the eyes of the residents (but also the image of destination in the eyes of visitors) and reduce their pride, and further community support for an event could be reduced. Negative impacts such as crowding or traffic jams do not receive the attention of either the community or the media in long term, it is the ASB which receives attention and damages the event, the community everyday life and the destination's image. Safety and security at destination are critical issues for residents' quality of life, as well as for tourists. Therefore, local authorities and tourism industry leaders need to manage ASB impact to maintain resident support and the attractiveness of the event among both locals and visitors. However, Arcodia and Whitford (2006) noted that festivals are primarily social phenomena with the potential to provide a variety of predominantly positive social impacts which further affect quality of life of local residents.

Research with focus on residents' perception regarding the impacts of festivals across different socio-demographic variables such as age, gender, education, occupation, household income is somewhat limited. Tosun (2002) found that residents in Central Florida with higher incomes showed higher levels of support for tourism than did those with lower incomes. In their study about social impacts of rural cultural festival in Texas Woosnam et al. (2013) found that long-time residents and long-time festival visitors indicated a higher degree of agreement with festival positive impacts to the community than did those who had not lived in the community as long.

Arcodia and Whitford (2006) noted that festival raises awareness and encourage a more effective use of community resources and expertise, contribute to development of social networks during organization of festivals which can be maintained even long time after festival ends. Also, festivals provide opportunities for training and development in a variety of skills for residents who are involved in organization of festival contributing to community well-being. Festivals impact positively community's quality of life by providing an opportunity to run away from daily routines and to socialise with family and friends within the larger community (Earls 1993). Like other researchers, Arcodia and Whitford (2006) discussed a range of negative socio-cultural impacts of festivals on the host community, but they also point out the role of festival management in determining social impacts on community, while enhancing benefits and minimizing social costs. Collaboration with community and consultation before, during, and after the festival are necessary to provide community well-being and support for the festival in long terms.

Gursoy and Kendall (2006) stated that community support for festivals is affected directly and/or indirectly by the level of community concern, eco-centric values, community attachment, perceived benefits, and perceived costs of the festival. In other words, the greater positive impacts or benefits of the event, the more positive and more supportive the host community will be. Loots et al. (2011) noted that the community will be more attached to an event if there is a positive connotation linked to event. They add that identification of the factors which influence community support can help the festival management in the planning and marketing festival as local support and consultation are likely to increase and prolong positive impacts on the local community and further will affect quality of residents' life. However, they conclude what is applicable to one event it is not necessarily of importance to the other events. Therefore, it is necessary to conduct research in the community where the festival is held and then results should be used by festival management and local government to improve community well-being and gain support for the specific festival.

11.2.3 Measuring Social Impacts of Events on Local Community

In recent years practitioners and academics have understood the value of the social and environmental impacts of events and, consequently, research into these areas has grown. Getz (2010) identified three main trends in studying festivals: the analysis of their influence on culture and society based on anthropological and sociological research, then studying economic issues and the analysis of festival organization and management. Studies regarding the impacts of festivals on the society may be grouped as studies dealing with motivation of festival visitors (Crompton and McKay 1997; Uysal et al. 1993), studies regarding the festival visitors' satisfaction (Mohr et al. 1993), studies referring to socio-demographic characteristics of festival audience (Formica and Uysal 1996; Peterson 1992), those describing the behaviours of the organizers or festival management (Molloy 2002; Saleh and Wood 1998) and researches on the perception of festivals by the host communities (Delamere 2001; Delamere et al. 2001; Gibson and Davidson 2004).

Deery and Jago (2010) noted that the aim of the previous research on social impacts of events on communities had been mainly focused on the development of scales to measure the social impacts of events on communities, testing measurement scales on resident perceptions and comparative studies of the social impacts of events (pre-and post-event studies). Adapted from the work Deery and Jago (2010), Table 11.1 summarised most frequently used scales to assess the social impacts of events.

Except for the work of Kim et al. (2006), there has been a lack of comparative studies among countries or regions that are hosts of events (like Olympic Games) and festivals of similar program, audience etc. This kind of comparative study would be interesting specifically in the context of post-communist countries in Central and Eastern Europe, like in the case of Serbia and Hungary, and hence could have theoretical as well as practical contribution.

Table 11.1 Measurement scale of events' social impacts on host communities

Authors	Scale	Research Settings	Measurement Scale characteristics	Research Conclusion
Delamere (1998), Delamere (2001), Delamere et al. (2001), Rollins and Delamere (2007)	Festival Social Impact Attitude Scale (FSIAS)	Edmonton fold festival, Alberta, Canada	Valid, reliable instrument. Sub-factors: Community and cultural/educational benefits and costs.	FSIAS can be modified to suit community, client and research needs.
Small and Edwards (2003), Fredline et al. (2005)	Social Impact Perception (SIP)	Cultural event (Australian Festival of the book)	Smaller scale reliable and valid.	Important to examine nonoccurrence of impacts.
		Australian Open Tennis (Melbourne)	Two cluster groups of unconcerned and positive.	
Fredline et al. (2003)	Modified FSIAS	Aust Grand Prix, Melbourne Moomba, Horsham Art Ist festival	Six factors: social/economic developments, injustice/ inconvenience, facilities, bad behavior and environmental impacts, longer term impacts, price of goods and services	
Wood (2005)	Four surveys (repeated)	Blackburn (UK)	Scale items valid/reliable.	Civic pride found to be an important impact of events.
Fredline and Faulkner (2000)	Survey, cluster analysis	Gold Coast Indy, Australia	Five clusters: ambivalent supporters, haters, realists, lovers, concerned for a reason.	

Source: Adapted from Deery and Jago (2010)

11.3 Research Methodology

11.3.1 Research Cases of Exit and SZIGET Music Festival

The second largest city in Serbia, Novi Sad is the economic, political and cultural centre of Vojvodina province. Since 2000, population of Novi Sad is constantly growing, reaching 270,500 inhabitants in 2015, including surrounding suburbs Sremski Karlovci, Veternik, Futog, and Petrovaradin (Statistical Report, Republic of Serbia, 2015). The urban centre is mainly inhabited by Serbs (78.8%), but has a diverse ethnic composition with an increasing number of Hungarians (3.9%), Slovaks (2.0%), Croats (1.6%) and Romanians (1.1%). The population of Novi Sad was on average 39.8 years old, with men slightly younger (38.3) than females (41.2). In 2015, the average size of household was 2.63. The inhabitants of Novi Sad were predominantly employed in manufacturing, agricultural, forestry and fishing industries while unemployment rate accounted for 17.1% in 2015.

Although numerous media and government have pointed out that Exit has significant impacts on Serbian economy, tourism industry of the city and Novi Sad image, there is a lack of research on this festival and its impacts in the academic circles in Serbia. There is a lack of research with a focus on social impacts of Exit festival on local community and its' quality of life, even though it is considered that Exit has a strong social mission.

Exit is a summer music festival held annually at the Petrovaradin fortress on Danube in the city of Novi Sad, Serbia. It started as a student movement fighting for democracy in Serbia and the Balkans. The festival was founded in 2000 when lasted for 100 days. The "zero" Exit was local event, and already in 2001 it became one of the most prominent music festivals in Europe. Festival lasts for 4 days the first weekend in July (from Thursday to Sunday). Exit won the "Best Major European Festival Award" on European Festival Awards 2013 as well as the "Best European Festival" award at the UK Festival Awards in 2007. It was ranked top 10 best major festivals at European Festival Awards 2009, 2010, 2011, 2012 and 2013 and one of the 10 Best Overseas Festivals at UK Festival Award 2014. Exit was officially proclaimed as the "Best Major European Festival" at the EU Festival Awards 2014. More than 2.5 million people from over 60 countries around the world have visited the festival so far. Many global media such as CNN, BBC, MTV, Guardian, the Sun, Euronews promote Exit as one of the leading music festivals in the world (www.exitfest.org/en/about-us).

With about 1.7 million inhabitants and more than 3 million of tourists in 2015, Budapest is the most inhabited city in Hungary and one of the largest cities in the European Union. This urban area populates predominantly Hungarians (80.8%), Romani (1.1%), Germans (1.0%), Romanians (0.4%) and other ethnicities (17.5%) (Census Statistics 2016). The average age of the resident population recorded in 2016 was 43. The annual unemployment rate accounted for 6.5% (Hungarian Central Statistical Office 2016).

Starting in 1993, Sziget festival became one of the largest music and cultural events in Europe. It is held every August in northern Budapest, Hungary, on the "Old Buda Island" on Danube. Likewise Exit festival, it has grown from a student event in 1993 to become one of the prominent European festivals, with about half of all visitors coming from outside Hungary, especially from Western Europe. The festival attracts almost 400,000 visitors from over 70 countries, providing a complete festival-holiday experience with live concerts, a widely international community and all touristic features the city should offer. It lasts for 7 days with approximately 50 program venues and around 200 programs daily. Sziget is not just about music, as it offers other **cultural programs**, like theatre, circus, or exhibitions (http://szigetfestival.com/_/info/about). In 2011, Sziget was ranked one of the five best festivals in Europe by The Independent. The 2011 festival won the European Festivals Award in the category *The Best Major European Festival* in early 2012.

11.3.2 Survey Design and Data Collection

The scale used in the study was inspired by the previous work of Delamere (1998, 2001) who developed the Festival Social Impact Attitude Scale (FSIAS). Original FSIAS scale comprises of 21 items related to social benefits and 26 items on social costs of festivals tested on the local community of Edmonton, Alberta, Canada. For this research, the original scale was modified to suit specific cases of EXIT and SZIGET music festivals.

Through overview of the relevant literature, prominently used scales to measure the social impacts of events on host communities were conducted preliminarily to expert discussion session. Namely, panel discussion with 5 academic representatives expertized in the regional tourism industry and event management was organized. Experts were invited to discuss the Festival Social Impact Attitude Scale (FSIAS) and suggest scale adjustment; 20 original items from the FSIAS (Delamere 2001) were kept and 11 additional items were proposed base on the previous research on the wider impact of events on local communities (Lankford and Howard 1994; Likert 1968; Mayfïeld and Crompton 1995).

Based on the preliminary research, including expert discussion group, the measurement scale with 31 items was suggested and psychometric properties of the scale were tested. Proposed scale has good internal consistency ($\alpha = 0.88$); Five point Likert scaling was used for ranking respondent's agreement/disagreement on festivals impacts on their local communities. In addition, questionnaire comprises a section on the socio demographic characteristics of respondents (gender, age, education, occupation, work experience) and their visitation experience with music festivals of interest.

The questionnaire was translated in Serbian and Hungarian language as the target research population was residents from Novi Sad and Budapest where investigated music festivals are hosted. The research was conducted in the period from June to September 2014 years. Under assumption that strongest impact of festivals on the local communities and their quality of life can be recorded in the period immediately pre-and after organization of event, time of research coincide with the summer months when events take place regularly (Fredline et al. 2003).

For the population size of 1.7 million residents of Budapest and 275,500 residents of Novi Sad, a sample size was calculated using confidence interval approach (Burns and Bush 1995). To obtain 95% accuracy at the 95% confidence level, targeted sample size of 384 (N) was required to validate a study on a population of 1, 000, 000 (N) and above.

Since complete census lists of Novi Sad and Budapest could not be access for employing more precise surveying methodology, convenience non-probability sampling method was used. The questionnaires were distributed electronically via social networks to residents of Novi Sad and Budapest. Specifically, all Facebook users who stated place of residence Budapest and Novi Sad were invited to take participation in the survey. The sample of 505 respondents was collected among which 301 were from Novi Sad and 204 residents of Budapest.

Subsample of Novi Sad respondents consist of 66.4% female and 33.6% male respondents; Budapest subsample has similar gender distribution with 58.8% female and male respondents 41.2%. In both research subsamples dominate subjects under the age of 31 years with 55.5% from Novi Sad and 54.5% from Budapest. Much of respondents are employed in private sector (40.9% from Novi Sad and 53% from Budapest) while high share of unemployed respondents (40.5% from Novi Sad; 27.9% from Budapest) represents students and youth who are loyal visitors to EXIT and SZIGET music festival. In the research sample dominate experienced respondents who visited investigated festivals more than three times: 43.2% of Novi Sad respondents visited Exit and 33.8% respondents from Budapest visited SZIGET multiple times (Table 11.2).

Preliminary data analyses include testing z-scores for univariate and Mahalanobis's distance for multivariate data screening and univariate (Kolmogorov-Smirnov (K-S) and multivariate (Mardia) normality testing. Finally, expectation-maximization procedure was used for regression imputation of missing data in the dataset as suggested by Kline (2005).

To investigate underlying factor structure of EXIT and SZIGET impacts on local communities of Serbia and Hungary, exploratory and confirmatory factor analyses were conducted. Principle axis factoring extraction method with Promax rotation was performed under assumption of correlation between latent factors. Data processing is conducted in SPSS 20.0.

11.4 Results

To explore underlying dimension of festival impact on local communities of Novi Sad and Budapest explanatory factor analysis (EFA) was carried out. Kaiser's measure of sampling adequacy and the Barlett's test of sphericity suggesting that the data were suitable for factor analysis (KMO = 0.927). Latent dimensions were extracted by principal components analysis with Oblimin rotation and the optimal number of dimensions was determined by the parallel analysis with 95% percentile criterion. This criterion suggested two-factor solution which explained 46.35% of total variance. Factor one consists of 22 items related to different positive aspects of music events on the local communities and their quality of life. Hence, factor is titled "social benefits"and it's explains 32.35% of the total variance. Factor two consists of nine items which describe negative impacts of festivals on the local communities, therefore named" social costs" (Table 11.3).

Arithmetic mean and standard deviation were calculated to describe Serbian and Hungarian residents' attitude towards impact of EXIT and SZIGET on their local communities while Student t test (t statistic) was employed to explore differences of

Table 11.2 Respondent's characteristics

City/Festival	Novi Sad/EXIT		Budapest/SZIGET	
Characteristics	N	(%)	N	(%)
Gender				
Female	200	66.4	120	58.8
Male	101	33.6	84	41.2
Age				
Less than 31	167	55.5	111	54.4
Between 31 and 41	92	30.5	56	27.5
More than 41	42	14.0	37	18.1
Years of residence in the cities				
Less than 10 years	76	25.3	68	33.3
Between 10 and 20 years	78	25.9	42	20.6
More than 20 years	147	48.8	94	46.1
Occupation				
Public sector and NGO	56	18.6	39	19.1
Private sector	123	40.9	108	53.0
Unemployment	122	40.5	57	27.9
Level of education				
High school	70	23.2	50	24.5
2-years higher education	31	10.3	59	28.9
Graduate studies	133	44.2	54	26.5
Post graduate studies	67	22.3	41	20.1
Work related to tourism sector?				
Yes	50	16.6	35	17.2
No	251	83.4	169	82.8
Visitation experience with the festival?				
Yes	216	71.8	147	72.1
No	85	28.2	57	27.9
Frequency of visits to the festival				
Never	85	28.2	57	27.9
Ones	34	11.3	27	13.3
Two times	27	9.0	32	15.7
Three times	25	8.3	19	9.3
More than three times	130	43.2	69	33.8
Total	**301**	**100.0**	**204**	**100.0**

Note: N stands for the number of respondents

local communities' attitudes towards costs and benefits of hosting the festivals. Attitude of residents from Novi Sad on social impacts of EXIT range from 2.55 to 4.75, whereas locals from Budapest grade impacts of SZIGET with a slightly lower average mark ranking from 2.25 to 4.48. Residents of Novi Sad rated both positive and negative impacts of the festivals with higher marks compared to locals of Budapest. Positive scores of F statistics imply that locals from Novi Sad perceive

Table 11.3 Results of the exploratory factor analysis for modified FSIAS

Factors	Variance explained	Eigen value	Parallel analysis 95 percentile of random Eigenvalues	Cronbach's alfa	Number of items
F1 Positive impact – social benefits	32.35	10.027	1.538	0.937	22
F2 Negative impact – social costs	14	4.342	1.472	0.863	9

Source: Survey research, 2014

impacts of EXIT music festival on their community to be more profound than locals from Budapest (Table 11.4).

Both subsample perceived the opportunity for additional income as the greatest benefits of hosting the festival (EXIT = 4.75; SZIGET = 4.48) with residents from Novi Sad rating this economic benefit significantly more important compared to residents of Budapest ($t = 19.34$; $p = 0.00$). For community of Novi Sad very important role of hosting the festival was promotion of the city internationally (EXIT = 4.43; SZIGET = 3.58; $t = 85.8$; $p = 0.00$). These results are in accordance with the finding of Magnússon (2010) who examined the impact of Carnival in Aalborg (Denmark) where Denmark local community stated that international promotion and improvement of the city image are very central implication of hosting an event. Further, respondents from Novi Sad held opinion that self-presentation as a special and unique hosting community (EXIT = 4.12; SZIGET = 3.64) are significant impacts of EXIT music festival on their community. Similarly, respondents from Budapest also sow the festival as an important instrument of city promotion internationally, but perceive this benefits as a less important for the well-being of the community compared to residents of Novi Sad ($t = 27.06$; $p = 0.00$).

Respondents from both cities believe that their local communities did not have any chance to meet musical performances which stayed in their cities during the festival (EXIT = 2.62; SZIGET = 3.17; $t = 22.65$, $p = 0.00$) nor that festivals have positive cultural influences on their communities (EXIT = 3.08; SZIGET = 2.57; $t = 21.16$, $p = 0.00$). Non-significant differences of t statistics on the local community involvement in the organization of the festivals indicate both communities perceived to be insufficiently involved in the organization of the festivals which resulted in low average marks for EXIT (Mean = 3.21) and for SZIGET (Mean = 3.25). Having low involvement in the organization of festivals, residents might perceive little personal benefits of hosting an event. Residents of Budapest felt that organization of the festival benefit their quality of life on contrary to residents from Novi Sad who were more satisfied as a community since hosting the event (EXIT = 3.71; SZIGET = 3.11; $t = 31.92$, $p = 0.00$). In addition, respondents from Budapest was not sure whether destination and event management acknowledge their attitudes toward organization of the festival while Novi Sad community hold more positive regarding this matter (EXIT = 3.47; SZIGET = 2.98; $t = 17.96$; $p = 0.00$).

Table 11.4 Descriptive statistics and T-test for EXIT and SZIGET festival

Label	Respondents attitude	Festival	Mean	SD	t-test	P
A1	Hosting festival improve promotion of the city internationally	EXIT	4.43	0.04	85.8	**0.00**
		SZIGET	3.58	0.08		
A2	Hosting festival improve the image of the city	EXIT	3.94	0.06	105.8	**0.00**
		SZIGET	2.88	0.08		
A3	Due to the organization of the festival, local population has the opportunity for additional income	EXIT	4.75	0.03	19.34	**0.00**
		SZIGET	4.48	0.05		
A4	Festival enables local community to present itself to others (visitors) as special and unique	EXIT	4.12	0.05	27.06	**0.00**
		SZIGET	3.64	0.08		
A5	The festival is of great importance for visitors to learn about local culture	EXIT	3.79	0.06	15.11	**0.00**
		SZIGET	3.38	0.08		
A6	**The local community can meet different cultures and have multicultural experiences during the festival**	**EXIT**	**2.95**	**0.07**	**1.882**	**0.17**
		SZIGET	3.11	0.08		
A7	Hosting festival improve the identity of local community	EXIT	3.79	0.06	7.04	**0.00**
		SZIGET	3.52	0.08		
A8	Festival program is always rich and diverse	EXIT	3.85	0.06	10.04	**0.00**
		SZIGET	3.52	0.08		
A9	The festival has a positive cultural influence on the local community	EXIT	3.08	0.07	21.16	**0.00**
		SZIGET	2.57	0.07		
A10	The festival represent a source of new ideas for the local community	EXIT	3.62	0.07	25.26	**0.00**
		SZIGET	3.04	0.09		
A11	**Local community has a sense of national pride when hosting festival in the city**	**EXIT**	**3.09**	**0.08**	**0.00**	**0.92**
		SZIGET	**3.10**	**0.08**		
A12	Noise level in the city increases during the festival	EXIT	3.96	0.06	9.55	**0.00**
		SZIGET	3.65	0.07		
A13	The local community gain a positive recognition for hosting a festival	EXIT	3.75	0.06	23.9	**0.00**
		SZIGET	3.27	0.07		
A14	**Prices of products (such as souvenirs) and services (such as food and beverage services in the restaurants or taxi services) increases during the festival**	**EXIT**	**3.63**	**0.07**	**0.065**	**0.42**
		SZIGET	**3.72**	**0.07**		
A15	The city is very crowded during the festival	EXIT	4.31	0.05	37.77	**0.00**
		SZIGET	3.75	0.08		
A16	Organization of the festival creates opportunity for new employability places for local population	EXIT	3.98	0.06	60.95	**0.00**
		SZIGET	3.13	0.08		
A17	**High security level of event visitors during a festival**	**EXIT**	**3.65**	**0.05**	**0.53**	**0.46**
		SZIGET	**3.58**	**0.07**		
A18	**Hosting festival gives opportunity to local residents to learn new things**	**EXIT**	**3.59**	**0.06**	**4.91**	**0.02**
		SZIGET	**3.38**	**0.07**		
A19	**High security level of local population during a festival**	**EXIT**	**3.29**	**0.06**	**2.41**	**0.12**
		SZIGET	**3.15**	**0.07**		

(continued)

Table 11.4 (continued)

Label	Respondents attitude	Festival	Mean	SD	t-test	P
A20	**Public spaces and facilities for relaxation, entertainment and recreation used by local communities are overcrowded at the time of the festival**	**EXIT**	**3.85**	**0.06**	**0.45**	**0.50**
		SZIGET	3.79	0.07		
A21	Impaired cleanliness and tidiness of the city during the festival – the amount of garbage increases in public areas	EXIT	3.25	0.06	21.25	**0.00**
		SZIGET	2.78	0.07		
A22	**Visitors of festival behave properly**	**EXIT**	**2.83**	**0.06**	**0.30**	**0.58**
		SZIGET	2.61	0.08		
A23	**The local community is involved in organisation of the festival**	**EXIT**	**3.20**	**0.07**	**0.22**	**0.63**
		SZIGET	**3.25**	**0.08**		
A24	**Organisation of festival disrupt normal routine and every day life of local community**	**EXIT**	**3.49**	**0.06**	**1.25**	**0.26**
		SZIGET	3.38	0.07		
A25	The local community has a chance to meet musical performers at the festival	EXIT	2.62	0.07	22.65	**0.00**
		SZIGET	3.17	0.08		
A26	Hosting festival improve the quality of life of local community	EXIT	3.71	0.06	31.92	**0.00**
		SZIGET	3.11	0.08		
A27	**Local traffic is overloaded and there are significant traffic jams during festivals**	**EXIT**	**3.05**	**0.07**	**2.03**	**0.15**
		SZIGET	2.90	0.08		
A28	The festival contributes to well being of the local community	EXIT	3.71	0.06	67.20	**0.00**
		SZIGET	2.84	0.08		
A29	Local community attitudes toward organization of the festival are acknowledged	EXIT	3.47	0.07	17.96	**0.00**
		SZIGET	2.98	0.08		
A30	The influx of festival goers reduces privacy within the local community	EXIT	3.72	0.06	31.30	**0.00**
		SZIGET	3.12	0.08		
A31	Crime rates in the city increases during the festival	EXIT	2.55	0.07	8.07	**0.00**
		SZIGET	**2.25**	**0.08**		

Respondents from Novi Sad and Budapest also mentioned several negative impacts of music festivals on their community such as high noise in the city during the festival (EXIT = 3.96; SZIGET = 3.65; $t = 9.55$, $p = 0.00$), crowded city during festival (EXIT = 4.31; SZIGET = 3.75; $t = 37.77$, $p = 0.00$) and reduced privacy of host community due to influx of festival goers (EXIT = 3.72; SZIGET = 3.12; $t = 31.3$, $p = 0.00$). Interestingly, neither residents of Novi Sad nor residents of Budapest believe that organization of the festival increase crime rate in their cities (EXIT = 2.55; SZIGET = 2.25).

Finally, the results showed that residents from both countries perceived more social benefits (F1) than social costs (F2) whereas respondents from Novi Sad rated positive and negative impacts of the festival slightly higher than respondents from Budapest; for EXIT festival F1 = 3.67 and F2 = 3.26, while for Sziget F1 = 3.35 and F2 = 3.00. In line with these findings, authors Bagiran and Kurgun (2013) argue that local communities tent to perceive social benefits slightly important than social costs.

11.5 Conclusions

This paper has presented and discussed the results of Serbian and Hungarian residents' attitude toward EXIT and SZIGET festival and their influence on community quality of life. The results of the study show that local population from Novi Sad and Budapest perceive more positive impacts of festivals than their negative effects. This may imply that residents from Novi Sad are more sensitive to festival impacts on their community. For example, residents of Novi Sad are concerned about noise and crowded public spaces during the time of the festival, while community of Budapest has no issue regarding this matter. As noted by Raj and Musgrave (2009) this could be due to different development stage of hosting destinations analyzed in the study. It is argued that resident's reaction to tourism become less negative during the time with the experience of event management to reduce these disruptive festival effects on the local community (Tassiopoulos and Johnson 2009).

Research also confirmed that locals perceive the festival as a contributing factor to development of tourism in the destination as well as promotion and image of the cities. Research also points out the areas that call for event management attention such as negative impacts of festivals which cannot be ignored as they can largely influence both well-being of local community and the quality of festival itself.

From the perspective of host community, festival should contribute to economic well-being of locals by providing more employability places and opportunities for additional income, thus improve host community standard of living. Also, a greater labor demand during the event could help in reducing unemployment. Through generated revenue, in the form of various taxes to the central budget, festivals can stimulate the growth of country economy (Gondos). From the perspective of environment, festivals might provide monetary resources for revitalisation of cultural heritage or maintenance of natural environment that contribute to community quality of life, or oppositely might cause devastation of natural and cultural goods on locations where festivals are being held.

Regarding social impacts, Williams (1998) noted that each arrival of foreign tourists in to a local community inevitably provokes positive and negative influences. The main positive influence refers to the increased knowledge and understanding of hosts societies and cultures, which refers to positive interaction etc. On the other hand, tourism can provide negative effects such as debasement and the commercialisation of culture, increased tensions between imported and traditional lifestyles, erosion of strength of a local language, new patterns of local consumption, and risks of promotion of antisocial activities (gambling, drugs, violence, etc.).

The festivals also have political impacts on host communities and country development through international promotion, the regional recognition as well as mutual understanding that might foster foreign policies and foreign relationship between countries.

Therefore, it is not surprising that local communities of both Novi Sad and Budapest perceive hosting EXIT and SZIGET music festivals as an ideal opportunity to promote culture of their cities internationally as well as to build distinctive image of their communities. The positive influence of festivals on the image of cities, their promotion and, consequently, tourism development is also confirmed in many previous related works (Getz 2008, 2010; Long and Robinson 2004; Quinn 2005). Moreover, Weaver and Robinson (1989) noticed that festivals can raise national pride and community spirit through self-promotion of local community, enhancement of unique community image and represent an opportunity for the community to discover and develop cultural skills and talents, as well as participate in new activities related to organization of the festival.

In addition to local community self-promotion internationally, residents from both investigated areas acknowledged music festivals to be significant source of additional income. However, majority of residents from Serbian and Hungary do not generate any direct economic benefits due to low involvement of local communities in the organization of the festival. Not only that residents perceive little chance to gain additional income, but they are also affected by increase in prices of products such as souvenirs and services such as food and beverage services in the restaurants or taxi services during the festival. Furthermore, insufficient involvement of local population in the organization of festivals consequently entails mixed feelings about whether organization of the festival can improve their quality of leaving.

This empowers negative resident's perception towards festival and its impacts on local community. Evidently this problem can be overcome by planning, developing and managing events from a community standpoint. Destination event management and local authorities should acknowledge that destination can't have a successful tourism endeavor unless the community is involved in it. This could be beneficial for both parties: local community can gain additional income by providing support in organization of the festival while event management can guide community perceptions on potential positive impact of festival organization. Finally, local community can generate hospitable experiences that drive a festival forward through word of mouth to 'must-attend' quality of event (Mason 2015). Hence, perception and attitudes of residents towards the impacts of tourism are likely to be an important planning and policy consideration for successful development, marketing, and operation of existing and future events programs (Ap 1992).

These results provide residents, destination and festival managers with important community perceptions pertaining to the festival. Residents' opinion and support for festival is of foremost importance as they are directly involved in creating experience for visitors and support for the event will probably influence the sustainability of the festival (Gursoy and Kendall 2006). From a theoretical point of view, this paper add knowledge to understanding of events impact on post-community societies of Central and Eastern Europe and can serve as a significant comparative material for similar analyses conducted earlier on a larger scale in Western Europe, the United States and Australia.

More importantly social impacts of festivals on local community are not universal; those that have significant impact on one community may have a negligible effect on the other. Also, cultural values of local community may influence attitudes towards the festivals. Hence, future studies should be aimed at exploring eventual differences in perception of festival impacts on local community across diverse groups of residents considering their cultural norms and values, socio demographic characteristics, previous experience with the festival etc. Due to the distinctiveness of segments mentioned above, these specific groups may have different perceptions on impacts of events on their community and quality of life. These differences should be acknowledged by destination and event management to maximize social benefits of festival for the whole society.

11.5.1 Limitations and Potential Future Research

This study has several limitations that present opportunities for additional community-oriented research on the event management of travel destinations. The current study is limited to two nations, particularly to Hungary and Serbia. Thus, future studies should pursue examining the impact of events on the quality of other local communities. Testing the FSIAS scale in different community environments as well as in different festival types would have a significant contribution to future research.

Further, a community's perceptions of the impacts of a festival are not static, but rather dynamic and festivals themselves evolve over time. Hence, in the future, a longitudinal study could be conducted to explore how local communities respond to events and its' changing impacts. This would also allow for a stronger causality assertions to be made whereas, in contrast, the cross-sectional nature of data in the present study limits the extent to which causality claims can be made.

Acknowledgements The authors appreciate the financial help provided via a research project of the ADEMAR group (University of Granada) under the auspices of the Andalusian Program for R&D, number P12-SEJ2592, and a Research Program from the Faculty of Education, Economy and Technology of Ceuta. The research work of our Serbian collaborator is supported by the Ministry of Education, Science and Technological Development, Republic of Serbia (project number 176020).

References

Andereck, K. L., & Nyaupane, G. (2011). Development of a tourism and quality-of-life instrument. In M. Budruk & R. Phillips (Eds.), *Quality-of-life community indicators for parks, recreation and tourism management* (Vol. 43, pp. 95–113). Dordrecht: Springer.

Anderson, T. D., & Solberg, H. A. (1999). Leisure events and regional economic impact. *World Leisure and Recreation, 41*(1), 20–28.

Ap, J. (1992). Residents' perceptions on tourism impacts. *Annals of Tourism Research, 19*(4), 665–690.

Arcodia, C., & Whitford, M. (2006). Festival attendance and the development of social capital. *Journal of Convention and Event Tourism, 8*(2), 1–18.

Armenski, T., Dragin, V., Pejović, L., Lukić, T., & Đurđev, B. (2011). Interaction between tourists and residents: Influence on tourism development. *Polish Sociological Review, 1*(173), 107–117.

Bagiran, D., & Kurgun, H. (2013). A research on social impacts of the Foça Rock Festival: The validity of the festival social impact attitude scale. *Current Issues in Tourism.* https://doi.org/10.1080/13683500.2013.800028.

Bole, D. (2008). Cultural industry as a result of new city tertiarization. *Acta Geographica Slovenica, 48*(2), 255–276.

Bowdin, G., Allen, J., O'Toole, W., Harris, R., & McDonnell, I. (2006). *Events managements* (2nd ed.). Oxford: Butterworth-Heinemann.

Burgan, B., & Mules, T. (2000). Event analysis: Understanding the divide between cost benefit and economic impact assessment. In J. Allen, R. Harris, L. K. Jago, & A. J. Veal (Eds.), *Events beyond 2000: Setting the agenda. Proceedings of conference on event evaluation, research and education*. Sydney: Australian Centre for Event Management School of Leisure, Sport and Tourism, University of Technology.

Burns, A. C., & Bush, R. F. (1995). *Marketing research*. Englewood Cliffs: Prentice Hall.

Census Statistics. (2016). *Population and vital events*. Hungarian Central Statistical Office. https://www.ksh.hu. Accessed 15 June 2017.

Crompton, J., & Mckay, S. (1997). Motives of visitors attending festival events. *Annals of Tourism Research, 24*(2), 425–439.

Deery, M., & Jago, L. (2010). Social impacts of events and the role of anti-social behavior. *International Journal of Event and Festival Management, 1*(1), 8–28.

Delamere, T. A. (1998). *Development of a scale to measure local resident attitudes toward the social impact of community festivals*. Edmonton: Faculty of Physical Education and Recreation.

Delamere, T. A. (1999). *Development of a scale to measure local resident perceptions of the social impacts of community festivals*. Paper presented at the Ninth Canadian Congress on Leisure Research. Wolfville, Nova Scotia: Acadia University. Abstract retrieved from http://lin.ca/Uploads/cclr9/CCLR9_11.pdf

Delamere, T. A. (2001). Development of a scale to measure resident attitudes toward the social impacts of community festivals, Part II: Verification of the scale. *Event Management, 7*, 25–38.

Delamere, T. A., Wankel, L. M., & Hinch, T. D. (2001). Development of a scale to measure resident attitudes toward the social impacts of community festivals, Part I: Item generation and purification of the measure. *Event Management, 7*(1), 11–24.

Dragićević, V., Bole, D., Bučić, A., & Prodanović, A. (2015). European capital of culture: Residents perception of social benefits and costs-Maribor 2012 case study. *Acta Geographica Slovenica, 55*(2), 283–302.

Dwyer, L., Mellor, R., Mistilis, N., & Mules, T. (2000). A framework for assessing "tangible" and "intangible" impacts of events and conventions. *Event Management, 6*(3), 175–189.

Dwyer, L., Forsyth, P., & Spurr, R. (2006). Assessing the economic impacts of events: A computable general equilibrium approach. *Journal of Travel Research, 45*(1), 59–66.

Earls, Z. (1993). First night celebration: Building community through the arts. *Festival and Event Tourism, 1*, 32–33.

Exit Festival. (2016). www.exitfest.org/en/about-us. Accessed 16 June 2017.

Formica, S., & Uysal, M. (1996). A market segmentation of festival visitors: Umbria jazz festival in Italy. *Festival Management and Event Tourism, 3*(4), 175–182.

Fredline, L., & Faulkner, B. (2000). Host community reactions: A cluster analysis. *Annals of Tourism Research, 27*(3), 763–784.

Fredline, L., Jago, L., & Deery, M. (2003). The development of a generic scale to measure the social impacts of events. *Event Management. An International Journal, 8*(1), 23–37.

Fredline, L., Deery, M., & Jago, L. (2005). *Testing of a compressed generic instrument to assess host community perceptions of events: A case study of the Australian open tennis tournament* (pp. 158–77). In Proceedings of the 3rd international event conference, the impacts of events: Triple bottom line evaluation and event legacies, UTS, Sydney, July

Getz, D. (1997). *Event management and event tourism*. New York: Cognisant.

Getz, D. (2008). Event tourism: Definition, evolution and research. *Tourism Management, 29*, 403–428.

Getz, D. (2010). The nature and scope of festival studies. *International Journal of Management Research, 5*(1), 1–47.

Gibson, C., & Davidson, D. (2004). Tamworth, Australia's 'country music capital': Place marketing, rurality, and resident reactions. *Journal of Rural Studies, 20*(4), 387–404.
Godfrey, J. (2002). *Standard of living or quality of life: Does one come first?* Ottawa: TD Bank Financial Group.
Gondos, B. (2014). *Relationship between tourism and quality of life – Researches at Lake Balaton.* Human capital without borders: Knowledge and learning for quality of life, 25–27 June, Portoroz, Slovenia.
Gursoy, D., & Kendall, K. (2006). Hosting mega events: Modelling locals' support. *Annals of Tourism Research, 33*(3), 603–623.
Gursoy, D., Kim, K., & Uysal, M. (2004). Perceived impacts of festivals and special events by organizers: An extension and validation. *Tourism Management, 25*, 171–182.
Herrero, L. C., Sanz, J. Á., Devesa, M., Bedate, A., & del Barrio, M. J. (2006). The economic impact of cultural events: A case-study of Salamanca 2002, European capital of culture. *European Urban and Regional Studies, 13*(1), 5–24.
Hungarian Central Statistical Office. (2016). *Labour market statistics.* www.ksh.hu/labour_market. Accessed 10 June 2017.
Jackson, J., Houghton, M., Russell, R., & Triandos, P. (2005). Innovations in measuring economic impacts of regional festivals: A do-it-yourself kit. *Journal of Travel Research, 43*(4), 327–327.
Kim, H. J., Gursoy, D., & Lee, S.-B. (2006). The impact of the 2002 World Cup on South Korea: comparisons of pre- and post-games. *Tourism Management, 27*(1), 86–96.
Kline, T. (2005). *Psychological testing: A practical approach to design and evaluation.* London: Sage.
Lankford, S. V., & Howard, D. R. (1994). Developing a tourism impact attitude scale. *Annals of Tourism Research, 21*(1), 121–139.
Likert, R. (1968). The method of constructing an attitude scale. In M. Fishbein (Ed.), *Reading in attitude theory and measurement.* New York: Wiley.
Long, P. T., & Perdue, R. R. (1990). The economic impact of rural festivals and special events: Assessing the spatial distribution of expenditures. *Journal of Travel Research, 61*, 19–14.
Long, P., & Robinson, M. (Eds.). (2004). *Festivals and tourism: Marketing, management and evaluation.* Sunderland: Business Education Publishers Ltd.
Loots, I., Ellis, S., & Slabbert, E. (2011). Factors predicting community support: The case of a South African arts festival. *Tourism and Management Studies, 7*, 121–130.
Lundberg, E. (2015). The level of tourism development and resident attitudes: A comparative case study of coastal destinations. *Scandinavian Journal of Hospitality and Tourism, 15*(3), 266–294.
Magnússon, I. (2010). *The social impacts of the Carnival in Aalborg, A quantitative event social impact study.* Master thesis, Aalborg University, Denmark.
Mason, P. (2015). The commercialization of music festivals and the rise of super concerts. *Huff Post Blog.* www.huffingtonpost.com/pete-mason/the-commercialization-of-_1_b_7873236.html. Accessed 10 May 2017.
Mayfield, T. R., & Crompton, J. L. (1995). Development of an instrument for identifying community reasons for staging a festival. *Journal of Travel Research, 33*, 37–44.
McDonnell, I., Allen, J., & O'Toole, W. (1999). *Festival and special event management.* Brisbane: Wiley.
Mings, R. C. (1988). Assessing the contribution of tourism to international understanding. *Journal of Travel Research, 17*(2), 33–38.
Mohr, K., Backman, K. F., Gahan, L. W., & Backman, S. J. (1993). An investigation of festival motivations and event satisfaction by visitor type. *Festival Management and Event Tourism, 1*(3), 89–97.
Molloy, J. (2002). Regional festivals: A look at community support, the isolation factor and funding sources. *Journal of Tourism Studies, 13*(2), 2–15.
Montgomery, J. (2007). *The new wealth of cities: City dynamics and the fifth wave.* Aldershot: Ashgate.
Mules, T., & Faulkner, B. (1996). An economic perspective on special events. *Tourism Economics, 2*(2), 107–117.

Peterson, R. A. (1992). Understanding audience segmentation: From elite and mass to omnivore and univore. *Poetics, 21*, 243–258.

Pfitzner, R., & Koenigstorfer, J. (2016). Quality of life of residents living in a city hosting mega-sport events: A longitudinal study. *BMC Public Health, 16*, 1102.

Quinn, B. (2005). Arts festivals and the city. *Urban Studies, 42*(5–6), 927–943.

Rahman, T., Mittelhammer, R. C., & Wandschneider, P. R. (2011). Measuring quality of life across countries: A multiple indicators and multiple causes approach. *Journal of Socio-Economics, 40*(1), 43–52.

Raj, R., & Musgrave, J. (2009). *Event management and sustainability*. Leeds: CABI.

Richards, G. (2000). The European cultural capital event: Strategic weapon in the cultural arms race? *Journal of Cultural Policy, 6*(2), 159–181.

Richards, G., & Wilson, J. (2004). The impact of cultural events on city image: Rotterdam, cultural Capital of Europe 2001. *Urban Studies, 41*(10), 1931.

Robertson, M., & Wardrop, K. M. (2012). Events and the destination dynamic: Edinburgh festivals, entrepreneurship and strategic marketing. *Festival and Events Management,* 115–121.

Rollins, R., & Delamere, T. A. (2007). Measuring the social impacts of festivals. *Annals of Tourism Research, 34*(3), 805–808.

Saayman, M. (2000). *En route with tourism*. Potchefstroom: Institute for Tourism and Leisure Studies.

Saleh, F., & Wood, C. (1998). Motives of volunteers in multicultural events: The case of Saskatoon folkfest. *Festival Management and Event Tourism, 5*, 59–70.

Small, K., & Edwards, D. (2003). Evaluating the sociocultural impacts of a festival on a host community: A case study of the Australian festival of the book. In T. Griffin & R. Harris (Eds.), *Proceedings of the 9th annual conference of the Asia Pacific Tourism Association* (pp. 580–593). Sydney: School of Leisure, Sport and Tourism, University of Technology Sydney.

Statistical Report. (2015). *Demographic indexes and employment statistics by industry sector*. Republic of Serbia.

Sziget Festival. (2016). http://szigetfestival.com/_/info/about. Accessed 8 Jan 2017.

Tassiopoulos, D., & Johnson, D. (2009). Social impacts of events. In *Event management and sustainability* (pp. 76–89). Wallingford: CABI.

Thyne, M., Lawson, R., & Todd, S. (2006). The use of conjoint analysis to assess the impact of the cross-cultural exchange between hosts and guests. *Tourism Management, 27*, 201–213.

Tosun, C. (2002). Host perceptions of impacts: A comparative tourism study. *Annals of Tourism Research, 29*(1), 231–253.

Uysal, M., Gahan, L., & Martin, B. (1993). An examination of event motivations. *Festival Management and Event Tourism, 1*, 5–10.

Van den Berg, M. (2012). Femininity as a city marketing strategy gender bending Rotterdam. *Urban Studies, 49*(1), 153–168.

Van Wynsberghe, R., Derom, I., & Maurer, E. (2012). Social leveraging of the 2010 Olympic Games: 'Sustainability' in a city of Vancouver initiative. *Journal of Policy Research in Tourism, Leisure and Events, 4*(2), 185–205.

Veenhoven, R. (1996). The study of life satisfaction. In: Saris, W.E Veenhoven, R. Scherpenzel, A.C. Bunting, B. A comparative study of satisfaction with life in Europe. Budapest: Eötvös University Press.

Weaver, G. D., & Robinson, R. (1989). *Special events: Guidelines for planning and development*. Columbia: University of Missouri.

Williams, S. (1998). *Tourism geography*. New York: Routledge.

Wood, E. (2005). Measuring the economic and social impacts of local authority events. *International Journal of Public Sector Management, 18*(1), 37–53.

Woosnam, K., Van Winkle, C., & An, S. (2013). Confirming the festival social impact attitude scale in the context of a rural Texas cultural festival. *Event Management, 17*, 257–270.

Ziakas, V. (2016). Fostering the social utility of events: An integrative framework for the strategic use of events in community development. *Current Issues in Tourism, 19*(11), 1136–1157.

Part III
Quality of Life in Tourism and Its Impact on Tourists' Well-being

Chapter 12
Seniors: Quality of Life and Travel/Tourism

Hyelin (Lina) Kim, Muzaffer Uysal, and M. Joseph Sirgy

Abstract The senior segment in travel and tourism is increasing in both size and profitability. Travel/tourism scholars have done much research in relation to quality of life and senior tourists. Determining what aspects of travel impacts the well-being of seniors should be valuable to program coordinators of retirement communities and tourism officials. In addition, destination promoters and service providers should benefit by knowing which aspect of travel is most conducive to enriching the physical and emotional well-being of senior travelers. With this regard, this chapter is designed to review the literature relevant to senior tourist behaviors, measures of seniors' quality of life and its relation to tourism, and how participating in leisure while traveling may enhance their well-being. Another goal of the chapter is to suggest future research directions that can be useful for tourism providers and professional associations (as well as government agencies) that deal with seniors, travel, and tourism.

Keywords Senior Tourists · Tourism · Quality of Life (QOL)

H. (Lina) Kim (✉)
William F. Harrah College of Hospitality, University of Nevada, Las Vegas, NV, USA
e-mail: hyelin.kim@unlv.edu

M. Uysal
Department of Hospitality & Tourism Management, Isenberg School of Management, University of Massachusetts, Amherst, MA, USA
e-mail: muysal@isenberg.umass.edu

M. Joseph Sirgy
Department of Marketing, Pamplin College of Business, Virginia Polytechnic Institute and State University, Blacksburg, VA, USA
e-mail: sirgy@vt.edu

A. M. Campón-Cerro et al. (eds.), *Best Practices in Hospitality and Tourism Marketing and Management*, Applying Quality of Life Research,
https://doi.org/10.1007/978-3-319-91692-7_12

12.1 Introduction

The travel and tourism industry has long recognized the importance of the mature market. If the tourism industry is going to better serve this market, industry officials must understand and meet the needs and expectations of senior travelers, and this requires systematic study of this market (Carneiro et al. 2013; Kim et al. 2015). Tourism researchers have also long recognized the existing link between travel and quality of life (QOL) of individuals. In the scholarly leisure literature, much research has supported the notion that seniors' involvement in leisure activity contributes to their subjective well-being (e.g., Fernandez-Ballesteros et al. 2001). However, there is only limited research focusing on how senior tourists' travel experiences affect their well-being. A recent study by Kim et al. (2015) showed that involvement in travel activity has a positive influence on seniors' overall QOL. Determining what aspects of travel impacts the QOL of seniors should be valuable to program coordinators of retirement communities and tourism officials. In addition, destination promoters and service providers should benefit by knowing which aspect of travel is most conducive to enriching the physical and emotional well-being of senior travelers. Thus, goal of this chapter is twofold: (1) to review the literature relevant to senior tourists and how participating in leisure while traveling may enhance their well-being in and (2) suggest future research directions that can be useful for tourism providers and professional associations (as well as government agencies) that deal with seniors, travel, and tourism.

To achieve these goals, the current study reviewed articles in leisure and tourism journals concerning (1) senior tourists' quality of life, (2) measures of seniors' quality of life, (3) life domains of seniors and how tourism experiences may influence these life domains. We then summarized the findings of the studies.

12.2 Senior Tourists and Quality of Life (QOL)

There are a number of definitions that are used to explain and describe the nature of the aging population in the United States and beyond. In the context of travel and tourism research, this aging segment of the population is associated with many labels: "the elderly market," "the baby boomers," "the mature market," "the graying market," "the senior market," "the older market," "the golden agers," "post-retirement age groups," among others (Hsu et al. 2007; Lee and Tideswell 2005; Shoemaker 2000). Although these terms are used interchangeably, the trend seems to point to the more frequent use of the "senior market" or simply "seniors." As the size of this market is increasing and projected to increase significantly by 2050, the demand for more quality and quantity leisure programs in tourism is likely to grow by leaps and bounds (Kim et al. 2015). Given the rising number of seniors, most of whom have much discretionary time, it is not surprising that this segment has been of interest to tourism researchers (Heo et al. 2013; Kohlbacher and Chéron 2012;

Lehto et al. 2008). There is no question that this aging trend is a phenomenon that tourism scholars and officials should attend to. Staying active and meaningfully engaged in leisure activities seem essential to good health and well-being of seniors (Global Cooalitaion on Aging 2013). There is much evidence in tourism that has firmly established the fact that travel is an important lifestyle activity that helps alleviates stress and increases physical and emotional well-being. For example, a recent study conducted by Global Cooalitaion on Aging (2013) reveals that Americans both aspire to travel in their retirement and understand the critical role that travel plays in their personal well-being, both physical and mental. This effect seems to be most pronounced in the developed, much more so than in the developing countries. Furthermore, research has also shown that travel is viewed by tourists as important for good health and personal happiness (Smith and Puczkó 2014). As such, there are a number of theories that have been used to explain how seniors' leisure activities during travel contribute to their personal well-being. These theories include activity theory and continuity theory.

Historically, the pioneering studies of Havighurst (1961) were the first to introduce *activity theory* proposing that an increase in time availability enables seniors to engage in leisure and non-leisure activities, which become a conduit for life satisfaction. Activity theory assumes that the way to achieve greater life satisfaction in older adulthood is through one's ability to maintain or increase involvement in social roles and leisure activities (e.g., Fernandez-Ballesteros et al. 2001). Activity theory was also used in response as a critique to disengagement theory, which argues that the disengagement from the daily routine of economic activity is a natural part of aging and is essential for inner fulfillment. (e.g., Ananian and Janke 2010). Even today, activity theory is the guiding force for much of the activity programming in senior centers, long-term care facilities, and retirement communities. The major tenet of this theory is to encourage seniors to stay as active as possible, and doing so should lead to more satisfying and fulfilling life. But, it is also acknowledged that some older adults or seniors may find the process of remaining active stressful rather than rewarding.

Another theory was also proposed around the same time of activity theory called *continuity theory* (Rowe and Kahn 1998). Continuity theory focuses on explaining how successful aging entails the use of health care, transportation, and leisure/recreation services to adapt to changes in aging. The authors (Rowe and Kahn 1998) have argued that successful aging is characterized by the ability of mature adults to avoid disease, maintain high physical and cognitive function, and continue engagement in life. In this regard, engagement refers to the constructive use of leisure time, a meaningful and rewarding way that contributes to personal well-being and successful aging. Nimrod (2008) tested patterns of continuity and change in leisure behavior of recently retired individuals. Four groups (reducers, concentrators, diffusers and expanders) were identified and their leisure participation and life satisfaction were measured. The research finding showed that the expanders and the concentrators enjoyed a significantly higher life satisfaction than the other groups. This result support the activity and continuity theory.

Activity theory and continuity theories discussed above support the general premise that engagement and activity involvement are linked to health and well-being in later life. In the discipline of leisure studies, many studies have supported these theories by demonstrating that a retired senior's participation in an activity contributes to his or her subjective well-being (e.g., Fernandez-Ballesteros et al. 2001; Menec and Chipperfield 1997; Silverstein and Parker 2002). For instance, Heo et al. (2013) segmented the senior population into three groups based on patterns of serious leisure involvement and examined how these three groups differ in terms of life satisfaction and health. The results suggested that the level of involvement in serious leisure had a positive impact on life satisfaction and health. Another study conducted by Yin (2008) examined the lives of retired seniors in Hong Kong's Aldrich Bay by testing the impact of both perceived leisure constraints and leisure satisfaction on life satisfaction. The results showed that leisure satisfaction made a major and significant contribution to seniors' overall life satisfaction.

The scholarly tourism literature has examined the interrelationships among senior tourists' behavior (especially focusing on motivation for travel), socio-demographic characteristics, destination choice, travel constraints, and well-being (e.g., Burton et al. 2006; De Vos et al. 2013; Jang et al. 2009; Kim et al. 2015; Lee and Tideswell 2005). This line of research found that that the most common travel motive for a senior involves relaxation (e.g., Chen and Wu 2009; Jang et al. 2009; Tung and Ritchie 2011), socialization (e.g., Jang et al. 2009; Wei and Milman 2002), ego-enhancement (e.g., Jang et al. 2009; Sangpikul 2008), novelty (Chen and Wu 2009), and health (e.g., Hsu et al. 2007; Sirakaya et al. 1996). These motivational factors can be characterized as "push factors." In contrast, "pull factors" include natural resources, historical sites, and facilities (e.g., Anderson and Langmeyer 1982; Wei and Milman 2002), as well as event attractiveness and cost (e.g., Sirakaya et al. 1996).

In terms of Maslow's hierarchy of needs, senior tourists' major motives tend to reflect higher-order needs (Csikszentmihalyi and LeFevre 1989; Maslow 1968). Cordes and Ibrahim (1999) have argued that seniors' travel motives should be viewed at a level higher than physiological needs; that is, travel needs reflect higher-order needs such as self-actualization needs, personal growth and development.

Only a few studies have focused on how seniors' travel experiences affect their well-being (e.g., Kim et al. 2015; Lee and Tideswell 2005; Milman 1998; Wei and Milman 2002). For example, Kim et al. (2015) examined the relationships between involvement in tourism activity, perceived value, and satisfaction with trip experience, leisure life satisfaction, overall QOL, and revisit intention among seniors. The study results suggested that the level of involvement of senior tourists positively influences their overall QOL and revisit intentions. A study conducted by Milman (1998) also identified the impact of travel experience on the subjective well-being of senior tourists. The results indicate that travel experience may increase the level of happiness after the trip.

12.3 Measures of Seniors' Quality of Life (QOL) and Its Relation to Tourism

Operationalizing overall QOL among seniors has received much attention (e.g., Diener et al. 1999; Stanley and Cheek 2003). In gerontology, overall QOL has been viewed as the subjective counterpart of a more public evaluation of "successful aging." Gerontology scholars have used many instruments to capture subjective well-being among seniors. For example, the Life Satisfaction Rating (LSR) developed by Neugarten et al. (1961), has been widely used to measure seniors' overall life satisfaction (e.g., Hsu 2010; Meadow and Cooper 1990). Items such as "Compared to other people, my life is better than most of them" and "I would say I am satisfied with my way of life" are included in the LSR measure.

Alternatively, the Reflective Life Satisfaction (RLS) measure is equally popular (Wood et al. 1969). The measure involves the following items: "As I look back on my life, I am fairly well satisfied"; "I have gotten pretty much what I expected out of my life"; "When I think back over my life, I did not get most of the important things I wanted"; "I have gotten more of the breaks in life than most of the people I know"; "In spite of what people say, the lot of the average man is getting worse, not better"; "Most of the things I do are boring or monotonous"; "These are the better years of my life"; "The things I do are as interesting to me as they ever were"; and "I am just as happy as when I was younger."

In addition, CASP-19 scale was designed to measure QOL and fulfillment of human needs in early old age. It involves four dimensions: control, autonomy, self-realization, and pleasure (Jivraj et al. 2014). Example items of the control dimension include: "My age prevents me from doing the things," and "I feel that what happens to me is out of my control." Examples of items reflecting the autonomy dimension include: "I feel that I can please myself in what I can do," and "I can do the things that I want to do." Items capturing the self-realization dimension include: "I feel that my life has meaning," and "I look back on life with a sense of happiness." Items capturing the pleasure dimension include: "I feel that the future looks good for me," and "I enjoy the things that I do."

Another popular measure of overall life satisfaction of seniors is the Satisfaction with Life Scale (SWLS) (Diener et al. 1985). SWLS includes items such as the following: "In most ways my life is close to my ideal"; "The conditions of my life are excellent and I am satisfied with my life"; "So far I have gotten the important things I want in life"; and "If I could live my life over, I would change almost nothing." There is a voluminous literature involving SWLS which provided much evidence of the reliability and validity of this measure.

In tourism studies, overall life satisfaction has been typically measured using survey items such as: "I felt good about my life shortly after the trip"; "Overall, I felt happy upon my return from that trip"; and "I felt that I lead a meaningful and fulfilling life" (e.g., Neal et al. 1999; Sirgy et al. 2011).

12.4 Senior Tourists and Domain Satisfaction

To understand how tourism influences the quality of life of the seniors, it is important to identify the main life domains of seniors and how tourism experiences may influence these life domains. Farquhar (1995) attempted to identify salient life domains for seniors. The study revealed that family, social contact, activities, health, and material circumstances as important domains affecting overall QOL. Brown et al. (2004) highlighted the following life domains: relationships with others, autonomy, health, mobility, family relationships, emotional well-being, independence, and leisure. Managerially speaking, these areas of life should be emphasized in tourism program development and the marketing of these programs. Moreover, Ferrans and Powers (1992) measured seniors' QOL in terms of their satisfaction with a select set of life domains: relationships with family members, friendships, ability to meet nonfinancial family responsibilities, health, leisure time activities, and religious life. In later life, physical health is perceived by senior tourists as more important than they are in earlier life. Smith et al. (1999) conducted a meta-analysis of QOL instruments showing that "health status" is a prominent construct of aging research. In addition, a number of studies emphasized physical and mental health as predominant life domains for seniors (e.g., Janke et al. 2008; Paillard-Borg et al. 2009; Werngren-Elgstrom et al. 2006). Based on a comprehensive review of the leisure and gerontology literature, the most commonly used life domains and indicators seem to include family, social, emotional, leisure, and health life domain as major determinants of overall QOL (Brown et al. 2004; Kelly-Gillespie 2009; Ku et al. 2008). Of course, seniors' tourism experiences are most likely to influence these life domains.

Family life is usually viewed in terms of relationships between family members and relatives (Brown et al. 2004). Andrews and Withey (1976) provided substantial evidence indicating that satisfaction with family life is a substantial factor in life satisfaction. Seniors do consider their relationship with spouse and other family members as important aspects in family life and overall life satisfaction. Specifically, research has suggested that there is a significant association between family conflict and QOL (e.g., Ejechi 2012). Family conflict decreases satisfaction with family life and overall QOL (Amato 2005). Tourism serves to strengthen familial relationships when seniors travel with family members or when they travel to visit family (e.g., Mancini et al. 2012; Smith and Puczkó 2012). As such, tourism programs should be developed and marketed in a manner to enhance family well-being.

The quality of *social life* typically involves quality of relationships with friends, interaction with others, and general satisfaction with one's friends. In regards to tourism, people are more likely to form new friendships and meet new people if they go on, for instance, singles' holiday tours or if they take part in group tours with similarly-minded people. For example, Dann (2001) found that seniors, while exploring opportunities for new experiences during tourism excursions, are likely to foster a sense of purpose through new friendships or making romance with other tourists of a similar age. As such, tourism programs should be developed and marketed in a manner to enhance social well-being.

The quality of *leisure life* of seniors is typically judged in terms of satisfaction with leisure life, available leisure time, and free time management. Seniors manage their free time by participating in various types of travel and leisure activities (McGuire et al. 1996). Much research have demonstrated that leisure and tourism are major elements of post-retirement life and do play a significant role in life satisfaction (e.g., Fernandez- Ballesteros et al. 2001; Kim et al. 2015; Nimrod 2008). For example, Kim et al. (2015) found that a senior's satisfaction with leisure life domain positively affects his/her overall life satisfaction. Mishra (1992) conducted a study to examine the relationship between leisure-life experience and QOL among seniors. The study results indicated that leisure-life experience has a positive influence on QOL. As such, tourism programs should be developed and marketed in a manner to enhance leisure well-being.

Spiritual well-being is conceived of as devotion to a deity or particular life philosophy (Sirgy 2002). It reflects fulfillment of spiritual needs as well as those activities related to their fulfillment. Teichmann et al. (2006) conducted a study that produced positive and significant correlations between spiritual well-being and subjective well-being. Moreover, the same study underscored a positive relationship between spiritual well-being and physical health and social relationships. As such, tourism programs should be developed and marketed in a manner to enhance spiritual well-being.

A study by Cummins (2005) reviewed the 32 QOL studies and classified 173 different terms into seven life domains. One of the findings showed that leisure and tourism activities are the significant predictor of satisfaction of *emotional well-being*, and 85% of the studies included emotional well-being in some form of satisfaction with activities related to leisure, spiritual life, and morale. Lee and Ishii-Kuntz (1987) emphasized the importance of emotional well-being of seniors. The authors tested the role of partners on emotional well-being of seniors by using a large sample (2872 seniors). The study underscored the notion that social interaction with friends has a strong effect on emotional well-being. As such, tourism programs should be developed and marketed in a manner to enhance emotional well-being.

Health life is one of the most important domains affecting life satisfaction among seniors. Several large-scale studies have provided evidence suggesting that satisfaction with health affects life satisfaction (e.g., Andrews and Withey 1976). Indeed, many QOL studies have linked health-related factors with seniors' QOL. In recent years, health and wellness tourism—including spas, clinics for medical procedures, and hiking—has rapidly grown (Sheldon and Bushell 2009; Smith and Puczkó 2009). The study by Hobson and Dietrich (1995) found that tourism is an important factor in pursuing health life, thus improving the quality of life. In addition, much research among seniors have indicated that physical health conditions lead seniors to experience stress, which adversely affects their subjective well-being (e.g., Berg et al. 2006; Lachman et al. 2008; Pearlin and Skaff 1996). For example, a study conducted by Windle et al. (2010) has demonstrated the negative effect of poor health on life satisfaction of seniors, and that this effect is moderated by resilience. As such, tourism programs should be developed and marketed in a manner to enhance health well-being.

In sum, based on the review of the literatures in tourism and gerontology, one can conclude that tourism experiences influence seniors' sense of well-being in family life, social life, leisure life, emotional life, and health life (e.g., Brown et al. 2004; Everard et al. 2000; Greenley et al. 1997; Ku et al. 2008; Kelly-Gillespie 2009). Moreover, we can safely conclude that senior tourists' overall QOL is mostly influenced directly or indirectly by evaluations of these salient life domains.

12.5 Conclusion and Future Research Directions

What can be inferred from the literature on seniors, their well-being, especially by partaking in leisure and tourism activities? First, regardless of the target group or segment, whether it is senior or general public, engaging in leisurely travel and tourism activities result in physiological and psychological benefits to participants. The central tenet implied in this assertion is that a leisure/tourism activity contributes significantly to the well-being of participants if it delivers not only functional benefits but also a range of other benefits related to both basic and growth needs (e.g., Bjork 2014; Chen and Petrick, 2013; Driver et al. 1991; Payne et al. 2010; Smith and Puczkó 2014;). This assertion should be further tested using samples from a variety of countries, given that much of the research is Western based. Determining the extent to which travel impacts the quality of life of seniors could be valuable to program coordinators, policy makers of retirement communities and homes to legitimize and develop leisure activities. In addition, destination promoters and service providers would benefit by knowing which salient dimensions of the travel experience are most conducive to enrich the physical and emotional well well-being of senior travelers.

Second, the review of the extant literature reveals that the assumed link between the travel behavior of seniors and their well-being may vary from one type of activity to another and from one form of travel experience to another, each yielding different benefits and value. Thus, the types of activities and their role in creating value for seniors should be of a major concern to researchers. Researchers should closely examine how engaging in what type of activity may contribute to the well-being of seniors and under what situations and cultural contexts this contribution may show variation.

Third, there are also measurement issues related to the use of certain scales. Researchers have to identify life domains that are most pertinent to seniors in particular setting and select those instruments with the most pertinent life domains. Both subjective and objective measures should also be used; they should complement each other in the assessment of seniors' well-being (Bimonte and Faralla 2012). Doing so should capture QOL of seniors, as travelers, more effectively.

Further research is needed and issues that need to be addressed are as follows:

- determining the impact of pleasure travel on the quality of life of the aging population;
- determining the extent of travel as a part of the senior lifestyle;
- determining the impact of pre-retirement travel planning, including savings for travel on post-retirement adjustment and travel behavior;
- identifying and alleviating barriers to travel for senior travelers and non-travelers;
- identifying the expenditure behavior of senior travelers;
- determining the extent to which travel experiences can replace lost roles and create new roles for the senior traveler;
- determining if travel businesses are meeting the physical, social and psychological needs of the elderly; and
- segmenting the senior population and determining the impact of inter-generational programming, and providing opportunities for inter-generational travel.

In addition, it is important to do research exploring opportunities to create a mechanism by which individuals would also do additional savings throughout their active years of work for travel goals to make their desire for travel a reality. The senior traveler will be a significant part of the future travel and tourism market, and we need to base our research and services on *facts* related to the needs, desires, expectations, and attitudes of the senior travelers.

The research issues addressed above cannot be the responsibility of one agent but several, including providers of services and goods, government and regulatory agents, intermediaries (such as booking agents and transportation agents), lodging establishments, destination promoters, researchers, community developers, and the travel participants themselves. In this vein, providers of tourism goods and services have a major role as facilitators to influence the consumption setting of the older adults in which experiences are created and behavioral outcomes are influenced.

References

Amato, P. R. (2005). The impact of family formation change on the cognitive, social, and emotional well-being of the next generation. *The Future of Children, 15*(2), 75–96.

Ananian, C. D., & Janke, M. (2010). Leisure in later life. In L. Payne, B. Ainsworth, & G. Godbey (Eds.), *Leisure, health, and wellness: Making the connections* (pp. 249–261). State College: Venture Publishing.

Anderson, B. B., & Langmeyer, L. (1982). The under-50 and over-50 travelers: A profile of similarities and differences. *Journal of Travel Research, 20*(4), 20–24.

Andrews, F. M., & Withey, S. B. (1976). *Social indicators of well-being America's perception of quality*. New York: Plenum Press.

Berg, A. I., Hassing, L., McClearn, G., & Johansson, B. (2006). What matters for life satisfaction in the oldest-old? *Aging and Mental Health, 10*(3), 257–264.

Bimonte, S., & Faralla, V. (2012). Tourist types and happiness; A comparative study in Maremma, Italy. *Annals of Tourism Research, 39*(4), 1929–1950.

Bjork, P. (2014). Tourist experience value: Tourist experience and life satisfaction. In N. Prebensen, J. Chen, & M. Uysal (Eds.), *Creating experience value in tourism* (pp. 22–32). Wallingford: CABI.

Brown, J., Blowling, A., & Flynn, T. N. (2004). *Models of quality of life: A taxonomy and systematic review of the literature review*. Sheffield: Report Commissioned by the European Forum on Population Ageing Research/Quality of Life.

Burton, K. D., Lydon, J. E., D'Alessandro, D. U., & Koestner, R. (2006). The differential effects of intrinsic and identified motivation on well-being and performance: Prospective, experimental, and implicit approaches to self-determination theory. *Journal of Personality and Social Psychology, 91*(4), 750.

Carneiro, M. J., Eusébio, C., Kastenholz, E., & Alvelos, H. (2013). Motivations to participate in social tourism programmes: A segmentation analysis of the senior market. *An International Journal of Tourism and Hospitality Research, 24*(3), 352–366.

Chen, C., & Petrick, J. F. (2013). Health and wellness benefits of travel experiences: A literature review. *Journal of Travel Research, 52*(6), 709–719.

Chen, C. F., & Wu, C. (2009). How motivations, constraints, and demographic factors predict seniors' overseas travel propensity. *Asia Pacific Management Review, 14*(3), 301–312.

Cordes, K. A., & Ibrahim, H. M. (1999). *Applications in recreation and leisure: For today and the future*. Boston: McGraw-Hill Book Company Europe.

Csikszentmihalyi, M., & LeFevre, J. (1989). Optimal experience in work and leisure. *Journal of Personality and Social Psychology, 56*(5), 815.

Cummins, R. A. (2005). *The domains of life satisfaction: An attempt to order chaos citation classics from social indicators research* (pp. 559–584). Dordrecht: Springer.

Dann, G. M. S. (2001). Senior tourism and quality of life. *Journal of Hospitality & Leisure Marketing, 9*(1/2), 5–19.

De Vos, J., Schwanen, T., Van Acker, V., & Witlox, F. (2013). Travel and subjective well-being: A focus on findings, methods and future research needs. *Transport Reviews, 33*(4), 421–442.

Diener, E., Emmons, R. A., Larsen, R. J., & Griffin, S. (1985). The satisfaction with life scale. *Journal of Personality Assessment, 49*, 71–75.

Diener, E., Suh, E. M., Lucas, R. E., & Smith, H. L. (1999). Subjective well-being: Three decades of progress. *Psychological Bulletin, 125*(2), 276–302.

Driver, B. L., Brown, P. J., & Peterson, G. L. (1991). *Benefits of leisure*. State College: Venture Publishing.

Ejechi, E. O. (2012). The quality of life of retired reengaged academics in Nigeria. *Educational Gerontology, 38*(5), 328–337.

Everard, K. M., Lach, H. W., Fisher, E. B., & Baum, M. C. (2000). Relationship of activity and social support to the functional health of older adults. *The Journals of Gerontology Series B, 55*(4), S208–S212.

Farquhar, M. (1995). Definitions of quality of life: A taxonomy. *Journal of Advanced Nursing, 22*(3), 502–508.

Fernandez-Ballesteros, R., Dolores Zamarrón, M., & Angel Ruíz, M. (2001). The contribution of sociodemographic and psychosocial factors to life satisfaction. *Ageing and Society, 21*(01), 25–43.

Ferrans, C. E., & Powers, M. J. (1992). Psychometric assessment of the quality of life index. *Research in Nursing & Health, 15*(1), 29–38.

Global Cooalitaion on Aging. (2013). *Journey to healthy aging: Planning for travel in retirement*. Transamerica Center for Retirement Studies, December 2013.

Greenley, J. R., Greenberg, J. S., & Brown, R. (1997). Measuring quality of life: A new and practical survey instrument. *Social Work, 42*, 244–254.

Havighurst, R. J. (1961). Successful aging. *The Gerontologist, 1*, 8–13.
Heo, J., Stebbins, R. A., Kim, J., & Lee, I. (2013). Serious leisure, life satisfaction, and health of older adults. *Leisure Sciences, 35*(1), 16–32.
Hobson, J. S., & Dietrich, U. C. (1995). Challenging the responsibility of using the traditional tenets of sun, sea, sand, and sex in tourism marketing. *Journal of Travel & Tourism Marketing, 3*(4), 21–38.
Hsu, H.-C. (2010). Trajectory of life satisfaction and its relationship with subjective economic status and successful aging. *Social Indicators Research, 99*(3), 455–468.
Hsu, C. H., Cai, L. A., & Wong, K. K. (2007). A model of senior tourism motivations—Anecdotes from Beijing and Shanghai. *Tourism Management, 28*(5), 1262–1273.
Jang, S. S., Bai, B., Hu, C., & Wu, C. (2009). Affect, travel motivation, and travel intention: A senior market. *Journal of Hospitality & Tourism Research, 33*(1), 51–73.
Janke, M. C., Nimrod, C., & Kleiber, D. A. (2008). Leisure activity and depressive symptoms of widowed and married women in later life. *Journal of Leisure Research, 40*(2), 250–266.
Jivraj, S., Nazroo, J., Vanhoutte, B., & Chandola, T. (2014). Aging and subjective well-being in later life. *The Journals of Gerontology Series B*, 1–12. *69*(9), 930–941.
Kelley-Gillespie, N. (2009). An integrated conceptual model of quality of life for older adults based on a synthesis of the literature. *Applied Research in Quality of Life, 4*(3), 259–282.
Kim, H., Woo, E., & Uysal, M. (2015). Tourism experience and quality of life among elderly tourists. *Tourism Management, 46*, 465–476.
Kohlbacher, F., & Chéron, E. (2012). Understanding "silver" consumers through cognitive age, health condition, financial status, and personal values: Empirical evidence from the world's most mature market Japan. *Journal of Consumer Behaviour, 11*(3), 179–188.
Ku, P. W., Fox, K. R., & McKenna, J. (2008). Assessing subjective well-being in Chinese olderadults: The Chinese aging well profile. *Social Indicators Research, 87*, 445–460.
Lachman, M. E., Röcke, C., Rosnick, C., & Ryff, C. D. (2008). Realism and illusion in Americans' temporal views of their life satisfaction: Age differences in reconstructing the past and anticipating the future. *Psychological Science, 19*(9), 889–897.
Lee, G. R., & Ishii-Kuntz, M. (1987). Social interaction, loneliness, and emotional well-being among the elderly. *Research on Aging, 9*(4), 459–482.
Lee, S. H., & Tideswell, C. (2005). Understanding attitudes towards leisure travel and the constraints faced by senior Koreans. *Journal of Vacation Marketing, 11*(3), 249–263.
Lehto, X. Y., Jang, S. S., Achana, F. T., & O'Leary, J. T. (2008). Exploring tourism experience sought: A cohort comparison of baby boomers and the silent generation. *Journal of Vacation Marketing, 14*(3), 237–252.
Mancini, J., George, D. V., & Jorgensen, B. (2012). Relational tourism: Observations on families and travel. In M. Uysal, R. Perdue, & M. J. Sirgy (Eds.), *Handbook of tourism and quality-of-life research: Enhancing the lives of tourists and residents of host communities* (pp. 309–320). Dordrecht: Springer.
Maslow, A. H. (1968). *Toward a psychology of being* (Vol. 16). New York: Van Nostrand Reinhold.
McGuire, F. A., Boyd, R., & Tedrick, R. T. (1996). *Leisure and aging: Ulyssean living in later life*. Champaign: Sagamore Publishing.
Meadow, H. L., & Cooper, P. D. (1990). Finding useful marketing measures for the future: Life satisfaction preparation for a marketing view. In H. L. Meadow & M. J. Sirgy (Eds.), *Quality-of-life studies in marketing and management* (pp. 645–656). Blacksburg: Virginia Tech, Center for Strategy and Marketing Studies.
Menec, V. H., & Chipperfield, J. G. (1997). Remaining active in later life the role of locus of control in seniors' leisure activity participation, health, and life satisfaction. *Journal of Aging and Health, 9*(1), 105–125.
Milman, A. (1998). The impact of tourism and travel experience on senior travelers' psychological well-being. *Journal of Travel Research, 37*(2), 166–170.

Mishra, S. (1992). A case study of retired government employees living in urban areas. *Activities, Adaption & Aging, 16*(4), 7–26.
Neal, J. D., Sirgy, M. J., & Uysal, M. (1999). The role of satisfaction with leisure travel/tourism services and experience in satisfaction with leisure life and overall life. *Journal of Business Research, 44*(3), 153–163.
Neugarten, B. L., Havighurst, R. J., & Tobin, S. S. (1961). The measurement of life satisfaction. *Journal of Gerontology, 16*, 34–143.
Nimrod, G. (2008). Retirement and tourism Themes in retirees' narratives. *Annals of Tourism Research, 35*(4), 859–878.
Paillard-Borg, S., Wang, H., Winblad, B., & Fratiglion, L. (2009). Pattern of participation in leisure activities among older people in relation to their health conditions and contextual factors: A survey in a Swedish urban area. *Aging & Society, 29*(5), 803–821.
Payne, L., Ainsworth, B., & Godbey, G. (2010). *Leisure, health, and wellness: Making the connections*. State College: Venture Publishing.
Pearlin, L. I., & Skaff, M. M. (1996). Stress and the life course: A paradigmatic alliance. *The Gerontologist, 36*(2), 239–247.
Rowe, J. W., & Kahn, R. L. (1998). *Successful ageing*. New York: Random House.
Sangpikul, A. (2008). Travel motivations of Japanese senior travellers to Thailand. *International Journal of Tourism Research, 10*(1), 81–94.
Sheldon, P., & Bushell, R. (2009). Introduction to wellness and tourism. In*Wellness and tourism: Mind, body, spirit, place* (pp. 3–18). New York: Cognizant Communication Corp.
Shoemaker, S. (2000). Segmenting the mature market: 10 years later. *Journal of Travel Research, 39*(1), 11–26.
Silverstein, M., & Parker, M. G. (2002). Leisure activities and quality of life among the oldest old in Sweden. *Reserch on Aging, 24*(5), 528–547.
Sirakaya, E., McLellan, R. W., & Uysal, M. (1996). Modeling vacation destination decisions: A behavioral approach. *Journal of Travel & Tourism Marketing, 5*(1–2), 57–75.
Sirgy, M. J. (2002). *The psychology of quality of life*. Dordrecht: Kluwer Academic.
Sirgy, M. J., Kruger, P. S., Lee, D., & Yu, G. B. (2011). How does a travel trip affect tourists' life satisfaction? *Journal of Travel Research, 50*(3), 261–275.
Smith, M. K., & Puczkó, L. (2009). *Health and wellness tourism*. London: Routledge.
Smith, M., & Puczkó, L. (2012). Budapest: from socialist heritage to cultural capital? *Current Issues in Tourism, 15*(1-2), 107–119.
Smith, M. K., & Puczkó, L. (2014). *Health, tourism and hospitality: Spas, wellness and medical travel*. London: Routledge.
Smith, K. W., Avis, N. E., & Assmann, S. F. (1999). Distinguishing between quality of life and health status in quality of life research: A meta-analysis. *Quality of Life Research, 8*(5), 447–459.
Stanley, M., & Cheek, J. (2003). Well-being and older people: A review of the literature. *Canadian Journal Occupational Therapy, 70*(1), 51–59.
Teichmann, M., Murdvee, M., & Saks, K. (2006). Spiritual needs and quality of life in Estonia. *Social Indicators Research, 76*(1), 147–163.
Tung, V. W. S., & Ritchie, J. B. (2011). Exploring the essence of memorable tourism experiences. *Annals of Tourism Research, 38*(4), 1367–1386.
Wei, S., & Milman, A. (2002). The impact of participation in activities while on vacation on Seniors' psychological well-being: A path model application. *Journal of Hospitality & Tourism Research, 26*(2), 175–185.
Werngren-Elgstrom, M., Brandt, A., & Iwarsson, S. (2006). Everyday activities and social contacts among older deaf sign language users: Relationships to health and well-being. *Occupational Therapy International, 13*(4), 207–223.
Windle, G., Woods, R. T., & Markland, D. A. (2010). Living with ill-health in older age: The role of a resilient personality. *Journal of Happiness Studies, 11*(6), 763–777.

Wood, V., Wylie, M., & Sheafer, B. (1969). An analysis of a short self-report measure of life satisfaction: Correlation with rater judgments. *Journal of Gerontology, 24*, 465–469.

Yin, L. (2008). The perceived leisure constraints of retired elderly people in Aldrich Bay. An honours project submitted in partial fulfilment of the requirement for the degree of bachelor of arts in physical education and recreation management (honours). Hong Kong Baptist University.

Chapter 13
The Blue Flag Label as a Tool to Improve the Quality of Life in the Sun-and-Sand Tourist Destinations

Antonio Chamorro-Mera, Verónica Nobre de Oliveira, and José Manuel García-Gallego

Abstract Environmental impacts generated by tourism can adversely affect competitiveness of tourism destinations, not only through the reduction in the quality of their tourism inputs, but also through a potential fall in demand as a consequence of the emergence of "environmentally sensitive" tourists. The Blue Flag is a tool for to public managers of tourist destinations in order to find a balance between environment and enjoyment of the tourist. It is an eco-labelling of beaches that demands the fulfilment of a set of requirements related to the quality of life: some of them referring directly to the environmental quality, and others to the additional comfort and services that tourists and residents can enjoy.

In order to know the effectiveness of the Blue Flag as a good practice of tourism management, it is important to understand how tourists' environmental concerns influence their choice of holiday destinations. This study evaluates the relative importance that have factors related with the quality of life and the environmental management of the tourism destination in comparison with other factors as massification, recreational activities and night-life. Through a survey to a sample of 819 Portuguese and Spanish tourists, three segments were found: "Concerned about massification", "Concerned about certified quality" and "Concerned about quality without willingness to pay more". The level of awareness of the Blue Flag is very high among tourists, but their willingness to pay a premium to stay in a tourism accommodation located near a beach with Blue Flag is not so high.

Keywords Tourism destination · Green tourism · Ecolabelling · Blue flag · Quality of life · Conjoint analysis

---

A. Chamorro-Mera (✉) · J. M. García-Gallego
University of Extremadura, Badajoz, Spain
e-mail: chamorro@unex.es; garciagallego@unex.es

V. Nobre de Oliveira
Instituto Politécnico de Leiría, Leiria, Portugal
e-mail: veronica.oliveira@ipleiria.pt

A. M. Campón-Cerro et al. (eds.), *Best Practices in Hospitality and Tourism Marketing and Management*, Applying Quality of Life Research,
https://doi.org/10.1007/978-3-319-91692-7_13

13.1 Introduction: Tourism, Environment and Quality of Life

The concept of quality of life (QOL) can be studied from two scientific approaches: individual QOL and social or community QOL. In the first approach, quality of life is concerned with individuals' subjective experience of their lives. The World Health Organization (1997) defined quality of life as an individual's perception of their position in life in the context of the culture and value systems in which they live and in relation to their goals, expectations, standards and concerns.

QOL is a multidimensional concept, beyond the individual satisfaction with his/her economic situation. Although there is a wide variety of measurement scales, it is common to include dimensions related to physical wellbeing (or health), material wellbeing, social wellbeing or emotional wellbeing, as indicated in the literature reviews performed by scholars such as Dodge et al. (2012), Dolnicar et al. (2012) or Felce and Perry (1995).

Although some of the natural environment conditions directly affect the QOL of individuals (such as air quality, noise or traffic congestion), they have indirect long-term effects on the health status of citizens. For this reason, most indices and scales have not considered the interrelationships between individual QOL and environmental changes, and not include explicitly the natural environment within the dimensions or domains that configure quality of life. Some other scales do include items relating to natural environment within the broader health domain, and only a few of them include the environment wellbeing or quality of environment as a specific dimension (Andereck and Nyaupane 2011; Lazim and Osman 2009; Palomar-Lever 2000; Rahman et al. 2011).

Furthermore, social or community QOL is a specific concept that has into account the life conditions of a territory (country, region, city or tourism destination) and that uses indicators that reflect people's objective circumstances in a given cultural or geographic environment. For instance, indicators such as gross income per capita, life expectancy at birth, infant mortality, mean years of schooling, doctors per capita, homicide rates, etc. Epley and Menon (2008, p. 281) consider that this concept of QOL measures "the liveability in the area or as one measure of the level of attractiveness".

Various indices of community QOL have been proposed by researchers (Diener and Suh 1997; Epley and Menon 2008; Hajduová et al. 2014), public policy institutes and government agencies, such as the Human Development Index (HDI) developed by the United Nations Development Program (UNDP). In contrast to the individual QOL, when assessing social QOL, aspects related to the environmental quality are considered. This is because, as indicated by Malkina-Pykh and Pykh (2008), it is generally accepted that most of the environmental problems do not directly affect individual QOL, but contribute rather to the health or quality of society. Among the measures that are used as environmental indicators are carbon dioxide emissions, water pollution, access to safe water supplies, deforestation or depletion of environmental resources.

From the community QOL perspective, the level of QOL may be managed by politicians and policymakers through economic, social and environmental policies. We agree with Epley and Menon (2008) when they suggest that QOL has become a potent marketing tool for cities and countries and that it can be used as a critical feature of marketing campaigns to promote a region, city or tourism destination.

Nowadays, environmental policy is closely related to the aim of increasing the QOL. One of the most important political and societal problems is how to improve the quality of life of population while living within the carrying capacity of the natural environment and without compromising the long-term human, economical, and ecological capital of the future. That is, how to balance economic wellbeing with environmental wellbeing.

In the case of tourism, the policies should aim at promoting sustainable tourism practices that minimize the negative impacts of tourism on the environment, while the positive economic impacts in the quality of life are kept for the residents of the tourist destinations (job creation, access to infrastructure, social and cultural services). There is a bidirectional relationship between the activities of tourism and the environment in the sense that the environmental impacts they generate may adversely affect the competitive position of the whole of the tourism destination and, therefore, the quality of life of residents. The reason is not only the reduction of the quality of tourism inputs, but also the potential decrease in consumption due to the existence of segments of "environmentally sensitive" tourists, who take into account issues such as environmental quality or sustainability in their choice of destination. In particular, the degradation in quality of the destination devalues the quality of the tourist's experience.

For example, when studying QOL of residents in a tourist destination, Kim et al. (2013) found that when residents perceive the positive economic, social, and cultural impact of tourism, satisfaction with related life domains (sense of material, community, and emotional well-being) increases too. However, when residents perceive the negative environmental impact of tourism, their sense of health and safety decreases as a result. Negative perceptions of environmental impact of tourism (e.g., tourists producing large quantities of waste products or destroying the beauty of the landscape by littering) were found to be a significant predictor of satisfaction with health and safety.

In order to improve the environmental indicators that determine the QOL of a tourist destination, in the last few decades several tools have been developed to implement good practices in tourist destinations management, such as environmental taxes, Best Practice Guidelines, Local Agenda 21, environmental management systems certification or environmental labels.

One of the most widespread environmental labels in the field of tourism is the Blue Flag, which identifies beaches that meet a set of requirements relating to four aspects: (1) quality of bathing water, (2) environmental management of the area, (3) information and environmental education for tourists and residents, and (4) security, services and facilities. A large part of the requirements relates to environmental indicators that affect QOL, such as the absence of wastewater discharges, the separate waste collection in the area or the promotion of sustainable transport. Another part of the requirements demanded by the Blue Flag refers to more general indicators of QOL, such as security and surveillance, cleaning, accessibility to the beach or the availability of drinking water in it.

To find out if these market-based tools can succeed as good management practices it is necessary to study the attitudes and behaviours of tourists and residents towards the environment, in general, and toward each particular tool. With this general context in mind, the purpose of this paper is to analyse the importance that tourists give to the blue flag when choosing a sun-and-sand tourist destination. The conclusions obtained will serve as a guide for politicians and policymakers regarding their decision about to the level of investment in environmental policies and quality of life.

13.2 Theoretical Context About Blue Flag

According to the International Standards Organization (ISO), the aim of an environmental label is to encourage the demand and the offer of products that cause less pressure on the environment throughout their life cycle, through the communication of verifiable, reliable, and not misleading information on the environmental aspects of the products and services. For tourism accommodation in particular, according to ECOTRANS, in Europe there are about 50 different ecolabeling systems; such as *European Ecolabel*, *Green Globe 21*, *Ecotel* or *Distintivo de Garantía de Calidad Ambiental*. Ecolabels effect on tourists decision making process has been analysed by different authors like Anderson et al. (2013) – about Green Coach Certification for Tourist transportation, among North American tour operators -, Fairweather et al. (2005) –among visitors to one important destination in New Zealand-, Reiser and Simmons (2005) –about Green Globe 21 ecolabel in New Zealand- and Sasidharana et al. (2002) –about the feasibility of adopting ecolabeling schemes for certifying tourism enterprises in developing countries.

Among these instruments, of particular relevance is the Blue Flag certification of beaches. It is awarded annually by the Foundation for Environmental Education to beaches and recreational harbours that meet a set of requirements relating to environmental conditions, safety, and comfort, and provide information targeted at increasing their visitors' environmental awareness. The Blue Flag was born in 1987 and in 2013 awarded to 3850 beaches and marinas in 46 countries from Europe, Africa, America and Oceania.

There are some studies on the value of the Blue Flag, with mixed results, some positive and some negative. Capacci et al. (2015) explore the relationship between Blue Flag achievement and inbound tourist flows by some panel data techniques covering a rather long time span (2000–2012). They compare the attractiveness of certified and non-certified Italian provinces and they suggest that current certification positively affects future foreign tourist decisions to visit the destination.

Lucrezi et al. (2015) interview beachgoers on Blue Flag and non-Blue Flag beaches in South Africa, to assess awareness, knowledge, and attitudes concerning the Blue Flag award, and perceptions of beach features that are also listed as Blue Flag criteria. They also interview Blue Flag managers to examine their opinion of and commitment to the award. Their results show that beachgoers and managers shared positive views of the Blue Flag award, but a lack of knowledge on the award's criteria by beachgoers was reflected in managerial and educational flaws by Blue Flag managers.

This positive assessment of the ecolabel can justify the prices of tourist services on the Blue Flag beaches being higher. In this sense, Rigall-i-Torrent et al. (2011) measured the effects of beach characteristics and hotel location with respect to the beach (such as beach length, width, sand type or beach services) on hotel prices. The study was conducted in Catalonia (Spain) and reveals, among other results, that a Blue Flag increases the price by around 11.5%.

However, there is also some criticism of the Blue Flag system. Mir-Gual et al. (2015) test if the Blue Flag management system really ensures an improvement of environmental and natural features of beaches, or if they are just a mechanism for improving the services and benefits to users. They criticize and warn that the concession of Blue Flag award is strictly focused on services offered to the tourists, and they do not take into account environmental and ecological issues related to the behavior of beaches as natural and fragile systems. They analyze 481 beaches of the Spanish coastline awarded with the Blue Flag over the period 2007–2012 and their results show that the beaches are not characterized for their naturalness; instead they show high levels of human influence and artificialization.

The merits of beach awards are also critically reviewed by McKenna et al. (2011). These authors collect various surveys of beach visitor motivation in Ireland, Wales, Turkey and the USA and they indicate that beach awards play an insignificant role in motivation to visit beaches. Other criteria, such as scenic setting, general ambience, proximity and range of activities available, are much more important than beach awards in attracting visitors to beaches. Moreover, some criteria closely identified with the Blue Flag, notably cleanliness and water quality, are revealed to be important, separately. These authors even suggest that, in some cases, the costs associated with achieving and maintaining such awards may exceed any benefits in terms of increased visitor numbers and spending.

As a consequence of the different results, further studies on the decisions of tourists and the effect of the Blue Flag are needed. It is very probable that the effect of the Blue Flag will not be universal and will vary according to the moment and place where the study will be conducted. Moreover, this effect will be different depending on the level of knowledge about the Blue Flag and other personal characteristics of tourists, such as nationality, socio-demographic profile, reasons for their trip or level of concern with the environment. This study aims at answering some of these questions.

13.3 Objective and Methods

13.3.1 Objectives

This study's main purpose was to evaluate the effect that obtaining a Blue Flag has on attracting tourists to a destination. In this way, we can evaluate if the blue flag may be a good tool to manage the quality of life in tourist destinations. Specifically, and as it was commented before, we set the following objectives:

- Quantifying the level of awareness of the Blue Flag.
- Estimating the importance of the environmental quality of a tourism destination certified with a Blue Flag as against other attributes that influence the choice of that destination.
- Analysing the willingness to pay more for tourism destinations certified with a Blue Flag.
- Identifying the existence of different segments of tourists according to their criteria for choosing destinations.

13.3.2 Methods

To estimate the relative importance of environmental quality as against other aspects of the tourism destination, we chose to use the technique of Conjoint Analysis. This reveals information about the structure of the preferences of tourists, and thus provides insight into the relative importance they give to the different attributes of the tourism destination. In simple terms, the technique consists of presenting to a sample of purchasers a set of products (or stimuli) and asking them to value them (rating or ranking) according to their preferences or purchasing intention. Each product is defined by a combination of attributes, each of which is represented at different levels.

The first step in applying this technique in the present study was to select the set of attributes that will define the different tourism destinations. For this, we first made a literature review of previous studies that have analysed the relevant attributes in the choice of tourism destinations (Table 13.1).

The attributes for choosing a tourist destination used in the 20 studies that have been analyzed can be grouped into 5 types: attributes related to environmental quality, attributes related to massification, attributes related to leisure activities, attributes related to infrastructure and attributes related to prices and fees.

Based on this review and given the objectives pursued in the study, we selected four attributes for inclusion and, for each of the attributes, three levels of presence were identified (Table 13.2).

(a) **Quality of water and beaches.** There have already been studies that have analysed this attribute (Adamowicz et al. 1994; Figini and Vici 2012; Huybers and

Table 13.1 Relevant attributes when choosing tourism destinations

Author	Attributes
Adamowicz et al. (1994)	Water quality
	Existence of a beach
Baarsma (2003)	Leisure
Brau et al. (2009)	Massification
	Characteristics of beach-front
	Environmental impact of bathing establishments and other beach services
	Night-life activities at the beach
	Cost of accommodation per person per night
Figini and Vici (2012)	Social events
	Environmental impact of bathing establishments and other beach services
	Health, sport and wellness tourism
	Cultural and leisure activities offered off-season
	Evening and night opening of shops
Figini et al. (2009)	Massification
	Environmental impact of bathing establishments and other beach services
	Use of the promenade next to the beach
	Entertainment and funfairs by the beach
	Taxes necessary to finance the scenarios
Hanley et al.(2002)	Massification
	Beauty of landscape
Huybers and Bennett (2000)	Activities
	Environmental conditions
	Development/crowdedness
	Rarity of natural attractions
Huybers (2003)	Superstructures
	Massification
	Type of activities that can be done
Kelly et al. (2007)	Leisure activities
Klenosky (2004)	Quality of the area for recreation
	Residential development
	Air quality
	Noise
Needham and Szuster (2011)	Use level/density
	Presence of litter
	Damage to reefs
	Condition of facilities
Ortega and Recio (2006)	Surroundings and location
	Offer and services of leisure
Picón and Varela (2000)	Night-life

(continued)

Table 13.1 (continued)

Author	Attributes
Rahemtulla (1998)	Marine life quality
	Rarity of wildlife
	Development of the beaches
	Local prices
Ramos et al. (2004)	Accommodation and its services
	Holiday atmosphere
	Prices of the product/service
	External services
Reig and Coenders (2002)	Beach and sea water quality
	Surroundings
Riganti (2008)	Rising cost of hotel room
Riera (2000)	Natural attributes
	Infrastructures
	Activities
Shoji and Yamaki (2004)	Environmental tax
Varela et al. (2004)	Entertainment and night-life

Bennett 2000; Rahemtulla 1998; Reig and Coenders 2002). They conclude that it is the key element for almost all segments of tourists when they are choosing a tourism destination. None of these studies, however, have associated this quality with an external certification such as the Blue Flag. Therefore, in the present work we included the following levels for the environmental quality attribute: low quality, good quality, and good quality with Blue Flag certification.

(b) **Massification.** This attribute refers to the number of visitors to be found in a tourism destination, together with the degree of urbanization and congestion of the zone's tourism infrastructures and facilities. There are studies showing that this is not one of the most important attributes in the choice of a tourism destination (Brau et al. 2009; Figini et al. 2009). But it has also been shown to have a major influence on tourists' level of satisfaction with the destination (Apostolakis and Jaffry 2005; Huybers and Bennett 2000; Klenosky 2004; Needham and Szuster 2011; Rahemtulla 1998), with it being expected that tourists' preferences will decrease as massification increases. Thus, we opted to include the following three levels of the massification attribute: not massified, moderately massified, and very massified.

(c) **Recreational activities and night-life.** This attribute refers to the number of leisure activities that exist in the tourism destination for recreation and leisure time. Several studies have shown that this is a fairly important attribute when choosing the destination (Brau et al. 2009; Figini et al. 2009; Picón and Varela 2000; Reig and Coenders 2002; Varela et al. 2004), especially for the younger segment of tourists. Thus, this attribute was included in the study with three possible options.

Table 13.2 Levels of the attributes

Quality of water and beaches	Low quality	This destination has a **low quality** of beach and of water for bathing. In addition, there is neither concern about informing and sensitizing tourists to environmental protection nor any environmental management measures.
	Good quality	This destination has a **good quality** of beach and water for bathing, although **it has not been awarded** the Blue Flag rating.
	Good quality with Blue Flag	This destination has been awarded the **Blue Flag logo**, which is a guarantee of compliance with stringent quality standards in water for bathing and beach, the existence of media for providing environmental information and of environmental education campaigns, the adoption of environmental management measures, the safety of bathers, and some other additional services and structures for tourists.
Massification	Not massified	A destination with **few tourists**, few buildings (few hotels, predominance of scattered houses). Here it is possible to "get away from it all", to rest completely; it is quiet and relaxed.
	Moderately massified	A destination with a **moderate number of tourists** and some areas of urban concentration, sometimes congestion of infrastructure (heavy traffic and jams) and facilities, but a relaxed atmosphere prevails.
	Very massified	A destination with a **large number of tourists**, with dense high-rise buildings near the beach; frequent congestion of infrastructure (heavy traffic and jams) and facilities. An atmosphere of movement and bustle.
Recreational activities and night-life	Few	A **few opportunities for recreational activities** at the beach and of local night-life (bars, restaurants, discotheques...).
	Some	There are **some recreational activities** offered at the beach and some local night-life (bars, restaurants, discotheques...)
	Many	There is a **great variety of recreational activities** at the beach (volleyball and beach soccer, surfing, sailing, areas for aerobics and dance classes,...) and a wide range of local night-life (bars, restaurants, discotheques,...).
Green tax	No tax	No environmental tax of any type.
	5%	Tourists **must pay 5% of the daily cost** of their accommodation as an environmental tax, destined to maintaining and improving the area's natural conditions.
	10%	Tourists **must pay 10% of the daily cost** of their accommodation as an environmental tax, destined to maintaining and improving the area's natural conditions.

(d) **Green Tax.** This attribute refers to the possibility that the tourism destination has implemented a tax surcharge on the price per night of accommodation, and which is earmarked by the competent Public Administration for investments to protect, conserve, and improve the zone's natural resources. The influence of this attribute has been analysed in several studies, such as those of Kelly et al. (2007), Mercado and Lassoie (2002), Reig and Coenders (2002), and Shoji and Yamaki (2004). In the light of this information, we included the attribute "*Green Tax*" in the study with three levels: no tax, 5% and 10% on the cost of accommodation.

Table 13.3 Stimuli presented to the respondents

Quality of water and beaches	Massification	Recreational activities	Environmental tax
Good quality – Blue Flag certified	Moderately massified	Few	10%
Good quality – Blue Flag certified	Very massified	Some	No tax
Good quality	Not massified	Some	10%
Good quality	Very massified	Few	5%
Good quality	Moderately massified	Many	No tax
Low quality	Very massified	Many	10%
Low quality	Not massified	Few	No tax
Good quality – Blue Flag certified	Not massified	Many	5%
Low quality	Moderately massified	Some	5%

Following the selection of attributes and levels, the second step in the application of Conjoint Analysis is to determine how to construct the stimuli. There are several procedures that can be followed for the presentation of the stimuli to elicit a valuation response from the interviewees. We used the full profile method. In this method, the respondent is presented with a single set of stimuli to evaluate. Each stimulus comprises information on all the attributes included in the study. In the present case therefore, each stimulus (tourism destination) consists of three levels each of quality, massification, recreational activities, and Green Tax. The number of possible stimuli was therefore 81 ($3 \times 3 \times 3 \times 3$). However, presenting so many stimuli to the respondent would overload the respondent with information, and adversely affect the quality of the responses. To avoid this problem, we performed an orthogonal design procedure which reduced the combinations to only 9 (Table 13.3). This reduction is carried out in such a way that the information acquired from the use of the resulting subset will be similar to that which would be acquired using all the stimuli. In particular, one ensures the presence of all the attributes and their corresponding levels with equal intensity in the stimuli with this design, without introducing a bias to any given level.

Initially, the tourism destinations were presented to the respondents in a similar form to how they are described in a travel agency brochure. Subsequently, to facilitate the decision-making process, they were presented in a summary form in the questionnaire, and the respondents were asked to list their preferences from 1 to 9.

The survey was directed at Portuguese and Spanish tourists. We worked with a sample of 819 tourists, chosen through convenience sampling, visiting in the District of Leiria (Portugal) and the Region of Extremadura (Spain), over the age of 18, who usually spend their holidays in sun-and-sand destinations. The fieldwork was carried out during 2010, through a self-administered personal survey.

By nationality, 54% were Portuguese, and 46% Spanish. By gender, 57% of the sample were women and 43% men. By age, 21% of the sample were from 18 to 25 years old, 31% from 26 to 35, 27% from 36 to 45, 16% from 46 to 55, and 5% were over 55. By educational level, the sample was distributed into higher education (45%), secondary education (37%), and primary education (18%). By monthly household net income, 20% had an income of less than €1000/month, 42% from €1001 to €2000/month, 19% from €2001 to €3000/month, and 16% above €3000/month.

13.4 Results

Overall, the results of the study showed the level of awareness of the Blue Flag to be very high among these Spanish and Portuguese tourists. Specifically, 84% of respondents stated they knew about the Blue Flag and understood what it means, only 9% said they had heard of it but did not know what it means, and the remaining 7% did not even know about it. By nationality, the Portuguese respondents had the higher level of awareness. Pearson's chi-squared test confirmed that these differences were statistically significant. This difference may reflect the geographical situation of the two nationalities in the sample: in Portugal, the sample was obtained in a coastal region, while in Spain it was obtained in an inland region (Fig. 13.1).

The respondents were presented with nine tourism destinations, and were asked to list them according to their preferences from 1 to 9. The scores provide an insight into the relative importance of the various attributes that describe the tourism destination and the utility of each level of the attributes. As expected, the results confirmed that the ideal sun-and-sand destination can be defined as one that has a Blue Flag, that ensures the good quality of its bathing water and its beach, that is not massified, that has an offer of recreational and leisure activities, and where tourists do not have to pay a Green Tax. But the analysis also allowed us to determine the

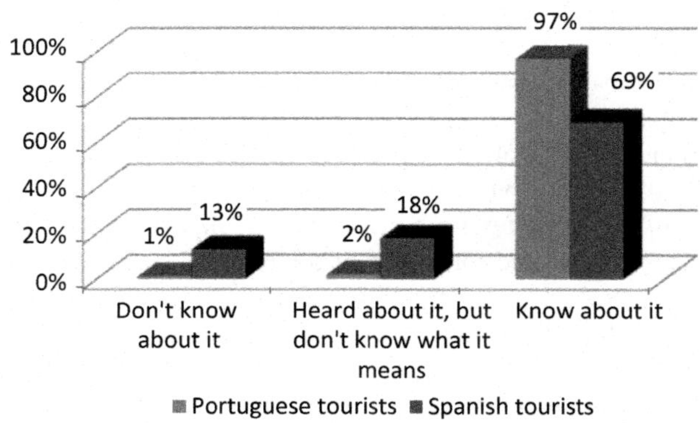

Fig. 13.1 Level of awareness of the Blue Flag

Table 13.4 Estimated utilities and relative importance of the attributes

Attribute	Level	Utility	Importance
Quality of the beach	Low	−2.5385	46.42%
	Good	0.9642	
	Blue Flag	1.5743	
Massification	Not massified	0.7957	25.12%
	Moderately massified	0.3423	
	Very massified	−1.1380	
Activities available	A lot	0.5922	16.78%
	Some	−0.0956	
	Few	−0.4965	
Environmental tax	No tax	−0.1062	11.68%
	5%	−0.2125	
	10%	−0.3187	
Constant		5.2125	

Kendall's tau and Pearson's R coefficients with significance <0.001

Table 13.5 Estimated utilities and relative importance by nationality

		Portugal		Spain	
Attribute	Level	Utility	Importance	Utility	Importance
Quality of the beach	Low	−2.678	47.86%	−2.377	44.77%
	Good	1.001		0.922	
	Blue Flag	1.677		1.455	
Massification	Not massified	0.832	24.28%	0.754	26.09%
	Moderately massified	0.289		0.404	
	Very massified	−1.121		−1.158	
Activities available	A lot	0.573	16.54%	0.614	17.06%
	Some	−0.058		−0.139	
	Few	−0.515		−0.475	
Environmental tax	No tax	−0.049	11.32%	−0.172	12.09%
	5%	−0.099		−0.344	
	10%	−0.148		−0.516	
Constante		5.099		5.344	

Kendall's tau and Pearson's R coefficients with significance <0.001

relative importance of each attribute. As seen in Table 13.4, the "*Quality of water and beaches*" is the key attribute in the formation of the tourists' preferences, determining 46.4% of those preferences. The next in importance is "*Massification*", which contributes 25% to the formation of the tourists' preferences. The attribute "*Recreational activities and night-life*" represents almost 17%, while the "*Green Tax*" attribute is the least important in the choice of a tourism destination (11.7%).

After determining the results for the overall sample, we proceeded to segment it according to the nationality of the tourist. The relative importance and the estimated utility for each attribute level are presented in Table 13.5, which shows that there are

Table 13.6 Estimated utilities and relative importance by segment

		Concerned about massification		Concerned about certified quality		Concerned about quality without willingness to pay more	
Attribute	Level	Utility	Importance	Utility	Importance	Utility	Importance
Quality of the beach	Low	−1.362	28.20%	−2.920	52.66%	−2.327	42.43%
	Good	0.701		0.908		1.232	
	Blue Flag	0.661		2.012		1.095	
Massification	Not massified	1.732	44.54%	0.970	24.96%	−0.103	14.90%
	Moderately massified	0.723		0.284		0.264	
	Very massified	−2.455		−1.255		−0.161	
Activities available	A lot	0.517	16.97%	0.471	13.90%	0.903	23.08%
	Some	−0.062		−0.089		−0.129	
	Few	−0.455		−0.382		−0.774	
Environmental tax	No tax	0.141	10.29%	0.171	8.47%	−0.860	19.59%
	5%	0.282		0.343		−1.720	
	10%	0.424		0.514		−2.581	
Constant		4.718		4.657		6.720	

Kendall's tau and Pearson's R coefficients with significance <0.001

no differences in the order of the attributes either according to their relative importance or according to the order of the estimated utilities of the different levels.

We next sought to identify groups of tourists who might have different preference structures. For this, we performed a Cluster Analysis using the k-means algorithm, with the data being each respondent's estimated utilities. From an analysis of the dendrogram, we considered it appropriate to use k = 3, thus determining three clearly distinct segments (Table 13.6).

Tourists in Segment 1 (14% of the sample) are characterized by attributing greater utility to those tourism destinations with "*good quality of water and beaches*", but without requiring the beaches to have been awarded a Blue Flag. They prefer destinations "*not massified*", with "*a lot of recreational activities and night-life*", and they do not mind paying an additional 10% onto the cost of their daily accommodation in the concept of a Green Tax. With respect to the relative importances, "*Massification*" is the key attribute in their choice of destination (44.5% of the preference structure). It is followed by "*Quality of water and beaches*" (28.2%), "*Recreational activities and night-life*" (17%), and "*Green Tax*" (10.3%). One can categorize this segment as tourists "*Concerned about massification*".

Tourists in Segment 2 (60% of the sample) preferred destinations with "*Blue Flag certification of good quality*", "*not massified*", with "*a lot of recreational activities and night-life*", and without it concerning them if they have to pay a 10% Green Tax. So this segment differs from the previous one in the value they attach to the Blue Flag as a way to ensure the environmental quality of the zone. With respect to the relative importances, the "*Quality of water and beaches*" is the key attribute in their choice of destination (52.7%). It is followed by "*Massification*" (25%), "*Recreational activities and night-life*" (14%), and "*Green Tax*" (8.5%). One can categorize this segment as tourists "*Concerned about certified quality*".

Finally, tourists in Segment 3 (26% of the sample) preferred destinations with "*good quality of water and beaches*", "*moderately massified*", and with "*a lot of recreational activities*", and they are unwilling to pay an additional Green Tax. With respect to the relative importances, the "*Quality of water and beaches*" is the key attribute in their choice of destination (42.4%). It is followed by "*Recreational activities and night-life*" (23.1%), "*Green Tax*" (19.6%), and "*Massification*" (15%). One can categorize this segment as tourists "*Concerned about quality without willingness to pay more*".

With respect to the profile of the tourists in each segment, gender does not influence the preferences for tourism destinations, but age, household income level, educational level, and the presence of under-age children do (Table 13.7).

Segment "*Concerned about quality without willingness to pay more*" is clearly differentiated from the other two segments because it includes a greater percentage of young people, of non-university educated tourists, and of families with older children (older than 14). This is perhaps the reason they are looking for a certain degree of massification. In contrast, Segment "*Concerned about certified quality*" differs from segment "*Concerned about massification*" in that it includes a greater proportion of families with small children.

To complete the results of the above analysis, we also asked respondents about their willingness to pay a premium to stay in a tourism establishment located near a Blue Flag beach. While 48% of the sample would be willing to do so, for most (60%) of this group the premium should not exceed 5% of the price per night of the accommodation (Fig. 13.2).

We used Pearson's chi-squared test to analyse the relationships between various sociodemographic variables of the tourist (gender, age, marital status, young children, teenagers, education and income) and the willingness to pay. The only significant variables were academic and household income, whereas there was no statistically significant relationship of the willingness to pay with gender, age, marital status, the number of young children, or the number of teenage children. Tourists with higher levels of education are more predisposed to pay a premium for the Blue Flag. And this predisposition to pay also increases as household income increases.

13.5 Conclusions and Practical Implications

Our results constitute support for the following conclusions:

- The quality of the sea water and beaches is the key attribute when choosing a tourism destination.

Table 13.7 Segment profiles

	Concerned about massification	Concerned about certified quality	Concerned about quality without willingness to pay more
Gender			
Female	53.4%	56.4%	58.5%
Male	46.6%	43.6%	41.5%
Age**			
≤ 25	18.6%	18.4%	28.6%
26–35	31.4%	31.4%	30.9%
36–45	30.5%	29.1%	18.9%
45–55	11.0%	16.5%	16.6%
> 55	8.5%	4.5%	5.1%
Household income**			
≤1000€/month	17.2%	17.7%	27.9%
1001–2000€/month	42.2%	43.8%	43.7%
2001–3000€/month	17.2%	21.4%	16.7%
>3000€/month	23.3%	17.1%	11.6%
Children 0–14 years**			
Yes	28.8%	38.0%	29.5%
Not	71.2%	62.0%	70.5%
Children >14 years*			
Yes	33.9%	27.9%	41.5%
Not	66.1%	72.1%	58.5%
Educational level**			
Elementary education	8.5%	7.0%	7.4%
Secondary school	33.1%	34.1%	46.8%
University	46.6%	47.9%	38.4%
Ph.D	11.9%	11.0%	7.4%

* Sig. < 0.01; **Sig. < 0.05.

- The possession of a Blue Flag gives additional value to the tourism destination for the tourists concerned about environmental quality when choosing the place for their holiday.
- The existence of a Green Tax is of little relevance in the choice of holiday destination compared to other attributes such as massification and the recreational activities and night-life offer.
- Tourists, on the whole, prefer destinations where they do not have to bear the payment of an additional tax, even though it is earmarked entirely for the conservation of the natural environment of the zone in which they spend their summer holiday.

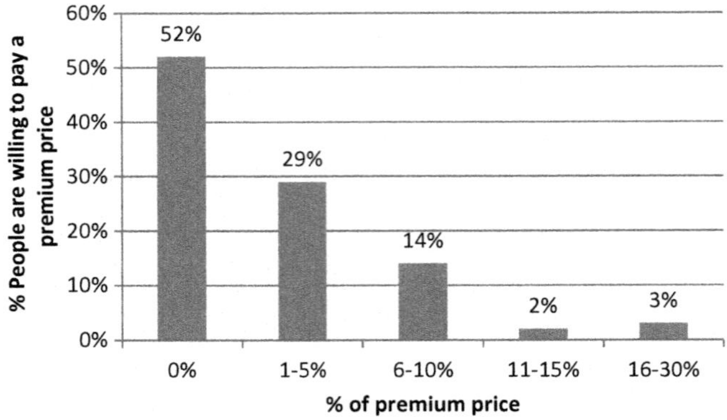

Fig. 13.2 Willingness to pay for accommodation on a Blue Flag beach

These results are similar to those obtained by other researchers in similar studies. For example, Rahemtulla (1998) found that the "Quality of the water and marine life" was the most important attribute in the choice of the Seychelles as a tourism destination, followed by the variety of wildlife, the development and massification of the beaches, and lastly of the prices. The author concluded that environmental quality contributes significantly to the choice of the tourism destination, and that tourists generally confer greater utility to beaches which are less developed and congested.

Huybers and Bennett (2000) also concluded that UK holidaymakers attribute greater utility and more willingness to pay for those destinations where the natural environment is presented as more unexplored and less massified. Huybers (2003) reports similar results with a sample of Australian tourists.

However, the studies of Brau et al. (2009) and Figini et al. (2009) for Rimini (Italy) describe results that differ partially. In those studies, tourists attached more importance to "Night-life activities", followed by the "Characteristics of the beach", while giving less importance to "Massification" and "Environmental impact".

With regard to the nationality of the tourists, our finding is similar to those of similar studies. In a study of the preferences of British, German, French, Italian, and Spanish tourists visiting the island of Tenerife, Ramos et al. (2004) finds that the nationality variable does not affect the tourists' preference levels. Neither do Mercado and Lassoie (2002) find any statistically significant differences in the importance attached to the quality of the water and the cleanness of the beaches according to the continent of origin (Europe, South America, and North America) of visitors to Punta Cana.

In relation to the segments of tourists here identified, the results highlight the existence of a large group of tourists that prefer destinations with "Blue Flag certification of good quality". This group is even willing to pay a Green Tax in order to visit a destination with this quality label.

Finally, with regard to the willingness to pay a higher price, tourists with higher levels of education are more predisposed to pay a premium for the Blue Flag. This result is consistent with previous studies. For example, Brau et al. (2009) find that tourists with a higher educational level are more concerned about the environment. This predisposition to pay also increases as household income increases. This is also consistent with the results of previous studies on environmentally friendly products and support for environmental causes (e.g., Daniere and Takahashi, 1999; Roberts, 1996; Yan, 2008).

Regarding practical implications, it can be assumed that the environmental impacts generated by tourism can adversely affect the competitive position of tourism destinations and the quality of life of their residents, not only through the reduction in the quality of their tourism inputs, but also through a potential fall in demand as a consequence of the emergence of segments of "*environmentally sensitive*" tourists. It is therefore important to understand how tourists' environmental concerns influence their choice of holiday destinations, as well as their decisions once they are there.

The Blue Flag can be considered as a good tool to manage the balance between the respect for the natural environment and the enjoyment of tourists and residents of a sun-and-sand tourist destination. It also can be considered as a good practice guide to assess the social or community QOL, i.e. the life conditions of a tourist destination. A review of the criteria required to obtain the Blue Flag reveals that obtaining this certification guarantees an improvement of the quality of life of tourists and residents. It serves to enhance and control the quality of bathing water and the conservation of natural environments, but it also serves to improve some indicators such as cleanliness, public safety, traffic noise, public transport services, urban accessibility, etc.

However, do tourists know and value the effort that must be made in order to obtain The Blue Flag? And, therefore, is it a useful tool for the public management of the quality of life of a tourist destination? The objective of this study was to evaluate the effect that the award of a Blue Flag has on the attractiveness of a tourism destination. Overall, the results have shown that Blue Flag certification is indeed of interest for managers of sun-and-sand destinations in that, a priori, it helps attract tourists and maintain the quality of life of the residents.

A first step needed for a system of environmental labelling to be of real value is for it to be clearly recognized by its target public. According to the present survey data, the Blue Flag system of certifying beach destinations has already attained this status.

A second step is to get the certification or label to be taken into account positively in the tourist's process of selecting a product. The present results are quite encouraging in this sense to the extent that a large segment of the tourists (60% of the sample) had a preference for destinations whose quality is guaranteed with a Blue Flag.

In addition, a system such as the Blue Flag will have a greater market value if the tourist is willing to choose a certified tourism destination even though they have to bear higher costs of accommodation. If the percentage of such a premium over the base cost of accommodation is fairly small, i.e., a surcharge of about 5%, then the results of the study are also positive.

One can therefore conclude that the Blue Flag is a good management tool for tourism destinations, and can be of clear interest for managers with which to help maintain or improve the attractiveness of their destination and the quality of life. A Blue Flag award can be used both by managers of the territory and by tourism firms as an instrument of communication in that, for potential visitors, it is a guarantee of quality and security, and differentiates the destination both from others that are nearby and from more distant competitors.

As the main limitation of this study it should be pointed out that the technique of Conjoint Analysis consists of a simplification of the decision-making process and therefore, it is possible that, for some tourists, other attributes of the tourist destination that have not been included in this research could be important. In addition, the environmental awareness of individuals varies considerably from one context to another. Because of that, the results cannot be extrapolated to tourists from other countries or to other types of tourist destinations. In this sense, a future line of research could be to carry out a similar study in countries where the actual implementation of the Blue Flag is smaller than in Spain and Portugal. It would be also relevant to conduct a similar study aimed at residents of a tourist destination.

Acknowledgments This research has been co-financed by the Extremadura Government and FEDER fund (European Regional Development Fund) (Code: GR15007).

References

Adamowicz, W., Louviere, J., & Williams, M. (1994). Combining revealed and stated preference methods for valuing environmental amenities. *Journal of Environmental Economics and Management, 26*, 271–292.

Andereck, K. L., & Nyaupane, G. P. (2011). Exploring the nature of tourism and quality of life perceptions among residents. *Journal of Travel Research, 50*, 248–260.

Anderson, L., Mastrangelo, C., Chase, L., Kestenbaum, D., & Kolodinsky, J. (2013). Eco-labeling motorcoach operators in the North American travel tour industry: Analyzing the role of tour operators. *Journal of Sustainable Tourism, 1*, 750–764.

Apostolakis, A., & Jaffry, S. (2005). A choice modelling application for Greek heritage attractions. *Journal of Travel Research, 43*, 309–318.

Baarsma, E. B. (2003). The valuation of the Ijmeer nature reserve using conjoint analysis. *Environment and Resource Economics, 25*, 343–356.

Brau, R., Scorcu, A., & Vici, L. (2009). Assessing visitor satisfaction with tourism rejuvenation policies: The case of Rimini, Italy. *Journal of Environmental Planning and Management, 52*, 25–42.

Capacci, S., Scorcu, A. E., & Vici, L. (2015). Seaside tourism and eco-labels: The economic impact of Blue Flags. *Tourism Management, 47*, 88–96.

Diener, E., & Suh, E. (1997). Measuring quality of life: Economic, social, and subjective indicators. *Social Indicators Research, 40*, 189–216.

Daniere, A. G., & Takahashi, L. M. (1999). Environmental behaviour in Bangkok, Thailand: A portrait of attitudes, values and behaviour. *Economic Development and Cultural Change, 47*, 525–557.

Dodge, R., Daly, A., Huyton, J., & Sanders, L. (2012). The challenge of defining wellbeing. *International Journal of Wellbeing, 2*, 222–235.

Dolnicar, S., Yanamandram, V., & Cliff, K. (2012). The contribution of vacations to quality of life. *Annals of Tourism Research, 39*, 59–83.

Epley, D., & Menon, M. (2008). A method of assembling cross-sectional indicators into community quality of life. *Social Indicators Research, 88*, 281–296.

Fairweather, J., Maslin, C., & Simmons, D. (2005). Environmental values and response to ecolabels among international visitors to New Zealand. *Journal of Sustainable Tourism, 13*, 82–98.

Felce, D., & Perry, J. (1995). Quality of life: Its definition and measurement. *Developmental Disabilities, 16*, 51–74.

Figini, P., & Vici, L. (2012). Off-season tourists and the cultural offer of a mass-tourism destination: The case of Rimini. *Tourism Management, 33*, 825–839.

Figini, P., Castellani, M., & Vici, L. (2009). Estimating tourism effects on residents: A choice modelling approach to the case of Rimini. In Á. Matias, P. Nijkamp, & M. Sarmento (Eds.), *Advances in tourism economics* (pp. 145–164). Heidelberg: Physica-Verlag.

Hajduová, Z., Andrejovský, P., & Beslerová, S. (2014). Development of quality of life economic indicators with regard to the environment. *Procedia – Social and Behavioral Sciences, 110*, 747–754.

Hanley, N., Wright, R., & Koop, G. (2002). Modelling recreation demand using choice experiments: Climbing in Scotland. *Environmental and Resource Economics, 22*, 449–466.

Huybers, T. (2003). Domestic tourism destination choices: A choice modelling analysis. *International Journal of Tourism Research, 5*, 445–459.

Huybers, T., & Bennett, J. (2000). Impact of the environment on holiday destination choices of prospective UK tourist: Implications for tropical North Queensland. *Tourism Economics, 6*, 21–46.

Kelly, J., Haider, W., Williams, P. W., & Englund, K. (2007). Stated preferences of tourists for eco-efficient destination planning options. *Journal of Tourism Management, 28*(2), 377–390.

Kim, K., Uysal, M., & Sirgy, M. J. (2013). How does tourism in a community impact the quality of life of community residents? *Tourism Management, 36*, 527–540.

Klenosky, D. (2004). *The impact of negative environmental factors on recreation choice behavior.* In Proceedings of the 2004 Northeastern Recreation Research Symposium, pp. 272–280.

Lazim, M. A., & Osman, M. T. A. (2009). A new Malaysian quality of life index based on fuzzy sets and hierarchical needs. *Social Indicators Research, 94*, 499–508.

Lucrezi, S., Saayman, M., & Van der Merwe, P. (2015). Managing beaches and beachgoers: Lessons from and for the Blue Flag award. *Tourism Management, 48*, 211–230.

Malkina-Pykh, I. G., & Pykh, Y. A. (2008). Quality-of-life indicators at different scales: Theoretical background. *Ecological Indicators, 8*, 854–862.

McKenna, J., Williams, A. T., & Cooper, J. A. G. (2011). Blue Flag or Red Herring: Do beach awards encourage the public to visit beaches? *Tourism Management, 32*, 576–588.

Mercado, L., & Lassoie, J. P. (2002). Assessing tourists' preferences for recreational and environmental management programs central to the sustainable development of a tourism area in the Dominican Republic. *Environment, Development and Sustainability, 4*, 253–278.

Mir-Gual, M., Pons, G. X., Martín-Prieto, J. A., & Rodríguez-Perea, A. (2015). A critical view of the Blue Flag beaches in Spain using environmental variables. *Ocean and Coastal Management, 105*, 106–115.

Needham, M. D., & Szuster, B. W. (2011). Situational influences on normative evaluations of coastal tourism and recreation management strategies in Hawai'i. *Tourism Management, 32*, 732–740.

Ortega, J. M., & Recio, M. M. (2006). *Análisis de los Patrones de Elección entre Ofertas de Turismo Rural como Estrategia de Segmentación* [Analysis of choice patterns among rural tourism offers as a strategy for segmentation]. Unpublished manuscript University of Almería, Department of Business Management, pp. 1255–1269.

Palomar-Lever, J. (2000). The development of an instrument to measure quality of life in Mexico City. *Social Indicators Research, 50*, 187–208.

Picón, E., & Varela, J. (2000). Segmenting markets with conjoint analysis: An application to tourism sector. *Psicothema, 12*, 453–458.

Rahemtulla, Y. G. (1998). *Environmental quality and tourism development in the Seychelles: An application of the stated preference Method.* Unpublished master dissertation. University of Alberta, Agricultural Economics Department of Rural Economy.

Rahman, T., Mittelhammer, R. C., & Wandschneider, P. R. (2011). Measuring quality of life across countries: A multiple indicators and multiple causes approach. *The Journal of Socio-Economics, 40*, 43–52.

Ramos, C., Ramos, A., & Ramos, R. (2004). Análisis de las Preferencias del Turista hacia un Destino Turístico Maduro [Analysis of tourist preferences toward a mature tourist destination]. *Investigaciones Europeas de Dirección y Economía de la Empresa, 10*, 131–139.

Reig, G. C., & Coenders, G. (2002). Segmentación del Mercado Turístico Según las Preferencias Ambientales [Tourism market segmentation according to environmental preferences]. *Cuadernos de Turismo, 9*, 109–121.

Reiser, A., & Simmons, D. (2005). A quasi-experimental method for testing the effectiveness of ecolabel promotion. *Journal of Sustainable Tourism, 13*, 590–616.

Riera, A. (2000). Modelos de Elección Discreta y Coste del Viaje: Los Espacios Naturales Protegidos en Mallorca [Discrete choice models and cost of travel: The protected natural areas in Mallorca]. *Revista de Economía Aplicada, 8*, 181–201.

Rigall-i-Torrent, R., Fluvià, M., Ballester, R., Saló, S., Ariza, E., & Espinet, J. M. (2011). The effects of beach characteristics and location with respect to hotel prices. *Tourism Management, 32*, 1150–1158.

Riganti, P. (2008). Assessing the impacts of cultural tourism on small and medium sized european cities: A valuation framework for the city of Syracuse. *International Journal Services Technology and Management, 10*(1), 61–82.

Roberts, J. A. (1996). Green consumers in the 1990s: Profile and implications for advertising. *Journal of Business Research, 36*, 217–231.

Sasidharana, V., Sirakayab, E., & Kerstettera, D. (2002). Developing countries and tourism ecolabels. *Tourism Management, 23*, 161–174.

Shoji, Y., & Yamaki, K. (2004). Visitor perceptions of the inscription on the world heritage list: The use of stated choice methods. *Working Papers of the Finnish Forest Research Institute, 2*, 305–310.

Varela, J. M., Picón, E. P., & Braña, T. T. (2004). Segmentation of the Spanish domestic tourism market. *Psicothema, 16*, 76–83.

World Health Organization. (1997). *WHOQOL measuring quality of life*. Geneva: World Health Organisation.

Yan, J. (2008). *Cultural and attitudinal influences on destination choice: Preferences of Chinese domestic tourists*. Unpublished doctoral dissertation, Faculty of Agricultural Sciences, Georg-August-University Göttingen, Germany.

Chapter 14
Impacts of Family Tourism on Families' Quality of Life – Differences According to the Family Economic Profile

Joana Lima, Celeste Eusébio, and Celeste Amorim Varum

Abstract Tourism plays a significant role in our lives and is increasingly becoming associated with Quality of Life (QOL). Tourism offers opportunities to explore new environments, participate in new activities and to meet people as well as relax. While the effects of tourism on the QOL of individuals are nowadays recognized, the effects of family tourism upon families' QOL are relatively blurred. This neglect is more worrying insofar as it is known that family tourism represents a significant share in the tourism market globally. This study aims to overcome this gap by analysing the effects of family tourism on some dimensions of families' QOL, using survey data collected from a sample of Portuguese families (N = 825). Moreover, we explore whether the impacts of family tourism on families' QOL vary across the economic profile of families. This study is of utmost relevance given that families with low income represent a significant share of the Portuguese population nowadays. The results reveal significant effects of family tourism on family cohesion and on the improvement of families' QOL. The effects differ between families, with families with scarce economic resources being those that feel the effects with greater intensity. The chapter concludes with a discussion on the implications of the results for the design of family tourism experiences and also identifying paths for future research.

Keywords Family tourism · Impacts · Family's QOL · Low income families

J. Lima (✉)
CIDEHUS Research Unit, University of Évora, Évora, Portugal

GOVCOPP Research Unit, University of Aveiro, Aveiro, Portugal
e-mail: jisl@uevora.pt

C. Eusébio · C. A. Varum
GOVCOPP Research Unit, University of Aveiro, Aveiro, Portugal
e-mail: celeste.eusebio@ua.pt; camorim@ua.pt

A. M. Campón-Cerro et al. (eds.), *Best Practices in Hospitality and Tourism Marketing and Management*, Applying Quality of Life Research,
https://doi.org/10.1007/978-3-319-91692-7_14

14.1 Introduction

Taking a holiday has become an important and expected part of life for most citizens. This importance of holidays and travel for the well-being of individuals has been formally accepted since 1948 with the recognition by the United Nations of vacations as a basic human right (article 24). This importance was reiterated by some governments, who over the years have been recognizing the right to paid leave (Hall and Brown 2006). There is a belief that the benefits that holidays bring are plentiful. Tourism offers opportunities to explore new environments and engage in new situations. When the tourism activity occurs in a family, taking a holiday can also benefit the family as a whole. The in-family experience tends to increase the sense of belonging and identification among its members, contributing to a shared vision of the world and new experiences. Indeed, family tourism nowadays accounts for a significant share of tourism flows (Gram 2005; Obrador 2012; Small 2008). In spite of this, there are few empirical studies about the consequences of tourism for the tourists (Alexander et al. 2010), with even fewer studies existing which examine the effects of family tourism, both for individuals and for families (Lima et al. 2012; Minnaert et al. 2009).

This study, based upon survey data collected from a sample of Portuguese families (N = 825), aims to overcome the aforementioned gap by analysing the effects of family tourism on families' Quality of Life (QOL) and how they differ across families' economic status. For those on a low income, a holiday is often far from reach and not something they would even be able to consider. Low-income families are often those most in need of a holiday, yet they are the least likely group to take one.

Due to the economic developments in the last decade or so, low income families nowadays represent a significant share of the population – 24.5% of the EU-28 population was living in households facing poverty or social exclusion in 2013 (Eurostat 2015). In Portugal in 2012, the poverty risk rate, after social transfers, of families with dependent children rose to 22.2% (INE 2014a). In 2013, the material deprivation rate in this country stood at 25.5% and 59.8% of families were financially unable to afford a week's annual holiday away from home (INE 2014b). Additionally, the fact that there are no studies on the effects of family tourism and on the different effects that family tourism may have on the Portuguese families' QOL was another foundation for the choice of this territory as the empirical context of this research.

In the following section a review the background literature on family, QOL and tourism, and also on the effects of family tourism on family QOL, identifying factors likely to influence those effects will be presented. In the Sect. 14.3 the methodology adopted will be described. The results are presented and discussed in Sect. 14.4. The results confirm the relevance of family holidays for the family's QOL and indicate the existence of the effects of family tourism on families' QOL, as well as the fact that these effects differ according to the economic status of the families. Sect. 14.5 concludes the article, discussing some implications of the results and identifying possible paths for future research.

14.2 Family Tourism and Its Effects on QOL

Family is a structuring social group in society because of its role as a space for the individual personal and social construction (Agate et al. 2007; Alarcão and Relvas 2002; Howard 2012). Despite the changes which the family has suffered in recent decades and the growing number of types of family that differ from the traditional concept of family, the structuring role of family on society maintains its importance. Families persist as dynamic entities, with their own identity, composed of members connected by biological and/or emotional bonds, coexisting for a certain period of time during which they build a life story that is unique and unrepeatable (Agate et al. 2007; Alarcão and Relvas 2002). The family is also a unit of analysis of great relevance for tourism. A significant part of tourism experiences occur as a family (Gram 2005). As Gram (2005: 6) stated, "the family is a unit of individuals who seek experiences together". Obrador (2012) and Small (2008) point out that, though family is the main segment for consuming many tourism products, tourism research has rarely considered family tourism (parents and children together).

Schanzel et al. (2012) point out three-dimensional dynamics that must be understood when studying the family as a tourist segment: the family is a social group that brings together dynamics between genders, generations and between different people. From the studies undertaken by Agate et al. (2007), Fu et al. (2014), Lehto et al. (2009), Minnaert et al. (2009), Obrador (2012) and Schänzel and Smith (2014), it is possible to conclude that the common assumption is that family vacations happen when at least one of the parents and children travel together for leisure purposes. Based on these definitions, the present study defines family tourism as the leisure travel, for a minimum of 4 nights away from home (EC 1987; Hazel 2005; UNWTO 2008), of a group constituted by at least one of the parents (or legal guardians) and their children (or the children in their care). Children were considered to be individuals under 18 years old.

As Richards (1999) argues, holidays attenuate two constraints of everyday life – time and place, creating conditions for individuals to engage in their personal and social fulfilment, potentially enhancing their subjective well-being and QOL (Genç 2012).

Regarding the concept of QOL, there is no consensual definition (Andereck and Nuaupane 2011; Dolnicar et al. 2013; Eusébio and Carneiro 2014). The World Health Organization QOL (WHOQOL) Group (The WHOQOL Group 1994: 29) suggests that this construct is a "measure of the individuals' perception of their position in life in the context of the culture and value systems in which they live and in relation to their goals, expectations, standards and concerns".

Confirming the importance of leisure activities, such as tourism, for the family, several studies in the leisure field concluded that there are very positive effects for the family (satisfaction, functioning and family stability) as a result of family leisure activities (Agate et al. 2007). Goeldner and Ritchie (2009) report that tourist experiences have a profound effect on individuals and on society, because these experiences are often among the most striking memories of people's lives. Shaw et al. (2008) consider that family holidays are important shared experiences that become family memories. Obrador (2012) states that, by allowing the spatial mobilization of the feeling of "being at home", family holidays facilitate authentic relationships in the family. Haldrup and Larsen (2003) add that family holidays support and stabilize family relations and bonds, which otherwise could turn out to be poor. These findings suggest the importance that family tourism can have for improving the QOL of families.

Some literature on tourism marketing focuses on the benefits of tourism activities (e.g., Pesonen et al. 2011). However, most of these studies are related to the benefits sought and there are a very limited number of studies analysing the obtained benefits (Alexander et al. 2010). Alexander et al. (2010), Ballantyne et al. (2011), Chon (1999), Genç (2012), Gilbert and Abdullah (2004), Lehto et al. (2009), McCabe et al. (2010), Minnaert (2006), Minnaert et al. (2009), Neal et al. (1999), Richards (1999) and Smith and Hughes (1999) are examples of studies about the effects of tourism practice for the visitors. These studies conclude that access to vacation away from the usual place of residence contributes to the personal and social development of individuals for physical and psychological well-being, QOL and relief from daily pressures. However, Gram (2005) and Lehto et al. (2009) recognized the existence of a gap in the literature on the effects of family tourism on the family.

In their review, Lima et al. (2012) identified 20 empirical studies on the effects of tourism for participants. These studies use two main units of analysis: the effects of tourism on individuals and the effects of tourism on the family, with the individual being the most analysed unit. Only 7 studies out of 20 discuss the effects of tourism for families (Gram 2005; Lehto et al. 2009; McCabe et al. 2010; Minnaert et al. 2009; Minnaert 2006, 2012; Smith and Hughes 1999).

Also, despite the growing number of studies examining the benefits derived from the practice of tourist activities for tourists and examining the relation between tourism and QOL, little research has been conducted specifically on the effects of tourism on the QOL of families (Gram 2005; Hazel 2005; Schänzel et al. 2005). The first empirical study on the benefits of tourism for families identified in this research is the notable contribution of Smith and Hughes (1999). Six more years passed until a new study was published on the matter. Additionally, although a significant number of studies recognized that "leisure life" is an important life domain affecting overall QOL, the concrete impact of a specific type of tourism (family tourism) on QOL is much less studied.

Uysal et al. (2016) mentioned that in the literature both objective and subjective indicators have been used to analyse the effect of tourism on QOL. However, there is a predominance of studies using subjective indicators. Several scales have been adopted for assessing QOL, such as comprehensive QOL scales, health-related or multicultural QOL indexes or the WHOQOL scales (e.g. Chen and Yao 2010; Eusébio and Carneiro 2011; Skevington et al. 2004). So, similarly to what happens in the concept of QOL, there is still no consensual group of indicators to assess QOL. The WHOQOL-BREF (one short version of the WHOQOL) is one of the scales most frequently used for the assessment of QOL and Eusébio and Carneiro (2011, 2014) argue that it should be more extensively tested and used in the area of tourism.

Table 14.1 Effects of tourism on family QOL

Domain	Type of effect	Studies that identify the effect
Overall QOL	Improvement	Lehto et al. (2009), McCabe et al. (2010), Minnaert (2006, 2012), Minnaert et al. (2009), and Smith and Hughes (1999)
Health (mental and/or physical)	Improvement	Lehto et al. (2009), McCabe et al. (2010), and Smith and Hughes (1999)
	Deterioration	Minnaert (2012) and Smith and Hughes (1999)
Environment	Increased information access[a]	McCabe et al. (2010)
	Deterioration in the financial resources[a]	Smith and Hughes (1999)
Family relationship	Increased family cohesion/ bonding	Gram (2005), Lehto et al. (2009), Minnaert (2006, 2012), and Smith and Hughes (1999)
	Formation of good memories (quality and shared time)	Lehto et al. (2009), McCabe et al. (2010), and Smith and Hughes (1999)
	Quality time dependent on the children's behaviour	Gram (2005)
	Increased feeling of sharing/ togetherness dependent on the intensity	Gram (2005)
	Increased feeling of sharing/ togetherness	Lehto et al. (2009), McCabe et al. (2010), Minnaert (2006, 2012), and Minnaert et al. (2009)

Legend: [a]*Effects on low-income families*

Table 14.1 summarises the conclusions from empirical studies regarding the main effects of tourism on families' QOL. These effects can be grouped in Overall QOL and QOL domains. The *Health* domain includes effects on the families' physical and mental health (mainly the reduction of stress associated with breaking stressful routines, but also an increased level of stress from "practical problems" – particularly detected in families inexperienced in travel). The *Environment* domain includes an increased access to information and negative effects on the family's financial situation, in some cases economically disadvantaged families. *Family relationships* includes effects of holidays on family cohesion/bonding (strengthening family bonds), on the good memories that the holiday provides as a result of the quality and shared time and on the opportunities for sharing moments and doing things together (Table 14.1).

Family vacations provide a temporary disconnection of the family from its usual work or other social networks, which usually represents a new configuration of mental and physical space among family members (Lehto et al. 2009). Consequently, Table 14.1 shows that the majority of studies report positive effects of tourism on families' QOL and that the main benefits from tourism observed on families' QOL, besides the general improvement in the overall QOL, are related to family interaction and cohesion/bonding, improvement of the relationship with children (family relationship domain) and escape from routine and stressful daily routine (health domain). However, very few studies raise concerns over potential negative effects from tourism, which should not be neglected in research and practice. In this line of thought, Gram (2005) draws attention to the fact that family holidays may contribute to family members feeling tired of each other as a result of an excessive time spent together and the behaviour of the children during the holidays.

Considering special types of families, such as economically and/or socially disadvantaged ones, other benefits related with the Environment domain of QOL (particularly the increased access to information) appear to be important and also the strengthening of family bonds appears as an important aspect to consider (Minnaert et al. 2009; Smith and Hughes 1999).

Dolnicar et al. (2012) and Moscardo (2009) argue that the intensity and type of tourism effects are different according to the travel behaviour and certain personal and social characteristics of the individuals. Uysal et al. (2016) also concluded, from the literature review made, that the impact of tourism experience on QOL depends on life cycles and other background variables (cultural proximity, demographics or the experience context) that potentially influence the importance of travel. Several authors (e.g. Alegre et al. 2010; Hall and Brown 2006; Haukeland 1990) concluded that low income is one of the major determinants of tourism participation.

The relevance of analysing the differing effects of tourism in families' QOL, according to families' economic status, increases in a context of economic crisis like the one that has existed in Europe since 2008, particularly in Portugal, with austerity measures and the disposable income of many families having decreased significantly, aggravating this constraint to tourism participation. As mentioned above, when considering special types of families, such as the economically and/or socially disadvantaged ones, the main benefits that tourism can bring to families in terms of promoting access to information and the possible strengthening of family bonds, are extremely important aspects to consider (Minnaert et al. 2009; Smith and Hughes 1999). This importance stems from the fact that information and family socialization is strongly structuring the reintegration of families in society and power bases to promote changes in attitudes that perpetuate a situation of social exclusion.

McCabe et al. (2010) examined the relationship between well-being, QOL and family holiday participation among low-income families in the UK. The results of this study demonstrated that the impact of the family holiday on family relationships and on the quality time spent together, having fun, is significant and that the emotional well-being factors, related to QOL issues, were more important than situational factors affecting families. This result seems to be related to the result obtained by Smith and Hughes (1999), showing that disadvantaged groups feel the effects of tourism participation with greater intensity. It can then be concluded that income can be a differentiating and determining variable in terms of families' tourist practices and that the effects of family tourism on families' QOL can differ according to the economic profile of the families.

In this study, it is considered that the effects of family tourism depend on several variables, in which the features of the particular experience during a family holiday may assume great importance, and are differentiated according to socio-demographic and economic characteristics of families. It is believed also that these factors will, in turn, influence the overall satisfaction of individuals with their QOL (improving life satisfaction and satisfaction with the holidays). Therefore, the main research question of this study is: Are the effects of family tourism on family QOL more intense for low-income families?

14.3 Methodology

14.3.1 Objectives/Aims

In order to extend the knowledge regarding the effects of family tourism on QOL, the aims of this chapter are to: (i) analyse the effects of family tourism in some domains of families' QOL and (ii) identify if there are statistical differences in the impact of family tourism on families' QOL according to the economic profile of the families. To accomplish these objectives a sample of Portuguese families were analysed. As mentioned above, in this research, similarly to McCabe et al. (2010), an adapted version of the WHOQOL-BREF scale was used to measure the impact that family holidays have on families' QOL. In this scale, two approaches are used to measure QOL: (i) overall QOL (through overall satisfaction with life) and (ii) several domains of QOL (e.g. health, social relationships and environment).

14.3.2 Data Collection

A survey was carried out to collect data from a sample of Portuguese families (N = 825). The population of the study is composed by families living in the Central Region of Portugal. In 2014, 21.8% of the resident population in Portugal lived in the Central Region (INE 2015). The importance of tourism and the challenges related to the QOL of the population, emphasized by the present economic situation, make Portugal an ideal test bed for this study.

The population defined for this study was Portuguese families with at least one child aged between 6 and 17 years old and with different socio-economic characteristics, resident in the Central Region of Portugal. Since it was not possible to survey all the families residing in this region, a multi-step cluster-sampling approach was undertaken. The choice of this sampling technique was based not only on the objectives of the study, but also on the characteristics of the population under study (large and dispersed, in spatial terms). The sample included households from municipalities of inland and of coastal areas, regions with higher levels of economic development (coastal areas) and regions currently facing demographic and economic problems (inland regions).

In the first phase, two NUTS III of the Central Region – Cova da Beira (inland) and Baixo Vouga (coastal) – were selected, within which two municipalities were randomly selected – Covilhã, Fundão, Aveiro and Ílhavo. Once the four municipalities were selected, a Group of schools[1] was randomly chosen within each municipality and within each Group of schools, two classes of each year of education (from 1st year to 12th grade) were randomly selected. In each selected class, questionnaires were distributed to all students so they could ask their parents or legal guardians to fill it in.

The distribution of questionnaires to the schools took about 2 months (between April to June 2014) and 2077 questionnaires were distributed to be filled in by the parents or legal guardians of the students. 825 questionnaires were returned completed and were considered, which represents a response rate of around 40%.

14.3.2.1 Questionnaire Design

The questionnaire included questions to measure the travel experience of those interviewed (number of family tourism trips undertaken in the last 4 years), questions regarding the last family holidays (type of destination, travel group, satisfaction with travel experience and tourists' perception of tourism impacts on family's QOL), and questions related to the socio-demographic profile of the respondents and the family. The literature review made it possible to support variables and for items to be included in questionnaires to operationalize the constructs related to the effects of family holidays on their QOL (Table 14.2). The respondents had to reply using a scale from 1 – "totally disagree" to 7 – "totally agree".

In order to analyse the validity and reliability of the questionnaire used in this research, a number of steps were undertaken. First, the literature review helped identify valid questions to obtain the required information. Second, a pilot test was conducted with 126 parents. Based on the inputs provided by the pilot test, the questionnaire proved to serve the research objectives, needing just some small language adjustments.

14.3.3 Data Analysis

Each family was classified according to its economic status. For this, the index of material deprivation was used. The "deprived families" are the families who suffered forced absence of at least three of nine items that comprise the Material Deprivation Rate and "other families" (or "families without deprivation"). The Material Deprivation Rate considered for this study included nine items: ability to

[1] Groups of schools or School groupings are "defined as organisational entities with their own powers of administration and management at pre-school or compulsory level around a common pedagogical project" (Ministry of Education 2007).

Table 14.2 Variables and items included in questionnaires to operationalize the constructs related to the effects of family holidays on their QOL

Construct	Items	Source[a]
Overall QOL	All in all, I feel that these holidays have enriched my life	Neal et al. (1999)
	I felt much better about life after these holidays	
Family relationship	Traveling together steghtned our family bonds	Lehto et al. (2009)
	Tension within my family was more relaxed while traveling together	Lehto et al. (2009)
	Family members feel close to each other after these holidays	Lehto et al. (2009)
	These holidays helped to discover new ways of dealing with each other	Minnaert (2006, 2008, 2012, 2013), Minnaert et al. (2009), Minnaert et al. (2010), Wigfall (2004) and Kim (2010)
	These holidays contributed to get tired of being with each other	Gram (2005)
	These holidays gave us the opportunity for fun and happy memories	McCabe et al. (2010)
Environment	These holidays contributed for reducing health expenditure of the household (eg: Stress medication)	INATEL (2009)
	These holidays contributed for improving the financial situation of the family	WHO (2004), Smith and Hughes (1999)
	These holidays contributed to increase our access to information	McCabe et al. (2010)
	These holidays gave us the opportunity to experience new places and different activities	McCabe et al. (2010)
	These holidays contributed to increase our opportunities of meeting new and different people	Minnaert (2006, 2008, 2012, 2013), Minnaert et al. (2009) and Minnaert et al. (2010)

Legend: [a]*The items were created, adapted or translated from the results obtained in the studies mentioned in this column*

face unexpected expenses, ability to pay for one week's annual holiday away from home, existence of arrears, capacity to have a meal with meat, chicken or fish every second day, capacity to keep home adequately warm, possession of a washing machine, a colour TV, a telephone or a personal car (Wolff 2009).

T-tests and Chi-square tests were applied to test the differences in travelling behaviour and perception of QOL effects of family tourism between the two groups of families. All assumptions of these statistical tests were analysed.

14.4 Results and Discussion

14.4.1 Sociodemographic Profile

The 825 households surveyed, comprising 3024 individuals, were residents in the districts of Aveiro, Covilhã, Fundão and Ílhavo.

When asked about their living conditions, particularly in relation to material deprivation, the responses of the surveyed families permit the conclusion that 18.7% of these families were materially deprived, meaning that 18.7% of surveyed households suffered the forced absence of at least three of nine items that comprise the material deprivation rate (Fig. 14.1). In this study, as mentioned in the previous section, these households will be considered the group of "deprived families" (N = 154) and the families that do not suffer material deprivation will be designated as "other families" (N = 669).

In terms of the household's average net monthly income, it is observed that the majority of respondents reported incomes below 2000 euros (74.8%) (Table 14.3). Most of the sample has relatively low income, since 71.4% reported a level of *per-capita* monthly income lower or equal to 500 euros and 60.0% of respondents indicated *per capita* net monthly income below or equal to 375 euros, well below the monthly value of the poverty line for the year 2011 – 416 euros (INE 2012).

In terms of gender, 22.6% of the respondents are male and 77.4% are female. It was observed that the average age of respondents is 43 years – individuals aged between 35 and 45 represent 60.5% of the sample, corresponding to what was expected, since the population of the study were families with school-age children (6–17 years). The sample includes mostly couples (married or unmarried – 81.5%),

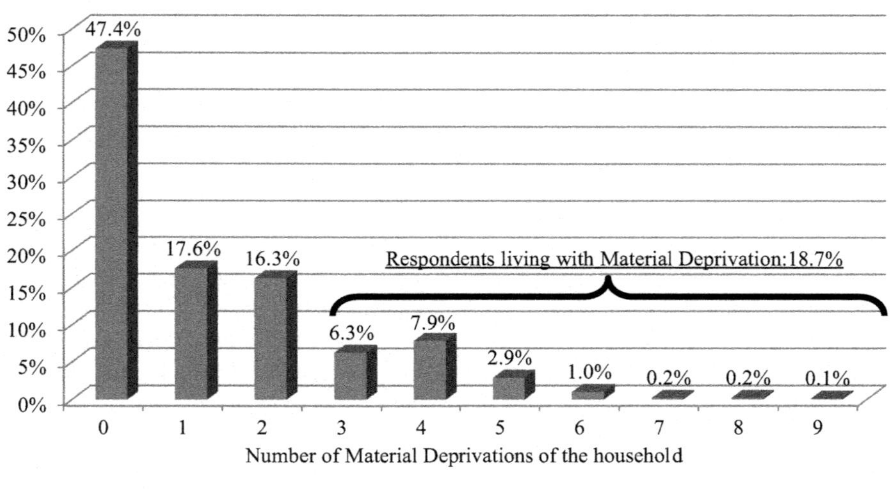

Fig. 14.1 Material deprivation of the households (number of deprivations)

Table 14.3 Sociodemographic profile of families who took holidays in the last 4 years

Sociodemographic variables for the respondentes and their families	Other families (N = 669)	Deprived families (N = 154)	All families (N = 823)	χ^2	Sig.	*t*	Sig.
Municipality of residence				15.87	0.001*	–	–
Aveiro	**21.20%**	9.10%	19.00%				
Fundão	31.60%	28.50%	31.00%				
Covilhã	20.90%	**28.60%**	22.40%				
Ílhavo	26.30%	**33.80%**	27.60%				
Gender				1.328	0.249	–	–
Feminine	76.60%	80.90%	77.40%				
Masculine	23.40%	19.10%	22.60%				
Marital status				16.6	0.001*	–	–
Single	5.10%	6.50%	5.40%				
Couple (married or not)	**83.90%**	70.60%	81.40%				
Divorced/ separated	10.10%	**20.90%**	12.10%				
Other	0.90%	2.00%	1.10%				
Situation regarding employment				33.04	0.000*	–	–
Unemployed	8.00%	**23.80%**	10.90%				
Retired	0.80%	1.40%	0.90%				
Employes	**73.90%**	60.90%	71.50%				
Entrepreneurs or self employed	11.60%	7.90%	10.90%				
Other	5.70%	6.00%	5.80%				
Level of formal education				47.87	0.000*	–	–
Higher education	**46.20%**	15.40%	40.60%				
Lower	53.80%	**84.60%**	59.40%				
Occupation				45.42	0.000*	–	–
Experts in intellectual professions & technicians and associate professionals	**45.50%**	12.90%	39.80%				
Other	54.50%	**87.10%**	60.20%				
Household's average net monthly income				183.5	0.000*	–	–
0–500€	3.2%	**30.8%**	8.2%				
501–1000€	18.5%	**41.1%**	22.7%				
1001–2000€	**48.4%**	23.3%	43.8%				
2001€ or more	**29.9%**	4.8%	25.3%				
Age	42.18	41.34	42.04	–	–	1.227	0.220

(continued)

Table 14.3 (continued)

Sociodemographic variables for the respondentes and their families	Other families (N = 669)	Deprived families (N = 154)	All families (N = 823)	χ^2	Sig.	*t*	Sig.
Number of elements of the household (share housing and general expenditures) aged <18 years	1.66	1.59	1.65	–	–	1.005	0.315
Number of elements of the household (share housing and general expenditures)	3.76	3.53	3.72	–	–	2.358	0.019*

Legend: % by column; In the dichotomous variables, we only present the values for the "Yes" category.
Legend: * p≤0.05; ** p≤0.1.

but also includes a relatively high proportion of divorced parents (12.1%), a result that is also a consequence of the country's social structure (INE, 2013) (Table 14.3).

Most respondents (40.6%) hold higher education and, the situation regarding employment and occupation is related to their level of qualifications: the majority of respondents are employed (71.4%); 32.1% are experts in intellectual professions and 27.8% are employees of personal services, protection and security (according to the CPP/2010 (INE 2011)). Included in the group of respondents who do not perform a professional activity, the unemployed (10.9%) are a significant segment, a result that reflects the economic situation faced by the country.

14.4.1.1 Differences Between the Families According to Their Economic Status

In relation to differences in the socio-demographic profile between the two segments of families analysed, some differences were observed (Table 14.3). The "deprived families" group includes more families living in Covilhã and Ílhavo, more respondents whose marital status is divorced/separated, smaller families and with net monthly incomes up to €1000. This segment also tends to concentrate more respondents with a level of education below higher education, whose professional situation is unemployed and with a different occupation from "experts in intellectual professions & technicians and associate professionals". The "other families" segment includes relatively more couples, with higher education, entrepreneurs or self-employed than the "deprived families" (Table 14.3).

Despite not having found statistically significant differences in terms of gender, age and number of household members aged under 18 years, the segment "deprived families" has a slightly higher concentration of female respondents, when compared to the totals (Table 14.3).

14.4.2 *Travel Behaviour and Experiences During the Last Family Holiday*

Regarding travel behaviour, 57.4% of the respondents had a family holiday (minimum of 4 nights out of the place of residence with the family) once a year for the last 4 years (Table 14.4). For 67.7% of the respondents these holidays happened in 2013 and the destination of the last family holiday was Portugal for 81.2% of the respondents, with the "other countries" that were mentioned being, particularly, Spain (6.6%), France (4.2%) and England/UK (1.3%) (Table 14.4).

The majority (66.1%) of the respondents were part of a travel party with a maximum of 4 elements. Regarding the composition of the travel group, in most cases (85.4%) this group comprised one to two children aged under 18 years. The average duration of the last family holiday of the respondents was 9.05 days, the 8-day stay being the most common. The most popular type of accommodation at the destination was the "Hotel or similar" for 30.7% of the respondents, followed by "house of friends or family" (28.0%) and "rented house" (27.2%). The means of transport most used during these family holidays were private car (89.0%), a result that can be justified by the fact that the car allows greater freedom of movement during the visit, particularly for families with children (Table 14.4).

14.4.2.1 Differences Between the Families According to Their Economic Status

There were also statistically significant differences observed between the two segments in terms of characteristics of the last family holiday. The "deprived families", when compared with the total number of families, concentrate relatively more families who had Portugal as the destination (90.9%), using the train as a means of transportation to the destination (5.9%) and who chose home of friends or family (36.0%) and camping (14.7%) as a means of accommodation. This group also includes relatively more families who made the last holiday more than a year and a half ago, are part of larger family groups when travelling and had a shorter duration of trip, when compared with the "other families" (Table 14.4). On the other hand, the "other families" concentrates more families who visited international destinations (21.1%), which are different environments from their usual environment, and consequently used the aircraft as a means of transportation to the destination (16.70%) and stayed overnight at "hotel or similar" (33.2%) (Table 14.4). These differences in the characteristics of travel behaviour of families show that the "other families" have holidays with more features contrasting with their everyday environment, eventually contributing to the existence of differences in the effects on families' QOL.

Table 14.4 Characteristics of the last family holiday between the two groups of families

Travel behaviour	Other families (N = 669)	Deprived families (N = 154)	All families (N = 813)	χ^2	Sig.	t	Sig.
Frequency of family holidays in the last 4 years				43.313	0.000*	–	–
Less than 1 holiday/year	9.90%	**26.00%**	13.00%				
1 holiday/year	56.50%	61.00%	57.30%				
2–3 holidays/year	**26.50%**	11.00%	23.60%				
4 or more holidays/year	**7.10%**	1.90%	6.10%				
Last family holidays:							
Visited country				11.859	0.001*	–	–
Portugal	78.90%	**90.90%**	81.10%				
Other	**21.10%**	9.10%	18.90%				
Means of transportation to the destination#						–	–
Plane	**16.70%**	7.80%	15.10%	7.697	0.006*		
Bus	3.00%	5.90%	3.50%	3.062	0.080**		
Private car	89.40%	86.90%	88.90%	0.765	0.382		
Train	2.20%	**5.90%**	2.90%	a)			
Main accommodation				22.353	0.000*	–	–
Hotel or similar	**33.20%**	19.30%	30.70%				
2nd residence (own)	5.70%	2.70%	5.20%				
House of friends or family	26.30%	**36.00%**	28.10%				
Camping	7.10%	**14.70%**	8.50%				
Other	27.70%	27.30%	27.60%				
How many years ago was the last family holiday?	1.16	1.70	1.34	–	–	−4.017	0.000*
Total number of the travel party	10.06	5.24	9.17	–	–	0.425	0.671
N° of family members in the travel party	2.37	2.64	2.42	–	–	−2.358	0.019*
N° of family members aged <18 years in the travel party	1.83	1.82	1.83	–	–	0.141	0.888
Duration of the holiday (days)	9.26	8.14	9.05	–	–	1.964	0.050*

Legend: #In the dichotomous variables, we only present the values for the "Yes" category
Note: % by column
Legend: * $p \leq 0.05$; ** $p \leq 0.1$.

14.4.3 Effects of the Family Holiday on QOL

Looking at "all families", the respondents mentioned that the last family holiday was, above all, an opportunity for the family to create good memories and/or fun, to strengthen emotional bonds, to experience new places and activities and for the family members to feel more union between them (Table 14.5). These results confirm findings from previous studies, such as the ones undertaken by Lehto et al. (2009), McCabe et al. (2010), Minnaert (2006, 2012) and Minnaert et al. (2009). On the other hand, the effects that respondents generally disagreed were a result from their last family holiday are improvements in the financial situation of the family (financial dimension of the QOL) and becoming tired of being with each other (negative effect on the family relationship domain of QOL) (Table 14.5).

However, three results appear behind the average values presented in Table 14.5:

(i) 40.3% of the respondents agreed (4.0 or more, on a scale from 1 'totally disagree' to 7 'totally agree') that the last family holiday contributed to improving the financial situation of the family, an effect also identified in the study undertaken by McCabe et al. (2010);
(ii) 56.3% of the respondents agreed (4.0 or more, on a scale from 1 'totally disagree' to 7 'totally agree') with the fact that those family holidays contributed to reducing household expenditure on health (e.g., medication to combat stress), an effect also identified for the senior population in the study undertaken by INATEL (2009);
(iii) all other items regarding the positive effects, which sought to measure the occurrence of certain effects of family holidays on the dimension of QOL, had more than 70% of the respondents agreeing with the existence of these effects' (agreement level greater than or equal to 4.0, on a scale from 1 'totally disagree' to 7 'totally agree'), a result that corroborates the conclusions of Lehto et al. (2009), McCabe et al. (2010), Minnaert (2006, 2012) and Minnaert et al. (2009).

Also noteworthy is the fact that 20.2% of the respondents agreed (4.0 or more, on a scale from 1 'totally disagree' to 7 'totally agree') that those holidays contributed to them getting tired of the other members of the family, a negative effect advocated by Gram (2005) that brings the attention to the importance of considering both the needs of the parents and the children for the family holidays to have more positive effects on the family.

14.4.3.1 Differences Between the Families According to Their Economic Profile

Regarding overall QOL, there were no differences between the two family segments, both of which reported high levels (average above 5.5) of satisfaction with life after the holiday (Table 14.5). It is, however, worth mentioning the relatively

Table 14.5 Effects of the last family holiday on the family's QOL

Effects on the Family's QOL		All families (N = 823)		Other families (N = 669)	Deprived families (N = 154)	*t*	Sig.
		N	AVG	AVG			
Overall QOL	All in all, I feel that these holidays have enriched my life	808	5.54	5.57	5.41	1.013	0.312
	I felt much better about life after these holidays	806	5.58	5.56	5.63	−0.467	0.641
Family relationship	Traveling together steghtned our family bonds	805	5.93	**5.96**	5.82	1.011	0.313
	Tension within my family was more relaxed while traveling together	803	4.93	4.86	**5.25**	−2.214	0,027*
	Family members feel close to each other after these holidays	803	5.67	**5.68**	5.60	0.586	0.558
	These holidays helped to discover new ways of dealing with each other	797	4.77	4.73	4.94	−1.294	0.196
	These holidays contributed to get tired of being with each other	803	2.09	2.03	2.34	−1.776	0.077**
	These holidays gave us the opportunity for fun and happy memories	804	6.15	**6.18**	6.00	1.477	0.141
Environment	These holidays contributed for reducing health expenditure of the household (eg: Stress medication)	798	3.76	3.66	**4.20**	−2.686	0,007*
	These holidays contributed for improving the financial situation of the family	798	2.99	2.93	**3.27**	−1.791	0,075**
	These holidays contributed to increase our access to information	803	4.61	4.6	4.66	−0.333	0.739
	These holidays gave us the opportunity to experience new places and different activities	803	5.89	**5.91**	5.80	0.77	0.442
	These holidays contributed to increase our opportunities of meeting new and different people	794	4.55	4.54	4.61	−0.463	0.644

Legend: AVG Average; $*p \le 0{,}05$; $**p \le 0{,}1$

higher intensity reported by the "deprived families" regarding the item "I felt much better about life after these holidays" (Table 14.5). These results corroborate Neal et al.'s (1999) findings about tourism helping to increase overall life satisfaction and clearly illustrate the increased importance tourism may have in improving the overall QOL of economically disadvantaged families, as evidenced, for example, in the studies conducted by McCabe et al. (2010) and Smith and Hughes (1999).

Comparing the effects that the last family holiday had on the two groups of families (materially deprived families and other families), significant differences were found in the contribution of the holidays to improving "the financial situation of the family", to reducing "health expenditure of the household" (e.g. stress medication) and for relaxing "tension within my family", noting that the "deprived families" are those who report a more intense perception of these effects (Table 14.5). These results confirm previous studies, such as those of Lehto et al. (2009), McCabe et al. (2010) and Minnaert et al. (2009), and show, clearly, the importance that a family holiday may have, particularly for this family segment, in the families' QOL.

It is also worth mentioning the fact that "deprived families" agreed relatively more with the effect "I felt much better about life after this trip" (Table 14.5). These results corroborate Neal et al.'s (1999) findings about tourism helping to increase overall life satisfaction and the increased importance of family tourism in increasing the QOL of economically disadvantaged families, as evidenced, for example, in the studies of McCabe et al. (2010) and Smith and Hughes (1999).

14.5 Conclusions and Implications

The obtained results confirm the relevance of family holidays for the family's QOL (McCabe et al. 2010; Minnaert et al. 2009; Smith and Hughes 1999), clearly indicating the existence of the effects of family tourism on families' QOL and that these effects differ according to the economic status of the families.

The sample was divided into two segments of families: "deprived families" and "other families", which were analysed separately, in order to observe differences in sociodemographic characteristics, travel behaviour and in the effects of family tourism on families' QOL. In terms of socio-demographic and economic characteristics, the results confirm the fact that the segment of "deprived families" are more exposed to contexts of poverty and social exclusion due to their sociodemographic characteristics and living conditions, while the "other families" have opposite characteristics.

Analysing the last family holiday, results clearly demonstrate the existence of differences in terms of travel behaviour of the two groups of families. Results show that the "Other families" have tourism practices with more contrasting features with their everyday environment, which could influence the type of experiences that families have during the holidays and the effects on the holidays on the families' QOL.

Considering the results of the effects of family holidays on families' QOL, it can be observed that the "deprived families" are those who feel the effects on the health and financial dimensions of the QOL with greater intensity. Regarding the effects on QOL more related with the family relationship – strengthening the emotional bonds among family members – the "deprived families" reported a less intense perception of these effects, except for the item regarding the relaxing of tension within the family. This result is contrary to previous studies about the increased intensity of the effects of tourism in the segments of disadvantaged population. It may be justified by the different travel behaviour observed, resulting in different experiences during the holidays and different effects on the families' QOL. This may indicate that the "deprived families" aren't having the type of family holidays that will maximize the effects on their QOL. Recognizing that family tourism can bring important contributions in terms of promoting socialization and the possible creation of social networks outside the usual circles for "deprived families" are key aspects that should be considered when designing tourism experiences as instrument for improving QOL, particularly for economically disadvantaged families.

Although there are no significant differences, "deprived families" agreed relatively more with the effect "I felt much better about life after this trip", confirming the results obtained in previous studies about the increased intensity of the effects of tourism in the segments of disadvantaged population (Neal et al. 1999; McCabe et al. 2010; Smith and Hughes 1999).

This study is exploratory in nature, but from the results presented above, it can be concluded that respondents perceive important effects of family tourism and that these effects are differentiated according to a series of factors, particularly the socioeconomic status of the family: there exists an increased importance of family tourism in increasing the QOL of economically disadvantaged families. Some other tendencies appear to exist regarding variables that may influence the perceptions of the effects of family holidays on the family's QOL. The features of a specific holiday and sociodemographic features seem to influence the perception of the effects family tourism may have on families' QOL. Tourism practices which contrast more with the families' everyday environment seem to contribute to a higher perception of the positive effects of family holidays on families' QOL and this also should be considered when designing tourism experiences, particularly when one of the aims is to improve the QOL of "deprived families".

In this context, social tourism programmes directed at economically disadvantaged families seem to be necessary as a strategy to promote what is nowadays considered a basic right of individuals and a dimension that characterizes modern society and QOL – access to tourism. Thus, results along with the literature review, make us believe that the activities to be integrated into social tourism programmes for families will be a key feature of these social tourism programmes, as a factor that will influence the type of experiences they have during the holidays and determine the effects of these holidays and their intensity. Also, the results permit the conclusion for the need to adapt the type of vacation to each kind of family (for example, there are different needs for different family members – children *vs.* adults, own time *vs.* socializing – when the objective is to maximize the effects that family tourism can bring to families' QOL. However, we recognize the need for more research on this issue in order to identify what kind of activities should be promoted for each type of family.

Although the results of this study are largely consistent with the relatively rare previous research, this study is only exploratory and limited in geographical terms of the considered sample. Therefore, further research is required in order to understand the real and complete effects and potential of family tourism as an instrument to enhance family QOL and well-being, particularly for materially deprived families. In a context where new approaches to enhancing family QOL, well-being and social inclusion are being sought (Lehto et al. 2009; Minnaert et al. 2009), the following types of studies are particularly pertinent: (i) studies that analyse/compare the effects of tourism reported by families in each phase of the tourist experience (before, during and after the holiday); (ii) research on the determinants of the effects of family tourism on family's QOL; and (iii) studies that analyse in-depth the tourism practices of disadvantaged families and the resulting benefits.

These types of studies would contribute decisively to understanding how to design family holiday programmes that maximize the positive effects for families, contributing to increasing the families' QOL, particularly those with material deprivation.

Acknowledgements This work was financially supported by the research unit on Governance, Competitiveness and Public Policy (project POCI-01-0145-FEDER-006939), funded by FEDER funds through COMPETE2020 – Programa Operacional Competitividade e Internacionalização (POCI) – and by national funds through FCT – Fundação para a Ciência e a Tecnologia.

References

Agate, S. T., Zabriskie, R. B., & Eggett, D. L. (2007). Praying, playing, and successful families. *Marriage & Family Review, 42*(2), 51–75.

Alarcão, M., & Relvas, A. P. (2002). *Novas formas de família*. Coimbra: Quarteto.

Alegre, J., Mateo, S., & Pou, L. (2010). An analysis of households' appraisal of their budget constraints for potential participation in tourism. *Tourism Management, 31*(1), 45–56.

Alexander, Z., Bakir, A., & Wickens, E. (2010). An investigation into the impact of vacation travel on the tourist. *International Journal of Tourism Research, 12*, 574–590.

Andereck, K. L., & Nuaupane, G. (2011). Quality-of-life community indicators for parks, recreation and tourism management. *Social Indicators Research Series, 43*, 95–113.

Ballantyne, R., Packer, J., & Sutherland, L. A. (2011). Visitors' memories of wildlife tourism: Implications for the design of powerful interpretive experiences. *Tourism Management, 32*, 770–779.

Chen, K.-H., & Yao, G. (2010). Investigating adolescent health-related quality of life: From a self-identity perspective. *Social Indicators Research, 96*(4), 403–415.

Chon, K. S. (1999). Special issue on tourism and quality-of-life issues. *Journal of Business Research, 44*, 135–136.

Dolnicar, S., Lazarevski, K., & Yanamandram, V. (2013). Quality of life and tourism: A conceptual framework and novel segmentation base. *Journal of Business Research, 66*(6), 724–729.

Dolnicar, S., Yanamandram, V., & Cliff, K. (2012). The contribution of vacations to quality of life. *Annals of Tourism Research, 39*, 59–83.

EC-European Commission. (1987). *Europeans and their holidays*. VII/165/87-EN. [EU Commission – Working Document]. http://aei.pitt.edu/10930/. Accessed Mar 2014.

Eurostat. (2015). Europe in figures—Eurostat yearbook, 2013. http://ec.europa.eu/eurostat/statistics-explained/index.php/Social_inclusion_statistics

Eusébio, C., & Carneiro, M. J. (2011). Determinants of tourism impact on tourists' quality of life. *International Journal of Leisure and Tourism Marketing, 2*(4), 313–323.

Eusébio, C., & Carneiro, M. J. (2014). The impact of tourism on quality of life. A segmentation analysis of the youth market. *Tourism Analysis, 19*(6), 741–758.

Fu, X., Lehto, X., & Park, O. (2014). What does vacation do to our family? Contrasting the perspectives of parents and children. *Journal of Travel & Tourism Marketing, 31*(4), 461–475.

Genç, R. (2012). Tourist consumption behavior of quality of life. In M. Uysal, R. Perdue, & M. J. Sirgy (Eds.), *Handbook of tourism and quality-of-life research: Enhancing the lives of tourists and residents of host communities* (pp. 135–148). Dordrecht: Springer.

Gilbert, D., & Abdullah, J. (2004). Holidaytaking and the sense of well-being. *Annals of Tourism Research, 31*, 103–121.

Goeldner, C. R., & Ritchie, J. R. B. (2009). *Tourism: Principles, practices and philosophies* (pp. 304–306). New York: Wiley.

Gram, M. (2005). Family holidays. A qualitative analysis of family holiday experiences. *Scandinavian Journal of Hospitality and Tourism, 5*, 2–22.

Haldrup, M., & Larsen, J. (2003). The family gaze. *Tourist Studies, 3*(1), 23–46.

Hall, D., & Brown, F. (2006). *Tourism and welfare: Ethics, responsibility and sustained well-being*. London: CAB International.

Haukeland, J. (1990). Non-travellers: The flip side of motivation. *Annals of Tourism Research, 17*(2), 172–184.

Hazel, N. (2005). Holidays for children and families in need: An exploration of the research and policy context for social tourism in the UK. *Children & Society, 19*, 225–236.

Howard, M. (2012). Foreword. In H. Schanzel, I. Yeoman, & E. Backer (Eds.), *Family tourism: Multidisciplinary perspectives* (pp. xvii–xviii). Bristol: Channel View Publications.

INATEL. (2009). *Estudo de impacto sócio-económico do Programa Turismo Sénior de 2001 a 2005*. University of Aveiro, Aveiro (not published).

INE – Instituto Nacional de Estatística. (2011). *Classificação Portuguesa das Profissões de* (p. 2010). Lisboa: Instituto Nacional de Estatística, I.P.

INE – Instituto Nacional de Estatística. (2013). *Destaque sobre Famílias nos Censos 2011: Diversidade e Mudança*. 20 de novembro de 2013. Lisboa: Instituto Nacional de Estatística, I.P.

INE – Instituto Nacional de Estatística. (2014a). *Indicadores da "Taxa de risco de pobreza (Após transferências sociais – %) por Composição do agregado doméstico privado; Anual"*. Base de dados ICOR – Inquérito às Condições de Vida e Rendimento.

INE – Instituto Nacional de Estatística. (2014b). *Rendimento e Condições de Vida 2013 (Dados Provisórios). Destaque de informação à comunicação social de 24 de março de 2014*. Lisboa: Instituto Nacional de Estatística, I.P.

INE – Instituto Nacional de Estatística. (2015). *Anuário Estatístico da Região Centro – 2014*. Lisboa: Instituto Nacional de Estatística, I.P.

Kim, J.-H. (2010). Determining the Factors Affecting the Memorable Nature of Travel Experiences. *Journal of Travel & Tourism Marketing, 27*(8), 780–796. https://doi.org/10.1080/10548408.2010.526897.

Lehto, X. Y., Choi, S., Lin, Y.-C., & Macdermid, S. M. (2009). Vacation and family functioning. *Annals of Tourism Research, 36*, 459–479.

Lima, J., Eusébio, C., & Amorim Varum, C. (2012). Effects of holidays on tourists: A review and directions for future research. *RT&D/Journal of Tourism and Development, 17*(18), 265–277.

McCabe, S., Joldersma, T., & Li, C. X. (2010). Understanding the benefits of social tourism: Linking participation to subjective well-being and quality of life. *International Journal of Tourism Research, 12*, 761–773.

Michalkó, G., Kiss, K., Kovács, B., & Sulyok, J. (2009). The impact of tourism on subjective quality of life among Hungarian population. *Hungarian Geographical Bulletin, 58*, 121–136.

Ministry of Education. (2007). *Improving school leadership – Country background report for Portugal.* OECD project "Improving School Leadership". OECD.

Minnaert, L. (2006). Social tourism: a potential policy to reduce social exclusion? The effects of visitor-related social tourism for low income groups on personal and family development. PhD Thesis, University of Westminster.

Minnaert, L. (2008). Holidays are for everyone. Research into the effects and the importance of holidays for people living in poverty. Brussels.

Minnaert, L. (2012). Social tourism as opportunity for unplanned learning and behavior change. *Journal of Travel Research. Published online version.* https://doi.org/10.1177/0047287511431324.

Minnaert, L. (Ed.) (2013). *Holidays are for everyone: developments in the facilitation of tourism for people in poverty*. Visit Flanders: Holiday Participation Centre.

Minnaert, L., Maitland, R., & Miller, G. (2009). Tourism and social policy – The value of social tourism. *Annals of Tourism Research, 36*, 316–334.

Minnaert, L., Stacey, J., Quinn, B., & Griffin, K. (2010). Social tourism for low-income groups: Benefits in a UK and Irish context. In S. Cole & N. Morgan (Eds.), *Tourism and inequality: Problems and prospects*. CAB International.

Moscardo, G. (2009). Tourism and quality of life: Towards a more critical approach. *Tourism and Hospitality Research, 9*, 159–170.

Neal, J. D., Sirgy, M. J., & Uysal, M. (1999). The role of satisfaction with leisure travel/tourism services and experience in satisfaction with leisure life and overall life. *Journal of Business Research, 44*, 153–163.

Obrador, P. (2012). The place of the family in tourism research: Domesticity and thick sociality by the pool. *Annals of Tourism Research, 39*, 401–420.

Pesonen, J., Laukkanen, T., & Komppula, R. (2011). Benefit segmentation of potential wellbeing tourists. *Journal of Vacation Marketing, 17*(4), 303–314.

Richards, G. (1999). Vacations and the quality of life: Patterns and structures. *Journal of Business Research, 44*, 189–198.

Schänzel, H. A., Smith, K. A., & Weaver, A. (2005). Family holidays: A research review and application to New Zealand. *Annals of Leisure Research, 8*(2–3), 105–123.

Schänzel, H., & Smith, K. A. (2014). The socialization of families away from home: Group dynamics and family functioning on holiday. *Leisure Sciences: An Interdisciplinary Journal, 36*(2), 126–143.

Schanzel, H., Yeoman, I., & Backer, E. (2012). Introduction. In H. Schanzel, I. Yeoman, & E. Backer (Eds.), *Family tourism: Multidisciplinary perspectives* (pp. 1–14). Bristol: Chanel View Publications.

Shaw, S. M., Havitz, M. E., & Delemere, F. M. (2008). "I decided to invest in my Kids' memories": Family vacations, memories, and the social construction of the family. *Tourism Culture & Communication, 8*(1), 13–26.

Skevington, S. M., Lotfy, M., & O'Connell, K. A. (2004). The World Health Organization's WHOQOL-BREF quality of life assessment: Psychometric properties and results of the international field trial: A report from the WHOQOL group. *Quality of Life Research, 13*, 299–310.

Small, J. (2008). The absence of childhood in tourism studies. *Annals of Tourism Research, 35*(3), 772–789.

Smith, V., & Hughes, H. (1999). Disadvantaged families and the meaning of the holiday. *International Journal of Tourism Research, 1*, 123–133.

UNWTO – World Tourism Organization. (2008). *2008 international recommendations for tourism statistics*. Madrid: UNWTO.

Uysal, M., Sirgy, M. J., Woo, E., & Kim, H. (2016). Quality of life (QOL) and well-being research in tourism. *Tourism Management, 53*, 244–261.

Wigfall, V. (2004). Extracts from 'Turning Lives Around' - Final Evaluation Report of Family Breaks Pilot Project for Family Holidays Association. Thomas Coram Research Unit.

Wolff, P. (2009). Population and social conditions, in Eurostat: Statistics in focus 46/2009. Available at: http://ec.europa.eu/eurostat/documents/3433488/5281381/KS-SF-09-046-EN.PDF/a710699c-8167-4ae8-87bc-26b71c91a74b. Accessed Jan 2016.

World Health Organization. (1994). *Quality of life assessment: An annotated biography*. Geneva: WHO (WHO/MNH/PFS/94.1).

World Health Organization – WHO. (2004). Quality of life (WHOQOL)-BREF. World Health Organization.

Chapter 15
A Quality-of-Life Perspective of Tourists in Traditional Wine Festivals: The Case of the Wine-Tasting Festival in Córdoba, Spain

Tomás López-Guzmán, Jesús C. Pérez-Gálvez, and Guzmán A. Muñoz-Fernández

Abstract In recent years the number of tourists that seek new experiences in their travels has increased. Therefore, there is a substantial increase in the trips related to gastronomy, wine and, in general, the experience related to culinary products. The objective of this chapter is to present a case study focussed on a traditional food and beverage festival, known as The Wine Tasting, in the city of Cordoba, where along with the attendance of the local community, a significant increase in tourists is being produced who find in this festival a meeting place to reinforce their knowledge about the wine and gastronomic products of this geographic area and to improve their quality-of-life, reinforcing at the same time their relations with the local community and, therefore, improving their knowledge of the culture of this geographic area. In this chapter, we present the results of an empiric study conducted during this festival with the objective of knowing the sociodemographic profile, the motivations and the satisfaction of the tourists that attend this festival.

Keywords Festival · Wine tourism · Culture · Spain

15.1 Introduction

At the beginning of the twenty-first century, tourism is evolving towards trips shorter in time, with greater frequency and where the travellers want to know in more depth other elements of that destination and, in this way, the tourism offer is creating new tourist products to respond to the current tastes of the consumer. Therefore, this activity is causing a segmentation of the traveller, and with it

---

T. López-Guzmán (✉) · J. C. Pérez-Gálvez · G. A. Muñoz-Fernández
University of Cordoba, Cordoba, Spain
e-mail: tomas.lopez@uco.es

A. M. Campón-Cerro et al. (eds.), *Best Practices in Hospitality and Tourism Marketing and Management*, Applying Quality of Life Research,
https://doi.org/10.1007/978-3-319-91692-7_15

different types emerge. Among the trends that are being detected in recent years is a growing interest by the tourists to get to know the gastronomy and the wines of certain geographic areas. The food, wine, tourism and its adjacent factors are the basic elements of the product (food and beverage tourism) which supplies an experience and a certain lifestyle of the visitors. Local gastronomy and tourism, linked with wine, appears as a perfect symbiosis so that the visitors can appreciate a different product, promoting sustainable economic development of certain geographic areas (Yuan and Jang 2008) because agricultural products of proximity are used. Recent studies (Hillel et al. 2013; Hollows et al. 2014) around this type of tourism suggest and promote the idea that gastronomy and wine can be, and often are, the principal motive for visiting a certain region and not being necessarily a secondary (or complementary) activity of the trip.

Food and beverage tourism presents a complete sensorial experience (Getz 2000): the visitor can experience the pleasure of taste, smell, touch, sight and sound. Gastronomy forms part of the social, economic and cultural history of towns and their inhabitants. And this is because it also reflects a certain lifestyle of the citizens of the different countries, since it is something rooted in their own culture and tradition. Following to Mitchell and Hall (2006), we can define food and beverage tourism as the visit to primary or secondary food producers, the participation in enogastronomic festivals and the search for restaurants or specific places where tasting food (and the entire experience that it entails) is the principal reason for travelling. That is to say, enogastronomic tourism is a tourist experience in which the person learns, appreciates and consumes typical products of that land.

Beverage food festivals have become an increasingly visible part of local and regional calendars (Hollows et al. 2014). Among them we have the Wine Festival of Montilla-Moriles, whose commercial name is *Cata de Vino Montilla-Moriles* (Montilla-Moriles Wine Tasting), which is held annually in the city of Cordoba (Spain) since 1982 and which is receiving in the recent editions around 80,000 visits. The purpose of this festival is double: on the one hand, to make the product known to the local community and the tourists; on the other hand, to reinforce the relations between the different companies. This festival, at the same time, also reinforces the Official "Montilla-Moriles" Wine Route which is one of the 21 official routes that exist in Spain. In this regard, this type of festivals reinforces belonging to a certain community and strengthens their cultural value in the society.

The principal objective of this chapter is to analyse the sociodemographic profile and the motivations of the tourists that visit this enogastronomic festival. In order to fulfil this objective, this chapter is structured, after this introduction, in a second section that includes a brief review of the existing literature; a third section refers to the methodology used and the fourth presents the results of the research. The chapter ends with the conclusions and the bibliographic references used.

15.2 Review of the Literature

15.2.1 Food and Beverage Tourism

The relationship between gastronomy, wine and tourism has been associated with a new tourism category called food and beverage tourism in which the motivation for travelling is to enjoy experiences obtained from culinary resources. The origin of the research in the field of enogastronomic tourism dates back to the mid-1990s of the last century, being basically located in Australia and New Zealand. One important study that was one of the first researches was centred, above all, on two aspects: the analysis of the socioeconomic impact of enogastronomic tourism and the study of the behaviour of tourists in the wineries (Getz 2000). Two of the studies that mark the beginning of the research in this field are: Wine Tourism around the World (Hall et al. 2000) and Food Tourism around the World (Hall et al. 2003).

Within food and beverage tourism, the authors have established different research lines. In this regard, we highlight the segmentation regarding the research lines of two different authors focussed on gastronomy and one author focussed on the analysis of wine tourism. In relation to wine tourism, Mitchell and Hall (2006) identified the following approaches in this field: wine tourism product; wine product and regional development; quantification of demand; segmentation of the wine tourist; behaviour of the visitors; nature of the visit to the wineries; and biodiversity and wine tourism. As for the food tourism, Henderson (2009) indicated that the papers that relate gastronomy to tourism can be grouped in four different research lines; namely; first, the analysis of the relationship between the concepts of gastronomy, tourism and tourists; second, the consideration of culinary resources as a tourist product; third, the consideration of gastronomy as a marketing element to attract the tourists; and fourth, food tourism as an instrument for development of certain geographic areas, including the activities of the primary sector. On the other hand, we can also highlight the research lines indicated by Tikkanen (2007), who considers that the relationship between tourism and gastronomy should be treated from four different areas: first, the use of gastronomy as an element of attraction to promote a destination, analysing such aspects as advertising of the typical culinary dishes; second, the use of gastronomy as a component of the tourist product itself, analysing related aspects such as the design of gastronomic routes, for example; third, the use of gastronomy as an experience for the traveller, especially in those places in which the kitchens of the great masters are found; fourth, the use of gastronomy as a cultural phenomenon, expressed in, for example, the holding of food festivals where the local community reinforces its relation with culinary tradition. In this article, the analysis of the sociodemographic profile and the motivations of the visitor are considered.

This type of tourism will have a greater or lesser degree of development according to the level of connection that the cuisine has with the culture of the place (Henderson 2014; Riley 2005) since the cuisine plays an important role in the satisfaction of the tourist experience and as part of the cultural heritage of the destination (Ignatov and Smith 2006) and to acquire knowledge of local community and to acquire knowledge on local food and culture (Mak et al. 2012). In summary, food and beverage tourism reinforces the importance of the local ingredients, helps to create a brand of the tourism destination and contributes to the learning and appreciation of its culinary resources.

15.2.2 Tourism and Enogastronomic Festivals

Food and beverage festivals are an important part of this type of tourism (Ignatov and Smith 2006). The tourist events have different functions such as the increment in the number of visitors to the region or to the city, the economic injection, the increase of employment, the improvement of the destination's image or the improvement of the social and cultural benefits of the local community as well as for the visitor (Çela et al. 2007). In this way, the gastronomic festivals are a good opportunity for the tourists to be able to enjoy the local cuisine and, therefore, have a different experience during their trip (Wu et al. 2014).

So that it can be affirmed that a festival is enogastronomic, it must offer food and wine from the geographic area and carry out scheduling with local and regional gastronomic themes (Lee and Arcodia 2011). In this way, greater satisfaction for the visitor is achieved, a concept that should be considered as the relationship between the degree of expectation that a tourist had before arriving at the festival and the perception that he received in it (Kim et al. 2015). Baker and Crompton (2000) point out four dimensions for determining the quality of the festival and, therefore, the visitor's satisfaction. These four dimensions are: the characteristics typical of the festival, the attractions that the festival has, the sources of information available within the festival area and the installations where the event is carried out. In turn, Wan and Chan (2013) define that the visitor's satisfaction with the festival is based on a series of attributes that encompasses, among others, the following aspects: locations and accessibility to it, culinary resources of the festival or the size of the event. Therefore, all these dimensions are going to determine the consumer's satisfaction with respect to the event (Yoon et al. 2010).

The satisfaction of the visitors in the gastronomic festivals has been analysed by different authors. Smith and Costello (2009) analyse the satisfaction in relation to gastronomy that they can taste in the festival as well as the quality/price of the products. Furthermore, Kim et al. (2015) analyse the level of satisfaction of visitors to a gastronomic festival through the establishment of a cluster analysis where three different segments of visitors are presented, according to their level of satisfaction and based on different attributes such as the reasons for which they attended the event, the distance from their place of origin, the overnight stay in the place of the event or the economic expense incurred.

15.3 Methodology

The methodology used in conducting this research was based on the field work carried out to know the profile and valuations of the tourists in relation to the Montilla-Moriles wine and food festival held in the city of Cordoba in April 2014. The field work was carried out within the wine festival grounds, specifically at the time in which the surveyed tourists were tasting the wine and gastronomy.

The structure of the survey used in the research was based on different prior papers (Carmichael 2005; Charters and Ali-Knight 2002; Dawson et al. 2011; Getz and Brown 2006) and responds to the four-section approach: (1) the analysis of the sociodemographic characteristics of the surveyed tourist; (2) the valuation of the different attributes of the gastronomic festival; (3) the motivations for attending; and (4) the satisfaction with it.

The surveys were done during the days of the festival, from the 24th to 27th of April 2014. The survey was distributed in two languages (Spanish and English). As mentioned, the survey was answered by the tourists from the festival grounds. The participants filled out the survey with complete independence, although the data collectors were present in case they had any difficulty in filling it out. The survey was completely anonymous. A pre-test of 20 surveys was conducted previously to detect possible deviations and errors. The total number of surveys obtained was 679 questionnaires. Among the foreign tourists surveyed stand out those coming from the United Kingdom, France and Italy.

The selection of the interviewees was made by random sampling among the visitors who met the condition of tourist. The data collectors randomly chose as survey sites a series of tables existing within the festival grounds in order to conduct it. The first question made by the data collectors to the selected persons was whether their usual residence was in the city of Cordoba, not handing out the survey to those visitors who responded affirmatively. No variable was stratified (for example, sex, age or country of origin) since in none of the editions of the Wine Tasting was this type of research conducted. The rate of rejections to the survey was low and not significant for any variable. The exact number of tourists that visited this festival in previous editions was not known although there is an estimate of 80,000 visitors, a figure used as the target population. It is not verified that up to now any similar study has been conducted, even though it is a festival consolidated over time. The survey was proportionally distributed during the days indicated, in two different shifts (mid-day and night). The number of surveys filled out were similar on the different days of the Tasting, with the exception of the date of 27 April (Sunday) where, due to the fact that it was only open in the mid-day shift, the number of surveys filled in was approximately half of those of the other days.

The items used were planned to respond to the indicators and measures proposed for the realisation of an analysis of the demand and were proposed with the aim of making systematic comparisons between different enogastronomic festivals (Getz and Brown 2006). A mixture of technical questions were used through a Likert 5-point scale with 1-minor, 5-major to assess the motivation and the characteristics

Table 15.1 Technical sheet of the research

Total number of visitors to the tasting (year 2013)	80,000 visitors
Sample	679 surveys
Procedure	Convenience sampling
Period of realisation	24, 25, 26 and 27 April 2014
Sampling error	3.74%
Confidence level	95.0% p = q = 0.5
Control of the sample	Realisation and supervision of work by the authors of the research

Source: Own elaboration

of the festival, yes/no answers and both closed and open questions where those surveyed could make comments on their enogastronomic experience. The total number of persons that visited the wine tasting in 2013 was, as indicated earlier, approximately 80,000. However, on those dates they did not differentiate between local visitors and tourists. Table 15.1 presents the technical sheet of the research. Convenience sampling was used, commonly adopted in this type of research where the persons surveyed are available to be surveyed in a certain space and time (Finn et al. 2000). The reliability index according to Cronbach's Alpha was 0.778. The high reliability index obtained reinforces the validity of the research work conducted (Nunnally and Bernstein 1994).

The data included were organised, tabulated and analysed using the IBM SPSS Statistics 19 program. The data processing was done through the use of univariate and bivariate statistical tools.

15.4 Results of the Research and Discussion

15.4.1 Sociodemographic Profile

Table 15.2 presents the sociodemographic characteristics of the tourist surveyed in the Cordoba wine and food festival according to sex, age, place of origin, professional category, educational and income levels.

The great majority of the tourists that visited this wine festival come from Spain (75.4%), followed by the United Kingdom and Italy. As for the main region of origin of the tourists, it is Andalusia, followed at a great distance by Madrid, Extremadura, Region of Valencia and Castilla-La Mancha. These data allow concluding that a greater promotion of the Montilla-Moriles Wine and Food Festival outside the territory of Andalusia would be necessary, both at the national and international level, in order to pursue greater tourist appeal. As for the educational level, tourists with university studies clearly stands out. They are mostly persons under 40 years of age, and a mode in the age bracket of 30–39 years. This result implies a great potentiality for the future consumption of this type of wine. As for the

Table 15.2 Sociodemographic characteristics of the tourist in the Cordoba Wine Festival

Variable	Category	Percentage	Variable	Category	Percentage
Sex (N = 668)	Male	52.2%	**Region (N = 508)**	Andalusia	46.5%
	Female	47.8%		Extremadura	5.6%
				Reg. of Valencia	5.4%
				Madrid	7.3%
				Castilla-La Mancha	5.2%
				Others	30.0%
Age (N = 671)	Less than 30	41.9%	**Professional category (N = 672)**	Independent professional	17.0%
	30–39 years	26.4%		Salaried employee	34.2%
	40–49 years	19.4%		Civil servant	15.2%
	50–59 years	8.6%		Housewife	3.4%
	60 years or more	3.7%		Retired	2.1%
				Student	24.2%
				Others	3.9%
Education (N = 662)	Primary	3.7%	**Country (N = 674)**	Spain	75.4%
	Secondary	18.7%		United Kingdom	7.3%
	University	77.6%		France	2.4%
				Italy	3.3%
				United States	2.5%
				Others	9.1%
Income (N = 575)	< €700/ month	26.8%			
	€700–€1000	15.7%			
	€1001–€1500	29.2%			
	€1501-€ 2500	19.1%			
	€2501-€ 3500	4.5%			
	More than €3500	4.7%			

Source: Own elaboration

purchasing power of the visitors, they are found in the bracket between 1000 and 1500 Euros.

A positive association was detected between income and age (Pearson's chi-squared coefficient = 82.287; p = 0.000), between the educational level and income (Pearson's chi-squared coefficient 25.308; p = 0.005), between the professional category and income (Pearson's chi-squared coefficient = 58.742; p = 0.000) and the professional category and sex (Pearson's chi-squared coefficient = 16.941; p = 0.005).

Table 15.3 Valuation of aspects of the Cordoba Wine Festival

Aspects	Valuation
Holding the tasting has a positive impact on the image that I have of Cordoba	4.37
It is necessary to incorporate to this type of event other sociocultural offers such as music	4.08
It is important to incorporate to this type of event other products related to gastronomy	4.07
The public administrations should form an active part in the organisation of this type of event	3.98
The good or bad organisation influences the number of visitors	3.92
The weather conditions influence the number of visitors	3.82
The ease of access, communication and parking influences the number of visitors	3.63
The lack of economic resources of the citizens influence the number of visitors	3.56
The greater or lesser presence in the communications media influences the number of visitors	3.52

Source: Own elaboration

The majority of the tourists surveyed already knew the city (80.3%) and are going to remain in the city for at least one night. We recall that one of the major goals of tourism of the city of Cordoba is to increase the loyalty and overnight stays, and events such as the festival can serve to achieve this objective. The majority visit the city accompanied by their partner (38.4%) or with work colleagues or friends (38.2%). Furthermore, 45.4% indicate that they are going to attend the wine festival for only one day. As for the way of learning about this event, the majority state that it was through friends (50.1%) and from their own experience of other years (24.3%). This datum corroborates the idea already noted on the necessity of making a better promotion of the Wine Tasting.

15.4.2 Valuation of the Wine and Food Festival

With respect to the Wine Festival of Cordoba, the principal valuations made by the surveyed tourists are shown in Table 15.3.

According to the responses it can be concluded that the celebration of the Cordoba Wine Festival produces a positive image of the city. The tourists indicate that it would be of interest to introduce in this Festival complementary activities such as music, as well as reinforce the gastronomy through a correct pairing between the wine and the traditional gastronomy of this geographical area. We use a Likert 5-point scale with 1-minor, 5-major.

As for the knowledge of the wine of the Denomination of Origin Montilla-Moriles, 77.4% of the tourists surveyed knew the wine of Montilla-Moriles before their visit to the city of Cordoba. Furthermore, 29.3% of the tourists surveyed consume wine more than once a week.

Table 15.4 Motivations for attending the Cordoba Wine Festival

Aspects	Valuation
Entertainment	4.07
Socialise with colleagues and friends	4.04
Learn the customs of this geographic area	3.79
It is another activity of my visit to Cordoba	3.79
Spend the day out	3.78
Taste different classes of wine	3.68
Taste gastronomic products	3.41
Learn about the world of wine	3.42
Contact exhibitors	2.74

Source: Own elaboration

15.4.3 Motivations for Attending the Food and Wine Festival

The reasons or the motives for the visit were reflected in the sixth question of the survey. For this, a total of 9 items were designed, on a measuring scale of the Likert 5-point type, where 1 is little and 5 is much, the relative importance of a series of factors in their decision to visit the wine festival, in which we tried to collect the most frequent and relevant reasons for the trip, analysed in previous research, adapting them and taking into account the specific characteristics of the tourist destination and of the visitors (Devesa et al. 2010; Gagić et al. 2013; Lee et al. 2004; Yuan and Jang 2008). Internal and external factors were included such as establishing the Crompton theory (1979) concerning the pull and push factors of motivation. *Cronbach's Alpha* coefficient of the final scale reached a value of 0.706, which indicates excellent internal consistency among the elements of the scale. The critical level (p) associated with the statistic F (127.889) of the variance analysis in order to compare the null hypothesis that all the elements of the scale have the same mean (ANOVA) is less than 0.001, not being possible to maintain the hypothesis that the means of the elements are equal. In Table 15.4, the principal motivations are presented, identifying two motivational dimensions (a primary hedonist-social dimension and the other enogastronomic) that allow segmenting the tourists surveyed according to the motivations that led them to visit this enogastronomic festival. We use a Likert 5-point scale with 1-minor, 5-major.

A factorial analysis was conducted on the modification scale to identify a small number of explanatory factors, and from which two different dimensions were extracted on the motivation in the Montilla-Moriles Wine Festival (Table 15.5).

Although interest resides in the factorial scores that are derived from these components as tools for establishing the strength of the motivations of each visitor, it is of interest to characterise each of the two extracted factors. We have called the first factor Enogastronomic Motives and it is related to a tourist who conceives the visit as an instrument to taste different classes of wine and gastronomic products of the

Table 15.5 Rotated component factor matrix – motivations for attending the Cordoba Wine Festival

	Factors		
Ítems	1	2	Motivational dimensions
Taste different classes of wine	0.636		**Food and wine**
Taste gastronomic products	0.669		
Learn about the world of wine	0.786		
Contact exhibitors	0.691		
Entertainment		0.836	**Hedonists and social**
Socialise with colleagues and friends		0.744	
Spend the day out		0.700	
Eigenvalues	2.004	1.880	
% variance explained	28.663	26.861	
% cumulative variance	28.663	55.494	
KMO	0.739		
Prueba de esfericidad de Barlett	Chi-cuadrado = 730.698. Sig < 0.001		
Extraction method: Main component analysis. Rotation method: Equamax with Kaiser			

Source: Own elaboration

land, and to broaden his knowledge on the world of wine. Chronbach's alpha coefficient (0.679) for the different items that make up this motivation dimension reveals that it represents a reliable subscale. The importance of this factor explains in itself 28.6% of the total variance of the motivation matrix. The second extracted factor, called Hedonist and Social Motives, relates to a tourist who conceives the visit as an instrument for sharing his time and his experiences with persons close to his environment, fundamentally spouse, family and/or friends, and to escape from routine. Chronbach's alpha coefficient (0.683) for this subscale also reveals good internal consistency. This factor would explain 26.8% of the total variance of the motivation matrix. The results are in line with the core of the motivational theory of Crompton (1979) which categorises in two large blocks the motives that have a bearing on tourist behaviour: socio-psychological motives, where the trip or the visit is a means for satisfying an individual's or group's needs of a social or psychological type, and cultural motives, in which the satisfaction obtained would be in relation to the attributes of the tourist destination.

The study of the motivations provides bases for establishing segmentation of the Montilla-Moriles Wine Festival as a tourist destination. To accomplish this, a non-hierarchical cluster analysis was conducted with factorial scores of the two factors. Under the criterion of maximising the variance between types and minimising the variance within each type, the best solution that fulfils the criteria is that which establishes three clusters. The characterisation of the clusters from the means of the motivation variables is shown in Table 15.6. The F statistic of the ANOVA allows contrasting that the compared means are not equal, but it does not specify where the detected differences are found. In order to know which mean differs from another, a particular type of contrast was used, called post hoc multiple comparisons or comparisons a posteriori. With the aim of making these comparisons, it cannot be

Table 15.6 Characterisation clusters from motivations for attending the Cordoba Wine Festival

	Clústers	ANOVA			
	1	2	3	ANOVA	
Motivations	Mean	Mean	Mean	F	Sig.
Taste different classes of wine	**4.40**(*)	3.34 (*)	3.07 (*)	98.606	<.001
Taste gastronomic products	**4.30**(*)	2.85 (*)	2.86 (*)	140.981	<.001
Learn about the world of wine	**4.31**(*)	2.71 (*)	2.97(*)	159.494	<.001
Contact exhibitors	**3.77**(*)	**1.73**(*)	**2.55**(*)	185.888	<.001
Entertainment	**4.45**(*)	**4.63**(*)	**2.97**(*)	274.051	<.001
Socialise with colleagues and friends	**4.42**(*)	**4.61**(*)	**2.96**(*)	197.093	<.001
Spend the day out	4.30 (*)	4.22(*)	**2.68**(*)	164.846	<.001

Source: Own elaboration
(*) The values in italic type present significant differences in two of three of the means clusters in the post hoc ANOVA. In order to be able to test for the significant differences between the different means the Games-Howell test was applied

Table 15.7 Robust homogeneity tests of variances and equality of means

Motivations	Homogeneity variances (Levene)		Equality of means (Welch)	
Taste different classes of wine	31.265	<.001	116.907	<.001
Taste gastronomic products	21.022	<.001	171.317	<.001
Learn about the world of wine	13.365	<.001	180.534	<.001
Contact exhibitors	16.034	<.001	202.673	<.001
Entertainment	07.290	<.001	209.248	<.001
Socialise with colleagues and friends	11.439	<.001	151.714	<.001
Spend the day out	03.341	<.005	116.907	<.005

Source: Own elaboration

assumed that the population variances are equal -the critical level associated to Levene's statistic is less than 0.5 for all cases, for which reason the equality of variances is rejected. The F statistic of the ANOVA is based on the fulfilling of two cases: normality and homoscedasticity. Given that it is not possible to assume that the population variances are equal, the Welch statistic was used as an alternative to the F statistic of the ANOVA -Table 15.7. Since the critical level associated to both statistics is less than 0.05, the hypothesis of equality of means can be rejected and it can be concluded that the averages of the motivational variables of the three compared clusters are not equal. In order to contrast the significant differences between the different means, the Games-Howell test was applied.

The first of the clusters presents significant values in nearly all the motivational variables, noting the highest score in the items: tasting different classes of wine, tasting gastronomic products, learning about the culture of wine and contact with exhibitors. Therefore, we have called it the enogastronomic visitor, relating to the factor or first motivational area and to a lesser degree to the second – it is the most numerous cluster, with 288 visitors. The second cluster is integrated by 199 of those surveyed; values with significant differences are observed in the variables of entertainment, socialising with family members and/or friends, and contact with exhibitors. It is characterised by a tourist who plans the visit to break from routine and to take advantage of being with family or friends. We have called this tourist the hedonist and social visitor, and it relates clearly with factor two of the factorial analysis. The third cluster is integrated by 192 visitors, being the least numerous and the one with lowest score in the majority of the variables, without being able to clearly relate it to any of the obtained areas. This cluster could be called visitor with other motivational reasons which the study could not detect. The results provide arguments so that the promoters of the Montilla-Moriles Wine Festival may pay more attention to the hedonist and social motivations, as there is an important segment of visitors who do not seek the singularity of the destination.

15.4.4 Satisfaction with the Wine Tasting

As for the degree of satisfaction with the visit to the wine tasting, the mean, on a Likert 5-point scale, is 4.19. Therefore 40% of the tourists surveyed are very satisfied with the visit, while 45% are satisfied. An association was detected between the degree of satisfaction and the country of origin (Pearson's chi-squared coefficient = 193.456; p = 0.000) and the degree of satisfaction and the level of income (Pearson's chi-squared coefficient = 40.066; p = 0.005).

Having established the groups of tourists, it is basic to analyse the relations that these clusters could have with the satisfaction of the visit (Table 15.8). The results show a quite positive valuation of the experience in the festival by the three segments or groups of identified tourists. With it, the valuation is higher in the first cluster, indicative of the greater relevance of the enogastronomic dimension, for which the satisfaction or experience of the visit seems to increase as this dimension increases. The significant mean of the second cluster reveals that the hedonist-social dimension is also a significant variable, the higher the desire of the tourist to share time with family and friends and to free himself from the tensions of daily life, the greater is his satisfaction. The third cluster seems to indicate that those visitors who show motivational reasons other than the identified dimensions value to a lesser degree their experience in the festival. The robustness tests on the means of the satisfaction variable show that the averages of the satisfaction variable in the three compared clusters are not equal (Table 15.9).

Table 15.8 Characterisation cluster from satisfaction of the visit

Degree of satisfaction of the visit	**Clúster de pertenencia**			**ANOVA**	
	1	**2**	**3**		
	Mean	**Mean**	**Mean**	**F**	**Sig.**
	4.44(*)	**4.13**(*)	**3.89**(*)	26.504	<.001

Source: Own elaboration
(*) The values in italic type present significant differences in two of three of the means clusters in the post hoc ANOVA. In order to be able to test for the significant differences between the different means the Games-Howell test was applied

Table 15.9 Robust homogeneity tests of variances and equality of means

Degree of satisfaction of the visit	Homogeneity variances (Levene)		Equality of means (Welch)	
	17.551	<.001	24.691	<.001

Source: Own elaboration

15.5 Conclusion

The heterogeneity of the preferences of consumers makes it necessary to go into depth in the knowledge of the reasons that may affect their election processes. In recent years wine and food festivals have become a vehicle for the promotion of agricultural products as well as the tourist destination. In this regard, different geographic areas in Spain present festivals in order to make their products known and, at the same time, to reinforce their importance in the tourist destinations, all related to the enograstronomic culture. In this chapter, an analysis is presented of the sociodemographic profile and of the motivation of the tourist who visits one of the most consolidated enogastronomic festivals that exists in Spain, the Montilla-Moriles Wine Tasting, which is held each year in the city of Cordoba and where both residents and visitors meet to get to know the native agricultural products of the area. The principal results of the research point to the high educational level; they are persons under 40 years of age, a positive aspect that reinforces the increasingly greater introduction of this type of wine in this population bracket. The results of the investigation show evidence on the diversity of reasons for which the visitors opt for attending a festival when choosing a certain tourist destination.

The heterogeneity in the preferences of the consumers makes it necessary to go into depth in knowing the reasons that might influence their processes of choosing to attend a festival. In this paper, we show the evidence on the diversity of reasons by which the visitors opt for the festival as a tourist destination. Based on them, two clear motivational dimensions have been identified in visiting the 31st edition of the Montilla-Moriles Wine Festival; the first, which we have call enogastronomic, which makes up 42.5% of the sample, includes the motivations clearly identify a tourist with the wine culture, that is, an enological tourist. The other motivational dimension, called hedonist-social, and which represents 29.3% of the sample, encompasses the tourists who attend for entertainment and social type motives. The third segment of tourists, 28.2% of the sample, have motivational reasons not clearly identified, which we call the visitor with other motivational reasons.

The results obtained are, with regard to the degree of satisfaction, generally high, although there are significant differences between the identified tourist segments, being clearly linked to the motivations of the visit. The highest degree of satisfaction, by far, corresponds to tourists that have an enogastronomic interest. The satisfaction decreases slightly, although it continues being high, in those tourists that basically seek entertainment, with the lowest degree for those that have no defined motivations for attending the festival.

The principal practical application of this research is to contribute to understanding the reasons for which the tourists participate in this type of festival with the purpose of conceiving tourist and cultural products, related to agriculture, that better satisfy the needs of the tourists and which, at the same time, is compatible with sustainable management.

The main limitation of this research is based on the scarcity of data existing with regards to the relationship between this wine festival and the characteristics of the attending tourists, as the researchers did not have prior information on the type of traveller that visits this festival, not even having data of a quantitative type. And precisely we consider that this limitation is one of the great contributions that this research provides.

As future research lines in the Montilla-Moriles Wine Tasting, two work lines are recommended: the first, to carry out a study of the tourists as well as the residents, to compare the valuations and motivations of both groups regarding the wine festival, whose conclusions allow the different public administrations and private companies that work in the field of tourism and in the promotion of the Denomination of Origen Montilla-Moriles to have greater awareness of the types of visitors, their motivations and their perceptions and, above all, to preserve and reinforce the Montilla-Moriles Wine Tasting; second, we recommend going into depth in the motivation-satisfaction binomial according to the place of origin of the tourist and his socioeconomic characteristics.

References

Baker, D. A., & Crompton, J. L. (2000). Quality, satisfaction and behavioral intentions. *Annals of Tourism Research, 27*(3), 785–804. https://doi.org/10.1016/S0160-7383(99)00108-5.

Carmichael, B. A. (2005). Understanding the wine tourism experience for winery visitors in the Niagara region, Ontario, Canada. *Tourism Geographies, 7*(2), 185–204. https://doi.org/10.10180/14616680500072414.

Çela, A., Knowles-Lankford, J., & Lankford, S. (2007). Local food festivals in Northeast Iowa communities: A visitor and economic impact study. *Managing Leisure, 12*(2–3), 171–186. https://doi.org/10.1080/13606710701339470.

Charters, S., & Ali-Knight, J. (2002). Who is the wine tourist? *Tourism Management, 23*, 311–319. https://doi.org/10.1016/S0261-5177(01)00079-6.

Crompton, J. L. (1979). Motivations for pleasure vacation. *Annals of Tourism Research, 1*(6), 336–344.

Dawson, H., Homes, M., Jacob, H., & Wade, R. I. (2011). Wine tourism: Winery visitation in the wine appellations of Ontario. *Journal of Vacation Marketing, 17*(3), 237–246.

Devesa, M., Laguna, M., & Palacios, A. (2010). The role of motivation in visitor satisfaction: Empirical evidence in rural tourism. *Tourism Management, 31*(4), 547–552. https://doi.org/10.1016/j.tourman.2009.06.006.

Finn, M., Walton, M., & Elliott-White, M. (2000). *Tourism and leisure research methods: Data collection, analysis and interpretation*. Harlow: Pearson Education.

Gagić, S. M., Tešanović, D. V., Ivokoz-Džigurski, A. C., Pivac, T. D., & Jovičić, A. D. (2013). Motives and attitudes of food and drink festival visitors: A case study of Serbia. *Journal of Food, Agriculture & Environment, 11*(1), 1055–1059.

Getz, D. (2000). *Explore wine tourism, management, development and destinations*. New York: Cognizant Communication Corporation.

Getz, D., & Brown, G. (2006). Critical success factors for wine tourism regions: A demand analysis. *Tourism Management, 27*(1), 146–158. https://doi.org/10.1016/j.tourman.2004.08.002.

Hall, C. M., Sharples, L., Camourne, B., & Macionis, N. (2000). *Wine tourism around the world: Development, management and markets*. Oxford: Elsevier.

Hall, C. M., Sharples, L., Mitchell, R., Macionis, N., & Cambourne, B. (2003). *Food tourism around the World*. Oxford: Butterworth-Heinemann.

Henderson, J. C. (2009). Food tourism reviewed. *British Food Journal, 111*(4), 317–326. https://doi.org/10.1108/00070700910951470.

Henderson, J. C. (2014). Food and culture: In search of a Singapore cuisine. *British Food Journal, 116*(6), 904–917. https://doi.org/10.1108/BFJ-12-2012-0291.

Hillel, D., Belhassen, Y., & Shani, A. (2013). What makes a gastronomic destination attractive? Evidence from the Israeli Negev. *Tourism Management, 36*, 200–209. https://doi.org/10.1016/j.tourman.2012.12.006.

Hollows, J., Jones, S., Taylor, B., & Dowthwaite, K. (2014). Making sense of urban food festivals: Cultural regeneration, disorder and hospitable cities. *Journal of Policy Research in Tourism, Leisure and Events, 6*(1), 1–14. https://doi.org/10.1080/19407963.2013.774406.

Ignatov, E., & Smith, S. (2006). Segmenting Canadian culinary tourists. *Current Issues in Tourism, 9*(3), 235–255.

Kim, Y. H., Duncan, J., & Chung, B. W. (2015). Involvement, satisfaction, perceived value, and revisit intention: A case study of a food festival. *Journal of Culinary Science & Technology, 13*(2), 133–158. https://doi.org/10.1080/15428052.2014.952482.

Lee, I., & Arcodia, C. (2011). The role of regional food festivals for destination branding. *International Journal of Tourism Research, 13*(4), 355–367. https://doi.org/10.1002/jtr.852.

Lee, C., Lee, Y., & Wicks, B. E. (2004). Segmentation of festival motivation by nationality and satisfaction. *Tourism Management, 25*(1), 61–70. https://doi.org/10.1016/S0261-5177(03)00060-8.

Mak, A. H. N., Lumbers, M., & Eves, A. (2012). Globalisation and food consumption in tourism. *Annals of Tourism Research, 39*(1), 171–196. https://doi.org/10.1016/j.annals.2011.05.010.

Mitchell, R., & Hall, C. M. (2006). Wine tourism research: The state of play. *Tourism Review International, 9*(4), 307–332.

Nunnally, J. C., & Bernstein, I. H. (1994). *Psychometric theory*. New York: McGraw-Hill.

Riley, M. (2005). Food and beverage management: A review of change. *International Journal of Contemporary Hospitality Management, 17*(1), 88–93. https://doi.org/10.1108/09566110510577707.

Smith, S., & Costello, C. (2009). Segmenting visitors to a culinary event: Motivations, travel behavior, and expenditures. *Journal of Hospitality Marketing & Management, 18*, 44–67. https://doi.org/10.1080/19368620801989022.

Tikkanen, I. (2007). Maslow's hierarchy and food tourism in Finland: Five cases. *British Food Journal, 109*(9), 721–734. https://doi.org/10.1108/00070700710780698.

Wan, Y. K. P., & Chan, S. H. J. (2013). Factors that affect the levels of tourists' satisfaction and loyalty towards food festivals: A case study of Macau. *International Journal of Tourism Research, 15*(3), 226–240. https://doi.org/10.1002/jtr.1863.

Wu, H. C., Wong, J. W. C., & Cheng, C. C. (2014). An empirical study of behavioral intentions in the food festival: The case of Macau. *Asia Pacific Journal of Tourism Research, 19*(11), 1278–1305. https://doi.org/10.1080/10941665.2013.844182.

Yoon, Y. S., Lee, J. S., & Lee, C. K. (2010). Measuring festival quality and value affecting visitors' satisfaction and loyalty using a structural approach. *International Journal of Hospitality Management, 29*(2), 335–342. https://doi.org/10.1016/j.ijhm.2009.10.002.

Yuan, J., & Jang, S. (2008). The effects of quality and satisfaction on awareness and behavioral intentions: Exploring the role of a wine festival. *Journal of Travel Research, 46*(3), 279–288.

Part IV
Cases Studies: From Theory to Practice on Quality of Life in Tourism

Chapter 16
Value for Time: Slowness, a Positive Way of Performing Tourism

Paola de Salvo, Viviana Calzati, and Stefano Soglia

Abstract Slowness involves a redefinition of existing touristic operations which are increasingly influenced by the tourist's heightened sense of responsibility towards the environment and the search for a quality experience (Dickinson JE, Les Lumsdon: Slow travel and tourism. Earthscan, London, 2010, Fullagar S, Markwell K, Wilson E: Slow tourism. Experience and mobilities. Channel View Publications, Bristol, 2012). The new cultural and behavioral model of slowness implies a fundamental change in the concept of the consumption of goods and services, with the concept of lifestyle being characterized by commitment, a strong sense of responsibility and the search for wellbeing in both life and work. The slow philosophy should not be interpreted as a temporary phenomenon, but rather as a life philosophy and a worldwide social movement that in recent years has characterized many socio-economic elements in local communities (Parkins W, Craig G: Slow living. Berg, Oxford, 2006). The characterizing theme of the paper is that QoL, collective well-being, cultural enrichment and slowness could become competitive factors in local development policies with particular reference to minor territories. The aim of the present work is to analyse how some minor areas, which some studies have defined as "slow territories," (Lancerini E: Territorio 34:9–15, 2005; Lanzani A: Territorio 34:19–36, 2005; Calzati V: Territori lenti: nuove traiettorie di sviluppo. In: Nocifora, E, de Salvo P, Calzati (eds), Territori lenti e turismo di qualità, prospettive innovative per lo sviluppo di un turismo sostenibile. Franco Angeli, Milano, pp 62–72, 2011; Calzati V, de Salvo P: Slow tourism: a new concept of sustainability, consumption and quality of life. In M. Clancy (ed), Slow tourism, food and

---

P. de Salvo
University of Perugia, Perugia, Italy
e-mail: paola.desalvo@unipg.it

V. Calzati
University of Bologna, Bologna, Italy
e-mail: viviana.calzati@unipv.it

S. Soglia (✉)
University of Siena, Siena, Italy
e-mail: info@stefanosoglia.info

A. M. Campón-Cerro et al. (eds.), *Best Practices in Hospitality and Tourism Marketing and Management*, Applying Quality of Life Research,
https://doi.org/10.1007/978-3-319-91692-7_16

cities: pace and the search for the good life. Routledge, London, 2012), are identifiable as locations able to promote a tourism of diversified typologies which are difficult to standardise (Savoja L: Turismo lento e turisti responsabili. Verso una nuova concezione di consume. In: Nocifora P, de Salvo E, Calzati V (eds), Territori lenti e turismo di qualità. Prospettive innovative per lo sviluppo di un turismo sostenibile. Franco Angeli, Milano, pp 86–99, 2011) in line with the new tendencies of slow tourism. In fact, such territories are characterized by a high quality of life, an elevated attention to the environment and landscape, to art and quality local products as well as offering a hospitable local community. These qualities of such zones appear to indicate that they are more capable, than other areas, of instigating itineraries orientated to achieving touristic development of a high quality and a sustainable nature. The paper presents a project of local touristic development carried out in Italy, in the Umbrian-Marche Apennine territory, with particular reference to *Value for Time* certification as applied to various accommodation structures in the territory. *Value for Time* identifies an area and the structures present in it, distinguishing them from their competitors and is a synthesis of objective values, together with cognitive and emotional elements with reference to the territory. *Value for Time certification* considers four main areas: People, Administration, Sustainability and Territory and aims to establish a reputation, offering added value to all components of the area and enhancing its cultural, social and economic identity.

Keywords QBO · Slow tourism · Quality of life · Slowness and territory

16.1 Quality of Life and Slow Tourism

In the course of the last 10 years, research on the Quality of Life (shown below as QoL) has been asserted as an emerging theme in the study of social, behavioral, environmental and political sciences. QoL is considered to be the emanation of a movement in social indicators, whose origins are to be found in the economic and sociological environments. These movements are based on the consideration that traditional economic indicators (GDP and GNP etc.…) do not take into account, as forms of wellbeing, values such as culture, creativity, life satisfaction and happiness, therefore expressing a measure which is quite inadequate in the identification of authentic wellbeing (Layard 2005; Sirgy 2002). The growth of material wealth measured exclusively with monetary indicators penalizes other forms of social richness (quality of life, good relationships, environmental quality, the democratic nature of institutions), highlighting that the wealth produced by economic systems cannot be reduced to only goods and services (Latouche 2007).

Recently, an intense debate has developed on the theme of wellbeing and the quality of life which, as well as giving birth to a new branch of economics ("happiness economics"), has also seen the contribution of sociologists (Baumann 2002; Veenhoven et al. 1993) and psychologists (Argyle 1987; Kahneman et al. 2003) who have established the foundations of Hedonistic Psychology.

It must be stressed that, on the one hand, the interchangeable terms QoL and wellbeing are often used on the part of researchers who are involved in these thematic fields and, on the other, that no subjective or objective dimension of these terms actually exists.

For example, when researchers refer to a QoL or wellbeing, they tend to elude to an objective dimension. If the reference is to QoL and collective wellbeing, the indicators used for economic wellbeing will be, for example, the family income, for leisure time wellbeing the indicator will be the number of parks, for environmental wellbeing the level of CO2 emissions and for the wellbeing associated with health it will be life expectancy.

However, if the researchers are referring to a subjective aspect of QoL or wellbeing, they use specific psychological constructs of subjective wellbeing, such as, happiness, life satisfaction, perceived QoL and hedonistic wellbeing (Uysal et al. 2016). In fact, in the literature, numerous studies also demonstrate the importance of the identification and quantification of subjective indicators of wellbeing and the overall subjective nature of the perception of wellbeing generally (Biswas-Diener and Diener 2006; Diener and Suh 1997; Wilkinson and Marmot 2003). In recent years, the number of studies related to the quality of life and the subjective perception of wellbeing have given rise to two different theoretical currents.

The first, attributable to the hedonistic perspective, analyzes the dimension of pleasure, intended as personal wellbeing (Kahneman et al. 1999) and refers principally to emotional dimensions and to life satisfaction. The second approach is defined as eudemonic (Ryan and Deci 2001) which includes not only individual satisfaction but also the pathway of development towards integration into the surrounding environment (Nussbaum and Sen 1993). The term is often considered to be similar to "happiness", but its semantic field is much broader: this implies a process of interaction between the wellbeing of the individual and that of the collective, in such a way that individual happiness is realized in the social environment. In the eudemonic approach, wellbeing does not necessarily coincide with pleasure, but it underlines the importance of the human capacity to achieve objectives that are relevant to the individual and to society, the enhancement of these capacities and the freedom of the individual, of social responsibilities and the role of interpersonal relationships that favor both the individual and the community. It is highlighted that in the investigation of wellbeing, the principal difficulty of research is "the absence of a relationship, or in the better cases, of a weak relationship, between its subjective and objective dimensions" (Kahn and Juster 2002, p. 629).

In this context, the value of tourism has also started concentrating more on non-economic indicators such as QoL, wellbeing and sustainability (Uysal et al. 2012). In fact, the influence and the incision tourism can have in facilitating and supporting some of the political imperatives related to QoL, for example, sustainability, the value of community heritage and local culture as well as the protection and safeguarding of cultural and natural resources is ever more evident.

New empirical studies and research have attempted to connect the behavior of the tourist to other life settings and of individual experiences to investigate in a more thorough way the consequences of touristic activity on others' lives (Sirgy 2010;

Uysal et al. 2012). Despite researchers' attention initially being given to the motivation and the satisfaction of the tourist, more recently their interest has been principally orientated to understanding the effects that touristic experiences have on the psychological states of the tourist (Dann 2012; Pearce and Lee 2005). Past studies were limited investigation to the possible connections between tourism and happiness, between subjective wellbeing and QoL and the factors that influence the relationship between tourism and QoL (Dolnicar et al. 2012). The positive effects of activities realized during leisure time have been more widely investigated (Adams et al. 2011; Kelley-Gillespie 2009; Iwasaki 2002, 2007; Iso-Ahola and Park 1996).

Effectively, the time dedicated to vacations proves to be significantly correlated to quality of life and a heightened sense of subjective wellbeing (Dolnicar et al. 2012, 2013; McCabe et al. 2010; Gilbert and Abdullah 2004; McConkey and Adams 2000; Hazel 2005; Neal et al. 2004). It is therefore evident that leisure time can be considered to be a long-term comprehensive experience which determines positive behavior towards life generally.

In this context, the implementation of slow tourism practices constitutes an ulterior opportunity to guarantee people's wellbeing. This bond is also indicated in the Report Stiglitz et al. (2009) where, in the attempt to define different dimensions of social wellbeing, the strong relationship to leisure time is obvious.

16.2 Slow Tourism: Theoretical Approaches

Numerous studies have attempted to define slow tourism by individualizing its principles, ideas and behaviors (Babou and Callot 2009; Blanco 2011; Conway and Timms 2010; Di Clemente et al. 2015; Dickinson et al. 2010; Dickinson and Lumsdon 2010; Lumsdon and McGrath 2011; Matos 2004; Oh et al. 2016; Savoja 2011), although in the scientific literature one unified and commonly shared definition still does not exist.

However, the various attempts at a conceptual systemization of slow tourism phenomenon do present common recurring conceptual areas, even though with various differentiated elements, which the authors summarize into three dimensions: sustainability and environment, modality and experience (Table 16.1).

Table 16.1 The dimensions of slow tourism based on a review of the literature

Dimension	Literature
Sustainability/ environment	Blanco (2011), Babou and Callot (2009), Conway and Timms (2010, 2012), Dickinson and Lumsdon (2010), Lumsdon and Mcgrath (2011), Matos (2004), Savoja (2011), and UNWTO (2012)
Modality	Babou and Callot (2009) and Lumsdon and McGrath (2011)
Experience	Gardner (2009), Heitmann et al. (2011), Lumsdon and McGrath (2011), Nocifora (2011), and Zago (2012)

Source: Calzati and de Salvo (2017)

With reference to the dimension of sustainability and environment Conway and Timms (2010) connect slow tourism to the sustainability of development of Campbell (1996) in which in the noted triangle of sustainability three elements are identified: environment, economy and equity. The same authors underline how the objectives of slow tourism can be similar to other alternative practices to mainstream tourism, such as ecotourism, responsible tourism and community tourism (Conway and Timms 2012).

Blanco (2011) also identifies slow tourism, as a practical touristic alternative to traditional tourism, implicating and requiring responsibility on the behalf of all stakeholders in the tourist market determining a significant change in their behaviors both in the economic field as well as in the cultural realm. In the same way, UNWTO (2012, 24) affirms that "Slow tourism allows a different set of exchanges and interactions from those available in the hurried contexts of mainstream tourism, offering economic benefits to the host and cultural benefits to the tourist".

Attention is drawn to how, at a fundamental level, both slow tourism and other forms of alternative tourism must define development initiatives in which sustainability is implicit in their practices. In the past, Matos (2004) already asserted the importance of sustainable development as one of the pillars of slow tourism. The role of sustainability in slow tourism was investigated by Savoja (2011, 99) who defines "slow tourism as a quality touristic form if it satisfies, not only tourists, but all the stakeholders involved, through the appeal to selective forms of limiting consumption as occurs in all recognizable forms of sustainable tourism". It also emerges how slowness in tourism corresponds to forms of limitation of consumption, limitations which are evident in the axiom the author refers to as "do fewer things but do them well" (Savoja 2011, 100). From Savoja's studies it is highlighted how slow tourists are amongst the most capable of evaluating how to bear imposed limitations and are the most convinced by the importance of the search for quality in experiences.

In this context, the question of touristic sustainability, which Savoja (2011) defines as the "required capacity", also comes to light in contrast to the well-known description of the "carrying capacity", which slow tourism represents as sustainable but unsatisfactory to tourists.

In the development of a conceptual framework for slow travel Lumsdon and McGrath (2011) identify four cornerstones: slowness and the value of time, the destination and on-site activities, the means of transport and the voyage experience and the environmental ethic. The authors indicate the importance of the environmental ethic, but also slowness and the experience, as the elements which permit the conception of a journey in an alternative manner.

In fact, the slow tourist is defined as a hard or soft traveler based on the importance given to the responsibility/sensitivity to environmental features in the organization and planning of the journey; these typologies do not constitute two distinct characteristics but rather the extremes of a continuum. (Dickinson et al. 2010). In fact, the bond between tourism and slowness requires a redefinition of the practices and the habits of the actual tourists, which are ever more influenced by a new sense of the environmental responsibility of the traveler (Babou and Callot 2009).

With reference to the aspect of the means of transport in the relationship between tourism and slowness, the studies of Babou and Callot (2009) highlight how a slow tourist chooses mainly activities, destinations and forms of transport which permit them to limit the impact of the journey on society and on the environment. As already pointed out, Lumsdon and McGrath (2011) also underline the importance of the means of transport considering it to be one of the four cornerstones of slow travel.

Finally, experience constitutes a further dimension through which one can understand slow tourism. Gardner (2009) sustains that the slow tourist represents one of the frames of mind of the traveler who attempts to utilize all the time necessary to discover the landscape and create relationships with the local community. Nocifora (2011) also defines slow tourism as touristic practice in which the scheduling of activities is more relaxed in order to facilitate the knowing/living/visiting of new locations through the construction of authentic relationships, giving value to the local space and rediscovering the relationship with others through mutual exchange. The slow tourist represents a possible answer to the needs of the post-contemporary tourist.

Zago (2012) considers that in order to be considered as such, a slow tourism experience must satisfy contemporarily six dimensions: relationship, authenticity, sustainability, time, slowness and emotion which, for the author, constitute the so called "castle" model. Finally, Heitmann et al. (2011) sustains the significant principle of slow tourism is attributable to a different idea of the journey which is not characterized by the number and quantity of experiences but in the living of a few experiences of quality. Slow tourism for Heitmann is a touristic practice which respects local cultures, history, environment and the values of social responsibility valorizing diversity and the relationship between people (tourists with other tourists and with the local community).

16.3 Slowness and Territory

The slow philosophy revolution also brings with it the opportunity to construct a slow society, that is, a society which is more attentive to the quality of life, to the ethics of responsibility and the values of solidarity. The theme of slowness is accompanied by various lifestyles, responsible consumption and a new idea of wellbeing, which may lead to the affirmation of a new humanism for a more supportive society. A new manner to conceive of the consumption of goods and services and the quality of life, where commitment, a strong sense of responsibility and the research for wellbeing in life and in the workplace, makes slowness a new behavioral cultural model (Calzati 2016).

Other researchers have demonstrated that in Western society people have begun to exchange material values in favor of a new life style characterized by more time, less stress and a better balance in daily life (Schor 1998; Hamilton 2003). In fact, "the beauty of the slow devolution is the counter-punch it could, in the long term, inflict on the culture of speed" (Osbaldiston 2013, 6). Hidden behind the concept of slowness is a desire to take back the rhythms, the places, the tastes and the emotions that highlight and reinforce the quality and the identity of a territory. The valorization of local identity and the constant search for quality can become the instruments to contain the phenomenon of globalization, which presents places which are changing rapidly and seem to be always less able to conserve their distinctive qualities (Knox 2005). Slowness does not refer merely to stillness (Bissell and Fuller 2011) but rather the creation of alternative locations, times, social contexts and experiences to counter the expectations of the daily life typical of fast, advanced, capitalistic society (Osbaldiston 2013; Presenza et al. 2015). The cittaslow movement: opportunities and challenges for the governance of tourism destinations. In this context, relevance is given to the responsibility and awareness of the individual which becomes collective, creating actual, significant relationships between people, culture, work, food and new touristic consumption (de Salvo 2011; Manella et al. 2017). In fact, in the growing relationship between tourism and slowness, actual touristic practices are increasingly influenced by a new sense of environmental responsibility on behalf of the tourist and in the search for experiences.

This new relationship between tourism and slowness establishes slow tourism as a touristic practice orientated to oppose the negative influences of popular mass tourism (de Salvo et al. 2013). This last phenomenon is characterized by the extensive development of structures and infrastructures motivated by a dominance of what are predominately economic interests, by a limited protection of environmental and social rights, by the dominance of highly seasonal use and the absence of shared responsibility in the benefits derived from the tourism practiced (Weaver 2000). Hence, slow tourism in port-modern culture is able to endorse the "genius loci", the spirit of place, to establish active relationships with the local community promoting slower rhythms of life and the slower consumption of the touristic product within a vision of real, and not presumed, sustainability (Hall 2009, 2010), also orientated towards the battle against the loss of the uniqueness of location (Woehler 2004).

The connection, therefore, between slow tourism, the sustainability of tourism and the characteristics of the supply of touristic services in a territory is quite evident. In fact, some territories have attempted to apply principles of sustainability or de-growth by orientating their development towards themes which address subjective wellbeing, the quality of life of the community, the valorization of territorial identity and responsible tourism (Beeton 2006). In this new scenario, some territories seem to be more adapted to slowness than others offering a tourism of a nonconformist quality, which is self-directed, self-motivated and difficult to standardize (Savoja 2011).

The identity, distinctiveness and specificity of such territories are difficult elements to reproduce elsewhere, capable of characterizing these areas and of activating trajectories of local development able to respond to the real demand for touristic consumption and for vacations which can be translated into an actual, unique style of consumption. These territories, described as "slow" (Lancerini 2005; Lanzani 2005; Beeton 2006; Calzati 2011) have a high quality of life, in their less frenetic rhythm of life, in their harmonic relationship between tradition and innovation, in the care for their urban fabric and safeguarding of the environment providing the incentives for an indisputable and recognizable touristic value.

Moreover, these locations are characterized by a strong local identity, the presence of typical local products of quality, a local hosting community and finally a model of hospitality composed of structures integrated into the local landscape. It is evident how "slow" territories can be places capable of achieving economic growth, social cohesion and environmental protection through the activation of pathways of sustainability able to define plausible, new courses for touristic development, through the assertion of alternative forms of tourism.

In conclusion, the theme of quality of life and quality of a territory and of its tourism is closely linked to the theme of slowness, a feature which already seems to have entered into the life style of post-modern society and to be a new challenge for the politics of future territorial development.

16.4 Results of the "District of Slowness: Methodology for the Certification of Slow Tourism in the Umbrian-Marche Apennine district" Project

The case study presents the results of the "District of Slowness: methodology for the certification of slow tourism in the Umbrian-Marche Apennine district" project released in Italy by the Cultural Association for the Development of the Umbrian-Marche Apennines,[1] in partnership with local stakeholders. The territory under investigation with its hamlets rich with local history, the cultural, environmental and gastronomic heritage is characterized as being a place of "the good life", for both the local community and for tourists. In consistency with that already presented, the Umbrian-Marche Apennines area is considered a "slow" minor territory characterized by a low demographic density and a rural context in which the historical-artistic patrimony is not well known but is of significant quality. The hospitality model which characterizes this area is composed of structures integrated into the local landscape (bed and breakfast, farm stays, holiday homes) and the

[1] The association "proposes to valorize, promote and develop, at both national and international level, the Umbrian-Marche Apennine territory, with particular attention being given to culture, craft activities, the sport and nature sectors, and to touristic and territorial development in the Provinces of Ancona, Pesaro-Urbino and Perugia and in the mountainous border zone of the Provincia di Macerata. In particular, cultural activities, in all their various manifestations, are called upon to present the best skills of the District's territory and to draw attention to the area's predicament, in order to relaunch the economy of the Umbrian-Marche mountain zone, utilizing every type of initiative that brings innovation, creativity and renovation to both its material and immaterial heritage, which is particularly rich. In order to achieve this result, the Association proposes to incentivize those touristic activities orientated towards so-called "slow tourism" which marries the reception of its locations to the relationship between visitor and host". (art. 2 Statute of the Association)

cultural activities are orientated to a valorization of local agro-food products, and local history and identity.

Involving 30 public institutions which subscribed to the Association (18 councils from the Marche Region and 10 from Umbria, together with two Comunità Montane from the Marche) and 25 tourist sector businesses (hotels, farm stays and other receptive structures, other than accommodation, restaurants), the objective of the project was to identify a certification method for slow tourism defined as "Value for Time", capable of attributing a "slow classification" to the touristic services both singular, and aggregated, from experiences through to events.

The slow classification was constructed with reference to four macro valuation areas and relative indicators to which points would be assigned that contribute to a final evaluation, based on which is attributed the certification. It is necessary to point out that the system of certification proposed is a process orientated to manage and improve the touristic services and the hospitality offered in a particular territory to the end of defining a touristic product capable of attracting the request for sustainable, slow, identifiable tourism of elevated quality.

16.4.1 P.A.S.T. Methodology

The "District of Slowness: methodology for the certification of slow tourism in the Umbrian-Marche Apennine district" project foresaw the elaboration of the methodology defined as PAST finalized to evaluating the class of slowness in the receptive structures in the territory. Twenty five structures were visited with the purpose of issuing Value for Time certificates, 6 in the province of Perugia (Gubbio and Parco del Monte Cucco zones) and the remaining in the hinterland of the Marche region.

From a synthesis of the different elements which can characterize a touristic service such as sustainability, authenticity and the cultural heritage of the territory, four macro valuation areas were defined. For each macro-area indicators were identified to which points were assigned which contributed to a final evaluation based on which is attributed the definitive certification of the Value for Time project. The four macro-areas are: People, Administration, Sustainability and Territory, summed up in the PAST acronym.

1. **People**: evaluates the contact with the local people, the degree of experientiality and the personalization of the activity
2. **Administration**: evaluates public politics; the environmental parameters; the scenic landscape context with respect to the local council area's identity
3. **Sustainability**: evaluates environmental, social and economic sustainability
4. **Territory**: evaluates the typology and the proposed touristic content, their coherence with local traditions, as well as the authenticity of the touristic experience (Fig. 16.1)

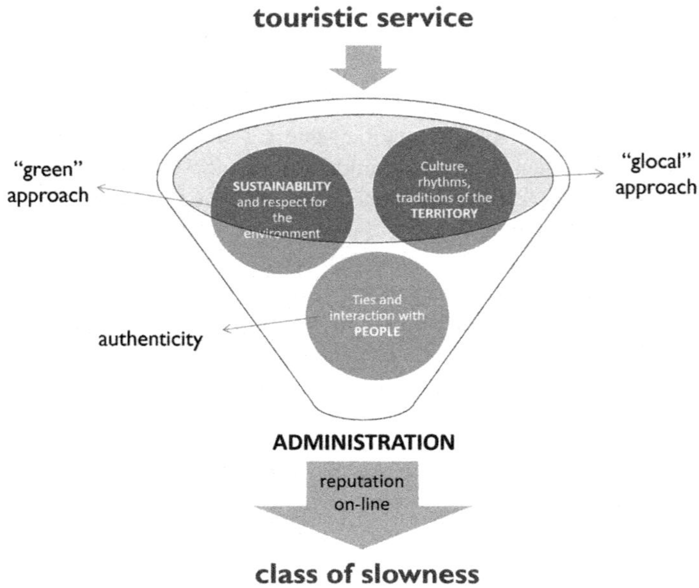

Fig. 16.1 Scheme of the PAST methodological process for the definition of the "class of slowness". (Source: Cultural Association for the Development of the Umbrian-Marche Apennines)

The four macro-areas identify the actual characters of the "slow" supply and demand and where the relative indicators attempt to evaluate and measure the degree of slowness in a structure and a touristic service.

The innovative element of this certification consists in the ability to make reference to a single component of the touristic offer of a territory, such as:

- Single service (e.g. receptive structure, restaurant, transport carrier etc.)
- Touristic service consortium (e.g. Package, card etc.) and a touristic experience (e.g. course, guided tour, etc.)
- Event (e.g. festival, competition, fair etc.)

The PAST methodology has actually been applied only to singular services, in particular to accommodation structures, but in the near future the experimental launch for its application also to combined touristic services, to experiences and to events will be carried out. The PAST method envisages a certification for increasing classes from C to A based on attributed points and also provides for periodic monitoring of the parameters in order to assign a revised valuation and classification.

The PAST methodology, by starting with an analysis of the parameters used for other forms of certification assigned, for example, by the DEKRA certification company and by Slow tourism theoretical models, such as CASTLE theorised by Zago (2012), has envisaged the selection of 41 indicators.

In the methodology adopted, after having identified the four macro-areas, an initial selection of indicators and the assignment of a points scale from 1 to 5 or from 1 to 3 for each indicator were established. This first check list was then tested on a group of four touristic structures and successively a definitive version was drawn up, officially recognized by the Brand Management Commitee and registered in the regulations.

With reference to the first marco-area which is People, 11 indicators have been identified and relative point assignment indicated (Table 16.2).

Ten indicators have been identified with reference to the second macro-area Administration, (Table 16.3).

In reference to the third marco-area which is Sustainability nine indicators were selected (Table 16.4).

Finally, 11 indicators have been identified with reference to the fourth marco-area, Territory (Table 16.5).

Apart from these 41 indicators, two further variables were identified which assign a valuation from clients based on the perception of the quality of the structure and of the service.

1. **Type of structure**: types of accommodation have been classified on a decreasing decimal scale, from the "slowest" being assigned 10 points, such as"albergo diffuso", to the fastest such as a hotel chain with a value of 0. With reference to dining facilities a decreasing scale of points from 1 to 5 have been ascribed, where the slow structure, with 5 points, offer the experience of "cooking with me" while a fast food restaurant is given the minimum score of 1 point (Table 16.6)

2. **On-line reputation**: value from 1 to 10 for accommodation structures and from 1 to 5 for restaurant activities, defined on the basis of the Travel Appeal Index,[2] whose objective-indicator is the synthesis of all the opinions expressed about the touristic activity on blogs, social networks and *rating* sites (e.g., Trip Advisor, Holiday Check, booking.com etc.).

As a corrective factor to the *rating* assigned periodically by the expert evaluators of the 41 factors described above, intervention is also made by "web 3.0", which through the judgements assigned by clients over a long period of time, allows a broader vision of the actual service supplied and that will tend increasingly to award

[2] TAI – Travel Appeal Index, of the Italian Company Travel Appeal (www.travelappeal.com), expresses in terms of a percentage, the on-line reputation of an accommodation structure or restaurant activity. The analysis carried out by Travel Appeal on an annual basis, to the ends of identifying the on-line reputation score has highlighted that, while the TAI over-all score of the thousands of structures analyzed in the Marche and Umbria Regions is 60.63%, the TAI score of the 23 accommodation structures (6 hotels and 16 other accommodation types) which requested slow tourism certification proved to be 50.85% (approximately 0.8% less than the regional average). It should be noted that the TAI score is expressed as a %. To make enable the calculation into the PAST methodology, the TAI scores for accommodation were transformed into decimal values, for the TAI for accommodation (TAI x 100, rounding to 0 decimal numbers), while for dining facilities the scores were converted to the 5 point scale. (TAI x 20, rounding to 0 decimal numbers)

Table 16.2 People macro-area: indicators and points

Macro-area		Indicators	Points
PEOPLE contact with local people; degree of experiential engagement; personalisation of activities and events	1.1	Organization for guests of initiatives in the territory (e.g. visits to craftspeople, hikes and excursions, farm visits and fruition of the territory)	5 high – 0 none
	1.2	Active participation of guests in activities and events organized by the actual structure (e.g. courses, workshops etc.)	From 0 to 5
	1.3	Type of management (family management/independent structure or chain)	3 for family management – 0 for chain activities
	1.4	Minimum number of participants required for an activity/experience.	5 if low – 0 for groups larger than 50
	1.5	Personalization of activities and service procedures (e.g. pillows, food, timetables etc.) already programmable and not as a response to an explicit/impromptu request	From 0 to 5
	1.6	Vacation programs (possible visits and activities) differentiated for the typology of tourist (e.g. children, sports, business, women, handicapped etc.)	1 point for every target group offered – up to a max of 3
	1.7	Sensorial installations and instruments (lighting, music, colors, perfumes, etc.)	From 0 to 3
	1.8	Presence of areas (internal or external) dedicated to: Meditation, reading, socialization, workshops	1 point for every specifically dedicated area – up to a max. of 4
	1.9	Capacity to transmit pleasant sensations, storytelling, reference to the territory, personality	From 0 to 6
	1.10	Motivated, independent, well-prepared, empathetic staff	From 0 to 5
	1.11	Employment of local workers and type of employment contract	3 i fall staff are local on permanent contracts or are owners
Total score			45

Source:Our own elaboration

Table 16.3 Administration macro-area: indicators and points

Macroarea		Indicators	Points
ADMISTRATION Public politics; environmental parameters; contextural landscape in respect to the local identity	2.1	Operations for the improvement of environmental sustainability carried out in the last 5 years (reduction of consumption, led-light public illumination, heating systems in school etc.)	From 0 to 5
	2.2	% of rubbish recycling	1 point for every 5% over the regional average for recycling – upto a max. of 5
	2.3	Territorial and environmental branding and recognition (e.g. Emas, Slow City, Orange flag, etc.)	1 point for every brand assigned – up to a max. of 5
	2.4	Presence of dumps and/or traditional (combustible fuels) electricity plants	0 if atleast one is present – 3 if absent
	2.5	Bicycle paths, horse trails, walking tracks with official signage	1 point for every path/trail +1 for each track up to a max. of 5
	2.6	Presence in local council territory of themed itineraries recognized, at least, at regional level	1 point for each itinerary up to a max. of 3
	2.7	Regulations within town planning/ building law with reference to environmental sustainability (saving of water resources, energy savings, landscape/scenic and environmental impact)	From 0 to 3
	2.8	Organization in the last 3 years of significant initiatives to raise awareness aimed at the territory to encourage the reduction of light and acoustic pollution, the consumption of public land, power and natural resources	From 0 to 3
	2.9	Level of intermodal transportation systems (public train/bus services; private means/public transport interface etc.)	From 0 to 3
	2.10	Realization in the last 3 years of informative material and/or educational activities about slow tourism in the territory	From 0 to 5
Total score			40

Source: Our own elaboration

Table 16.4 Sustainability macro-area: indicators and points

Macro-area		Indicators	Points
SUSTAINABILITY: environmental, social and economic	3.1	Affiliations and quality certification for services (Ospitalità Italiana, Ecolabel, etc.)	1 for each certification allocated up to a max. of 5
	3.2	Heat saving systems or systems for heat production from alternative energy sources (exterior insulation and finishing system, thermostats for heating regulation, pellet stoves, etc.)	1 point for each significant system utilised. Up to 4
	3.3	Devices for the reduction of environmental impact (e.g. measuring caps for detergents, biodegradable detergents, Ecolabel toilet paper, biodegradable plastic etc.)	1 point for each significant system utilised. Up to 4
	3.4	Practicing of rubbish recycling	1 point for each material group (over 2) up to a max. of 4 points
	3.5	Actions are taken to inform and encourage guests to recycle rubbish and save energy and water	From 0 to 3
	3.6	Systems are in use to reduce the use of water (flow reduction valves, filtered drinking water in jugs, double flush systems installed in toilets, roof water catchment etc.)	From 0 to 4
	3.7	Systems are in use to limit the waste of lighting energy (e.g. presence sensor controls, led lights or low energy consumption bulbs, timers, etc.)	From 0 to 4
	3.8	Clients are encouraged and facilitated in the use of public transport or alternative means of transport to the car (e.g. electrical vehicles, bicycles etc.)	From 0 to 3
	3.9	Alternative systems are in use for the generation of electricity (solar panels, windmills, biomass, etc.)	1 point for each significant system employed. Up to 4.
Total score			35

Source: Our own elaboration

who is congruent with the promises made to their clientele, who are ever more demanding with respect to their motivations for the "slow" journey.

Some indicators prove to be characteristic not only of the PAST method, but also constitute a precise challenge for the structures holding a certificate, to better their

Table 16.5 Territory macro-area: indicators and points

Macroarea		Indicators	Points
TERRITORY Relation to local traditions; typology and themes; degree of authenticity	4.1	Coordination with the territorial system (reciprocal osmosis: The transposition of proposals to local public services and the realization of initiatives in the territorial setting)	From 0 to 5
	4.2	Web sites with settings and proposals pertinent to the slow thematic and to local traditions	From 0 to 5
	4.3	Use of local enogastronomical/agro-food products	From 0 to 3 or 5. 1 point for every 10% of products above 40%
	4.4	Typical period furnishings	From 0 to 3
	4.5	Heritage buildings and/or quality architecture	From 0 to 3. 1 point for every 30 years since construction
	4.6	Level of maintenance, comfort, furnishings quality, touch of class	From 0 to 4
	4.7	Adoption of provisions to encourage de-seasonalization (including the opening during off-peak/low season periods)	From 0 to 4
	4.8	Information/formation for staff relative to the slow tourism thematic	From 0 to 3
	4.9	Adoption of a business objective characterized by the approach to slow tourism, announced and expressed through initiatives and other instruments	From 0 to 3
	4.10	Making available of informative material on slow tourism activities in the territory at the reception and/or in the rooms	From 0 to 4
	4.11	Purchase of and/or promotion of available enogastonomic and local handcrafted products[a]	3 if actually on sale. 1 if only in promotion
Total points			40

Source: Our own elaboration
[a]The term "local" refers to the territory in Umbro-Marche District

actual offer with a view to the diversification and the personalization of their services.

16.4.2 Value for Time *Certification*

The certification proposed for the project has been defined as VALUE for TIME (abbreviated to VxT) and indicates the "class of slowness" assigned to the hospitality structure. With this term, which is easy to understand also for the international

Table 16.6 Point variability by structure typology

	Typology	Points
Accommodation	Hotel chain	1
	Tourist village	2
	Standard hotel	3
	Charme or historical hotel	4
	Private room rental and camping	5
	Small family hotel	6
	Country house, historical residence	7
	Farmstay	8
	B&B	9
	Albergo diffuso	10
Dining facilities	Restaurant chain	1
	Standard restaurant	2
	Tavern, historical restaurant, typical trattoria	3
	Farm stay restaurant	4
	Cooking with me	5

Source: Our own elaboration

clientele, the intention is to elude to the concept *value for money,* typical of mainstream touristic consumerist practice in general and at the same time to refer to the reciprocal *time for values*, that is "to take the time for values" in relationships, authenticity and the territorial traditions, and in real slow practices, also including slow food.

VxT assigns the values A (gold), B (silver) or C (bronze) relative to the decreasing points gained.

A certification system is an important instrument in the process of the implementation of quality for the touristic offer in a territory, in that it is aimed to award excellence but also to stimulate and give visibility to new touristic practices such as for example, slow tourism, allowing for a relative improvement.

Between August 2014 – March 2015 a team of assessors went to the various accommodation facilities on order to assign scores to the different indicators in the 4 macro-areas. Successively, the resulting check list was sent to the controlling body for the brand, which through the implementation of the valuation method, undertook to assign a final score attributing to each reception facility its relative "slowness classification".

The final calculation is obtained using a total of the 41 evaluation indicators, together with the points derived from the typology of the structure and the on-line reputation, realized by means of an allocation scheme, which also generates a polar diagram with a synthesis of the score obtained in the single macro-areas of the PAST Method.[3] (Fig. 16.2).

[3] It should be observed that for the accommodation facilities the maximum number of points that may be assigned is 180, while for dining facilities it is 170. The minimum value was established by the Brand Management Committee based upon the pre-tests carried out on defining experimental facilities.

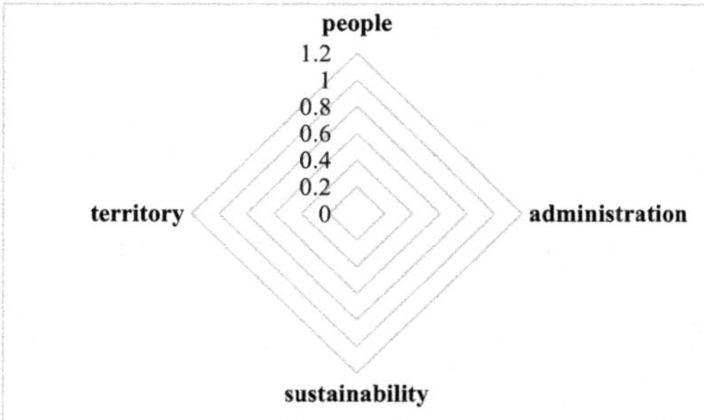

type of structure	1 to 10 points	1 to 5 points
reputation on-line	1 to 10 points	1 to 5 points

total POINTS GAINED	
Accomodation	**Restaurant**
180	**170**

Fig. 16.2 Synthesis of the scores relative to structure typology and on-line reputation, together with the total score and the polar diagram of the points for each single macro-area. (Source: Our own elaboration)

The VxT, as defined in the *Branding Regulations,* is subject to periodic modification in the case of a change in the check-list parameters, both for actions undertaken by the individual structures offering services, as well as for modifications to the territorial data base following choices carried out by local administrations (for example due to the opening of a thermal power plant or the increase in bicycle pathways). This highlights that the choices of local authorities and the strategies of private operators need to be jointly planned. In fact, in the application of some of the parameters provided for in the certification system, collective decisions activated in a territory also influence the slowness *ranking* of a touristic subject or product undergoing evaluation. For example, if political decisions are adopted in favor of energy savings or the use of a "slow" transport means in a particular territory, a benefit is also registered in the factors which define the class of slowness of the hotel.

The *Brand Management Committee* supervises the application of the provisions made in the Regulations for branding and the evaluations to be made during the visits carried out by experts to ascertain certification. The *Committee* also has the function of attributing the VxT classification based on the score received.

The first certificates were issued in November 2015 following the assignment of the scores given both for the accommodation and the dining facilities of each structure. It should be noted that, of the 19 structures visited in the Marche, 12 offer both accommodation and dining facilities and therefore have two scores while the 6 solely receptive structures and the one structure with only dining facilities have been assigned a single score. Of these structures 2 have attained Class A, 9 Class B, 6 Class C and 2 were deemed ineligible due to not attaining the minimum score necessary to obtain a certificate (Graph 16.1).

The Brand Management Committee decided to also assign a Class C to structure n.17, despite the score obtained by the dining facilities being less than the minimum

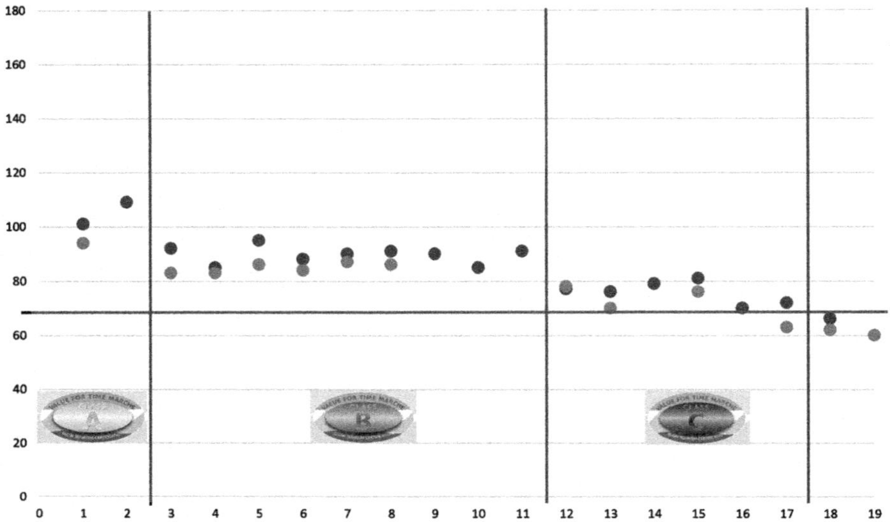

Legend
Points achieved for receptive facilities
Points achieved for dining facilities

Graph 16.1 Distribution of VxT certifications by class assigned. (Source: Our own elaboration)

value of 70 points its reception facilities were assigned a higher-than-minimum score for accommodation.

In reference to the structures in Umbria, as yet it has not been possible to assign any Value for Time certification, due to the difficulty of designating points in macro-area A this being the task of local administrative bodies, which to date demonstrate buearocratic difficulties and long response times.

16.4.3 Lessons Learned

The project "District of Slowness: methodology for the certification of slow tourism in the Umbrian-Marche Apennine district" in line with the slowness framework, is integrated into a vision of local development that promotes subjective wellbeing, the quality of community life, the valorization of local territorial identity and responsible tourism. In this context the touristic activities are influenced by an increasing sense of the responsibility of the tourist towards the environment and the search for a quality experience. In fact, tourism which combines the hedonistic aspects of holidays together with an eudaimonistic ethic, based on quality hospitality and an attention to quality living, where the tourist plays an active role in the vacation through the application of a responsible approach, becomes a possible model for local development in which the theme of the quality of life has a central role. The indicators identified by the PAST methodology result in being increasingly congruent with this new vision of local development.

For example *the minimum number of participants required for the activity/experience (Indicator 1.4)* proposed to its guests by a structure results as being important in that it allows a guest to live an emotionally captivating and intensely real life experience. Moreover, in consistency with the philosophy of slow tourism, it is important to provide services that are able, not only to respond to the specific needs of tourists but also to permit the tourist to feel received as a guest and not merely as a client. The PAST Method, therefore, attributes importance to *the activities and the processes built into program possibilities which personalize the services (e.g. pillows, food, timetables etc.) and not only as a response to an explicit/impromptu request (Indicator 1.5).*

As previously pointed out, in slow touristic operations, the aspect of environmental sustainability performs a central role, which should also be assumed in local touristic development politics which need to be orientated towards creating a more sustainable socio-economic context. Therefore, *the organization in the last 3 years of significant initiatives to raise awareness aimed at the territory in order to encourage the reduction of light and acoustic pollution, the consumption of public land, power and natural resources (Indicator 2.8)* becomes significant.

Moreover, sustainability (macro-area S) is strictly linked to the responsibility of choices made by the hospitality structures, which assume particular relevance with *Indicator 3.3 Devices for the reduction of environmental impact (e.g. measuring caps for detergents, biodegradable detergents, Ecolabel toilet paper, biodegradable plastic etc.)*

The ability of the territory to establish networks with the view to valorizing and promoting quality services and products is revealed by the adhesion to environmental/quality branding/certification schemes.

Therefore, *the presence of branding and territorial and environmental recognition (Indicator 2.3)* and the *affiliations and quality certification of the service (Indicator 3.1)* are considered to be bonus activities.

A marked alliance of the tourist with the territory is a particularity of slow tourism. The integration of and constructive dialogue between the various local socio-economic components proves to be important, indicating a *coordination with the territorial system (reciprocal osmosis: the transposition of proposals to local public services and the realization of initiatives in the territorial setting) (Indicator 4.1)* assuming a positive value.

Furthermore the PAST methodology highlights the importance of the collaboration between local administrations and tourist facilities which becomes of strategic importance in the planning and realization of tourism development politics at a local level. In fact, if the public stakeholder does not take an active part in the touristic development process, and therefore also in planning for slow tourism, the excellent quality of the private structures is insufficient if not integrated into a broader context of territorial quality. A possible appeal on behalf of private subjects for the furnishing of the data and information necessary to obtain certification, could give impetus to the response and the commitment of public institutions.

In closing, it should be underlined that the PAST Methodology could be experimented and adopted in other territories which identify slow tourism as a strategy for sustainable, local, touristic development capable of raising both competitivity and visibility.

References

Adams, K. B., Leibbrandt, S., & Moon, H. (2011). A critical review of the literature on social and leisure activity and wellbeing in later life. *Ageing and Society, 31*(04), 683–712.

Argyle, M. (1987). *The psychology of happiness*. London/New York: Methuen.

Babou, I., & Callot, P. (2009). Slow tourism, slow (r)evolution? Nouvelles mobilities touristiques. *Cahier Espaces, 100*(56), 48–54.

Baumann, Z. (2002). *La solitudine del cittadino globale*. Milano: Feltrinelli.

Beeton, S. (2006). *Community development through tourism*. Collingwood: Landlinks Press.

Bissell, D., & Fuller, G. (2011). *Stillness in a mobile world*. New York: Taylor & Francis.

Biswas-Diener, R., & Diener, E. (2006). The subjective well-being of the homeless and lessons for happiness. *Social Indicators Research, 76*(2), 185–205.

Blanco, L. (2011). Una aproximacion al turismo slow. El turismo slow en las Cittaslow de Espana. *Investigaciones Turisticas, 1*, 122–133.

Calzati, V. (2011). Territori lenti: nuove traiettorie di sviluppo. In E. Nocifora, P. de Salvo, & Calzati (Eds.), *Territori lenti e turismo di qualità, prospettive innovative per lo sviluppo di un turismo sostenibile* (pp. 62–72). Milano: Franco Angeli.

Calzati, V. (2016). *Nuove pratiche turistiche e slow tourism. Il caso della Valnerina in Umbria*. Milano: FrancoAngeli.

Calzati, V., & de Salvo, P. (Eds.). (2012). *Le strategie per una valorizzazione sostenibile del territorio*. Milano: Franco Angeli.

Calzati, V., & de Salvo, P. (2017). Slow tourism: A new concept of sustainability, consumption and quality of life. In M. Clancy (Ed.), *Slow tourism, food and cities: Pace and the search for the good life*. London: Routledge.

Campbell, S. (1996). Green cities, growing cities, just cities? Urban planning and the contradictions of sustainable development. *Journal of the American Planning Association, 62*(3), 296–312.

Conway, D., & Timms, B. (2010). Re-branding alternative tourism in the Caribbean: The case for slow tourism. *Tourism and Hospitality Research, 10*(4), 329–344.

Conway, D., & Timms, B. (2012). Slow tourism at the Caribbean's. Geographical margins. *Tourism Geographies, 14*(3), 396–418.

Dann, G. M. S. (2012). Tourist motivation and quality-of-life: In search of the missing link. In M. Uysal, R. Perdue, & J. Sirgy (Eds.), *Handbook of tourism and quality-of-life research: Enhancing the lives of tourists and residents of host communities* (pp. 233–245). Dordrecht: Springer Science & Business Media.

de Salvo, P. (2011). Cittàslow: un modello alternativo di sviluppo urbano lento e sostenibile. In E. Nocifora, P. de Salvo, & V. Calzati (Eds.), *Territori lenti e turismo di qualità. Prospettive innovative per lo sviluppo di un turismo sostenibile* (pp. 47–58). Milano: Franco Angeli.

de Salvo, P., Clemente, E. D., & ManuelHernández-Mogollón, J. (2013). "Repellent" tourists versus "slow" tourists. *The European Journal of Tourism Hospitality and Recreation, 4*(2), 131–148.

Di Clemente, E., Hernández-Mogollón, J. M., de Salvo, P., & Campón-Cerro, A. M. (2015). Slow tourism: An alternative model for local and tourist development. In J. Mondéjar-Jiménez, G. Ferrari, M.-d.-V. Segarra-Oña, & A. Peiró-Signes (Eds.), *Sustainable performance and tourism: A collection of tools and best practicesed* (pp. 23–37). Chartridge: Books Oxford.

Dickinson, J. E., & Lumsdon, L. (2010). *Slow travel and tourism*. London: Earthscan.
Dickinson, J. E., Robbins, D., & Lumsdon, L. (2010). Holiday travel discourses and climate change. *Journal of Transport Geography, 18*(3), 482–489.
Diener, E., & Suh, E. (1997). Measuring quality of life: Economic, social, and subjective indicators. *Social Indicators Research, 40*, 189–216.
Dolnicar, S., Yanamandram, V., & Cliff, K. (2012). The contribution of vacations to quality of life. *Annals of Tourism Research, 39*(1), 59–83.
Dolnicar, S., Lazarevski, K., & Yanamandram, V. (2013). Quality of life and tourism: A conceptual framework and novel segmentation base. *Journal of Business Research, 66*(6), 724–729.
Fullagar, S., Markwell, K., & Wilson, E. (2012). *Slow tourism. Experience and Mobilities*. Bristol: Channel view Publications.
Gardner, N. (2009). A manifesto for slow travel. *Hidden Europe Magazine, 25*, 10–14.
Gilbert, D., & Abdullah, J. (2004). Holiday taking and the sense of well-being. *Annals of Tourism Research, 31*(1), 103–121.
Hall, C. M. (2009). Degrowing tourism: Descroissance, sustainable consumption and steady state tourism. *Anatolia, 20*(1), 46–61.
Hall, C. M. (2010). Changing paradigms and global change: From sustainable to steady-state tourism. *Tourism Recreation Research, 35*(2), 131–145.
Hamilton, C. (2003). *Growth fetish*. Sydney: Allen & Unwin.
Hazel, N. (2005). Holidays for children and families in need: An exploration of the research and policy contexts for social tourism in the UK. *Children and Society, 19*, 225–236.
Heitmann, S., Robinson, P., & Povey, G. (2011). Slow food, slow cities and slow tourism. In P. Robinson, S. Heitmann, & P. Dieke (Eds.), *Research themes for tourism* (pp. 114–127). Oxford: CABI.
Iso-Ahola, S. E., & Park, C. J. (1996). Leisure-related social support and self-determination as buffers of stress-illness relationship. *Journal of Leisure Research, 28*, 169–187.
Iwasaki, Y. (2002). Testing independent and buffer models of the influence of leisure participation on stress-coping and adaptational outcomes. *Journal of Park and Recreation Administration, 20*, 90–129.
Iwasaki, Y. (2007). Leisure and quality of life in an international and multicultural context: What are major pathways linking leisure to quality of life? *Social Indicators Research, 82*(2), 33–264.
Kahn, R. L., & Juster, T. (2002). Well-being: Concepts and measures. *Journal of Social Issues, 58*, 627–644.
Kahneman, D., Edward, D., & Norbert, S. (1999). *Well-being: The foundations of hedonic psychology*. New York: Russell Sage Foundation.
Kahneman, D., David, K., & Tversky, A. (2003). Experienced utility and objective happiness: A moment-based approach. *The Psychology of Economic Decisions, 1*, 187–208.
Kelley-Gillespie, N. (2009). An integrated conceptual model of quality of life for older adults based on a synthesis of the literature. *Applied Research in Quality of Life, 4*, 259–282.
Knox, P. L. (2005). Creating ordinary places: Slow cities in a fast world. *Journal of Urban Design, 10*(1), 1–11.
Lancerini, E. (2005). Territori lenti: contributi per una nuova geografia dei paesaggi abitati italiani. *Territorio, 34*, 9–15.
Lanzani, A. (2005). Geografie, paesaggi, pratiche dell'abitare e progetti di sviluppo. *Territorio, 34*, 19–36.
Latouche, S. (2007). *La scommessa della decrescita*. Milano: Feltrinelli.
Layard, R. (2005). *Happiness: Lessons from a new science*. London: Penguin.
Lumsdon, L., & McGrath, P. (2011). Developing a conceptual framework for slow travel: A grounded theory approach. *Journal of Sustainable Tourism, 19*(3), 265–279.
Manella, G., de Salvo, P., & Calzati, V. (2017). Verso modelli di governo urbano sostenibile e solidale:il caso Cittaslow in Emilia-Romagna. *Sociologia Urbana e Rurale, 112*, 117–130.
Matos, R. (2004). Can "slow tourism" bring new life to alpine regions? In W. Klaus & C. Mathies (Eds.), *The tourism and leisure industry shaping the future* (pp. 93–104). New York: Haworth Press.

McCabe, S., Joldersma, T., & Li, C. (2010). Understanding the benefits of social tourism: Linking participation to subjective well-being and quality of life. *International Journal of Tourism Research, 12*(6), 761–773.
McConkey, R., & Adams, L. (2000). Matching short break services for children with learning disabilities to family needs and preferences. *Child: Care, Health and Development, 26*, 429–443.
Neal, J. D., Sirgy, J., & Uysal, M. (2004). Measuring the effect of tourism services on travelers' quality of life: Further validation. *Social Indicators Research, 69*(3), 243–277.
Nocifora, E. (2011). La costruzione sociale della qualità territoriale. Il turismo della lentezza come conquista del turista esparto. In E. Nocifora, P. de Salvo, & V. Calzati (Eds.), *Territori lenti e turismo di qualità, prospettive innovative per lo sviluppo di un turismo sostenibile* (pp. 6–30). Milano: Franco Angeli.
Nussbaum, M., & Sen, A. (1993). *The quality of life*. Oxford: University Press.
Oh, H., George, A., & Seyhmus, B. (2016). Motivations and goals of slow tourism. *Journal of Travel Research, 55*(2), 205–219.
Osbaldiston, N. (2013). Culture of the slow. In *Social deceleration in an accelerated world.* Hampshire: Palgrave Macmillan.
Parkins, W., & Craig, G. (2006). *Slow living*. Oxford: Berg.
Pearce, P. L., & Lee, U.-I. (2005). Developing the travel career approach to tourist motivation. *Journal of Travel Research, 43*, 226–237.
Presenza, A., Tindara, A., & Roberto, M. (2015). The cittaslow movement: Opportunities and challenges for the governance of tourism destinations. *Tourism Planning & Development, 12*(4), 479–488.
Ryan, R. M., & Deci, E. L. (2001). On happiness and human potentials: A review of research on hedonic and eudaimonic well-being. *Annual Review of Psychology, 52*, 14–166.
Savoja, L. (2011). Turismo lento e turisti responsabili. Verso una nuova concezione di consume. In E. Nocifora, P. de Salvo, & V. Calzati (Eds.), *Territori lenti e turismo di qualità. Prospettive innovative per lo sviluppo di un turismo sostenibile* (pp. 86–99). Milano: Franco Angeli.
Schor, J. (1998). *The overspent American: Why we want what we don't need.* New York: Harper, Perennial.
Sirgy, M. J. (2002). *The psychology of quality of life*. Dordrecht: Kluwer Academic.
Sirgy, M. J. (2010). Toward a quality-of-life theory of leisure travel satisfaction. *Journal of Travel Research, 49*, 246–260.
Stiglitz, J. E., Amartya, S., & Jean-Paul, F. 2009. Report by the Commission on the Measurement of Economic Performance and Social Progress, Paris.
UNWTO. (2012). Asia-Pacific Newsletter, Issue 27.
Uysal, M., Perdue, R., & Joseph Sirgy, M. (Eds.). (2012). *Handbook of tourism and quality-of-life research: Enhancing the lives of tourists and residents of host communities*. Berlin: Springer Science & Business Media.
Uysal, M., Joseph Sirgy, M., Woo, E., & Kim, H. L. (2016). Quality of life (QOL) and well-being research in tourism. *Tourism Management, 53*, 244–261.
Veenhoven, R., Ehrhardt, J., Ho, M. S. D., & de Vries, A. (1993). *Happiness in nations: Subjective appreciation of life in 56 nations* (pp. 1946–1992). Rotterdam: Erasmus University Press.
Weaver, D. B. (2000). A broad context model of destination development scenarios. *Tourism Management, 21*(3), 217–224.
Wilkinson, R. G., & Marmot, M. (2003). *Social determinants of health: The solid facts.* Copenhagen: World Health Organization.
Woehler, K. (2004). The rediscovery of slowness, or leisure time as one's own and as self-aggrandizement? In K. Weiermair & C. Mathies (Eds.), *The tourism an leisure industry: Shaping the future* (pp. 83–92). New York/London/Oxford: The Hanwoth Hospitality Press.
Zago, M. (2012). Definire e operativizzare lo slow tourism: il modello Castle. In E. Nocifora, P. de Salvo, & V. Calzati (Eds.), *Territori lenti e turismo di qualità. Prospettive innovative per lo sviluppo di un turismo sostenibile* (pp. 155–169). Milano: Franco Angeli.

Chapter 17
Agritourism and Quality-of-Life for Farmers

Lisa Chase

Abstract Agritourism is growing in popularity throughout the United States of America, Europe, and many other countries around the world. By blending tourism with agriculture, agritourism enterprises allow farmers to diversify core operations and keep farmland in production while educating visitors, preserving scenic vistas, and maintaining farming traditions. However, agritourism comes with challenges and is not for every farm. It requires different skills than traditional farming operations, and farmers interested in agritourism often have difficulty finding support for technical assistance and networking opportunities to ensure best practices.

This case study examines the impacts of agritourism on the quality-of-life (QOL) of farmers in the Northeastern region of the U.S. Survey findings indicate that agritourism can have both positive and negative impacts on QOL; however the positive impacts outweigh the negative impacts for many farmers. Specifically, the personal satisfaction gains are typically greater than concerns about extra time required for agritourism enterprises. These findings have important implications for helping farmers and rural communities develop agritourism in ways that emphasize positive impacts and minimize potential negative effects. Methods and findings from this case study can be readily transferred to other locations to examine quality-of-life impacts of agritourism on farmers in a variety of settings around the world.

Keywords Agritourism · Direct sales · Food tourism · Quality-of-life

17.1 Introduction

As the economic and social fabric of rural communities has undergone changes in the past century, many communities have experienced a transition from economic dependence on natural resource extraction (e.g., agriculture, timber) to service-based economies, particularly tourism. Population shifts transforming rural areas

L. Chase (✉)
Vermont Tourism Research Center, University of Vermont Extension, Brattleboro, VT, USA
e-mail: Lisa.Chase@uvm.edu

A. M. Campón-Cerro et al. (eds.), *Best Practices in Hospitality and Tourism Marketing and Management*, Applying Quality of Life Research,
https://doi.org/10.1007/978-3-319-91692-7_17

into suburban sprawl have made it increasingly difficult for some small and mid-size farms to remain viable. In response, entrepreneurial farmers and ranchers have merged farming, ranching, and tourism into the alternative agricultural enterprise known as agritourism (Chase and Grubinger 2014). The growing interest in local food systems has provided new economic opportunities for small and medium-sized farms throughout the country (Kloppenburg et al. 2000).

Agritourism can be defined as "a commercial enterprise on a working farm or ranch conducted for the enjoyment, education, and/or active involvement of the visitor, generating supplemental income for the farm or ranch (Chase 2008)." It has also been defined as: "A farm combining primary elements and characteristics of agriculture and tourism and providing members of the general public a place to purchase farm products and/or enjoy a recreational, entertaining or educational experience (Jensen et al. 2013)."

In many parts of the world, production of specific types of food and drink are the crux of agritourism in that region. In the European Union, protected designation of origin (PDO), protected geographical indication (PGI), and traditional specialties guaranteed (TSG) require that the names and labels of certain foods and drinks can only be used when they are produced in a specific region, sometimes following specific protocols. Well-known examples include Champagne and Cognac in France and Asiago, Gorgonzola, and Parmigiano-Reggiano cheese in Italy.

Widespread use of the term agritourism around the world may have its origin in the Italian agriturismo law passed in 1985, which encourages overnight farms stays as a way for Italian farmers to diversify their incomes so they can maintain farming practices, landscapes, and barns and other agricultural buildings. Agriturismo has become increasing popular in Tuscany, Italy and many other places around the globe.

Agritourism can take many forms and includes many kinds of activities, such as overnight farm stays, hay rides, corn mazes, and use of farm land for bird watching, bike riding, hiking, horseback riding, hunting, snowmobiling and other recreational activities. Some farms may charge for these activities or use them as tools to promote retail sales. Agritourism also includes educational programs for the public, school children, seniors, and all types of visitors, often involving exhibits, demonstrations, and workshops around specific topics and skills. On-farm classes teach visitors how to milk cows, make cheese, prune raspberry bushes, and bake apple pies, for example.

On-farm retail sales offer a unique 'shopping experience' that helps farms compete with traditional retail stores. The experience of visiting the farm, seeing its environs and talking with the farmers and their employees while shopping can be of value by itself; in many cases that value to the consumer is further enhanced by educational activities on the farm. These can include observing or petting animals, touring the farm or its facilities, and picking your own produce. Pick-your-own, or U-pick enterprises exemplify the overlap between marketing of farm products and marketing a farm experience. Some customers may be primarily motivated by the opportunity to purchase super-fresh fruit, while others are more attracted to the chance to spend time outdoors in a farm field (Fig. 17.1).

Fig. 17.1 Pick-your-own strawberries. (Photo by Vern Grubinger)

Agritourism on any given farm often goes beyond food; it may also be about cultural heritage, family entertainment and enjoyment of natural resources. In other words, it's a multi-faceted experience that's connected to, and takes place on, a farm. During that experience, farm visitors may learn basic information about food production. They also take in the sights, sounds, smells, and tastes of a farm, and along the way they may develop an appreciation for the hard work involved in producing food.

Agritourism may or may not be closely connected to the marketing of agricultural products. Farms that produce wholesale commodity products, like fluid milk, may offer tours, accommodations or recreation, but they usually don't, or can't, sell their primary product directly to their visitors. When schoolchildren take a field trip to a farm to learn how fruits and vegetables are grown, or how cows are milked, the focus is education, not marketing. Offering a tangible product may be part of the experience, perhaps an apple, a carrot or some cheese. The goal of this kind of visit is to help children understand where food comes from.

For other farms, the visitor experience *is* the marketing strategy for their products. Pick-your-own apple orchards do more than just sell fruit; they sell an experience that goes with it. The experience may include a beautiful setting for a family excursion, an apple cider making demonstration, samples of hot cider, or the chance to see the farm's horses or tractors at work.

In some cases, agritourism may not involve the farm product but there may still be indirect market benefits to the farmer. For example, after touring a vineyard, some visitors will purchase a bottle of wine, but others may not. However, their experience may lead them to buy wine from that vineyard at a later date. Visitors to a dairy farm, who can't purchase the milk directly, might be more inclined to buy locally-produced cheese that was made using that farm's milk.

Agritourism includes a range of experiences, some are directly connected to the marketing of a farm's product and some are not. In essence, they provide authentic experiences related to agriculture that enhance marketing of farm products, educate the public about farming, and improve public support for agriculture. But agritourism comes with challenges and farms must carefully weigh the benefits with the costs to understand how agritourism will impact their quality-of-life (QOL) (Chase and Kuehn 2010).

Quality-of-life is a central concern for individuals and communities (Chase et al. 2010), including farmers making decisions about agritourism. However, QOL is a particularly difficult concept to measure as it has multiple definitions and meanings, and can be examined at several scales ranging from an individual to a community to a country (Chase et al. 2012a, b). Costanza et al. (2007) describe QOL as "a multi-scale, multi-dimensional concept that contains interacting objective and subjective elements." To measure QOL, indicators are used that can be divided into subjective and objective categories. Subjective indicators reflect an individual's perceptions of satisfaction in several life domains including work life, family life, social life, and leisure life. Objective indicators include external evaluations of income levels, family life, social life, and health (Sirgy et al. 2000).

The objective of this chapter is to examine quality-of-life of farmers with agritourism as a component of farm viability. As such, the focus is on subjective quality-of-life indicators that reflect an individual's perceptions of satisfaction in work and leisure. This chapter begins with a brief history of agritourism in the United States, followed by a discussion of QOL and the benefits and challenges of agritourism. Background is presented on the case study, a University of Vermont Extension program to support agritourism in the northeastern region of the United States of America. Next, methods and results focused on QOL indicators are shared. Discussion and implication assess the contributions of the QOL indicators and the need for further research and outreach to improve our understanding of, and ability to, measure quality-of-life. The chapter concludes with lessons learned regarding agritourism and quality-of-life.

17.2 History of Agritourism in the United States

Although the term agritourism is relatively new, the concept of travel to celebrate and learn about agriculture has existed for centuries. Native American tribes in what is now the United States traveled long distances to participate in planting and harvesting feasts and ceremonies. Maple syrup production in the late winter was a time of reunion and renewal for tribes such as the Ojibwe and Abenaki. Family groups, reunited with their bands after the winter, would gather for the ritualized work of collecting sap and boiling it into maple syrup. European settlers in rural America

Fig. 17.2 Morse Farm Maple Sugarworks. (Photo by Lisa Chase)

learned about maple syrup from Native Americans and created their own cultural traditions and sugaring celebrations. Today, sugarmakers attract visitors with on-farm breakfasts and accommodations, sugarhouse tours and direct sales of maple syrup, maple candy, and other maple products (Fig. 17.2). This combination of activities is a major source of farm income in areas where sugar maples are abundant.

Throughout the nineteenth century, many large farmhouses also served as country inns. Immigrants traveling westward would spend their nights at these farms along their route, paying or working for room and board. In the late 1800s, as the United States became increasingly urbanized, families living in cities would visit farms or ranches for a few weeks or months in the summer to escape the heat and hectic pace of city life, and learn about farming and rural life during their stay. Some urban families would visit the same farm or ranch year after year, developing close relationships as their children grew up together during these annual visits.

A typical farm stay in the Northeast in the late 1800s is described by the Adams Farm in Wilmington, Vermont: "Walter and Ada Adams opened the Adams Farm homestead to the public during the late 1890s, for summer guests to get away and beat the heat of the city. Families would bring their children and spend a week or two enjoying Vermont's beauty, swimming in the Deerfield River and Lake Raponda, gathering eggs, playing with lambs, and eating fresh delicious home baked foods from the farm kitchen (Adams Family Farm n.d.)."

The Adams family continued to provide summer farm stays into the next century and they also opened up their farmhouse to winter visitors who traveled to Vermont.

Many came for the sport of skiing starting in the 1950s. The Adams farm took a brief break from agritourism in 1969 when they expanded their dairy herd and shifted their primary focus to dairying. A decade later, milk prices fell and the Adams family invited guests back onto the farm, this time for winter sleigh rides. Nearby ski areas provided the Adams Farm with a steady stream of visitors who bought maple syrup produced on the farm. Run by the fifth generation of the Adams family today, the farm continues to offer horse-drawn sleigh rides and direct sales of maple syrup. For more than a century, agritourism in a variety of forms has provided supplemental income for the Adams family, helping them keep their land in farming even when commodity prices dropped and other farming ventures became unprofitable.

While farm stays were becoming popular in the Northeast in the late 1800s, dude ranches in the American West were beginning to attract wealthy Easterners and Europeans on hunting trips and sightseeing excursions. To supplement their income, Western ranchers began taking in paying guests or 'dudes' who would share their homes and learn about the ranching lifestyle, horseback riding, herding cattle, hunting, and fishing. Famous dudes such as Theodore Roosevelt helped popularized dude ranches in the early 1900s and railroads made travel to dude ranches feasible. Tourists arrived on trains with their steamer trunks and often stayed for the entire summer, as dude ranches became the main tourist attraction in the Rocky Mountain area during the 1920s and 1930s.

Today, farm and ranch stays continue to be a major component of agritourism in rural America. To improve farm stay product development and marketing, farms and ranches in the United States often look to Asia and Europe, especially Italy, Greece, France, and Ireland. Farmstays dominate the agritourism market in many European countries where agricultural and culinary tourism complement each other. Culinary tourism, the pursuit of unique and memorable dining experiences often while traveling, emphasizes fresh foods creatively prepared (World Food Travel Association n.d.) and is a hot trend in tourism throughout the world. Projected growth in culinary travel brings external resources into local food systems, as farmers earn revenues by selling experiences and products to people from 'away'. For example, California's success in attracting tourists to wine tastings at vineyards by marketing the Napa Valley Wine Trail has been extended to other specialty food products, including the Wisconsin Cheese Tour and the Oregon Beer Trail.

Food festivals are another part of culinary agritourism, where crops and foods with special significance to an area are celebrated and promoted. Some of these festivals have been around for a long time while many are relative newcomers. The Apple Blossom Festival was started by the first apple shipper in Wenatchee, Washington, in 1919. The Florida Strawberry Festival was established in 1930 in Plant City, Florida, where 10,000 acres of the fruit are grown nearby. In 1967 the Morton Pumpkin Festival began in the Illinois town where most of the world's canning pumpkins are processed. In California, the Gilroy Garlic Festival started in

1979 and the Stockton Asparagus Festival in 1986. The Chatsworth, New Jersey, Cranberry Festival began in 1983 to celebrate one of the state's most valuable fruit crops. West Stockbridge, Massachusetts, kicked off its Zucchini Festival in 2003. While some of these festivals attract tens of thousands of people, there are hundreds if not thousands of small town events celebrating crops and foods in their own unique ways.

Some food celebrations are less festival and more feast. They may be more exclusive, perhaps requiring reservations and fetching a high price. For example, 'feasts in the field' are dinners that take place in farmers' fields or barns. Some are gourmet affairs, where accomplished chefs create multiple course meals made with locally-sourced products and served with local wines. Others may be family-style meals made with the farm's products, perhaps ground beef and sweet corn. From festivals to feasts and everything in between, recent studies of consumers and tourists indicate that demand is increasing for agricultural products and experiences, especially those focused on local foods and authentic experiences (Mandala Research 2013).

17.3 Quality-of-Life and the Benefits and Challenges of Agritourism

The blending of agriculture, marketing, and tourism poses both challenges and opportunities. The benefits and costs of agritourism businesses are important to assess when considering new enterprises (Table 17.1). For example, farmers taking on more interactions with the public have to deal with interruptions in daily operations and public scrutiny of farming practices. On-farm marketing and agritourism require different skills than other aspects of farming. These are areas in which many farmers do not have training. They also require different or expanded uses of land on farms such as parking areas, housing, and trails. It may require additional signage and restrooms. An agritourism enterprise that is not a farm's main marketing method may be viewed as an additional business, on top of the farming business. It can require additional investment, human capital, and cash flow to generate additional returns.

Agritourism is important to quality-of-life for economic and cultural reasons, promoting experiential education, preserving traditional land use, and contributing to a rural sense of place. In many cases, agritourism allows farmers to diversify their core operations and keep farmland in production while preserving scenic vistas and maintaining farming traditions. Although agritourism is growing rapidly in the northeast region of the U.S., the industry remains underdeveloped in many states, lacking technical assistance support, infrastructure, and networking opportunities to ensure best practices (Kuehn and Hilchey 2001).

Table 17.1 Benefits and costs of an agritourism business

Benefits	Costs
Provides potential additional income	Provides a low financial return, at least at first
Creates a physical operation that appreciates in value	Interferes with farming or ranching operations
Efficiently uses underutilized facilities, equipment, land, and talents	Hard work! Adds workload to family members
Allows you to be your own boss	Demands your full and constant attention, interfering with family time and activities
Allows you to work your own hours	Steals your privacy people are always around.
Allows you to express yourself creatively	Requires you always to be "on"-upbeat, available, and attentive
Allows you to live your own creation	Involves risk and liability.
Is personally rewarding	Can create staffing problems
Generates new opportunities for spouse and children	Generates excessive paperwork
Maintains family attention and interest on the farm or ranch	
Provides the opportunity to meet people – visitors as well as agritourism and nature tourism professionals	
Provides the chance to play a significant role in community activities	
Provides the chance to educate people about rural living, nature, and the agriculture industry, which in turn can lead to improved local policies	
Provides the chance to learn about outside perspectives, which in turn can lead to better educated rural residents and improved local policies	
Promotes the agriculture industry	
Models sustainable local industries	

17.4 Case Study: Impacts of Agritourism on the Quality-of-Life of Farmers in the Northeastern U.S.

To address these concerns about agritourism and help farmers assess the benefits and challenges of developing agritourism enterprises on their farms, Extension educators and farmers in Northeastern states collaboratively developed a program of agritourism training modules consisting of workshops and follow-up technical support. With funding from a United States Department of Agriculture (USDA) Sustainable Agriculture Research and Education (SARE) grant and additional resources, 19 workshops were held in 10 states (Maine, Maryland, Delaware, Vermont, New Hampshire, New York, Massachusetts, Connecticut, West Virginia, and Rhode Island) between January 2009 and March 2010. Evaluations were conducted on-site immediately following the workshops to assess short-term outcomes.

An internet survey was conducted 1 year later to assess medium- and long-term outcomes. Both the on-site and internet evaluations included questions about improvements in farm viability, which was defined as increases in profitability and/or increases in quality-of-life indicators including personal time and personal satisfaction.

17.4.1 Methods

To measure changes in QOL, an index of indicators was needed for the internet survey. Researchers typically use indicators as a way to quantify quality-of-life concerns and considerations, rather than directly attempting to measure these abstract concepts (Wong 2006). A literature review on quality-of-life revealed extensive works examining both subjective and objective aspects of quality-of-life, ranging from individual to county to national data (Sirgy et al. 2000). However, indicators measuring changes in quality-of-life as a result of an intervention (e.g., an Extension program) were not found through the extensive literature review. For the purpose of measuring impacts of a one-time Extension program on quality-of-life, an index of indicators with straightforward questions is needed. Our study addresses this need by developing such an index and applying it to an Extension program on agritourism in the Northeast.

A total number of 763 farmers, service providers, and others participated in the 19 workshops. A questionnaire was handed out at the end of each workshop (conducted between January 2009 and March 2010) to collect baseline data on farm operations, and to assess the knowledge gained from the workshop and the likelihood of adopting new practices. All participants had the opportunity to participate in the survey, and 143 completed questionnaires were received from farm operators, 129 of which included contact information for farmers willing to complete an online follow-up survey, which was administered in January 2010. Five follow-up e-mail reminders were sent to the 129 farmer every 2 weeks after the initial mailing, following recommendations from the Tailored Design Method (Dillman 2007). Of the 129 surveys distributed to farmer participants at the workshops, 62 responded for a response rate of 48%. Non-respondents were then contacted via phone, which boosted the sample to 98 respondents for the follow-up survey.

The on-line survey included questions on demographics (gender, year of birth, number of people in household, years of education); involvement of household members in the business; perceived impact of the farmer's business on local networking and the community; and impact of the economy, weather, workshop, and family life on the business. Farmers were asked to describe any business income and expenses during the previous 12 months that resulted from the workshop or technical assistance received. Questions regarding how the respondent's business has impacted the local community and business networking used a five-point scale ranging from highly negative impact to highly positive impact. An identical scale was used to identify the impact of the economy, weather, workshop, and changes in family life on the business during the previous year. Respondents were asked to identify changes in seven variables related to personal time and personal satisfaction over the past year using a five-point scale ranging from greatly decreased to greatly increased. To measure quality-of-life, a new set of indicators was developed based on related literature and our direct experience working with numerous agritourism stakeholders including farmers, consumers, visitors, community members, and Extension educators.

A principal components factor analysis with Varimax rotation was used to identify factor composition for "changes in personal time" and "changes in personal satisfaction." The mean value for each factor was obtained by averaging the variables included in each factor (averaging was used to maintain the five-point scale and enable interpretation of results). Cronbach's alpha was used to identify the reliability of the two factors; an alpha of 0.7 or higher indicates adequate internal consistency of factors (Hair et al. 1998).

17.4.2 Results

17.4.2.1 Response and Demographics

Of the 98 farms responding to both the on-line and phone surveys, 76 reported that they had assessed their business, implemented improvements, and/or created or changed a business plan.

Most of the survey respondents owned a farmstand (32% of respondents), u-pick operation (29%), farm-stay bed and breakfast (14%), greenhouse/plant nursery (11%), Christmas tree farm (11%), or operated farm tours (10%). Smaller percentages (less than 8%) of respondents owned a winery, retail store, or corn maze; functioned as Community Supported Agriculture (CSA); or sold maple products. Seventy-two percent of the respondents were female, 79% were married, and the average age was 55. The average respondent had 16 years of education, with 69% having 4 years or more of college education. The average household size of respondents was 2.5 people, ranging from one to six household members. Respondents indicated that household members were moderately involved in their agritourism business (i.e., most household members sometimes assisted with farm operations).

17.4.2.2 Impact Variables

Results indicated that 64% of farms had implemented agritourism improvements or new ventures. Examples included involvement in local schools, social media marketing, maple tours for the off-season, pairing and tasting events, and educational nature trails. Farm owners were asked how certain external elements (e.g., the economy, the workshop) impacted their business, and how their business impacted others (e.g., networking opportunities among local businesses). The economy and the

Table 17.2 Means for independent variables related to impacts on and from respondents' businesses

Question type	Variable	n	Mean	Standard error
Impact of variable on business[a]	The economy	61	−0.61	0.118
	The weather	62	−0.61	0.109
	The workshop	61	0.66	0.061
	Changes in family life	62	0.21	0.083
Impact of business on variable[a]	Networking opportunities among local businesses	52	0.73	0.073
	Marketing and packaging opportunities among local businesses	52	0.44	0.080
	The local economy	52	0.52	0.101
	The number of jobs available in your community	52	0.33	0.094
	Your neighbors	49	0.59	0.105
	Other people in your community or area	51	0.84	0.076

[a]The following scale was used for these variables: −2 = highly negative impact, −1 = negative impact, 0 = no impact, 1 = positive impact, 2 = highly positive impact

weather were identified as having a negative impact on the farm business during the previous year, both having a mean value of −0.61 (Table 17.2). In contrast, the workshop was identified as having a positive impact on the farm business (mean = 0.66); changes in family life had a slightly positive impact (0.21). Respondents indicated that their business had a positive impact on networking opportunities, marketing, the economy, job availability, and residents.

17.4.2.3 Time and Satisfaction Factors

QOL indicators included a series of questions about personal time and satisfaction (Table 17.3). Over two-thirds of respondents reported increased enjoyment from sharing farm life and/or heritage with visitors and 71% reported increased enjoyment from meeting new people through their business. Over half reported increased personal satisfaction from their business, while 45% reported no change and 2% reported a decrease. However, the increases in QOL indicators were tempered by 29% reporting a decrease in the amount of free time they have and only 9% reporting an increase in their free time after diversifying to include or expand agritourism on their farm. The majority of respondents (62%) reported no change in free time. Regarding the amount of time respondents spent with family during both work and free time, 72% reported no change, 16% reported an increase and 12% reported a decrease.

Principal components factor analysis revealed two factors: "changes in personal time" and "changes in personal satisfaction" (Table 17.3). Changes in personal time included the variables of "changes in the amount of time I spend with my family (during both work and freetime)" and "changes in the amount of free time I have."

Table 17.3 Factor and variable means related to personal time and personal satisfaction

Factor	Variable	n	Variable mean	Factor mean	Cronbach's alpha
Changes in personal time[a]	Changes in the amount of time I spend with my family (during both work and free time)	42	0.07	−0.08	0.722
	Changes in the amount of free time I have	42	−0.24		
Changes in personal satisfaction[a]	Changes in the amount of personal satisfaction I receive from my business	41	0.59	0.64	0.876
	Changes in my enjoyment in sharing farm life and/or heritage with visitors	41	0.80		
	Changes in my satisfaction with preserving the agricultural landscapes of my farm	41	0.88		
	Changes in the wages I receive from my business	41	0.05		
	Changes in my enjoyment with meeting new people through my business	41	0.90		

[a]Based on the following scale: −2 = greatly decreased, −1 = decreased, 0 = no change, 1 = increased, 2 = greatly increased

The factor mean was −0.08, a neutral value indicating that the average respondent had neither increases nor decreases in their amount of family time or free time. The 29% reporting a decrease in the amount of free time was offset by those reporting increases or no change in the amount of free time combined with those reporting no change or increases in the amount of time spent with family during both work and free time. The reliability of this factor was moderately high at alpha = 0.722.

The "changes in personal satisfaction" factor included the variables "changes in the amount of personal satisfaction I receive from my business," "changes in my enjoyment in sharing farm life and/or heritage with visitors," "changes in my satisfaction with preserving the agricultural landscapes of my farm," "changes in the wages I receive from my business," and "changes in my enjoyment with meeting new people through my business." The factor mean was 0.64, a positive value that indicates that the average respondent had an increase in the satisfaction they received from their business. The reliability of this factor was high (alpha = 0.876).

17.4.3 Discussion and Implications

In summary, results indicated that 76 farmers had assessed their business, implemented improvements, created a new businesses plan, or changed an existing business plan related to agritourism. Examples of agritourism ventures included farm stays, involvement in local schools, social media marketing, hosting fundraising events for non-profits, online newsletters to keep customers up-to-date on farm activities and varieties at their peak, educational nature trails, maple tours for the off-season, farm education retreats, pairing and tasting events, monthly dinners on the farm with a local chef, educational programs for children, and farm infrastructure improvements including roads, buildings, parking lots, farm stores and restrooms.

Because diversifying to include agritourism may not necessarily improve farm viability over the long-term, we examined farm viability by measuring increased profitability and increased quality- of-life. To assess changes in quality-of-life, the survey included a series of questions about "changes in personal time" and "changes in personal satisfaction." Changes in personal time included the variables of "changes in the amount of time I spend with my family (during both work and free time)" and "changes in the amount of free time I have." The factor mean was −0.08, a neutral value that indicates that the average respondent had neither increases nor decreases in their amount of family time or free time. "Changes in personal satisfaction" included the variables "changes in the amount of personal satisfaction I receive from my business," "changes in my enjoyment in sharing farm life and/or heritage with visitors," "changes in my satisfaction with preserving the agricultural landscapes of my farm," "changes in the wages I receive from my business," and "changes in my enjoyment with meeting new people through my business." The factor mean was 0.64, a positive value that indicates that the average respondent had an increase in the personal satisfaction they received from their business. Overall, 51 farmers reported increases in quality-of-life indicators as a result of changes made to their farm business based on the workshops and technical assistance.

Defining farm viability as increases in profitability and/or quality-of-life, we found that 72 farmers reported improved farm viability as a result of changes made based on workshops and/or technical assistance, with 38 reporting both increased profitability and quality-of-life indicators, 21 reporting increased profitability only and 13 reporting increases in quality-of-life indicators only.

17.5 Lessons Learned

The rapid growth in agritourism has some farmers concerned, especially when the diversification and expansion move beyond 'authentic' agriculture, which has different meanings to different people. Agritourism suffers from two types of image problems. Both deal with the idea of an 'authentic' farm. The first concern is that 'agri-tainment' on a working farm will take away from the core business of food and fiber production on the farm. But this doesn't have to be the case. Agritourism in Europe is typically far-removed from the corn mazes, hay rides, and other forms of entertainment often found on American farms that host visitors. Rather, European farm visitors stay overnight and immerse themselves in a true farm experience; they don't visit just to play for a few hours. There's no rush to install catapults for smashing pumpkins, or apple cider doughnut machines on European farms. Similar to the American concept of fast food, agri-tainment can provide a fast farm experience. It may seem satisfying in the short-term and it can fit into our fast-paced schedules but, like fast food, it may not nourish us over the long term. A fast farm agri-tainment visit can lack substance and authenticity; it can be a distraction, not a true educational experience.

Another concern about agritourism is that a tourist attraction may pose as a farm in order to draw visitors. For example, a bed-and-breakfast owner with a few acres of land may plant a vegetable garden and put up some pickles and jams. Does that make it an authentic farm experience? Is the public's knowledge of, and respect for, food production actually diminished by hobby farms? Such concerns lead some farmers to avoid the term agritourism even while welcoming visitors onto their farms for educational, enriching, and authentic agrarian experiences.

Despite these challenges, the benefits of agritourism for farmers and their communities are numerous, from increased economic activity to the preservation of rural lifestyles and landscapes. Interactions with consumers build new connections that give farmers and their work visibility and public support that they might not have otherwise. Agritourism can provide opportunities for income generation beyond the growing season, creating potential to hire year-round rather than seasonal employees. By adding agritourism to their farm enterprise, farmers may be able to include additional family members in the business, enhancing the likelihood that farms will be passed on to the next generation.

The La Mota Ranch just outside of Hebbronville, Texas is a prime example of the benefits of agritourism for multiple generations. The cattle ranch was founded in the 1890s and is still owned and managed by descendants of the original owners. La Mota's primary business is its purebred and commercial cattle herds. Being amateur historians, La Mota's owners, the Hellen family, saw the value in promoting the unique mixture of Mexican and Texan ranching history along the South Texas border. They were further encouraged by the state legislature's recognition of the area's historical significance, so they capitalized on their natural amenities, historic buildings, and local color to create ranch tours. The added income from running tours has allowed the Hellen family to keep the ranch working, and the involvement of the entire family in the tourist enterprise has made the business strong. The La Mota Ranch is an agritourism leader in their region and has helped other businesses with similar goals through a regional agritourism collaboration known as the Llanos Mesteños South Texas Heritage Trail (Chase et al. 2012a, b).

On the other side of the country, Karen Fortin of Carman Brook Maple & Dairy Farm in the remote northwest corner of Vermont credits direct sales of maple syrup on their farm for broadening her children's cultural awareness and sensitivity. While Karen educates visitors from around the world about traditional Native American methods of making maple syrup, she and her family learn about the traditions and lifestyles of visitors who come from Canada, Europe and Asia. According to Karen, "Inviting visitors to our farm has opened up new worlds to us. Living in this rural part of Vermont, my kids would have only known our neighbors, who are a lot like us. Now we have friends from around the world." Contributions to quality-of-life like that are part of the reason why farms offer agritourism.

But it is important to keep in mind that agritourism is not for all farms, or even most farms. Throughout the U.S., regions with the strongest record of direct sales and agritourism account for only about 20% of farms selling direct to the public; and those tend to be small farms for the most part. In one-third of the states, fewer than 5% of farms engage with the public (United States Department of Agriculture 2009). The challenges are many for those farmers who do decide to open their farms to visitors. They need to develop new skills for marketing and hospitality, expand infrastructure on the farm to accommodate visitors, and deal with zoning and liability issues, all in addition to the primary function of producing food, fiber or fuel.

For those farms who do engage with the public, the contributions to quality-of-life can be great – for the farmers, for consumers, and for the broader community. Agritourism enterprises allow farmers to diversify their core operations and add jobs, often keeping family members employed on the farm. By adding new revenues, these additional enterprises help keep farm land in production, preserving scenic vistas and maintaining rural traditions. At the same time, the public is educated about the importance of agriculture to our economy, culture, and quality-of-life.

References

Adams Family Farm. (n.d.). *Farm history*. http://adamsfamilyfarm.com/farm-history/. Accessed July 2013.

Chase, L. C. (2008). Agritourism. In G. A. Goreham (Ed.), *Encyclopedia of rural America: The land and people* (2nd ed., pp. 70–74). Millerton: Grey House Publishing. Excerpted with permission.

Chase, L. C., & Grubinger, V. (2014). *Food, farms, and community: Exploring food systems*. Durham: University of New Hampshire Press. Excerpted with permission.

Chase, L. C., & Kuehn, D. (2010). Measuring outcomes of extension conferences: A case study of the National Extension Tourism Conference. *Journal of Extension, 48*(3), 3FEA6. http://www.joe.org/joe/2010june/a6.php. Accessed 23 June 2017. Excerpted with permission.

Chase, L. C., Boumans, R., & Morse, S. (2010). Participatory modeling as a tool for community development planning: Tourism in the northern forest. *Community Development: Journal of the Community Development Society, 41*(3), 385–397.

Chase, L. C., Amsden, B., & Phillips, R. (2012a). Stakeholder engagement in tourism planning and development. In M. Uysal, R. R. Perdue, & J. Sirgy (Eds.), *Handbook on tourism and quality of life research: Enhancing the lives of tourists and residents of host communities* (pp. 475–490). New York: Springer.

Chase, L. C., Ramaswamy, V. M., Burr, S. W., Zeitlin, J., Green, G. P., & Dougherty, M. (2012b, June). *Successes and challenges in agritourism*. University of Vermont Extension. http://www.uvm.edu/tourismresearch/agritourism/agchecklists/AgritourismSuccessesChallenges.pdf. Accessed 22 June 2017.

Costanza, R., Fisher, B., Ali, S., Beer, C., Bond, L., Boumans, R., Danigelis, N., Dickinson, J., Elliott, C., Farley, J., Gayer, D. E., MacDonald Glenn, L., Hudspeth, T., Mahoney, D., McCahill, L., McIntosh, B., Reed, B., Rizvi, S. A. T., Rizzo, D. M., Simpatico, T., & Snapp, R. (2007). Quality of life: An approach integrating opportunities, human needs, and subjective well-being. *Ecological Economics, 61*, 267–276.

Dillman, D. (2007). *Mail and internet surveys: The tailored design method* (2nd ed.). Hoboken: Wiley.

Hair, J. F., Anderson, R. E., Tatham, R. L., & Black, W. C. (1998). *Multivariate data analysis* (5th ed.). Upper Saddle River: Prentice Hall.

Jensen, K., Bruch, M., Menard, J., & English, B. (2013). *A snapshot of Tennessee agritourism: 2013 update*. Knoxville: University of Tennessee.

Kloppenburg, J., Lezberg, S., & DeMa, K. (2000). Tasting food, tasting sustainability: Defining the attributes of an alternative food system with competent, ordinary people. *Human Organization, 59*(2), 177–186.

Kuehn, D., & Hilchey, D. (2001). Agritourism in New York: Management and operations. New York Sea Grant, New York. Retrieved from http://www.seagrant.sunysb.edu/Images/Uploads/PDFs/themeareas/CoastalEco/AgritourismInNY.pdf

Mandala Research. (2013, August 27). new study of traveler eating interests shows promoting culinary activities can pay off: Almost A Third of Travelers Choose Destinations Based on Eating Opportunities. www.MandalaResearch.com. Accessed 23 June 2017.

Sirgy, M. J., Rahtz, D. R., Cicic, M., & Underwood, R. (2000). A method for assessing residents' satisfaction with community-based services: A quality-of-life perspective. *Social Indicators Research, 49*, 279–316.

United States Department of Agriculture. (2009). *2007 census of agriculture*. Washington, DC: United States Department of Agriculture.

Wong, C. (2006). *Quantitative indicators for urban and regional planning: The interplay of policy and methods*. London: Routledge.

World Food Travel Association. (n.d.) What is food tourism? http://www.worldfoodtravel.org. Accessed July 2013.

Chapter 18
The Old Havana: Economic and Social Impact of Tourism Management on the Quality of Life of Residents

Yamilé Pérez Guilarte and Rubén Camilo Lois González

Abstract The Old Havana, a World Heritage Site since 1982, is one of the main tourist attractions in Cuba, but it is also a space with a marked residential nature. In recent years, the process of recovering this site and restoring it for tourist use has represented a major challenge, both economically and socially. The current situation in the country, resulting from new Cuban government policies, has led to great interest in developing public and private initiatives that enhance tourism in this area. This chapter presents Old Havana as a case study and addresses the economic and social impact that the tourism management carried out by the Office of the Historian of the City of Havana (OHCH) has had on its residents. The chapter opens by introducing historic centres and impacts of tourism, especially in Latin America. It then goes on to introduce the special features of tourism in Cuba. Next, it addresses the social impact on the Cuban population of the tourism policy implemented in the early 1990s, which focused on promoting international tourism at the expense of domestic tourism. It also describes the scenario that resulted from creating designated tourist areas, isolated from the Cuban population, which prevented visitor exchange with residents and cultural enrichment. Next, it discusses the tourism management model developed by the OHCH, which constitutes an outstanding example of sustainable tourism management practice. The chapter closes by presenting a series of final considerations regarding the future of tourism in Cuba, based on the current context.

Keywords Old Havana · Rehabilitation process · Tourist management · Social programme

Y. Pérez Guilarte (✉)
University Institute for Studies and Development of Galicia, University of Santiago de Compostela, Santiago de Compostela, Spain

R. C. Lois González
Faculty of Geography and History, University of Santiago de Compostela, Santiago de Compostela, Spain
e-mail: rubencamilo.lois@usc.es

A. M. Campón-Cerro et al. (eds.), *Best Practices in Hospitality and Tourism Marketing and Management*, Applying Quality of Life Research,
https://doi.org/10.1007/978-3-319-91692-7_18

18.1 Introduction

The historic city centres of Latin America share a common history of neglect, marginalization and vulnerability that has impacted the populations that reside therein. This situation has occurred as a result of the process of decline associated with factors such as the growth of the city, the deterioration of the buildings or natural disasters (Pérez 2014). However, in recent times the situation seems to have become more complex and different types of city centres are appearing: reasonably renovated city centres that suffer from continuous renovation and degradation processes, and a third group that is in a state of extreme deterioration (Vergara 2008).

Tourism is one of the main drivers for the interventions in historic city centres, and one of the main added values in the renewal processes that we have just mentioned. In the majority of cases, its influence is due to the recovery of architectural heritage and public spaces which allows the promotion of metropolitan tourism (Etulain and González 2012). In this regard, the enhancement of historic heritage allows the strengthening of a population's local identity as a whole, although the development of tourism may also cause social problems associated with gentrification processes or the trivialization of spaces, turning them into purely tourist sites and devoid of identity (Santos and Lois 2005).

An example of creating spaces solely for tourist use, was the tourist model developed by the Cuban government in the 1990s. As an alternative to the economic crisis resulting from the disintegration of the former Soviet Union, the development of international tourism was established as a priority. However, this model not only directed the tourist activity towards foreigners but also restricted it for locals, leading to an intense process of marginalisation of the Cuban population. Tourism thereby created an important social problem in the country that lasted for almost 20 years, until 2008 when the Cuban government authorised Cubans to access tourist services. In addition to this social problem, the tourism model did not have an important economic impact on the population. It could therefore be said that the sustainable tourism dimension aimed at improving the receptor community's quality of life, has not been reflected in the model established in Cuba.

Taking into account this problem, we proposed, as research questions, ascertaining whether any subsequent tourist strategy capable of reversing this situation was implemented, and if it had a positive impact on Cuban residents' quality of life. In this regard, we can only point to, at a national level, the exceptional case of the Historic City Centre of Havana. This is the largest and most successful model of local development undertaken in contemporary Cuba (Monreal 2007). Therefore, the objective of this chapter is to study the economic and social impact of tourism management on the quality of life of residents in the Old Havana. The tourist model developed by the Office of the Historian of the City of Havana (OHCH) will be presented as a case study to illustrate the way they deal with the improvement of the community's quality of life.

18.2 Theory Note: Historic City Centres and Tourism

The historic centre of a city is its prime symbolic space and is, to a large extent, the collective memory of the society that inhabits it (De la Calle and García 1998; Levy 1987). Santos and Lois (2005) state that historic cities whose emergence took place in the majority of cases in the pre-industrial period, are a unique social product. Their landscape features are the result of the juxtaposition of different building layers corresponding to different historical phases (Lois 2004). Functionally, they were spaces marked by diversity, polyfunctionality and modernity; although at present, social changes are generating a series of conflicts and misadaptations (Lois and Santos 2006). Taking into account the nature of the historic city centres, Troitiño (1992) differentiates between those who retain their functionality and those who do not. Taking this into account, the following functional types are suggested:

- Old towns which are no longer the economic city centre, but retain a symbolic and cultural centrality.
- Old towns that preserve certain heritage and functional centrality.
- Old towns which continue to be the functional centre of the current city.

The fact that some historic city centres lost their administrative centrality led the public management to focus on the new urban areas (Carrión 2009). Thus, the lack of investment in infrastructure and services and the maintenance of public spaces in the historical centres became evident. Also, the narrow streets and old buildings structures were unable to provide appropriate space for contemporary lifestyle patterns. For these reasons, the inhabitants with greater buying power began to abandon historic city centres as places of residence (Etulain and González 2012). This situation dragged the commercial activity and service companies with it, meaning the loss of historic city centres as points of reference, and resulting in their process of deterioration (Vergara 2008).

The processes of abandonment in which many historic Latin American and European city centres were in after the World Wars, started to reverse at the end of the 70s and the early 80s (Etulain and González 2012). In this period, many interventions took place resulting in renewal processes, usage replacement and the enhancement of central spaces. Its objective was to try to reconstruct both the materiality and the image of these undervalued areas, to become attractive sites for entertainment, visual and aesthetic consumption (Girola et al. 2011). Tourism became the priority sector of a large part of the rehabilitation activities in historic city centres. However, these processes were mainly oriented towards the protection of tangible heritage while abandoning other important functions. As a result, well preserved urban spaces but devoid of life and economic activities as well as tourist activities appeared, leading to a museumisation of historic city centres (Santos and Lois 2005).

With time the museumisation of historic city centres begins to be questioned and they start to be reclaimed as living centres, as a result of the society that inhabits them. The 1977 Charter of Quito, states that the protagonists of the city centres are their inhabitants and that one of the essential elements of a city centres' rehabilitation and its renewal must be its residential use (ICOMOS 2007). In this regard, it should be mentioned that in some historic city centres there has been a *gentrification* phenomenon. This is the result of the eviction of residents from damaged buildings so they can be remodelled and re-functionalised, to be inhabited by a population of greater buying power at a later date. Therefore, this phenomenon is accompanied by the displacement or eviction of the former residents (Sabatini et al. 2009), altering the richness of the primary housing function of these places.

In Latin America the characteristics of interventions in historic city centres vary according to the place. For example, in the Historic City Centre of Colonia del Sacramento in Uruguay villagers have been handing over their spaces to new inhabitants. At the same time many heritage structures have had their exterior kept and preserved, but emptied of content for refunctionalisation (Etulain and González 2012). In the Historic City Centre of Quito, together with the promotion of tourism in refunctionalised buildings, university buildings have been introduced, providing this space with new purposes and integrating tourism into the local development. Additionally, there are more comprehensive examples such as the recovery of the Historic City Centre of Old Havana. In this case, the actions have been focused on public spaces, buildings of heritage value, and the promotion of uses and activities with the participation of residents. Tourism is the economic pillar of the rehabilitation process of Old Havana (Palet et al. 2006; Monreal 2007).

The management of historic city centres is a complex task taking into account the diversity of actors, situations and realities. For example, a European historic city centre does not possess the same characteristics as a Latin American one. These differences also arise between different countries and even between cities in the same country (Etulain and González 2012). In this context, each territory must regulate the development of the tourist activity according to its own scenario. Tourism planning and management should ensure a satisfactory experience for visitors, but respect the environment of the resident community, according to the principles that govern the development of sustainable tourism (UNWTO 1997, 2004).

18.3 The Problem: Particularities of Tourism in Cuba

Tourism has been gradually acquiring a key role in the Cuban economy. In the last 10 years Cuba has received more than 2 million international visitors annually, and in 2014 this figure surpassed for the first time in its history the 3 million visitor mark (ONEI 2015). Ninety-five percent of arrivals have as their main motivation holidays and leisure, Canada being the main market source of tourists. However, with the recent restoration of relations between Cuba and the United States there has been an increase in the number of U.S. visitors, and the forecasts predict continuous growth. The second most important market (14%) is comprised of Cubans residing abroad (Perelló 2013). The European market comprises 30% of tourists, led by the United Kingdom, Germany, France, Italy and Spain (ONEI 2015).

Until the end of the 1950s, Cuba was the main tourist destination in the Caribbean. In 1957 the highest number of arrivals was reached with 272,265 visitors, of whom 85% were US citizens, attracted mostly by advertising offering Havana as the gambling and prostitution centre of the Caribbean (Baroni 2009; MINTUR 2015). However, with the triumph of the Cuban revolution in 1959, major changes took place. Among them are (Soler 2001): promotion of domestic tourism, change of beach ownership to become publicly owned, development of an incipient "Socialist tourism", emphasis on agricultural industrialisation and mechanisation, and loss of hotel competitiveness.

In the 1960s, the number of foreign tourists continued to trend downwards, due to the breakdown in relations with the United States, as a primary market source. In 1970 small groups from Canada and some countries of Latin America began to arrive, while visitors from Europe increased. In February 1982, the 50 Law Decree on foreign investment which came into force in 1988 was issued (Soler 2001). This law regulated the economic partnership between Cuban and foreign entities and was considered an instrument to expand exports and tourism more dynamically.

The disintegration of the Soviet Union in 1991 hit the Cuban economy, which lost 80% of its exports and imports, meaning a sharp decline of 35% of GDP (Navarro 2008). From that time onwards, the Cuban Government began to consider tourism as an alternative to the economic recovery and reactivation. However, the development was based on attracting international tourists, to the detriment of domestic tourism that had been promoted since the triumph of the revolution (Pérez 2014). Therefore, the tourism offered was designed taking into account the needs of international tourists, and not only that, but it forbade Cubans access to the main tourist facilities. In this way, tourists were people with certain privileges that residents did not have. This situation had strong social implications, as the fact that Cubans could not enjoy tourism in their own country created a major upset in the Cuban population.

This model promoted the creation of totally tourist areas, basically beach oriented, preventing it from differing itself from other Caribbean destinations which employ this same tourist formula (UNWTO and SEGIB 2010). This was a competitive disadvantage. It is well known that people are increasingly travelling away from crowded places, to find experiences that allow them to enjoy the customs and mix with the population (Pérez 2014). The places where the coexistence of both areas was inevitable were strongly policed to prevent any kind of relationship between visitors and residents. In 2008 this policy changed and Cuban citizens were allowed access to tourist services, although in practice they do not have the financial resources to enjoy them.

In regards to the levels of income, it should be noted that in addition to the aforementioned social problems, this tourism model did not have a relevant economic impact on the population. It is, however, true that the Cubans benefited by being hired in different public tourism or joint venture facilities, but as in other sectors, wages do not match the cost of living. Therefore, workers rely on customer tips, and often turn to fraudulent procedures that can affect the quality of the service. This wage imbalance has been maintained until today, being one of the most significant problems in Cuban society.

The private tourism sector was promoted by new laws or reforms of existing laws which have been adopted since 1994 (Carranza et al. 1995; Burgos 2011). It encouraged the creation of small private businesses such as restaurants called "paladares" or the rental of private homes to foreigners. However, then came a process of stagnation in the granting of licences for these purposes (MTSS and MFP 1996). This situation lasted for more than 10 years until 2011 when, as part of the new economic and social policy of the Cuban Government, the promotion of private business creation was restarted (PCC 2011). It is then when private business such as: the paladares, private accommodation in homes, shops, transportation services, rides in carriages or vintage cars among others, started to surge.

It could be said that the sustainable tourism dimension that looks for an improvement in the quality of life of the receiving community, has not been reflected in the model established in Cuba. In this regard, it can only be highlighted at a national level the exceptional case of the Historic City Centre of Havana. This is the largest and most successful model of local development undertaken in contemporary Cuba (Monreal 2007). Old Havana is one of the places with the most favourable conditions to territorially strengthen economic support of dynamic, diversified, and mutually reinforced activities, with the intensive use of knowledge (Monreal and Carranza 2003). Tourism is the economic engine driver of this model, but also the respect for the population's well-being is a fundamental pillar of the rehabilitation policy.

18.4 A Solution: The Case of the Old Havana Rehabilitation Process

The historic centre of Havana with an area of 214 ha (2.14 km^2) is located in Old Havana municipality, occupying 50% of the space. Unlike other historic city centres of Latin America, and in general of the central areas of big cities, it has an intense residential purpose. Its population of 66,742 inhabitants (OHCH 2011a) represents 74% of the municipal population (ONEI 2015). The gross density in the area is 310 inhabitants per ha, with net densities at building block level that vary between 100 and 1000 (OHCH 2011a).

Since the end of the eighteenth century to the early decades of the twentieth century, the area of the old city maintained population stability of between 40,000 and 50,000 inhabitants. However, from 1920 until 1943 a growth in population took place, reaching the figure of 72,000 inhabitants. This increase was a result of the construction boom, the process of property speculation and the conversion of former palaces into citadels and other housing solutions. Since the 1950s there has been a slight reduction in the number of inhabitants, as a result of the expansion of the city to the suburbs and a steady number of about 60,000 inhabitants in the area (OHCH 2015). However, in qualitative terms, it must be mentioned that the historic

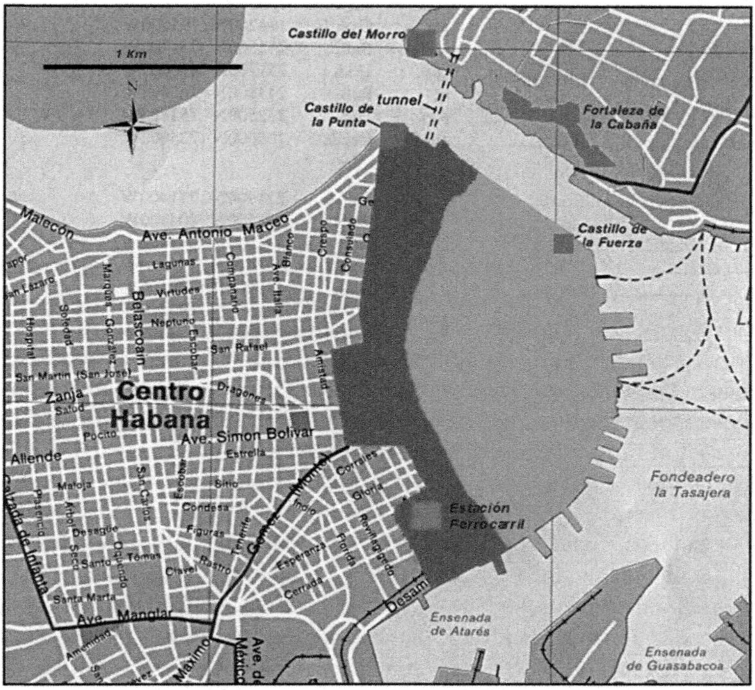

Within the Wall | *Las Murallas* neighbourhood | Historic Centre

Fig. 18.1 Delimitation of the historic city centre of Havana. (Source: Own work as per University of Texas (2014) and OHCH (2011a))

city centre shows similar indicators to those in other central urban areas, as for example, the aging of the population. Similarly, there has been a reduction in family size, which is evidenced by the fact that 16% of families are single households (OHCH 2015).

The historic city centre has 3370 buildings, of which 551 have a high heritage value. It consists of two areas clearly differentiated from the urban point of view: the old city within the walls, and the surrounding strip that was urbanised after the demolition of the city walls and built between mid-nineteenth century and the first decades of the twentieth century (OHCH 2011a). The area of Havana within the wall extends from the western edge of the bay, including the current maritime border, up to the axis through which the old wall ran (Fig. 18.1). The other area encompasses the Las Murallas neighbourhood (in Spanish, *barrio Las Murallas*) ranging from the San Salvador de la Punta Castle to the courtyard of the Central Train Station. The Bay of Havana Fortification System is also part of the historic city centre.

The decline of the historic city centre as the main residential area began in the mid nineteenth century with the growth of the city to the West and the emergence of exclusive neighbourhoods. Many of the single-family palaces were sold and became tenancy houses or citadels. The lower floors domestic use began to suffer transformations, being converted into warehouses and workshops depending on the port activity. New buildings for these purposes were also built, and the industrial function acquired greater relevance. With the arrival of the twentieth century, it became an area characterised by a high density of low income population (Rojas and Rodríguez 2004).

More critical issues included poor housing conditions, the deterioration of existing accessibility, and the health and educational facilities in the community. Similarly, there were flaws in the infrastructure needed for the elderly, the disabled and other vulnerable groups. Nor were there sufficient sports facilities, and resources for environmental care were scarce. In addition, there was an overload in damaged technological networks and infrastructure, which were insufficient to even provide an acceptable local performance. Another serious problem was the lack of supply of potable water, mitigated in part by the use of water tank trucks (OHCH 2006a).

In this context, Cuban avant-garde intellectuals in the 1930s started to raise awareness of the urgency of protecting buildings and historical monuments and deepening and disseminating Cuban culture and nationality. One of the biggest victories of that movement, led by Doctor Emilio Roig de Leuschenring (1889–1964), would be the foundation of the Havana Historian Office (OHCH) in 1938. After the disappearance of the historian Roig, the work of the institution continued with the appointment in 1967 of Dr. Eusebio Leal Spengler as the historian of the City of Havana (Rojas and Rodríguez 2004). Leal continues in this role and he is the highest authority in the comprehensive restoration of the historic city centre.

From then onwards, the restoration works of the General Captains old Palace in Armas Square began. This work continued with other later works, carried out jointly with institutions and agencies of the Cuban State and society. At this time, the proposal to award the Historic City Centre of Havana the National Monument distinction was submitted and was granted in 1978. In 1981, with the decision to allocate a significant budget to the restoration of the historic city centre, the Office was appointed to lead the rehabilitation from an urban perspective. The implementation of scientifically well-founded concepts was endorsed by UNESCO in 1982, listing the Historic City Centre of Havana and its Fortifications System as a World Heritage Site (Leal 2007).

The Old Havana Comprehensive Revitalisation program continued with the Five-year Restoration Plans (1981–1986 and 1986–1991) based on a strategy of recovery of public spaces, that would change the image of the main squares and establish the lines of what would become the old town heritage rehabilitation (OHCH 2015). In 1993 the Council of State approved the number 143 Law Decree, declaring the historic city centre A Conservation Prioritised Area (Leal 2007). From this moment, the Historian Office was awarded powers of attorney to develop self-funded comprehensive rehabilitation plans, a unique management formula which was introduced for the first time in Cuba. Also in November 1995 through the 2951 Agreement, the Council of Ministers proclaimed the historic city centre Area of High Significance for Tourism.

In the Historian's Office, the Master Plan is the entity that controls the uses of the land and is responsible for maintaining the management's integrity. In 1998 it developed the Special Development Plan (PED), a practical guide to govern actions in the territory, ensuring the coherence of interventions and physical recovery. The rehabilitation was structured by linking comprehensive development criteria, self-financing recovery mechanisms and cultural development, from five key policies (OHCH 2006b):

- Safeguard the national identity drawn from the research, promotion and development of culture.
- Protect the inherited heritage, rehabilitating the land through a legally binding continuing Special Plan of Comprehensive Development.
- Avoid the displacement of the local population, protecting it from the impact of outsourcing and establishing appropriate density and quality of life.
- Provide the territory with technical infrastructure and basic services that ensure its operation responding to contemporary needs.
- Achieve a self-funded comprehensive development making heritage investment recoverable and productive.

The continuity of this planning was followed by the 2001 Strategic Plan, where policies and actions in each of the main lines of action were laid out. However, a decade later the new Special Plan of Comprehensive Development (PEDI) was developed. This tool organises and directs the revitalisation process through the identification of a series of actions to develop from the physical point of view, in particular those planned in the short term (2011–2015) (OHCH 2011a). Its adoption was the result of a public consultation process, which has involved entities from the Historian Office, the Physical Planning and Cultural Heritage System, and the local government and its sectoral directorates. In addition, people residing or employed in entities in the historic centre participated by expressing their opinion through a questionnaire (OHCH 2011b).

With the increase of powers of the Historian Office regarding tourism, real estate and tertiary sector administration, the company Habaguanex was created in 1994 to find the financial resources that would make possible the self-financing of the work. Also, exclusive powers were granted to create the necessary companies to raise funds. In this way, a structure of hotels, restaurants, markets and other services was created; and also former hotels and small hostels located in mansions and palaces were repossessed (Rojas and Rodríguez 2004).

With revenue from tourism operations, from taxes on productive companies in the territory to the self-employed, investment increased significantly in the area. Figure 18.2 shows the case of the renovation of the Old Square *(in Spanish, Plaza Vieja)* and the Old Warehouses of San José *(in Spanish, Antiguos Almacenes de San José)*. As originally planned, the Old Square has become a space with a traditional image, a strong cultural, service and housing purpose; becoming one of the main attractions of the old part of the city. Furthermore, the restoration of the Old Warehouses of San José, an example of the industrial architecture of the late nineteenth century, gave rise to the process of restructuring the old port structures into

Fig. 18.2 Restoration works in Old Havana. Note: Old Square (left) and Old Warehouses of San José (right). (Source: Havana Historian Office. Master Plan (OHCH 2015))

cultural and leisure facilities. The former warehouse became the new headquarters of the Artisans Market, thus marking the first step in the recovery of the waterfront of the historic city (OHCH 2015).

In regards to the waterfront of the historic city centre, it is interesting to note the project of the OHCH for the redevelopment of the port of Havana, from a commercial to a tourist purpose. The recent opening of the Mariel Port, located 46 km from Havana, will allow the movement of all commercial activity from the port of Havana to Mariel. In this way, the Havana coast and its surroundings will have a tourist-recreational function. This is a typical urban renewal action as those undertaken in Europe, in cities such as A Coruña, Hamburg or Rotterdam, with the aim of freeing port space for citizens (Pérez 2014).

The waterfront of the historic city centre will feature a series of structures that will enable the diversification of touristic space, making use of architectural and industrial heritage located in this area and incorporating new products/services. The main functions defined for the waterfront are (Oliva 2013): Promenade, cruise liner terminal, poly-functional areas (recreational, commercial-gastronomic and cultural), tourist accommodation, markets, real estate offices, parking lots, a wharf for transfers between the two sides of the bay, and sporting and recreational yacht harbours (Fig. 18.3). However, work is being undertaken in sections, so the transformation will take place gradually.

Fig. 18.3 New purposes of Old Havana waterfront
Note: Floating promenade (top) and wharf (below)
Source: Oliva (2013)

18.5 Implications of the Rehabilitation Process on the Residents' Quality of Life

In order to ascertain the impact of tourist policies on the History City Centre of Havana's residents, we used the results of a survey of the local population carried out by the Office of the Historian's Master Plan. The objective was to ascertain the resident population's opinion of the tourist activity. The survey was carried out

Table 18.1 Reasons expressed by interviewees for working in tourism

Reasons	%
Greater economic benefits	70.8
Good working conditions	35.2
Cultural exchange	30.0
Meeting people from other countries	23.6

Source: Echarri (2006)

among 378 residents of the Historic City Centre in 2003, by means of simple random sampling with a significance level of 95% (Echarri 2006).

In the case of 88.8% of respondents, they would like to have activities related to tourism in their neighbourhood. In relation to tourism's benefits for the Historic City Centre, 85.7% replied that it is a source of economic income for the community, 33.7% believed that it favoured the preservation of heritage and 32.6% that it helped to promote Cuban culture abroad. Despite this, 9.9% of the interviewed residents expressed their discontent, claiming that it led to greater segregation and increased deterioration in the Historic City Centre.

Resident support for tourism is shown by their interest in working in this sector. In the case of 71.4% of interviewees, they expressed this intention, especially in relation to gastronomy and commerce. Table 18.1 shows the main reasons why residents work in tourism. Economic reasons are important, being mentioned by 70.8% of those interviewed. They also associated tourism with other reasons, such as: good working conditions, cultural exchange and the possibility of meeting people from other countries.

Another important study used in this chapter, to illustrate the comprehensive rehabilitation process' effect on residents, is the project "The capacity and number of visitors in Havana's Historic City Centre." The proposal was developed at the University of Havana's Tourism Faculty, based on the analysis of sustainability indicators using the methodology of Echarri (2006). Therefore, analysing as indicators the number of workers employed by Habaguanex and the number of tourism-related licenses granted to the self-employed, reflects the improvements experienced by residents in terms of employment and the possibilities of setting up private businesses.

Figure 18.4 shows the evolution of the number of workers employed by the Habaguanex tourist company (Delis 2015; Echarri 2006). As we can see, the number of workers grew by a factor of 3.7 from 1996 to 2014, as a result of an increase in tourist services. In relation to these workers, the Office of the Historian's Master Plan indicates that 50% are residents of the Historic City Centre (Delis 2015). In general, more than 13,000 direct jobs and another 2000 indirect ones have been created in the construction, tourism, and culture sectors thanks to the rehabilitation process (Leal 2007). In any case, these workers employed by OHCH are not exempt from the aforementioned wage problems. This is therefore an issue that still has to be solved, if this comprehensive rehabilitation process is to have a greater impact on the residents' quality of life.

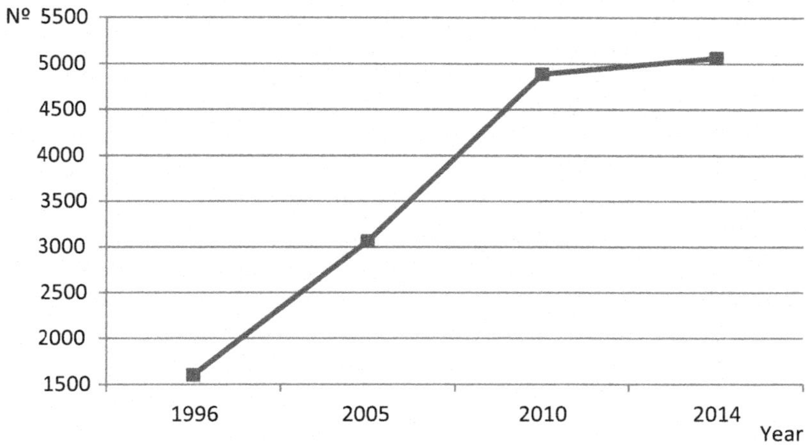

Fig. 18.4 Number of workers in Habaguanex tourist company. (Source: Echarri (2006) and Delis (2015))

Table 18.2 Licenses most frequently requested by the self-employed

Type of activity	%
Hiring employees	21
Gastronomic activities	11
Transport activities	9
Renting homes, rooms or spaces	9

Source: Delis (2015)

In relation to the number of tourism-related licenses granted to the self-employed, 954 had been approved by the end of October 2010, according to Old Havana's Municipal Tax Administration Office. This figure rose to 85% at the end of 2012, when, after being opened up to the private sector, 6157 licenses were registered. 4535 of them belonged to residents of the historic centre, 74% of the total (Marrero 2014). As Table 18.2 shows, the licenses most frequently requested by the self-employed were those required to hire employees (21%), those linked to gastronomic activities (11%), transport (9%) and for renting homes, rooms or spaces (9%). In 2014, there were 564 private management rooms, only being surpassed by the State-managed rooms by 3.9% (Delis 2015). This behaviour is a result of government regulations that have allowed rapid growth within the non-State sector. Some experts interviewed believe that private management will experience notable increases in the coming years and may even exceed the State supply.

In addition, the rehabilitation process of the historic city centre included a social program in which social centres for the most vulnerable population sectors have been built. In this way, institutions such as the following were founded: health centres for pregnant women at risk, for children with special needs, and retirement homes and day care centres for the elderly. Public libraries, playgrounds and gardens, concert venues, museums and other cultural institutions have also been created for both tourist and resident use. It should be noted that the museums as well as their cultural activity also welcome primary school students in a teaching program called "Classroom in the Museum" (OHCH 2011a).

Also, the homes of people who live in renewal areas have been rehabilitated, improving their living conditions. According to Delis (2015), 115 buildings were reconverted for residential purposes during 2008. In this sense, there is still much to be done to meet the demands of the population in terms of housing rehabilitation, and in general in buildings located within the historic city centre. Similarly, models of citizen participation need to be introduced, in the context of a decision-making process which is still very centralised and designed according to major general objectives only.

18.6 Final Considerations and Lessons Learned

As has been analysed in this chapter, the conception of tourism as a promoter of the rehabilitation project of Old Havana has resulted in economic development, while maintaining its functions as a residential area and ensuring the quality of life of its inhabitants. The model of tourism marketing and management implemented by the Office of the Historian of Havana strongly involved the local community. Firstly, inhabitants of the Old Havana were prioritized as employees to work in the tourist businesses. Secondly, facilities such as concert venues, museums, playgrounds, gardens among others were created for both tourist and resident use. Finally, the homes of people who lived in renewal areas have been rehabilitated, improving their living conditions.

Currently, the economic impact is even greater, since the promotion of the private sector by the Cuban Government has facilitated the proliferation of restaurants, shops, rooms for rent and other tourist activities in Old Havana. However, the relationships between the public and private sector is an emerging issue in a society in which for many years policies have been handed down unilaterally by government institutions. In this sense, the union of these new entrepreneurs and business associations, for example, could be an initiative to promote their participation in the decision-making process with regards to tourism planning and management in the future.

The Havana Historian Office model has achieved the integration of the resident population with the rehabilitation project, which means that its inhabitants are welcoming of tourism. This fact could be exploited further to the benefit of the receiving communities and visitors. In addition to the creation of common spaces for visitors and residents where they can interact, activities designed around the knowledge of Cuban culture at the hands of local residents could be created. In this way, cultural activities should be more flexible to allow promoting initiatives such as visits to artists' workshops and gastronomic tours among other activities. When people travel they increasingly demand this type of experience which allows them to experience the traditions and lifestyle of a destination in conjunction with the locals.

Old Havana has all the ingredients to develop traditional cultural tourism based on its rich material heritage, but at the same time it has the potential to differentiate itself from other destinations in the region if they know how to leverage their intangible heritage. The work done by the OHCH to develop tourism, while maintaining a "living" historic city centre so far has been commendable, although with some outstanding issues. However, it is faced with an imminent challenge. The number of visitors to the city is growing and it is expected that with the opening of the United States market this trend will continue. Therefore, taking into account these forecasts, the necessary measures should be anticipated and taken so this World Heritage Site can offer visitors a quality experience, and at the same time preserve its vitality and uniqueness.

References

Baroni, P. (2009). *The historic city centre: singularities and recovery*. http://www.nuevomundo.revues.org/index48472.html. Accessed 16 June 2015.

Burgos, M. (2011). El derecho en Cuba socialista: reflexiones desde perspectivas crítico-dialécticas. In B. Bernal (Coord.), *Cuba hoy: ¿perspectivas de cambio?* (pp. 23–85). México, D.F.: UNAM.

Carranza, J., Gutiérrez, L., & Monreal, P. (1995). *Cuba la reestructuración de la economía (una propuesta para el debate)*. Madrid: IEPALA Editorial.

Carrión, F. (2009). La centralidad histórica: entre el nacionalismo del pasado (monumento) y el sentido social de hoy (centro vivo). *Revista Centro-h, 3*, 7–12.

De la Calle, M., & García, M. (1998). Ciudades históricas: patrimonio cultural y recurso turístico. *Ería, 47*, 249–266.

Delis, C. D. (2015). *Evaluación de indicadores de sostenibilidad turística para el Centro Histórico de La Habana en el período 2010–2014*. Dissertation, University of Havana.

Echarri, M. (2006). *Análisis geográfico del turismo en ciudades patrimoniales. Caso de estudio: Centro Histórico de La Habana*. Dissertation, University of Havana.

Etulain, J. C., & González, A. (2012). Rupturas y reintegraciones socio-territoriales en la intervención de los centros históricos latinoamericanos. In *Actas 7mo Congreso de Medio Ambiente AUGM* (pp. 1–21). La Plata: UNLP.

Girola, M. F., Yacovino, M. P., & Laborde, S. (2011). Recentrando la centralidad: procesos de recualificación urbana y espacio público en la ciudad de Buenos Aires desde una perspectiva etnográfica. *Cuaderno Urbano, Cultura, Sociedad, 10*(10), 9–29.

ICOMOS. (2007). The 1977 charter of Quito. Chilean Committee of the International Council on Monuments and Sites. http://icomoschile.blogspot.com/2007/09/carta-de-quito-1977.html. Accessed 3 May 2015.

Leal, E. (2007). *La Rehabilitación del Centro Histórico: una obra esencialmente humana*. La Habana: City of Havana Historian Office. http://www.cccb.org/rcs_gene/eusebioleal.pdf. Accessed 24 May 2015.

Levy, J. P. (1987). *Centres Villes en Mutation*. París: CNRS.

Lois, R. C. (2004). Process of urban transformation in the historical cities of Spain. In M. Pacione (Ed.), *Changing cities. International perspectives* (pp. 161–172). Glasgow: IGU Urban Commission and Strathclyde University Pubs.

Lois, R. C., & Santos, X. M. (Eds.). (2006). *Modelos de gestión: soluciones institucionales para las ciudades históricas*. Santiago de Compostela: Ayuntamiento de Santiago de Compostela y Câmara Municipal de Porto.

Marrero, Y. (2014). *Impactos de la actividad por cuenta propia vinculada al turismo en el Centro Histórico de La Habana*. Dissertation, University of Havana.

MINTUR. (2015). Ministry of Tourism of Cuba. http://www.cubagob.cu/des_eco/turismo.htm. Accessed 5 Sept 2015.

Monreal, P. (2007). La Oficina del Historiador de la Ciudad de La Habana: Apuntes sobre un caso de escalamiento institucional. In E. Hershberg (Coord.), *Innovación y construcción institucional. Latinoamérica y el Este de Asia* (pp. 19–40). Barcelona: Icaria Editorial.

Monreal, P., & Carranza, J. (2003). El centro histórico de La Habana Vieja como acelerador de desarrollo. *Cultura y Desarrollo, 3*, 52–56.

MTSS & MFP. (1996). Legal ruling No.1/1996. Ministry of Labour and Social Security (MTSS) and Ministry of Finance and Price (MFP) of Cuba.

Navarro, E. (Ed.). (2008). *Turismo, cooperación y posibilidades de desarrollo en playas del este (La Habana-Cuba) y su zona de influencia*. Málaga: Servicio de Publicaciones. Centro de Ediciones de la Diputación Provincial de Málaga.

OHCH. (2006a). *Una experiencia singular. Valoraciones sobre el modelo de gestión integral de La Habana Vieja, Patrimonio de la Humanidad*. La Habana: Oficina Regional de Cultura para América Latina de la UNESCO.

OHCH. (2006b). Desarrollo integral del Centro Histórico de la Habana Vieja. City of Havana Historian Office. http://habitat.aq.upm.es/bpal/onu06/bp1315.html. Accessed 25 Feb 2015.

OHCH. (2011a). PEDI. Plan Especial de Desarrollo Integral. City of Havana Historian Office. http://www.planmaestro.ohc.cu/recursos/papel/libros/pedi.pdf. Accessed 10 Mar 2015.

OHCH. (2011b). Cuestionario de consulta ciudadana. City of Havana Historian Office http://www.planmaestro.ohc.cu/recursos/papel/formularios/cpcuestionario.pdf. Accessed 21 Mar 2015.

OHCH. (2015). Plan Maestro para la Rehabilitación Integral de la Habana Vieja. Población y vivienda en el centro histórico. City of Havana Historian Office. http://www.planmaestro.ohc.cu/index.php/territorio/demografia. Accessed 25 June 2015.

Oliva, J. (2013). *El proyecto turístico "Habana Puerto Viejo". Una diversificación del espacio turístico del Centro Histórico de La Habana*. La Habana: Universidad de La Habana.

ONEI. (2015). National Office of Statistics and Information of Cuba. http://www.one.cu. Accessed 10 Sept 2015.

Palet, M., Sardiñas, O., & García, M. (2006). La restauración como actor principal de la revalorización del espacio local. La Habana Vieja, patrimonio vivo. In A. Bergara (Ed.), *Renovación de centros históricos en grandes ciudades latinoamericanas* (pp. 54–83). Barranquilla: Uninorte.

PCC. (2011). VI Congreso del Partido Comunista de Cuba. Lineamientos de la política, económica y social del Partido y la Revolución. http://www.cubadebate.cu/wp-content/uploads/2011/05/folleto-lineamientos-vi-cong.pdf. Accessed 5 Sept 2015.

Perelló, J. L. (2013). *Actualización del sector turístico cubano al cierre del primer semestre de 2013. Documento de Trabajo*. La Habana: Centro de Estudios Turísticos de la Universidad de La Habana.

Pérez, Y. (2014). *Nuevas tendencias del turismo cultural. El papel de la investigación turística en ciudades patrimoniales: los casos de Santiago de Compostela y La Habana Vieja*. Dissertation, University of Santiago de Compostela. http://dspace.usc.es/handle/10347/11872. Accessed 8 Mar 2015.

Rojas, R., & Rodríguez, P. (2004). Desafío de una utopía. City of Havana Historian Office. http://www.planmaestro.ohc.cu/recursos/papel/libros/desafioutopia.pdf. Accessed 10 June 2015.

Sabatini, F., Sarella, M., & Vásquez, H. (2009). Gentrification without expulsion or the historical crossroads of the Latin American City. *Revista_180, 24*, 18–25.

Santos X.M., & Lois, R.C. (Coords.) (2005). *Desarrollo Turístico sostenible en ciudades históricas*. Santiago de Compostela: Ayuntamiento de Santiago de Compostela.

Soler, O. (2001). *El turismo en Cuba. Economía y estrategia sociopolítica*. La Habana: Escuela de Altos Estudios de Hotelería y Turismo.

Troitiño, M. A. (1992). *Cascos antiguos y Centros históricos: problemas, políticas y dinámicas urbanas*. Madrid: MOPU.

University of Texas. (2014). *Perry-Castañeda Library map collection*. http://www.lib.utexas.edu/maps/. Accessed 10 Mar 2014.

UNWTO. (1997). *Desarrollo Turístico Sostenible*. Guía para planificadores locales. Madrid: World Tourism Organisation.

UNWTO. (2004). *Indicators of sustainable development for tourism destinations. A Guidebook*. Madrid: World Tourism Organisation.

UNWTO and SEGIB. (2010). *Turismo en Iberoamérica en 2009*. UNWTO and Ibero-American General Secretariat (SEGIB). http://segib.org/es/node/3300. Accessed 10 Sept 2015.

Vergara, A. (2008). *Renovación de centros históricos en grandes ciudades latinoamericanas*. Barranquilla: Uninorte.